N JUMP MANGA

ONE PIECE

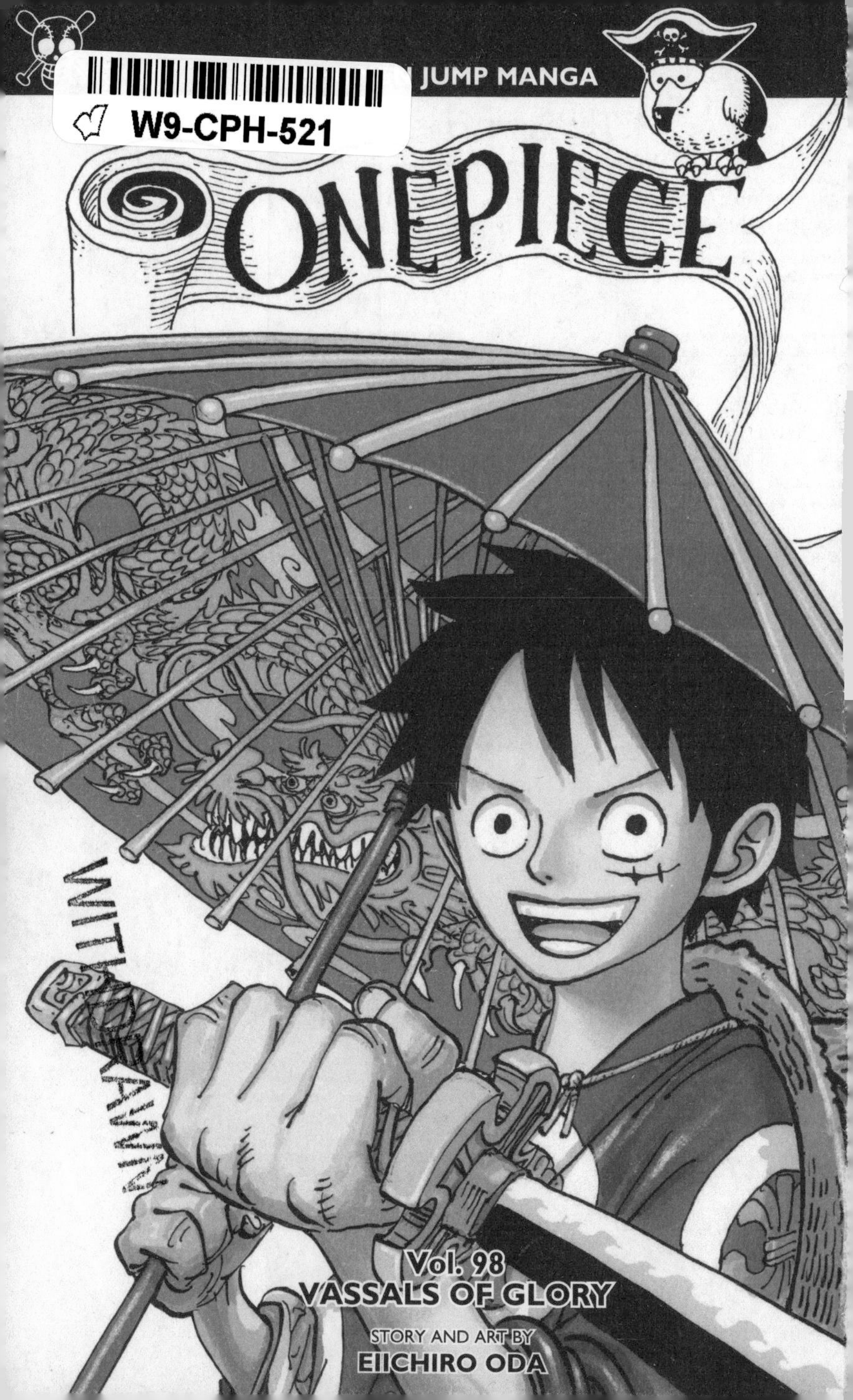

Vol. 98
VASSALS OF GLORY

STORY AND ART BY

EIICHIRO ODA

The Straw Hat Crew

Chopperemon [Ninja]
Tony Tony Chopper

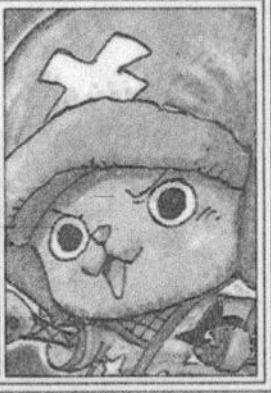

Studied powerful medicines in the Birdie Kingdom as he waited to rejoin the crew.

Ship's Doctor, Bounty: 100 berries

Luffytaro [Ronin]
Monkey D. Luffy

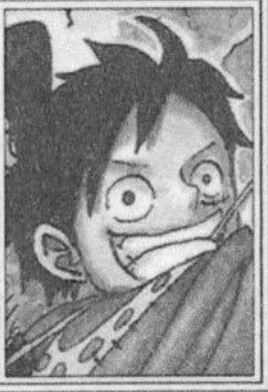

A young man dreaming of being the Pirate King. After two years of training he rejoins his friends in search of the New World!

Captain, Bounty: 1.5 billion berries

)robi [Geisha]
ico Robin

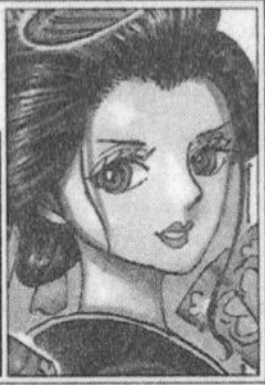

ent time on the island of Baltigo th Dragon, Luffy's father and ader of the Revolutionary Army.

cheologist, Bounty: 130 million berries

Zolojuro [Ronin]
Roronoa Zolo

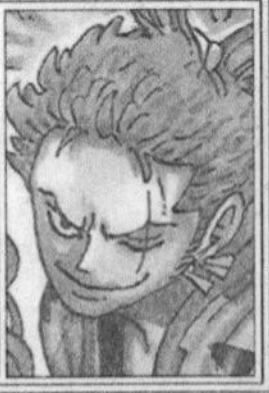

Swallowed his pride on Gloom Island and trained under Mihawk before rejoining Luffy.

Fighter, Bounty: 320 million berries

anosuke [Carpenter]
anky

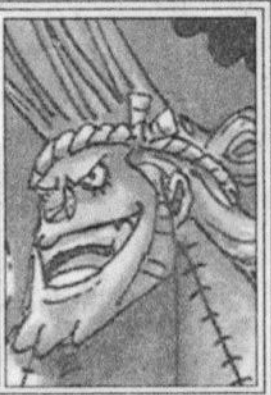

pgraded himself into "Armored ranky" in the Future Land, aldimore.

hipwright, Bounty: 94 million berries

Onami [Kunoichi]
Nami

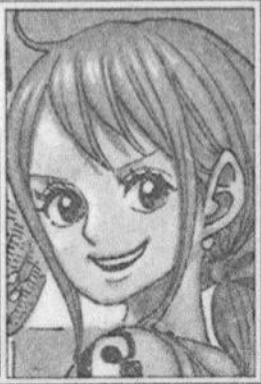

Learned about the climates of the New World on Weatheria, a Sky Island that studies the atmosphere.

Navigator, Bounty: 66 million berries

Bonekichi [Ghost]
Brook

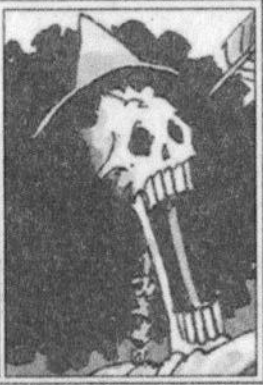

Originally captured by Long-Arm bandits for a freak show, he is now the mega-star "Soul King" Brook.

Musician, Bounty: 83 million berries

Usohachi [Toad Oil Salesman]
Usopp

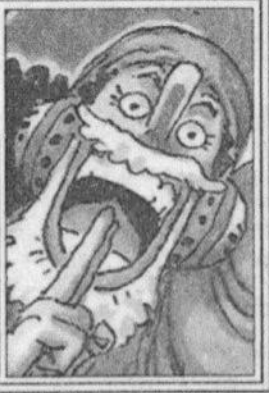

Received Heraclesun's lessons on the Bowin Islands in his quest to be the "king of the snipers."

Sniper, Bounty: 200 million berries

Jimbei, First Son of the Sea [Former Warlord]

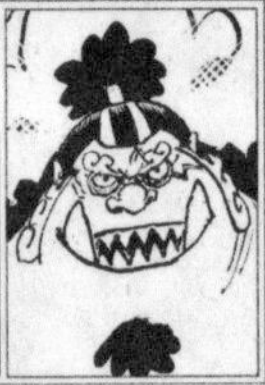

A man loyal to the code. Acted as rear guard against Big Mom to help Luffy escape, then rejoined before the raid.

Helmsman, Bounty: 438 million berries

Sangoro [Soba Cook]
Sanji

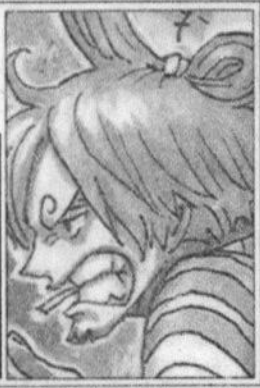

Honed his skills fighting with the masters of Newcomer Kenpo in the Kamabakka Kingdom.

Cook, Bounty: 330 million berries

Shanks

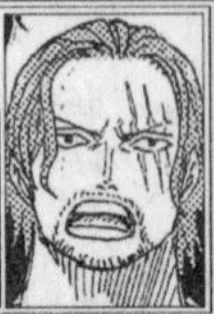

One of the Four Emperors. Waits for Luffy in the "New World," the second half of the Grand Line.

Captain of the Red-Haired Pirates

Land of Wano (Kozuki Clan)

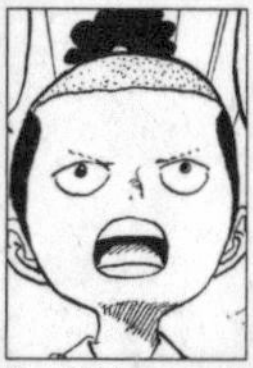
Kozuki Momonosuke
Daimyo (Heir) to Kuri in Wano

Akazaya Nine

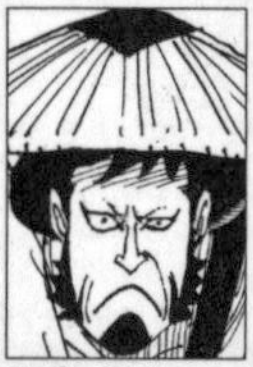
Foxfire Kin'emon
Samurai of Wano

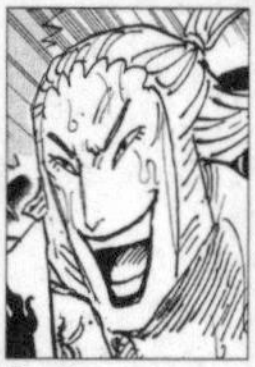
Denjiro
Formerly Kyoshiro

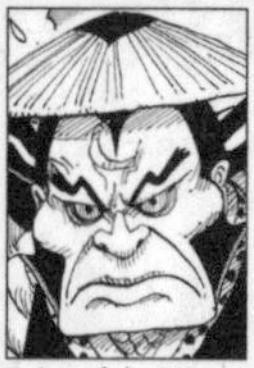
Raizo of the Mist
Ninja of Wano

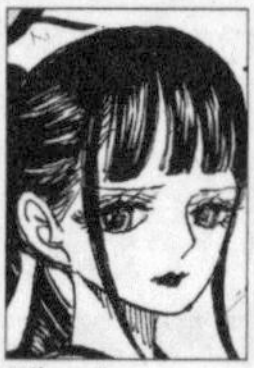
Kikunojo
Samurai of Wano

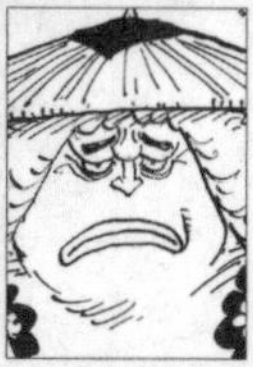
Ashura Doji (Shutenmaru)
Chief, Atamayama Thieves Brigade

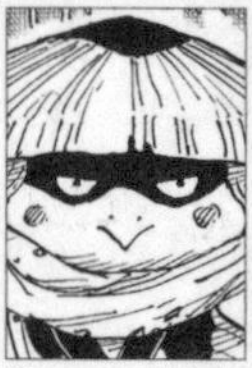
Kawamatsu
Samurai of Wano

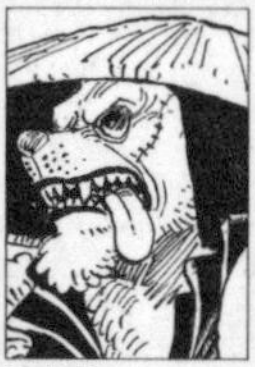
Duke Dogstorm
King of the Day, Mokomo

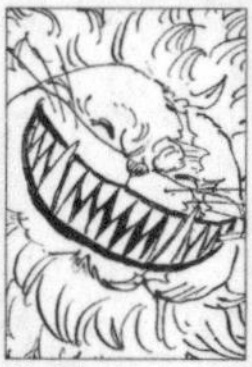
Cat Viper
King of the Night, Mokomo

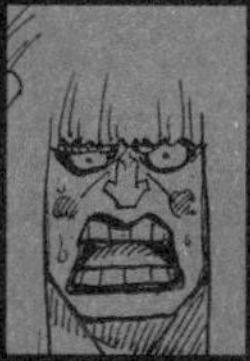
Evening Shower Kanjuro
Samurai of Wano

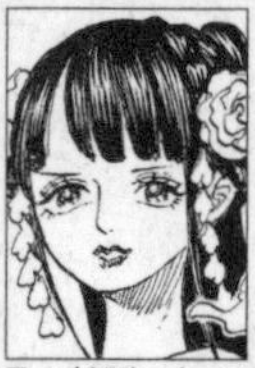
Kozuki Hiyori
Momonosuke's Little Sister

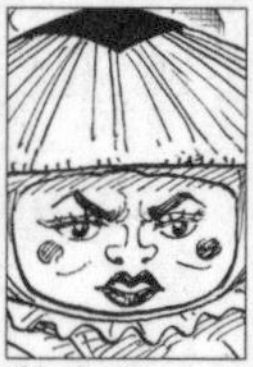
Shinobu
Veteran Kunoichi

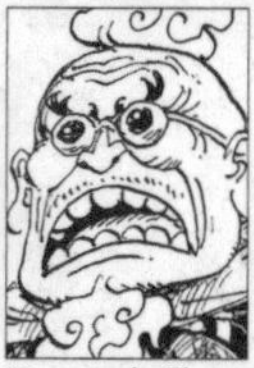
Hyogoro the Flower
Senior Yakuza Boss

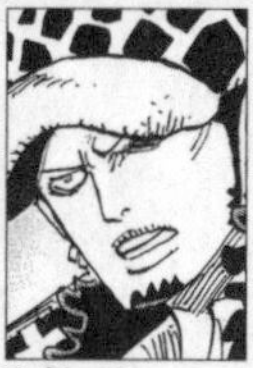
Trafalgar Law
Captain, Heart Pirates

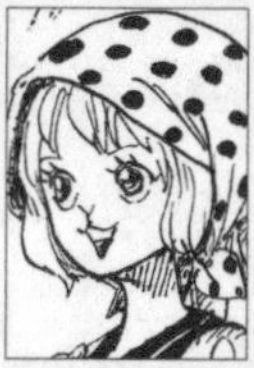
Carrot (Bunny Mink)
Battlebeast Tribe, Kingsbird

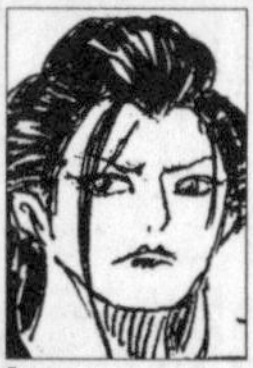
Izo
Former 16th Div. Leader, Whitebeard Pirates

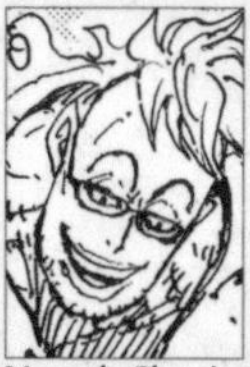
Marco the Phoenix
Former 1st Div. Leader, Whitebeard Pirates

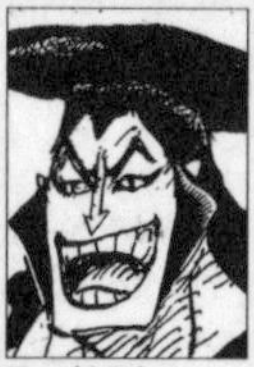
Kozuki Oden
Heir to the Shogunate of Wano

Kid Pirates

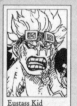

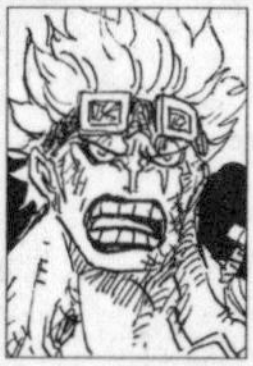
Eustass Kid
Captain, Kid Pirates

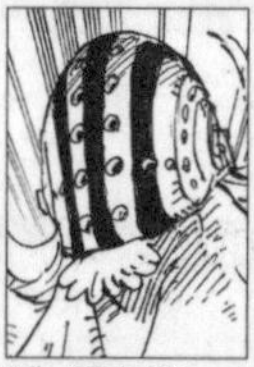
Killer (Hitokiri Kamazo)
Fighter, Kid Pirates

Animal Kingdom Pirates

Lead Performers

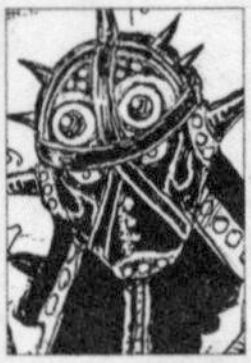
King the Wildfire

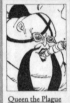

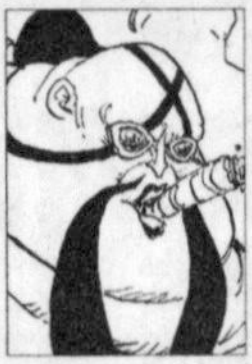
Queen the Plague

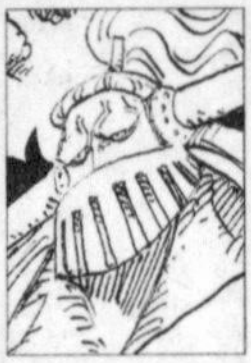
Jack the Drought

Kaido, King of the Beasts (Emperor of the Sea)

A pirate known as the "strongest creature alive." Despite numerous tortures and death sentences, none have been able to kill him.

Captain, Animal Kingdom Pirates

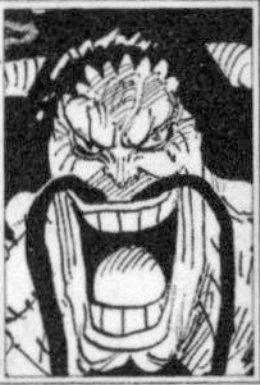

Tobi Roppo

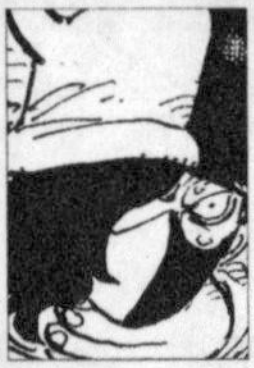
Page One

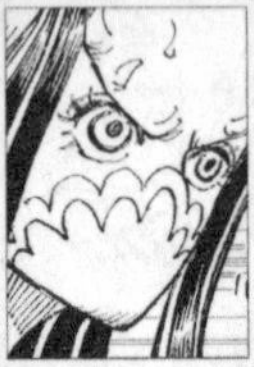
Ulti

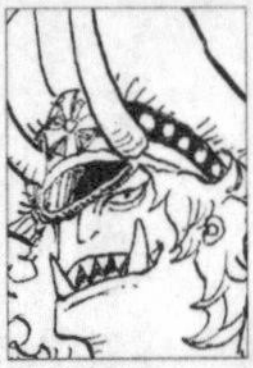
Sasaki

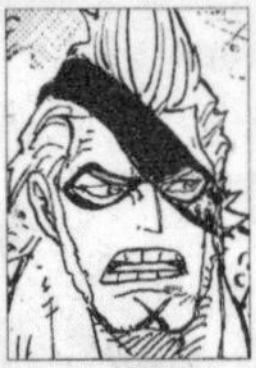
X. (Diez) Drake

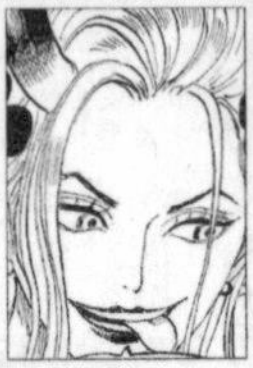
Black Maria

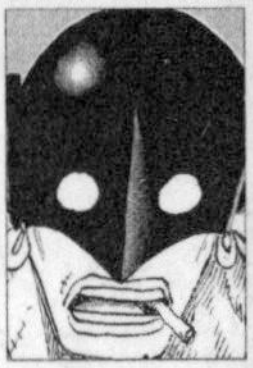
Who's-Who

Headliners

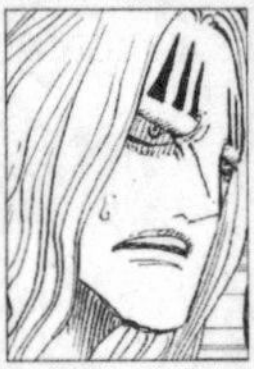
Basil Hawkins

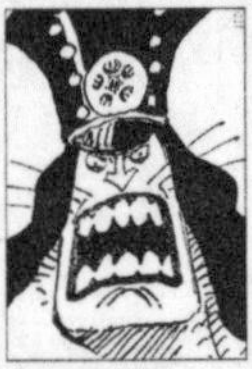
Holdem

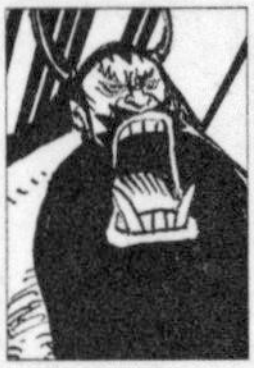
Babanuki

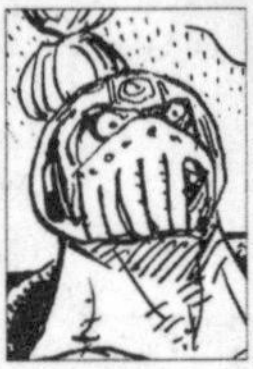
Daifugo

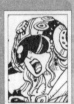

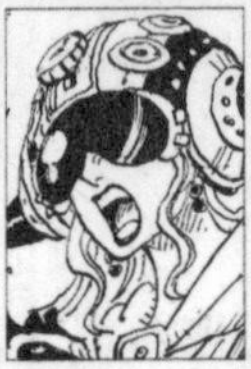
Solitaire

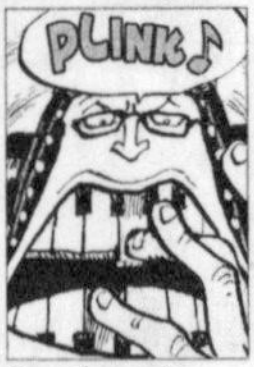
PLINK♪
Scratchmen Apoo

Captain, On-Air Pirates

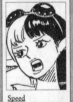

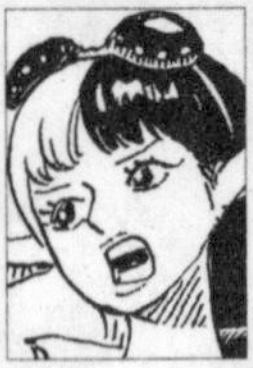
Speed

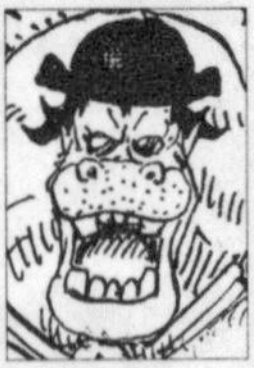
Dobon

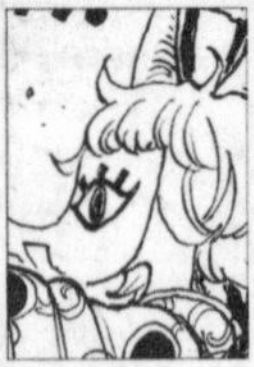
Bao Huang

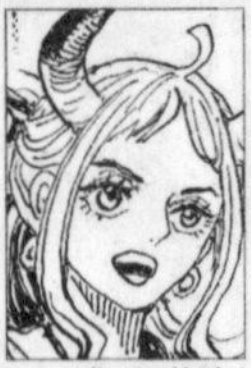
Yamato (Alias: Kozuki Oden)

Kaido's Daughter

Despite this, the Akazaya samurai head to Onigashima undaunted to avenge their slain liege. But Kanjuro is revealed to be a traitor!! Then Luffy's crew arrives to help the crestfallen Akazaya, providing a ray of hope. Kanjuro kidnaps Momonosuke and takes him away to Orochi. The alliance pursues in order to carry out their sneak attack on Onigashima, with powerful new companions among the vanguard!! The fighting on the island is difficult due to the Emperors' followers, but then Luffy meets a surprising individual: Kaido's daughter, Yamato!

Big Mom Pirates

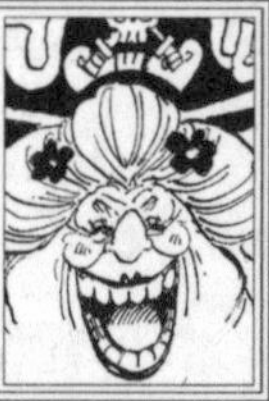

Big Mom
(Emperor of the Sea)

One of the Four Emperors. Uses the Soul-Soul Fruit that extracts life span from others.

Captain, Big Mom Pirates

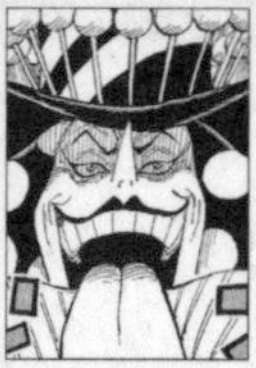

C. Perospero

1st Son of Charlotte

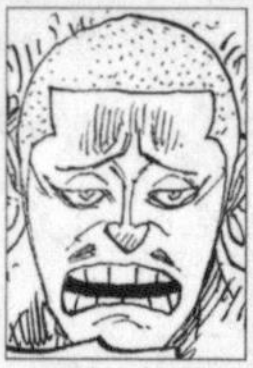

C. Daifuku

3rd Son of Charlotte

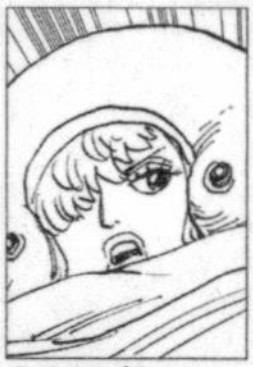

C. Smoothie

14th Daughter of Charlotte

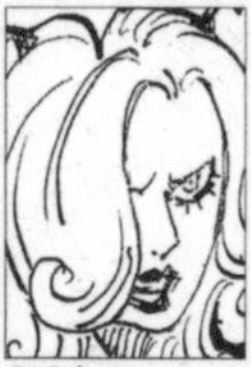

C. Galette

18th Daughter of Charlotte

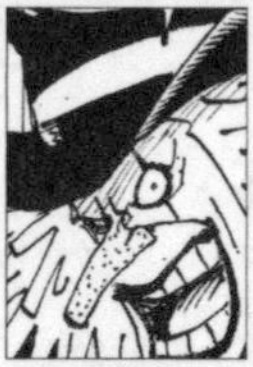

C. Montd'or

19th Son of Charlotte

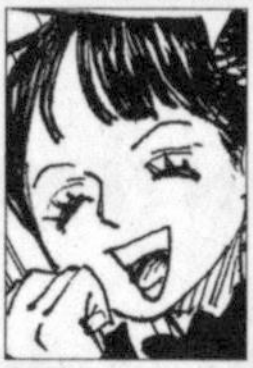

C. Flampe

36th Daughter of Charlotte

Land of Wano (Kurozumi Clan)

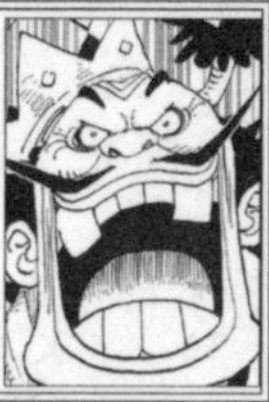

Kurozumi Orochi

The ruler of Wano, using Kaido's help. He cunningly schemed to overthrow his archenemy, the Kozuki Clan.

Shogun of Wano

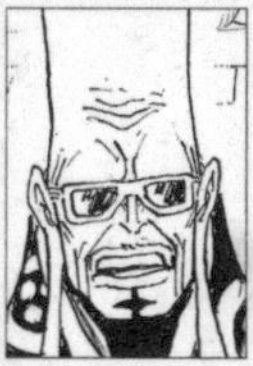

Fukurokuju

Leader, Orochi Oniwabanshu

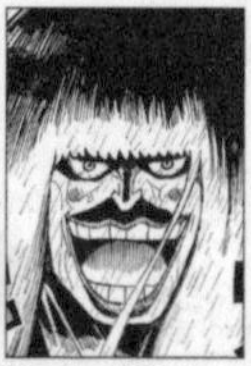

Kurozumi Kanjuro

Orochi's Spy

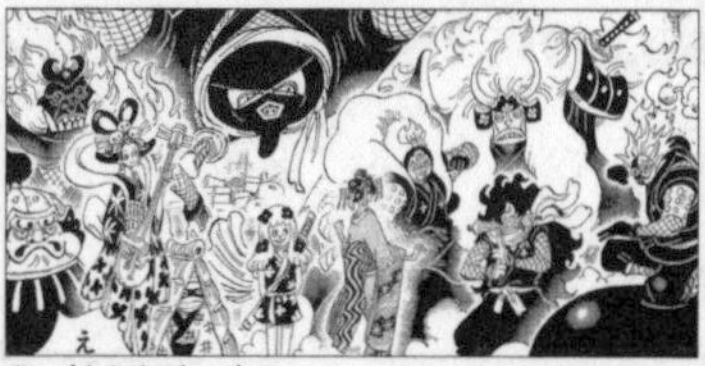

Orochi Oniwabanshu

Shogun of Wano's Private Ninja Squad

Story

After two years of hard training, the Straw Hat pirates are back together, first at the Sabaody Archipelago and then through Fish-Man Island to their next stage: the New World!!

Luffy and crew disembark on Wano for the purpose of defeating Kaido, one of the Four Emperors. They begin to recruit allies for a raid in two weeks' time. But Kaido's side finds out, and the plan is in peril. With great effort, the alliance rebounds and gathers members to await the day of the raid. But on the big day, the Straw Hats are a no-show because of Orochi's schemes...

Vol. 98
VASSALS OF GLORY

CONTENTS

ONE PIECE vol.98

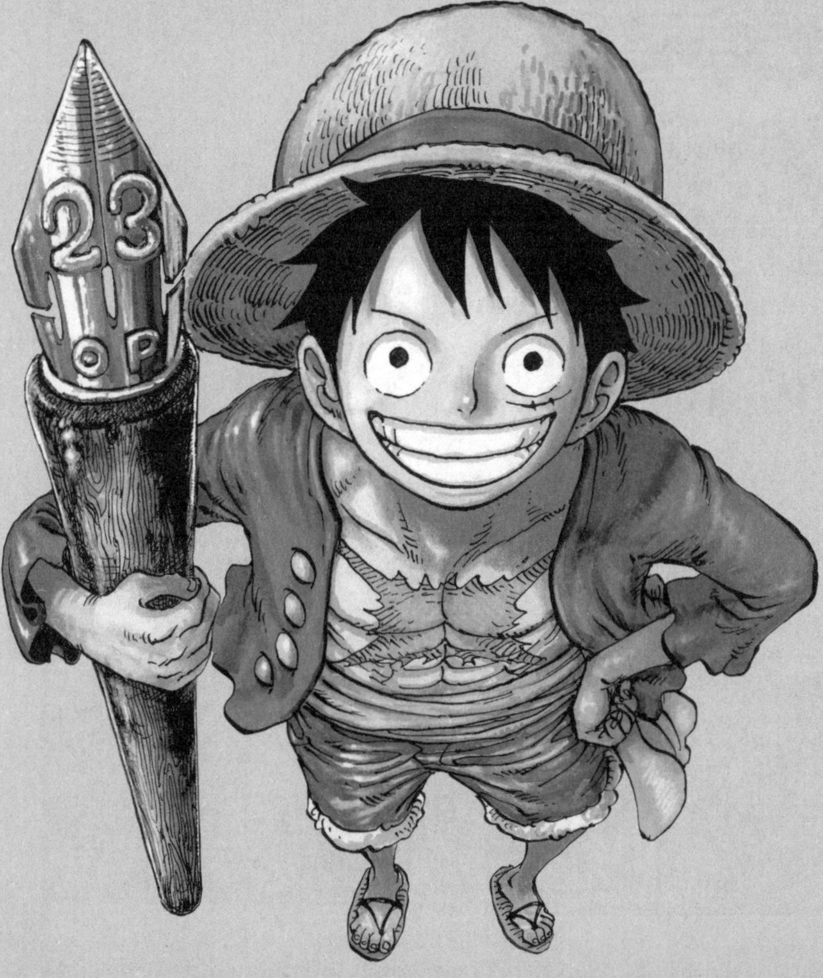
23
OP

NEW ONIGASHIMA PROJECT

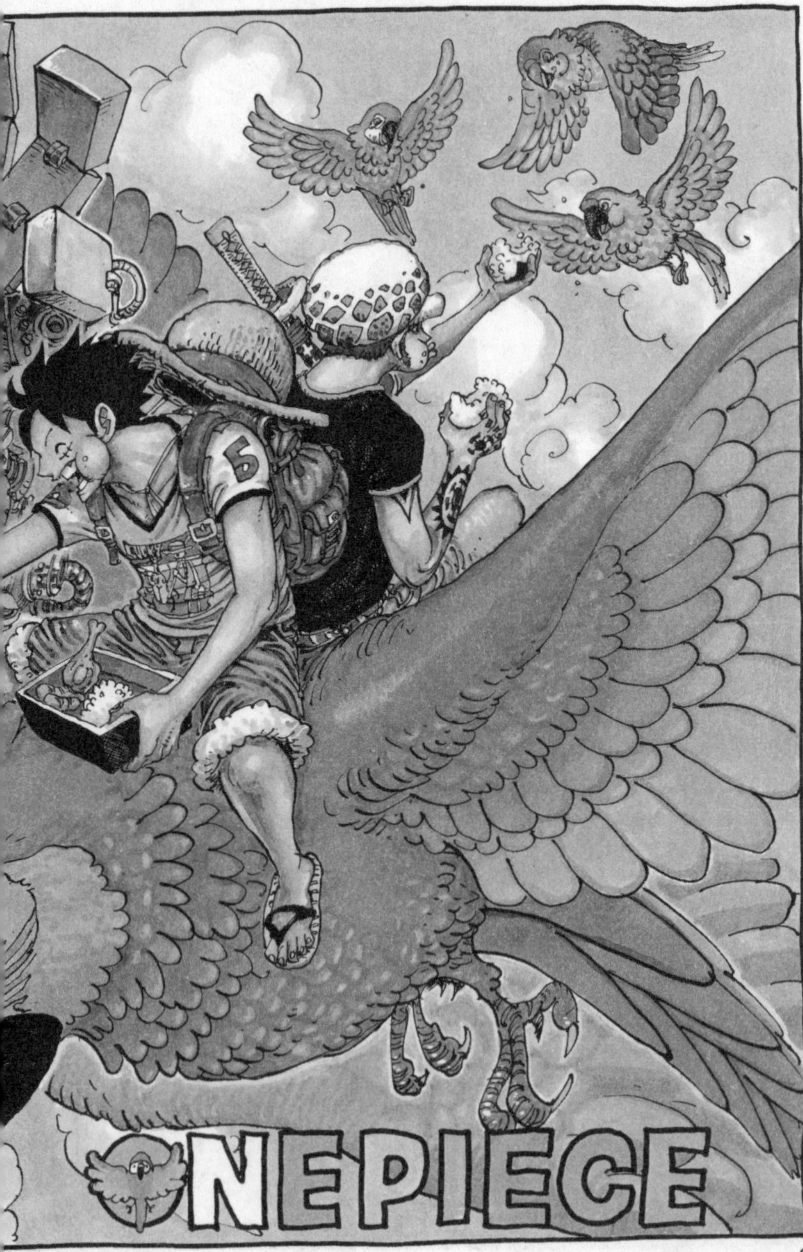
ONE PIECE

Chapter 985:

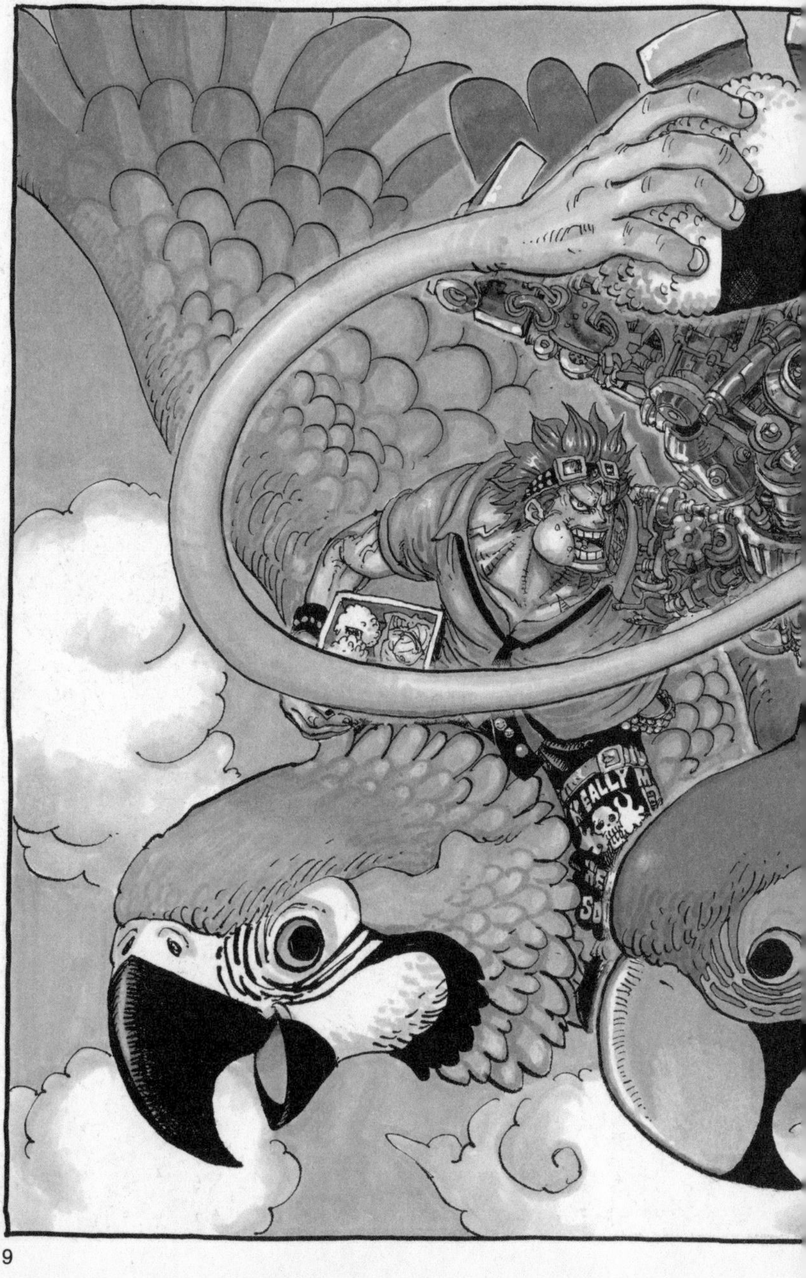

vol.98
ONE PIECE

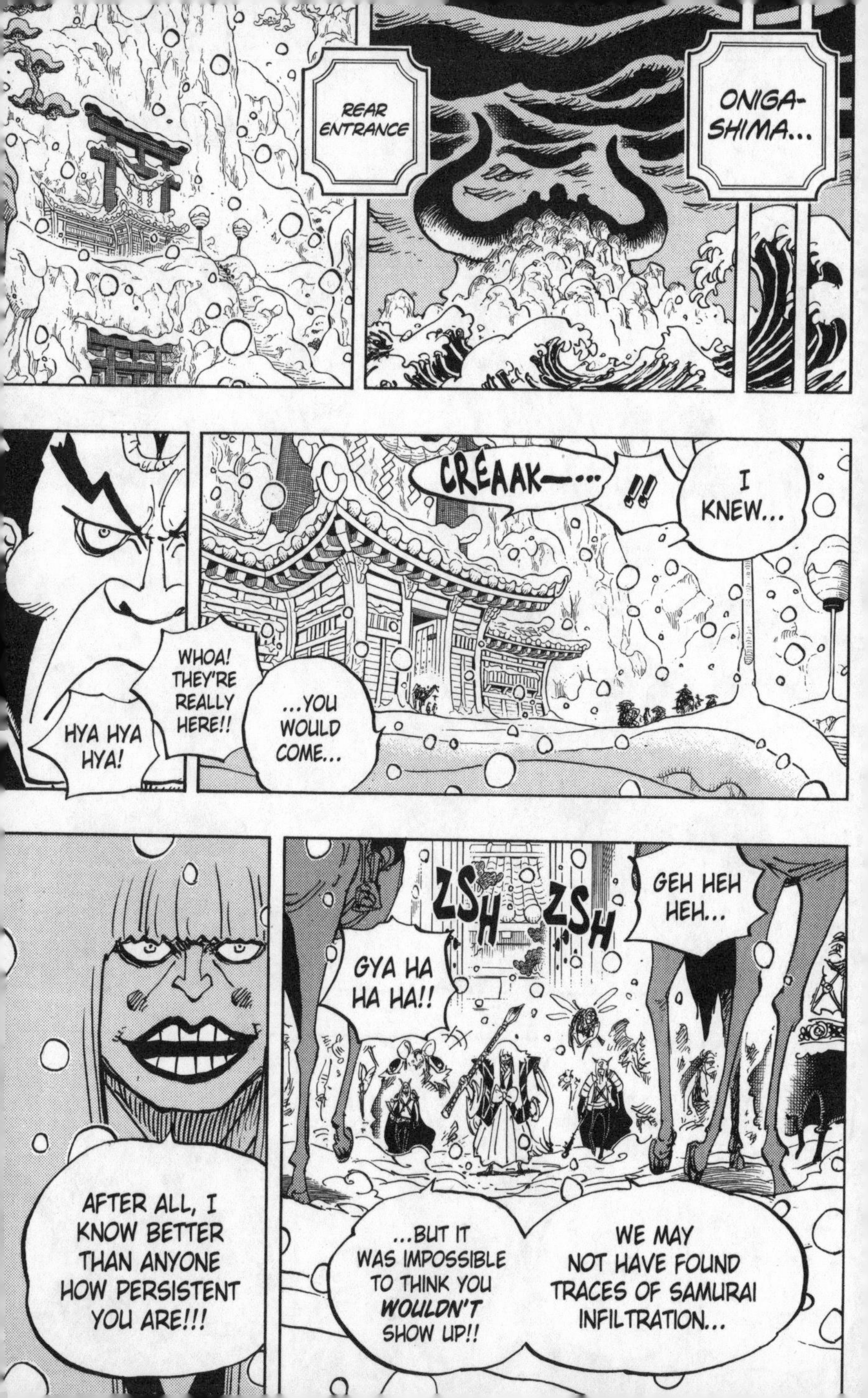
ONIGA-SHIMA...
REAR ENTRANCE
I KNEW...
CREAAK—...
!!
...YOU WOULD COME...
WHOA! THEY'RE REALLY HERE!!
HYA HYA HYA!
GEH HEH HEH...
ZSH ZSH
GYA HA HA HA!!
WE MAY NOT HAVE FOUND TRACES OF SAMURAI INFILTRATION...
...BUT IT WAS IMPOSSIBLE TO THINK YOU *WOULDN'T* SHOW UP!!
AFTER ALL, I KNOW BETTER THAN ANYONE HOW PERSISTENT YOU ARE!!!

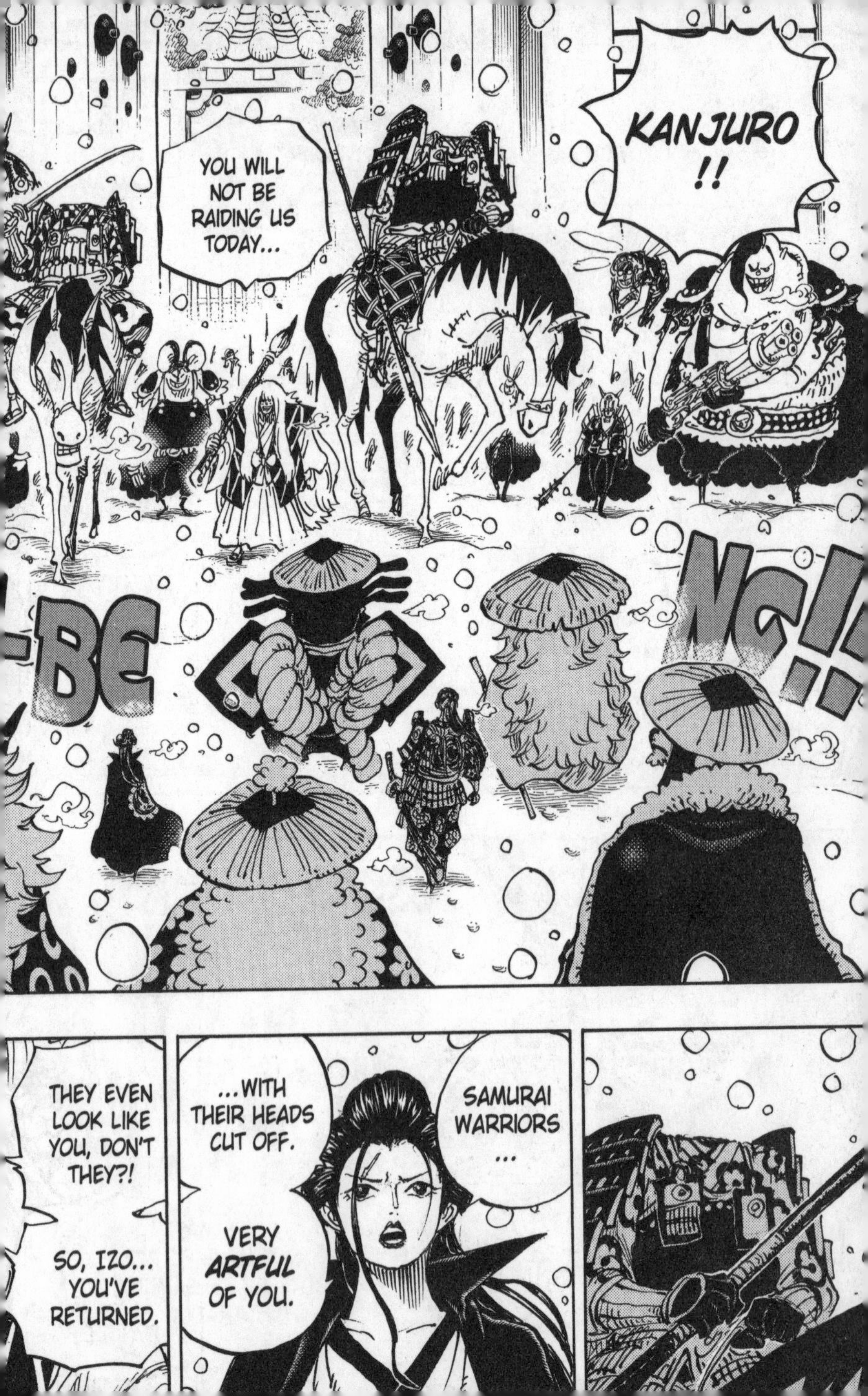
KANJURO !!
YOU WILL NOT BE RAIDING US TODAY...
-BE
NG!!
SAMURAI WARRIORS ...
...WITH THEIR HEADS CUT OFF.
VERY *ARTFUL* OF YOU.
THEY EVEN LOOK LIKE YOU, DON'T THEY?!
SO, IZO... YOU'VE RETURNED.

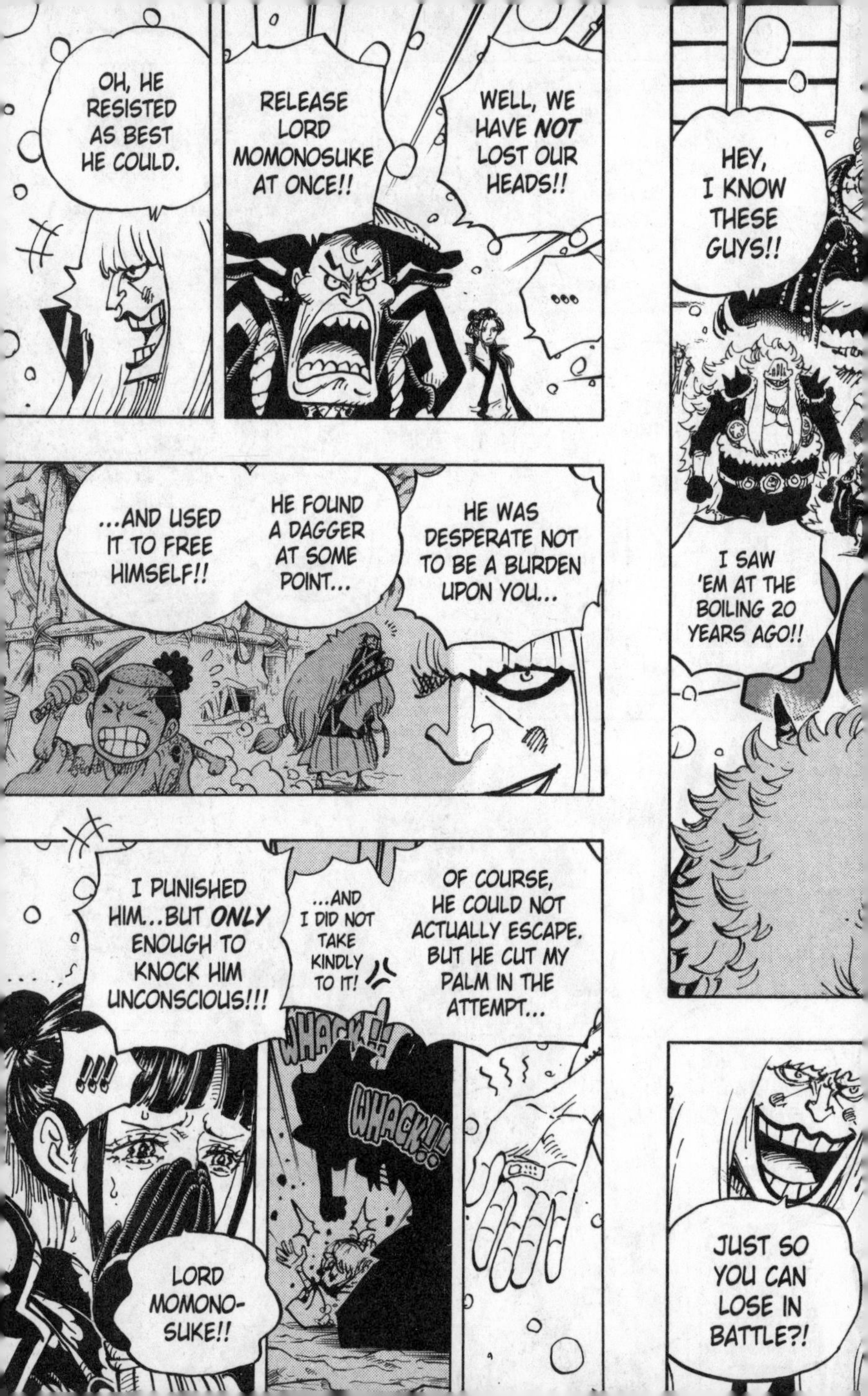
HEY, I KNOW THESE GUYS!!
I SAW 'EM AT THE BOILING 20 YEARS AGO!!
JUST SO YOU CAN LOSE IN BATTLE?!
WELL, WE HAVE **NOT** LOST OUR HEADS!!
RELEASE LORD MOMONOSUKE AT ONCE!!
...
OH, HE RESISTED AS BEST HE COULD.
HE WAS DESPERATE NOT TO BE A BURDEN UPON YOU...
HE FOUND A DAGGER AT SOME POINT...
...AND USED IT TO FREE HIMSELF!!
OF COURSE, HE COULD NOT ACTUALLY ESCAPE. BUT HE CUT MY PALM IN THE ATTEMPT...
...AND I DID NOT TAKE KINDLY TO IT!
I PUNISHED HIM...BUT **ONLY** ENOUGH TO KNOCK HIM UNCONSCIOUS!!!
WHACK!!
WHACK!!
!!!
LORD MOMONO-SUKE!!

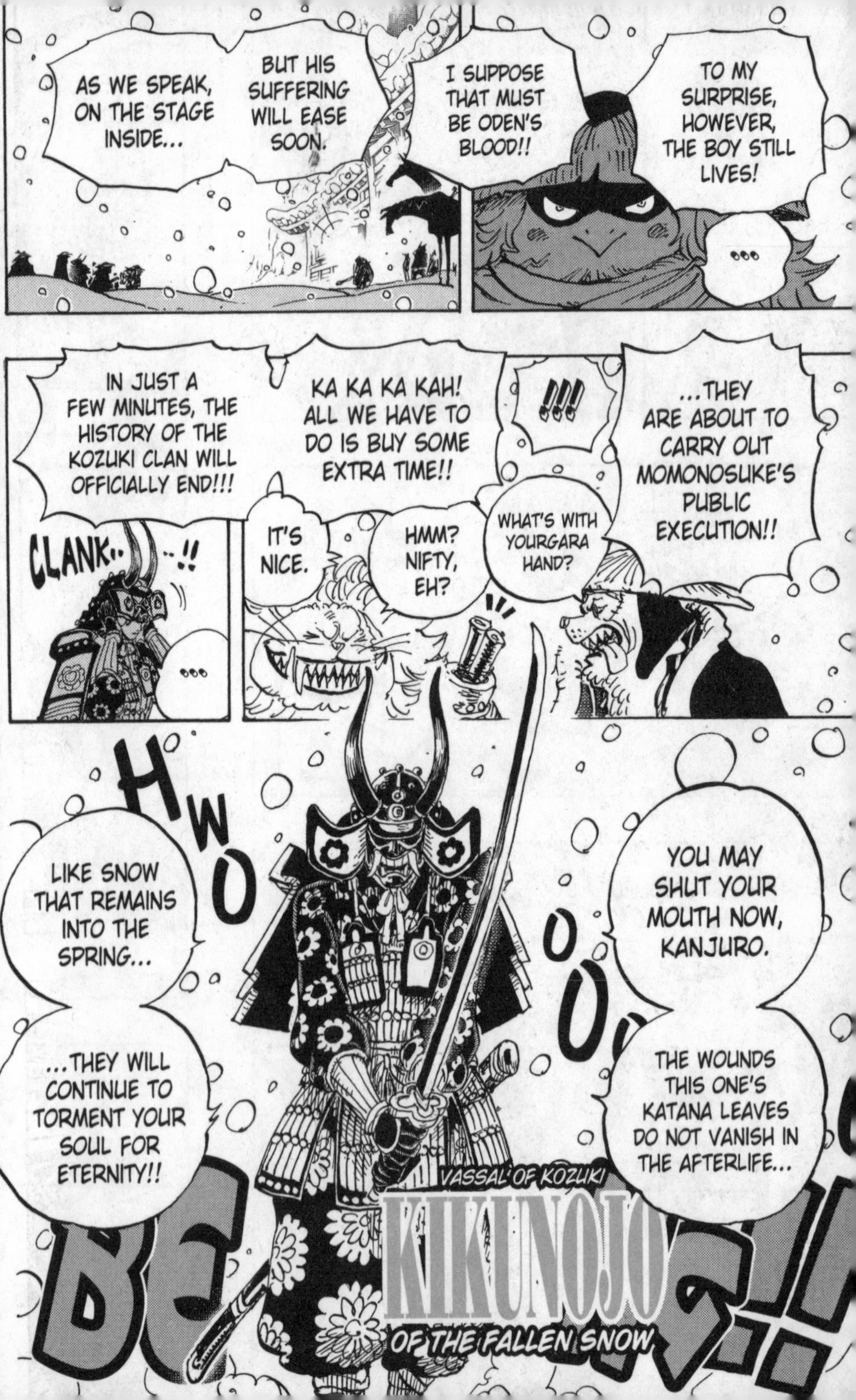
TO MY SURPRISE, HOWEVER, THE BOY STILL LIVES!
...
I SUPPOSE THAT MUST BE ODEN'S BLOOD!!
BUT HIS SUFFERING WILL EASE SOON.
AS WE SPEAK, ON THE STAGE INSIDE...
...THEY ARE ABOUT TO CARRY OUT MOMONOSUKE'S PUBLIC EXECUTION!!
!!!
KA KA KA KAH! ALL WE HAVE TO DO IS BUY SOME EXTRA TIME!!
IN JUST A FEW MINUTES, THE HISTORY OF THE KOZUKI CLAN WILL OFFICIALLY END!!!
WHAT'S WITH YOURGARA HAND?
HMM? NIFTY, EH?
IT'S NICE.
CLANK..
..!!
...
YOU MAY SHUT YOUR MOUTH NOW, KANJURO.
THE WOUNDS THIS ONE'S KATANA LEAVES DO NOT VANISH IN THE AFTERLIFE...
LIKE SNOW THAT REMAINS INTO THE SPRING...
...THEY WILL CONTINUE TO TORMENT YOUR SOUL FOR ETERNITY!!
HWOOOO
VASSAL OF KOZUKI
KIKUNOJO
OF THE FALLEN SNOW

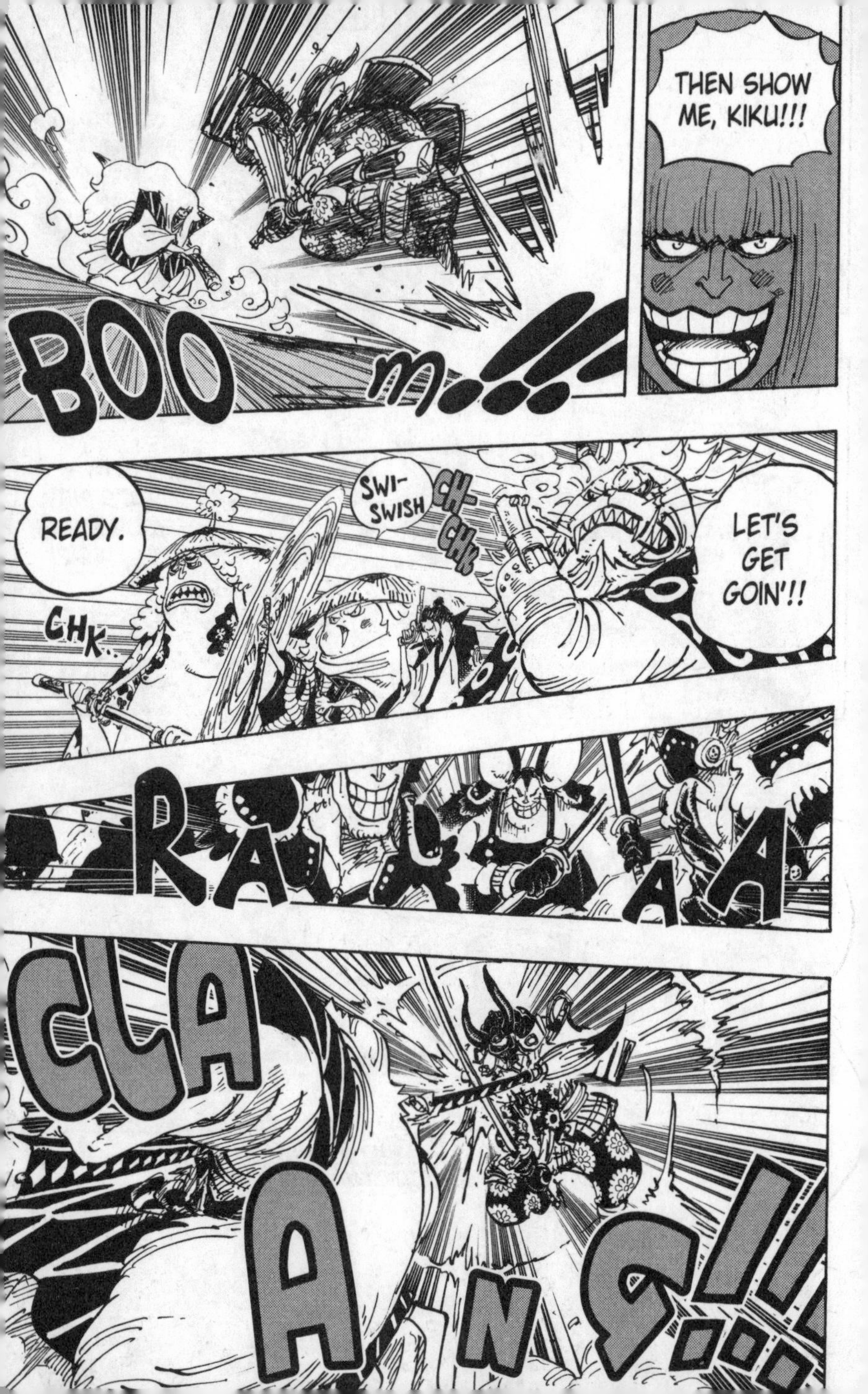
THEN SHOW ME, KIKU!!!
BOOm!!!
LET'S GET GOIN'!!
CH-CHK
SWI-SWISH
READY.
CHK...
RAAA
CLAANG!!

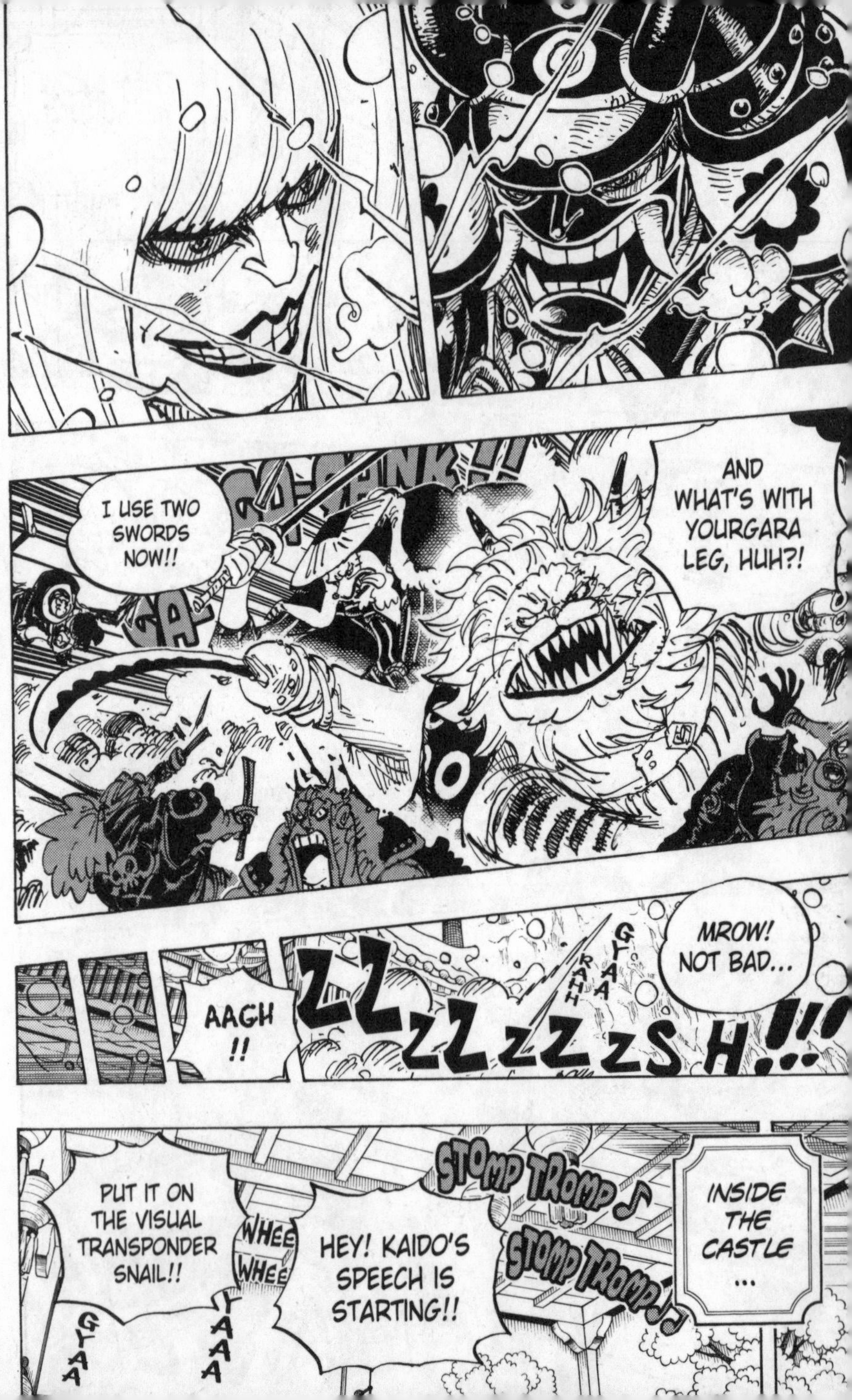
AND WHAT'S WITH YOURGARA LEG, HUH?!
I USE TWO SWORDS NOW!!
GA
MROW! NOT BAD...
GYAA
RAHH
ZZZZZZSH!!!
AAGH !!
INSIDE THE CASTLE ...
STOMP TROMP
STOMP TROMP
HEY! KAIDO'S SPEECH IS STARTING!!
WHEE WHEE
PUT IT ON THE VISUAL TRANSPONDER SNAIL!!
YAAA
GYAA

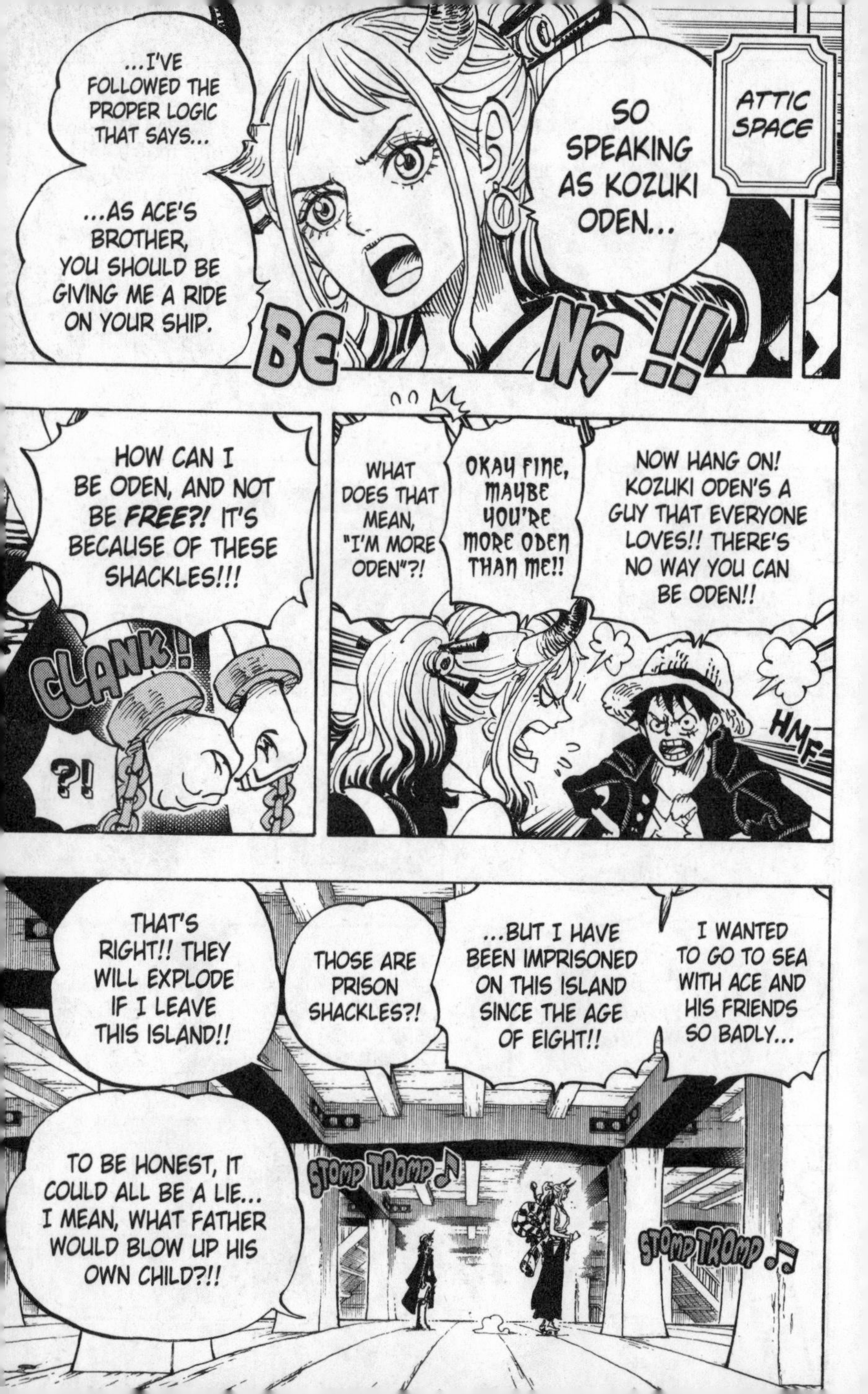
ATTIC SPACE
SO SPEAKING AS KOZUKI ODEN...
...I'VE FOLLOWED THE PROPER LOGIC THAT SAYS...
...AS ACE'S BROTHER, YOU SHOULD BE GIVING ME A RIDE ON YOUR SHIP.
BENG!!
NOW HANG ON! KOZUKI ODEN'S A GUY THAT EVERYONE LOVES!! THERE'S NO WAY YOU CAN BE ODEN!!
OKAY FINE, MAYBE YOU'RE MORE ODEN THAN ME!!
WHAT DOES THAT MEAN, "I'M MORE ODEN"?!
HMF
HOW CAN I BE ODEN, AND NOT BE *FREE?!* IT'S BECAUSE OF THESE SHACKLES!!!
CLANK!
?!
I WANTED TO GO TO SEA WITH ACE AND HIS FRIENDS SO BADLY...
...BUT I HAVE BEEN IMPRISONED ON THIS ISLAND SINCE THE AGE OF EIGHT!!
THOSE ARE PRISON SHACKLES?!
THAT'S RIGHT!! THEY WILL EXPLODE IF I LEAVE THIS ISLAND!!
STOMP TRAMP ♪
STOMP TRAMP ♪
TO BE HONEST, IT COULD ALL BE A LIE... I MEAN, WHAT FATHER WOULD BLOW UP HIS OWN CHILD?!!

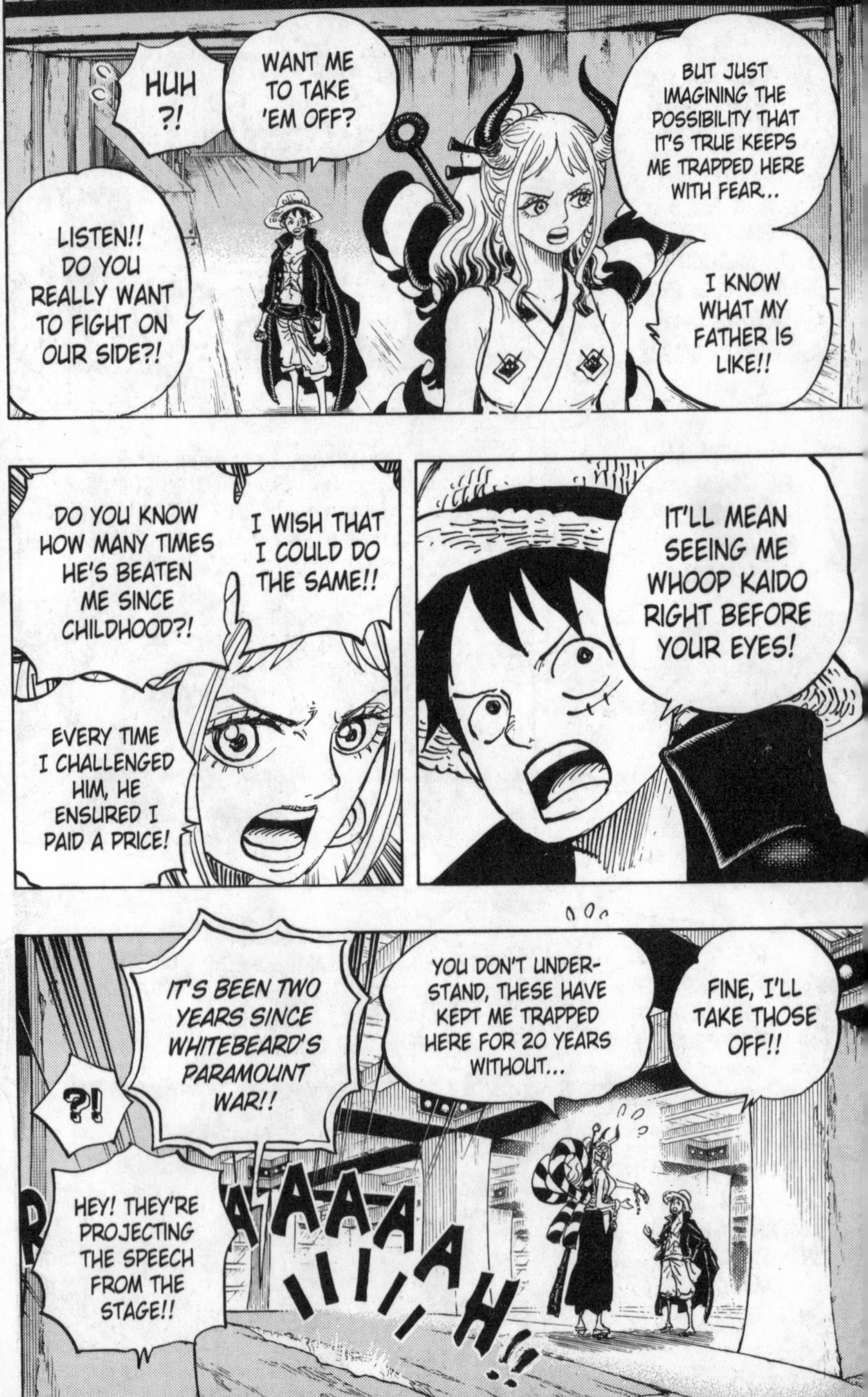
BUT JUST IMAGINING THE POSSIBILITY THAT IT'S TRUE KEEPS ME TRAPPED HERE WITH FEAR...
WANT ME TO TAKE 'EM OFF?
HUH ?!
I KNOW WHAT MY FATHER IS LIKE!!
LISTEN!! DO YOU REALLY WANT TO FIGHT ON OUR SIDE?!
IT'LL MEAN SEEING ME WHOOP KAIDO RIGHT BEFORE YOUR EYES!
I WISH THAT I COULD DO THE SAME!!
DO YOU KNOW HOW MANY TIMES HE'S BEATEN ME SINCE CHILDHOOD?!
EVERY TIME I CHALLENGED HIM, HE ENSURED I PAID A PRICE!
FINE, I'LL TAKE THOSE OFF!!
YOU DON'T UNDER-STAND, THESE HAVE KEPT ME TRAPPED HERE FOR 20 YEARS WITHOUT...
IT'S BEEN TWO YEARS SINCE WHITEBEARD'S PARAMOUNT WAR!!
?!
HEY! THEY'RE PROJECTING THE SPEECH FROM THE STAGE!!
AAAAAIIIIIIAH!!

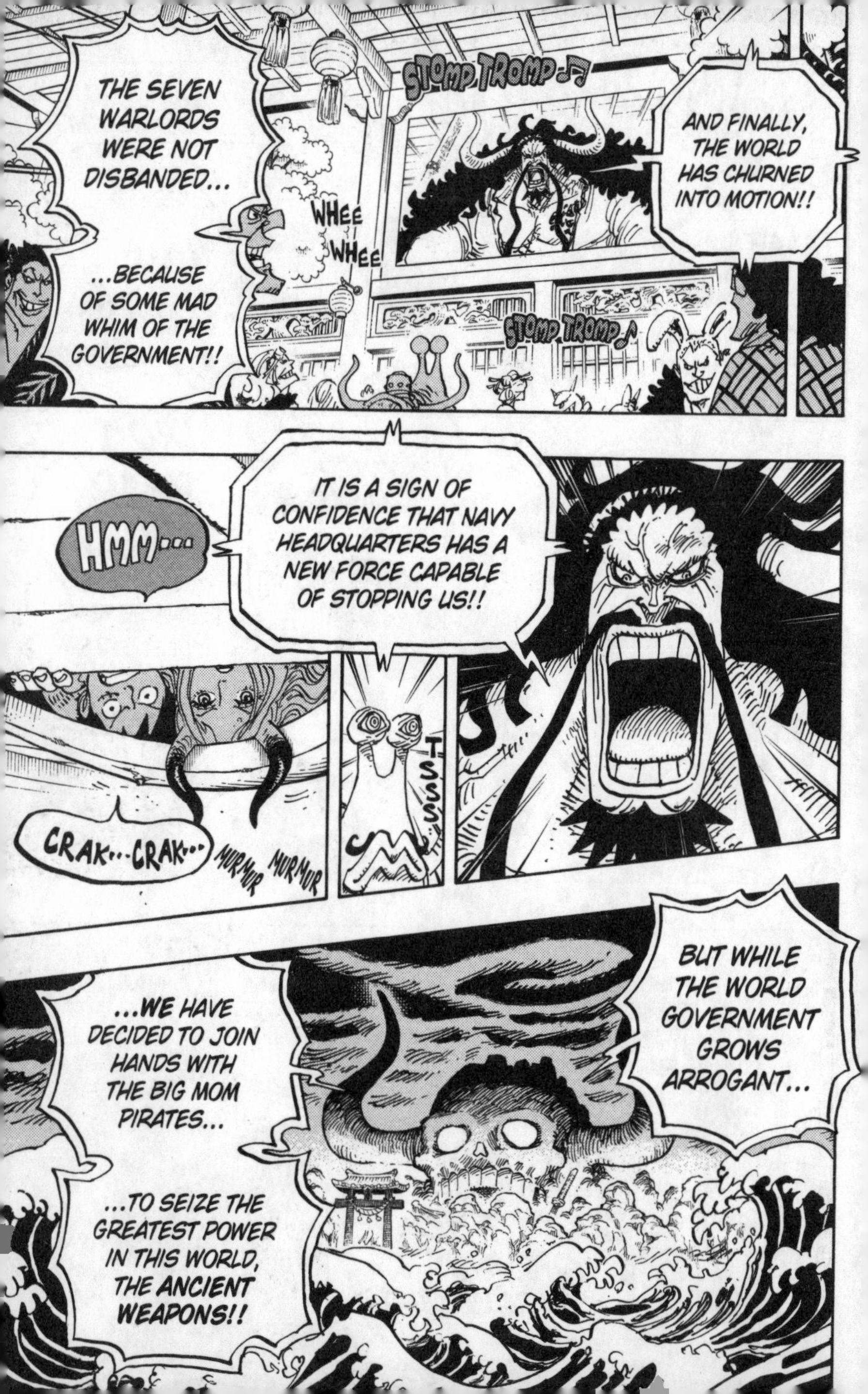

AND FINALLY, THE WORLD HAS CHURNED INTO MOTION!!
STOMP TROMP
THE SEVEN WARLORDS WERE NOT DISBANDED...
...BECAUSE OF SOME MAD WHIM OF THE GOVERNMENT!!
WHEE WHEE
STOMP TROMP
IT IS A SIGN OF CONFIDENCE THAT NAVY HEADQUARTERS HAS A NEW FORCE CAPABLE OF STOPPING US!!
HMM...
TSSS
CRAK...CRAK...
MURMUR MURMUR
BUT WHILE THE WORLD GOVERNMENT GROWS ARROGANT...
...WE HAVE DECIDED TO JOIN HANDS WITH THE BIG MOM PIRATES...
...TO SEIZE THE GREATEST POWER IN THIS WORLD, THE ANCIENT WEAPONS!!

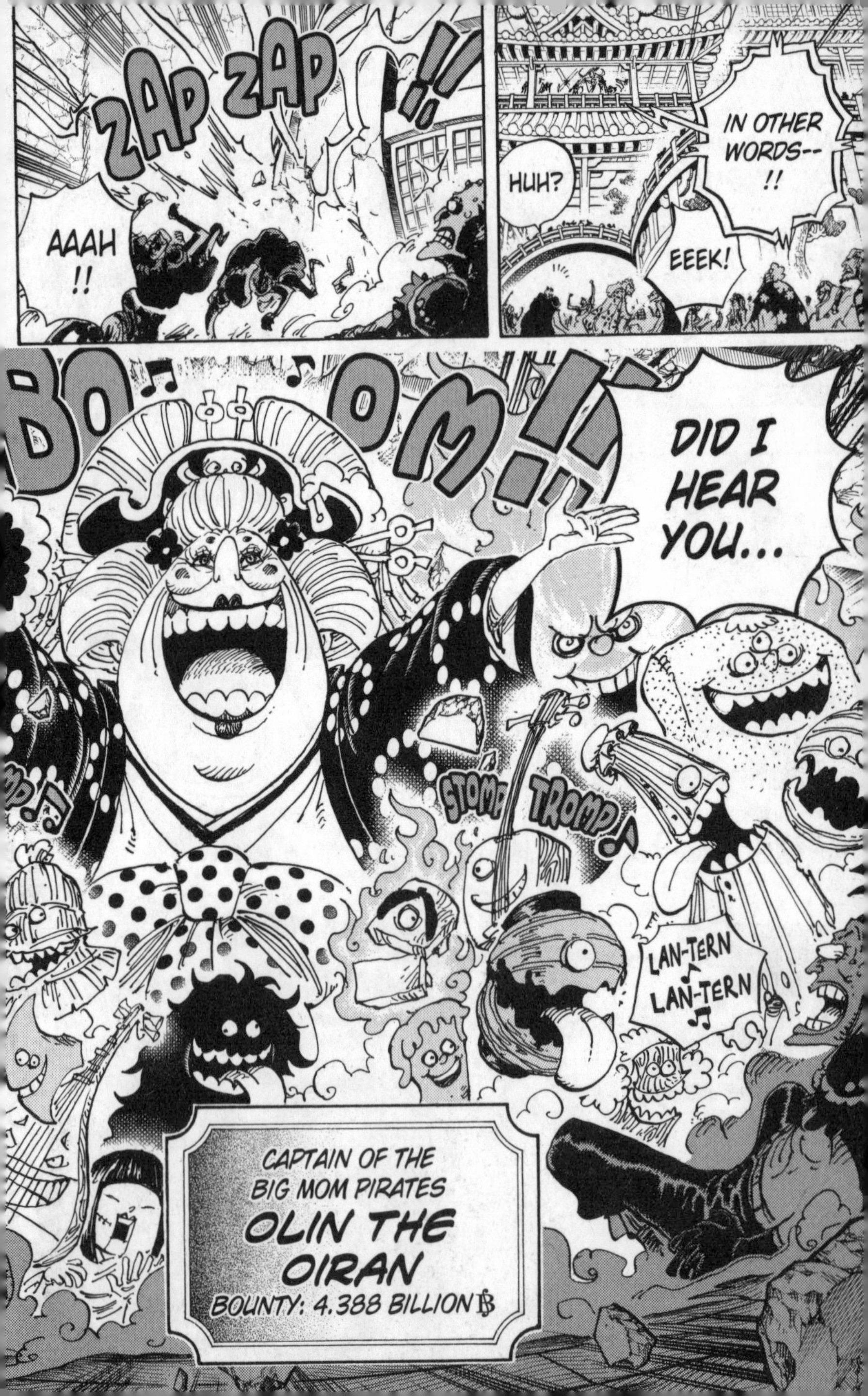
IN OTHER WORDS--!!
HUH?
EEEK!
ZAP ZAP!!
AAAH!!
DID I HEAR YOU...
BOOM!!
STOMP TROMP♪
LAN-TERN♪ LAN-TERN♫
CAPTAIN OF THE BIG MOM PIRATES
OLIN THE OIRAN
BOUNTY: 4.388 BILLION ฿

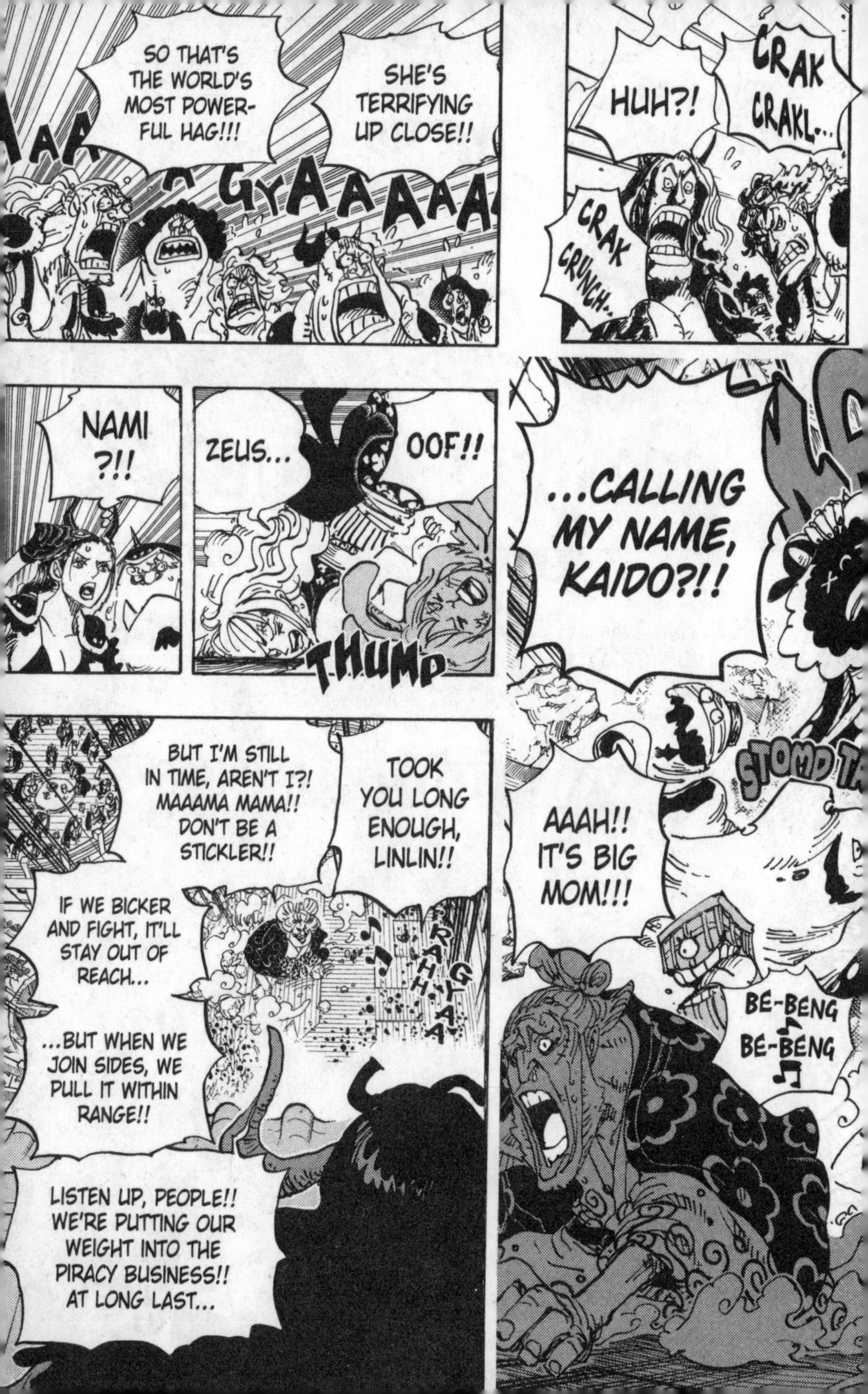
CRAK CRAKL...
HUH?!
CRAK CRUNCH...
SHE'S TERRIFYING UP CLOSE!!
SO THAT'S THE WORLD'S MOST POWER-FUL HAG!!!
GYAAAAAA
...CALLING MY NAME, KAIDO?!!
AAAH!! IT'S BIG MOM!!!
BE-BENG BE-BENG
OOF!!
ZEUS...
THUMP
NAMI ?!!
TOOK YOU LONG ENOUGH, LINLIN!!
BUT I'M STILL IN TIME, AREN'T I?! MAAAMA MAMA!! DON'T BE A STICKLER!!
IF WE BICKER AND FIGHT, IT'LL STAY OUT OF REACH...
...BUT WHEN WE JOIN SIDES, WE PULL IT WITHIN RANGE!!
LISTEN UP, PEOPLE!! WE'RE PUTTING OUR WEIGHT INTO THE PIRACY BUSINESS!! AT LONG LAST...

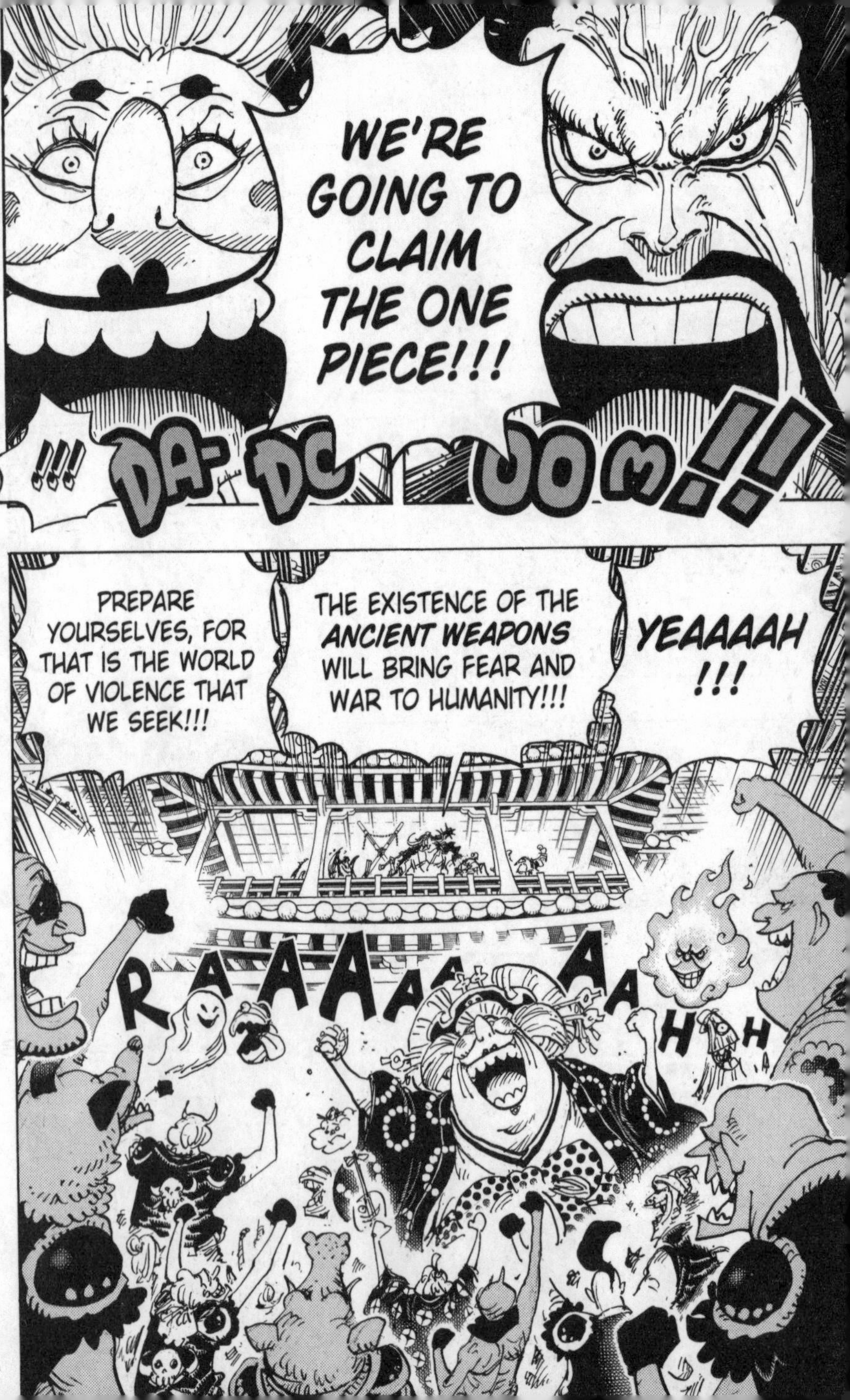
WE'RE GOING TO CLAIM THE ONE PIECE!!!
!!!
DA-DOOM!!
YEAAAAH !!!
THE EXISTENCE OF THE *ANCIENT WEAPONS* WILL BRING FEAR AND WAR TO HUMANITY!!!
PREPARE YOURSELVES, FOR THAT IS THE WORLD OF VIOLENCE THAT WE SEEK!!!
RAAAAAAAHH

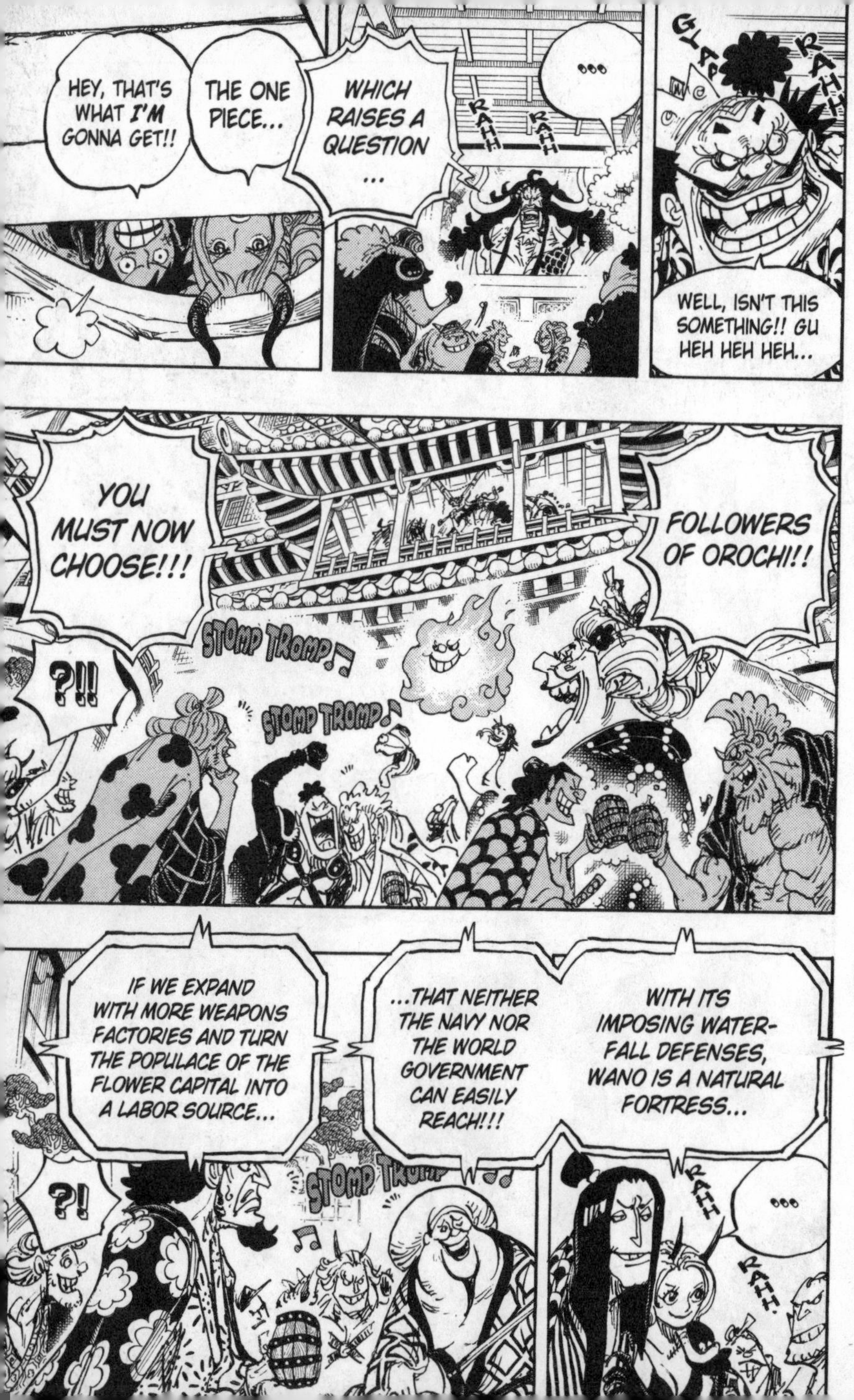
GYAPP
RAHH
WELL, ISN'T THIS SOMETHING!! GU HEH HEH HEH...
...
RAHH
RAHH
WHICH RAISES A QUESTION ...
THE ONE PIECE...
HEY, THAT'S WHAT *I'M* GONNA GET!!
FOLLOWERS OF OROCHI!!
YOU MUST NOW CHOOSE!!!
STOMP TROMP♪
STOMP TROMP♪
?!!
...
RAHH
RAHH
WITH ITS IMPOSING WATER-FALL DEFENSES, WANO IS A NATURAL FORTRESS...
...THAT NEITHER THE NAVY NOR THE WORLD GOVERNMENT CAN EASILY REACH!!!
IF WE EXPAND WITH MORE WEAPONS FACTORIES AND TURN THE POPULACE OF THE FLOWER CAPITAL INTO A LABOR SOURCE...
STOMP TROMP
?!

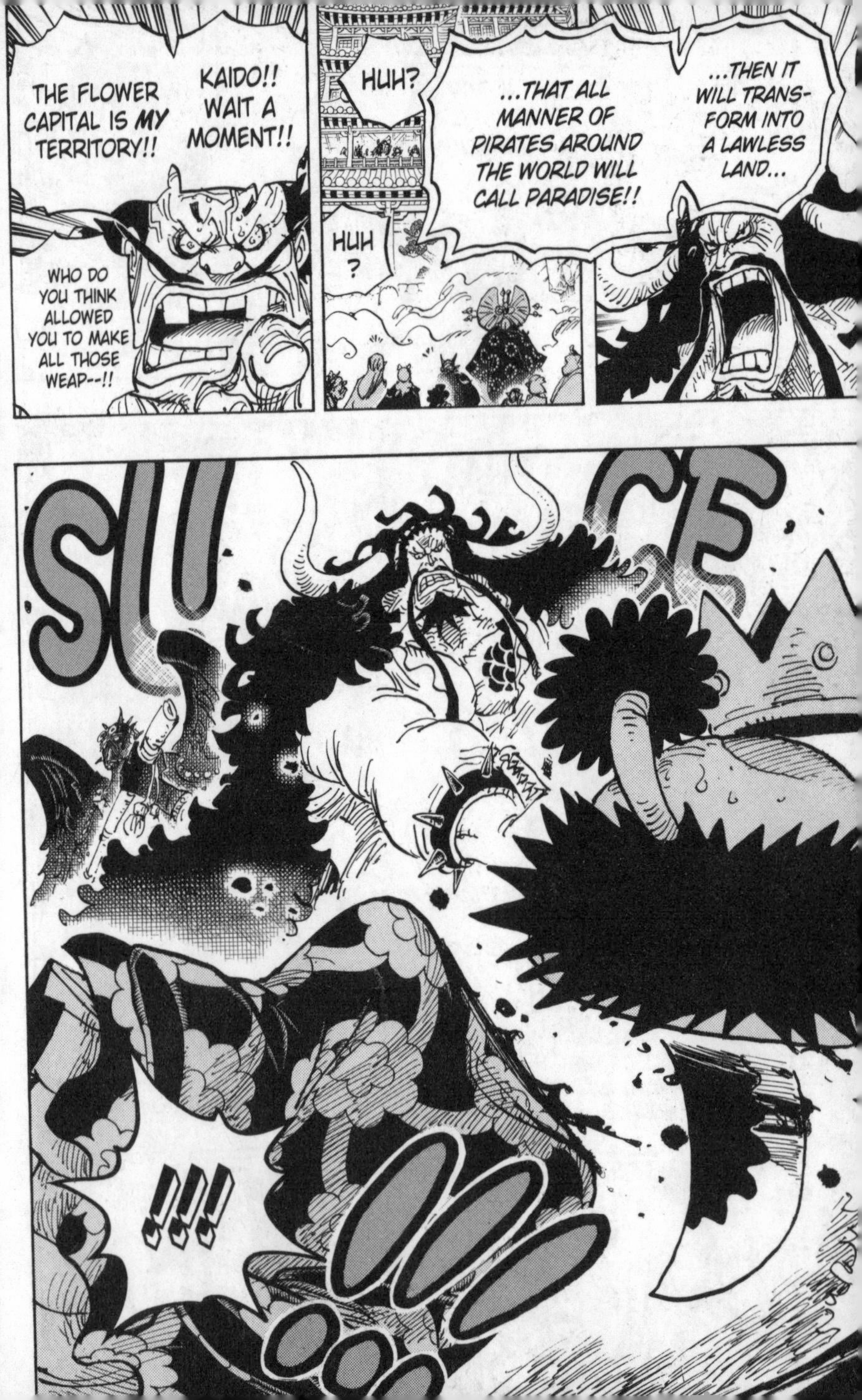
...THEN IT WILL TRANS- FORM INTO A LAWLESS LAND...
...THAT ALL MANNER OF PIRATES AROUND THE WORLD WILL CALL PARADISE!!
HUH?
HUH ?
KAIDO!! WAIT A MOMENT!!
THE FLOWER CAPITAL IS **MY** TERRITORY!!
WHO DO YOU THINK ALLOWED YOU TO MAKE ALL THOSE WEAP--!!
SLICE
!!!

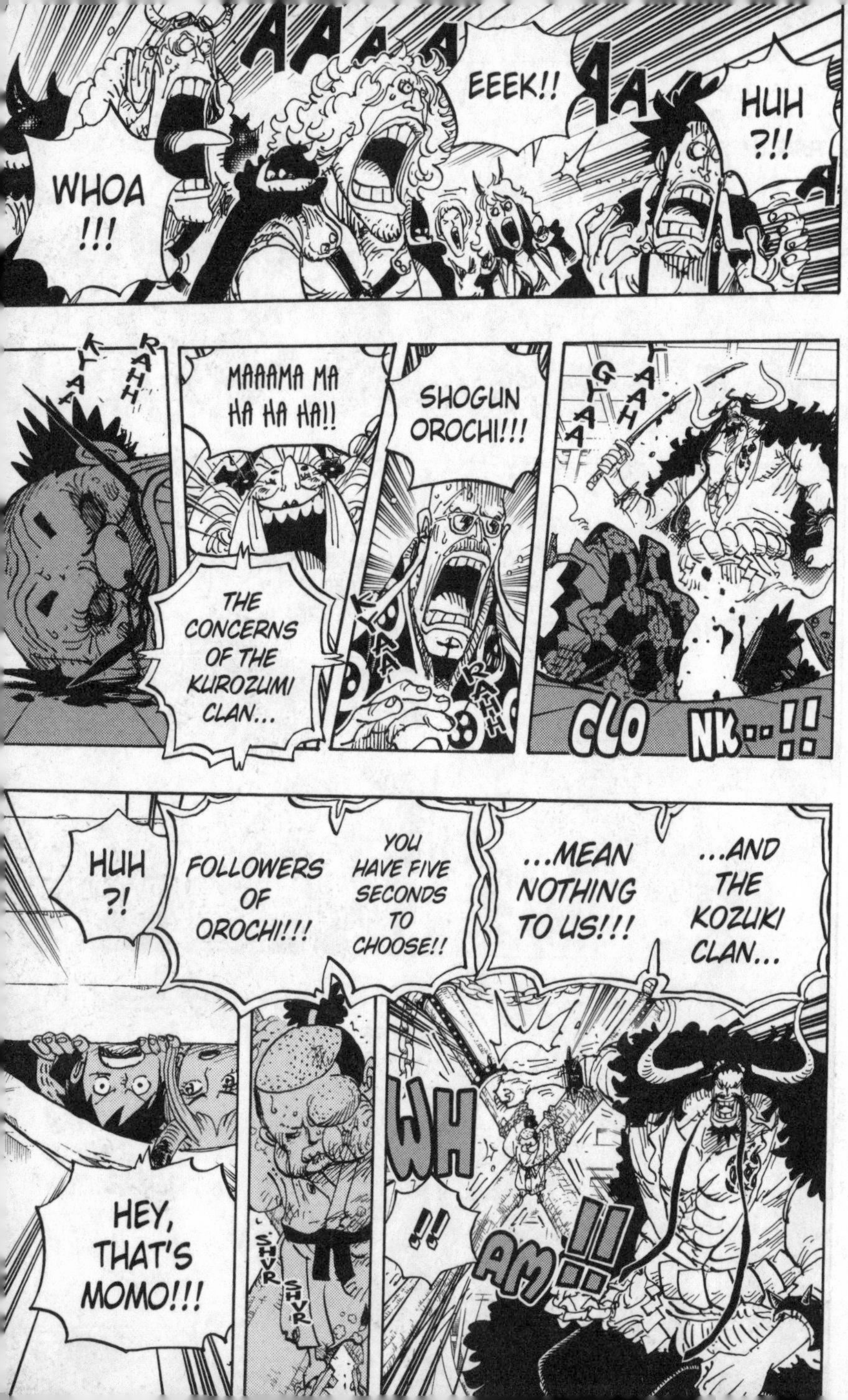
HUH ?!!
AA
EEEK!!
AAAA
WHOA !!!
GYAAA
YAAH
CLONK..!!
SHOGUN OROCHI!!!
KYAA
RAHH
MAAAMA MA HA HA HA!!
THE CONCERNS OF THE KUROZUMI CLAN...
KYAA
RAHH
...AND THE KOZUKI CLAN...
...MEAN NOTHING TO US!!!
YOU HAVE FIVE SECONDS TO CHOOSE!!
FOLLOWERS OF OROCHI!!!
HUH ?!
WHAM!!
SHVR
SHVR
HEY, THAT'S MOMO!!!

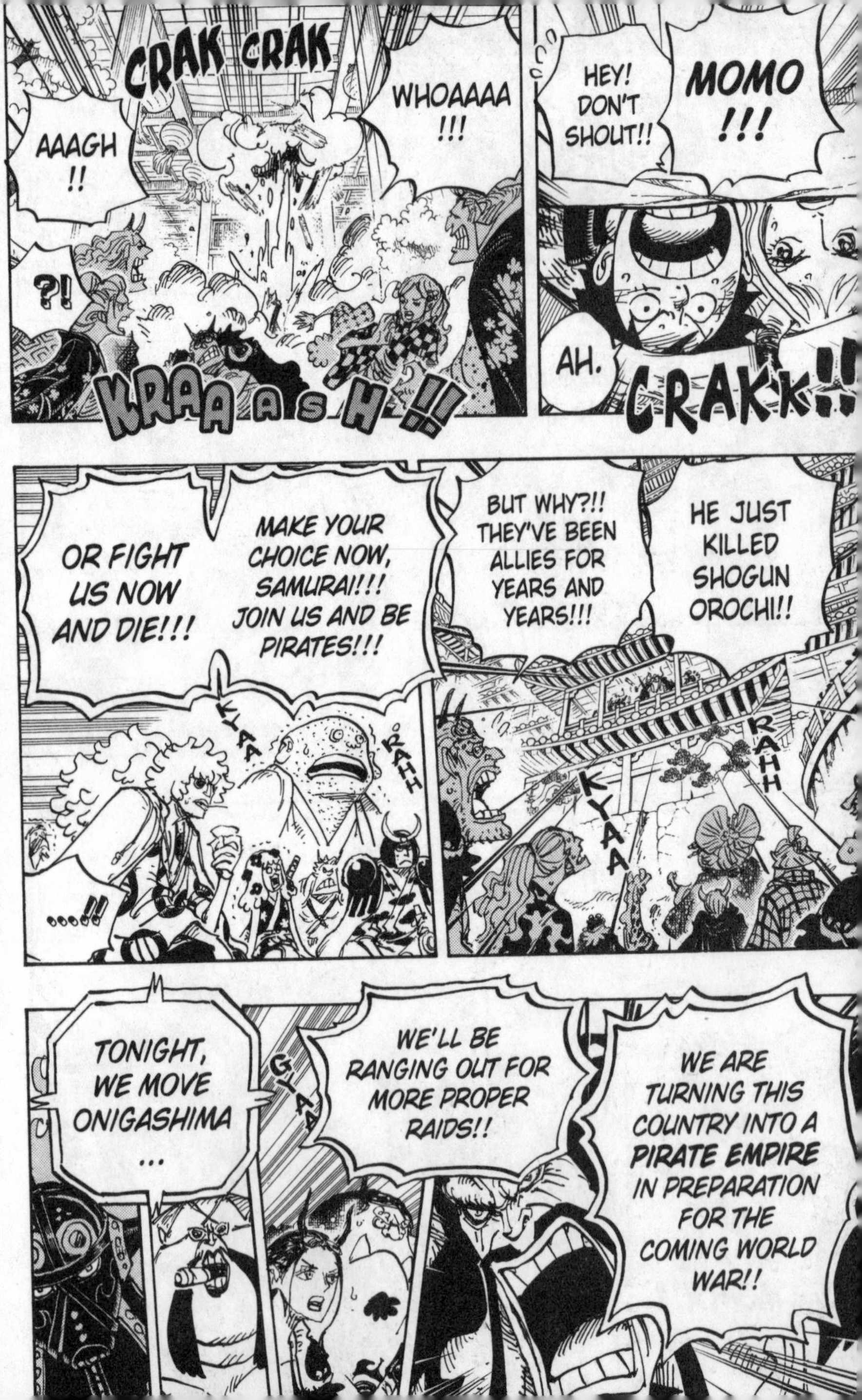
MOMO!!!
HEY! DON'T SHOUT!!
AH.
CRAKK!!
WHOAAAA!!!
CRAK CRAK
AAAGH!!
?!
KRAAASH!!
HE JUST KILLED SHOGUN OROCHI!!
BUT WHY?!! THEY'VE BEEN ALLIES FOR YEARS AND YEARS!!!
RAHH
KYAA
MAKE YOUR CHOICE NOW, SAMURAI!!! JOIN US AND BE PIRATES!!!
OR FIGHT US NOW AND DIE!!!
RAHH
KYAA
...!!
WE ARE TURNING THIS COUNTRY INTO A PIRATE EMPIRE IN PREPARATION FOR THE COMING WORLD WAR!!
WE'LL BE RANGING OUT FOR MORE PROPER RAIDS!!
GIAA
TONIGHT, WE MOVE ONIGASHIMA ...

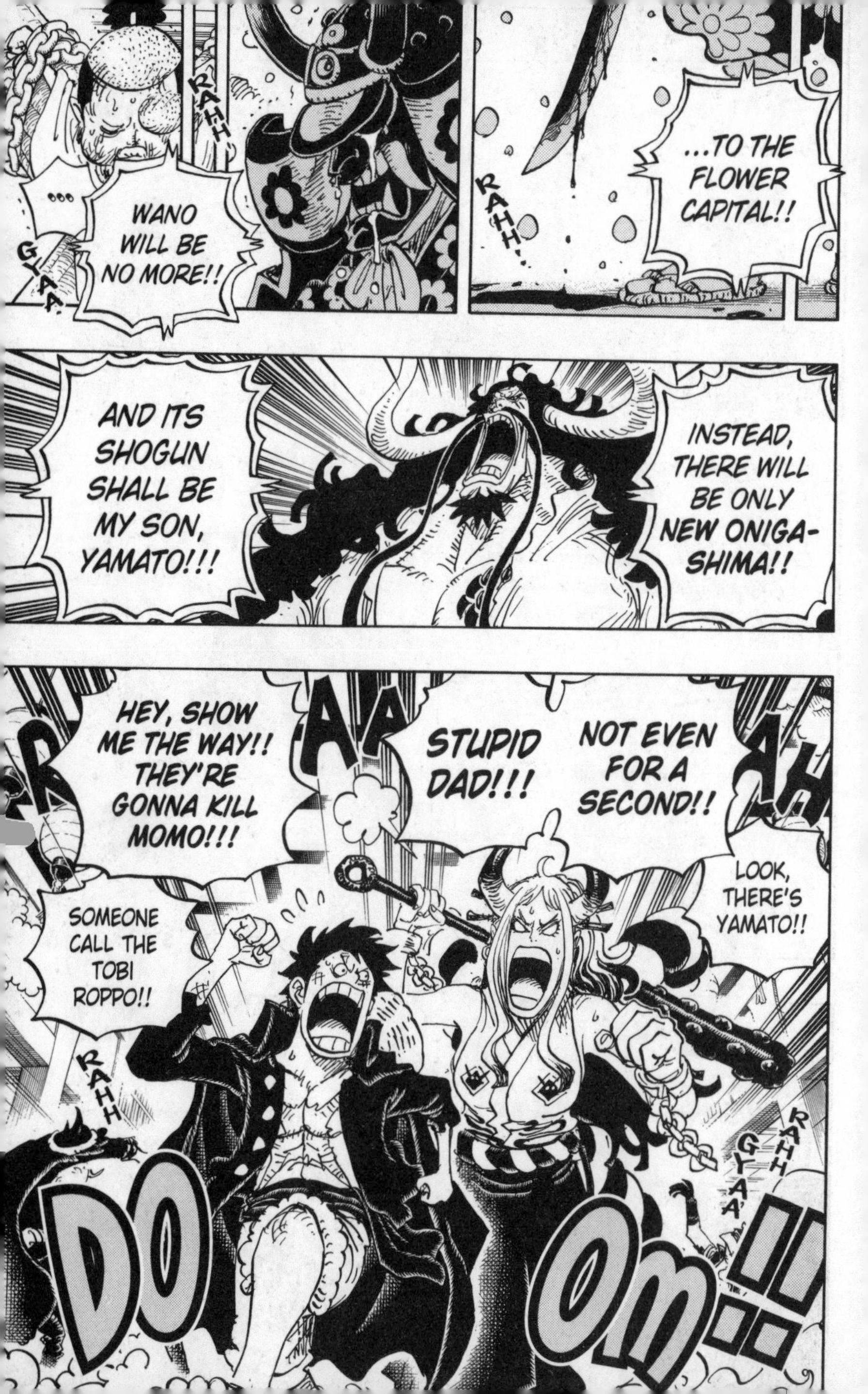
RAHH
...TO THE FLOWER CAPITAL!!
RAHH
WANO WILL BE NO MORE!!
...
GYAA
INSTEAD, THERE WILL BE ONLY NEW ONIGA-SHIMA!!
AND ITS SHOGUN SHALL BE MY SON, YAMATO!!!
NOT EVEN FOR A SECOND!!
LOOK, THERE'S YAMATO!!
STUPID DAD!!!
HEY, SHOW ME THE WAY!! THEY'RE GONNA KILL MOMO!!!
SOMEONE CALL THE TOBI ROPPO!!
RAHH
RAHH
GYAA
DOOM!!

SBS Question Corner

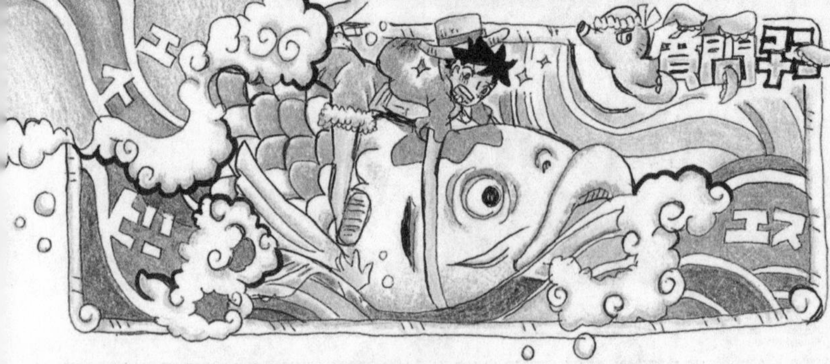

(Sankoko, Gunma)

Q: Oda Sensei! Look, over there! It's a UFO!! Let's start the SBS.

--The Man Respected by Higuma

A: What was that?!⚡ That was like an elementary school trick!! And you fooled me!! Dammit!! Oh, it says he's 11... So he is in elementary school...

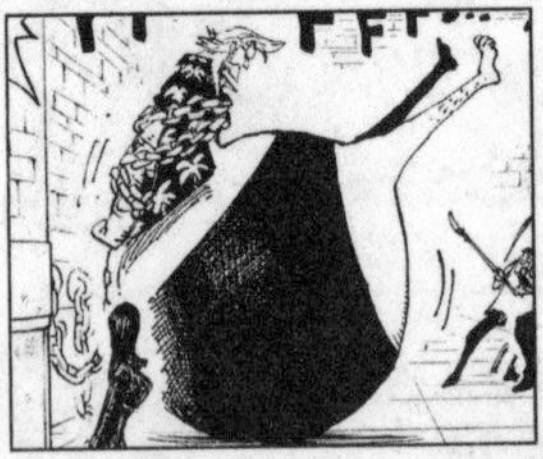

Q: Oda Sensei, hello! My mom farts around the clock all day long. Do you think she has the power of the Toot-Toot Fruit?

--Hata

A: No, that's just a sign of good gut health. Next question.

Q: Oda Sensei, hello! According to my grandma, Yamato's birthday is November 3. Is that true?

--Hata

A: Yep. Why wouldn't it be November 3?

Q: Please draw Law making a sour face after eating a pickled plum!

A:

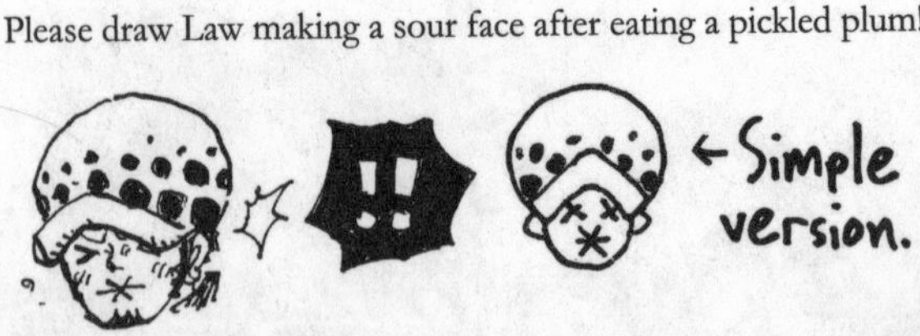
← Simple version.

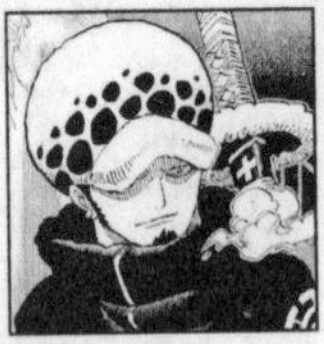

Q: I'm so, so, soooo curious about Broth Splatterina, the first crush of both Kid and Killer! What does she look like? I bet she's really cute!

--Onimaru

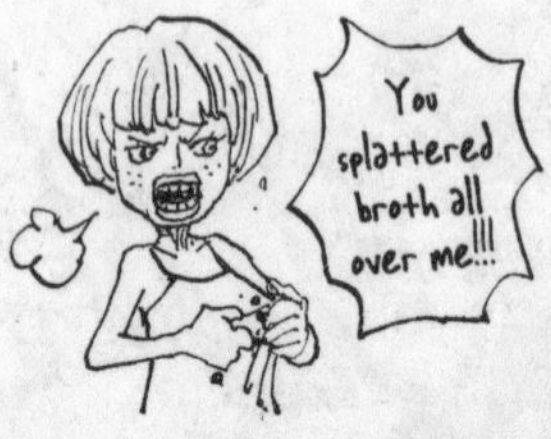
You splattered broth all over me!!!

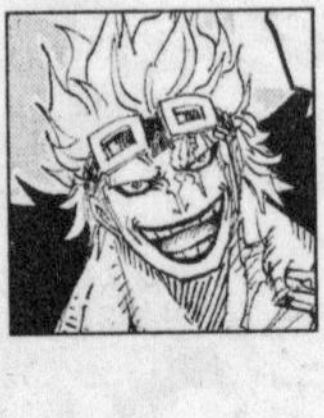

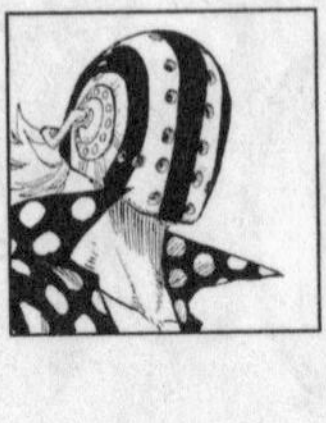

Chapter 986:
MY NAME

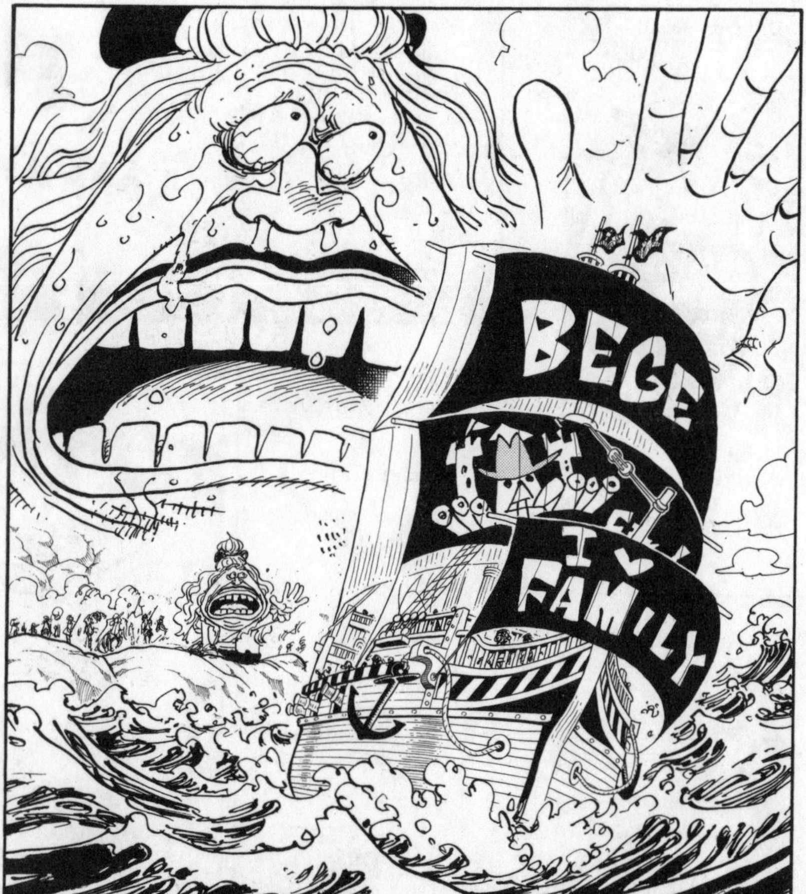
BEGE
I ♥ FAMILY

GANG BEGE'S OH MY FAMILY
VOL. 31: "ESCAPE FROM THE NAVY AND THE WEIRD MAN CALLING HIMSELF OUR FATHER!!"

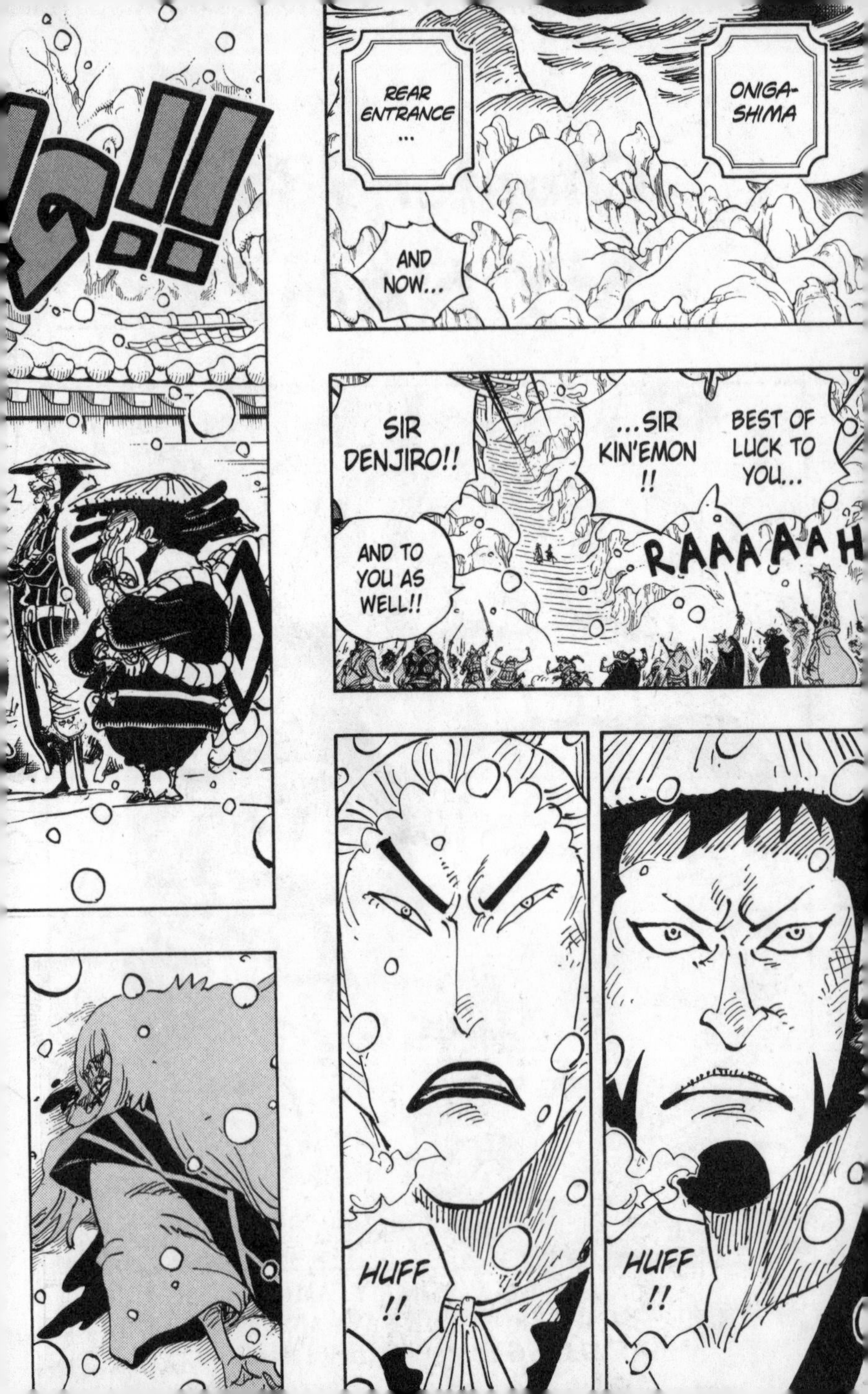
ONIGA-SHIMA
REAR ENTRANCE ...
AND NOW...
BEST OF LUCK TO YOU...
...SIR KIN'EMON !!
SIR DENJIRO!!
RAAAAAH
AND TO YOU AS WELL!!
HUFF !!
HUFF !!

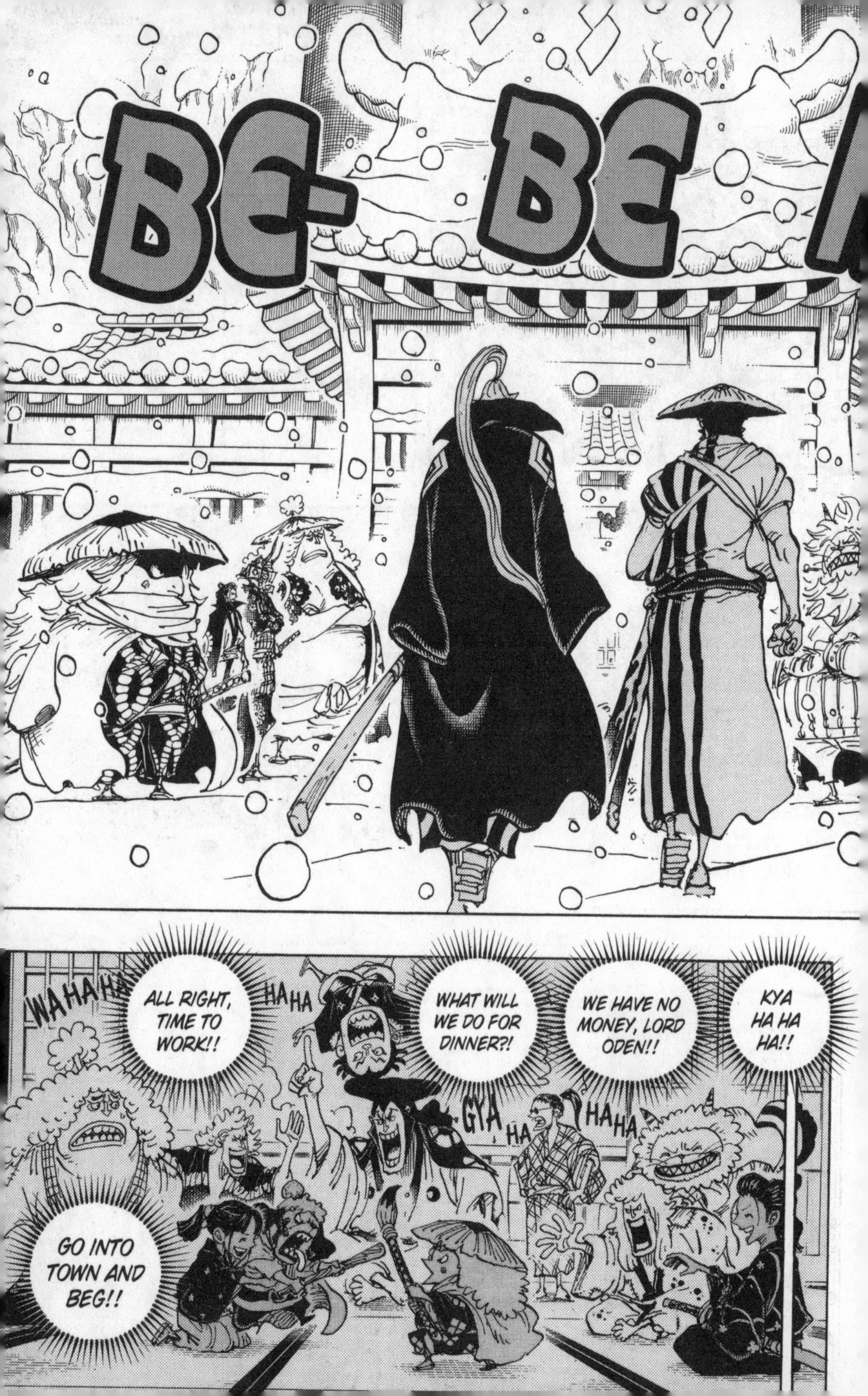
BE- BE
KYA HA HA HA!!
WE HAVE NO MONEY, LORD ODEN!!
WHAT WILL WE DO FOR DINNER?!
HA HA
ALL RIGHT, TIME TO WORK!!
WAHAHA
HAHA
GYA HA
GO INTO TOWN AND BEG!!

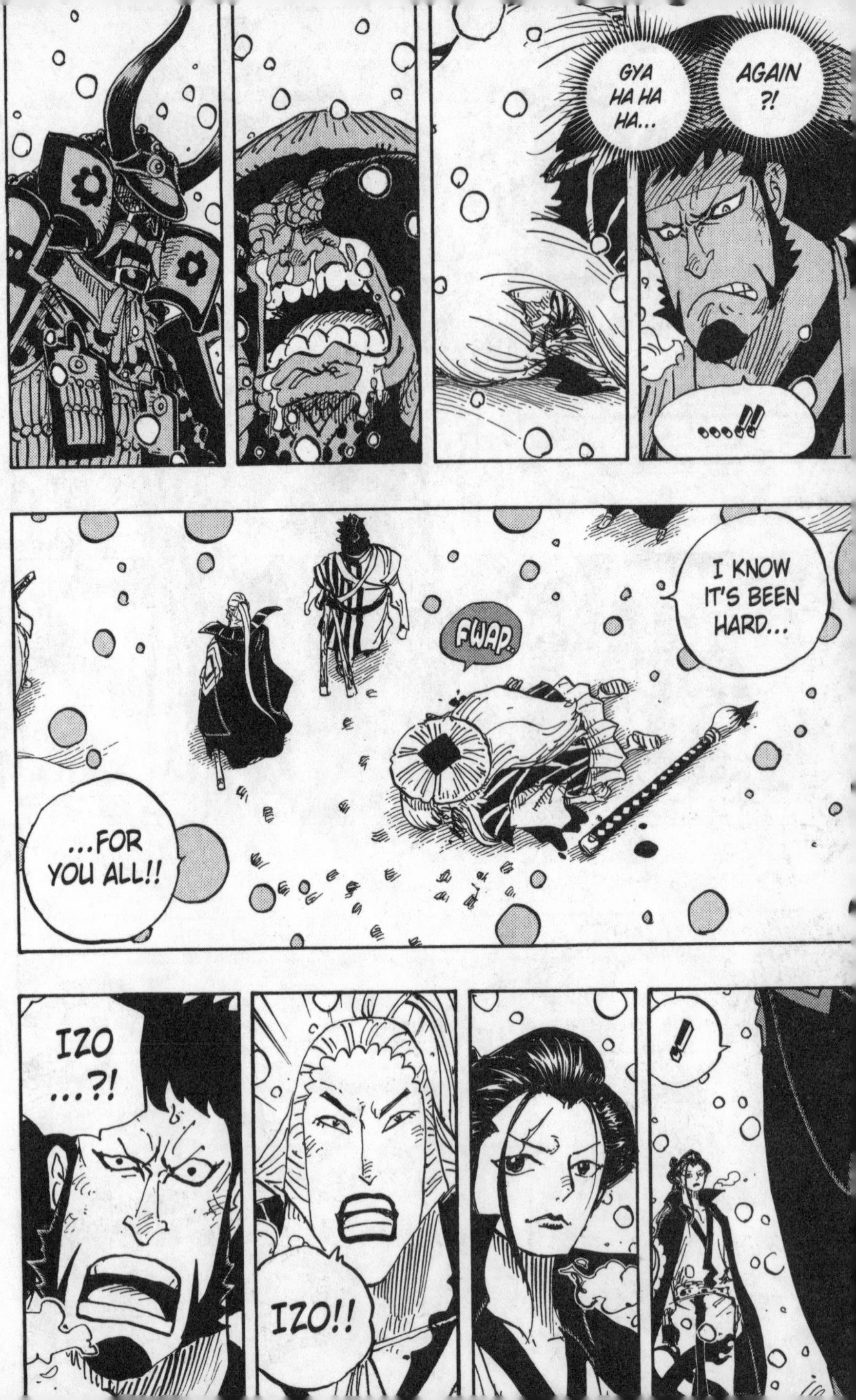
AGAIN ?!
GYA HA HA HA...
.....!!
I KNOW IT'S BEEN HARD...
FWAP
...FOR YOU ALL!!
!
IZO!!
IZO ...?!

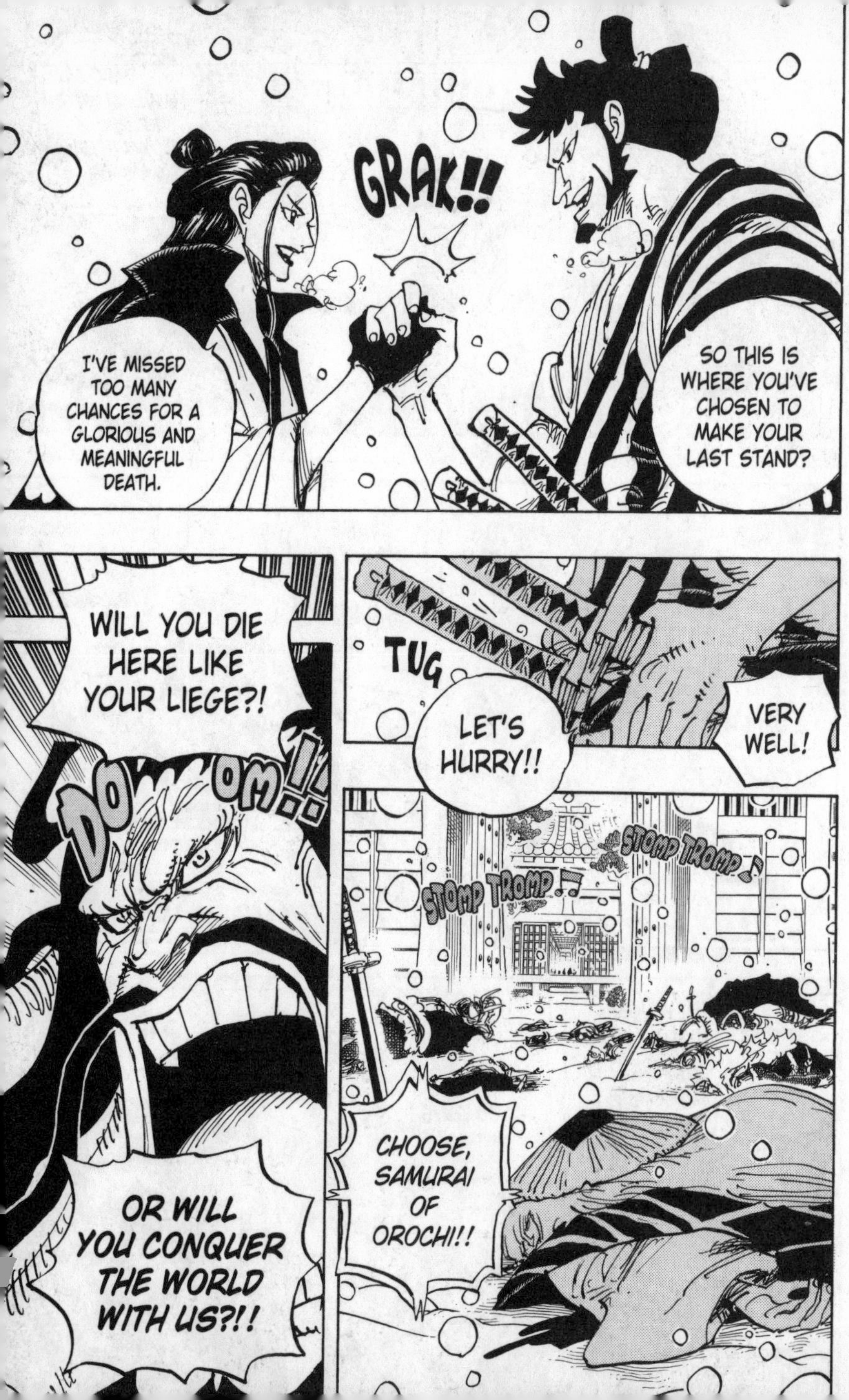
SO THIS IS WHERE YOU'VE CHOSEN TO MAKE YOUR LAST STAND?
GRAK!!
I'VE MISSED TOO MANY CHANCES FOR A GLORIOUS AND MEANINGFUL DEATH.
VERY WELL!
TUG
LET'S HURRY!!
STOMP TROMP
STOMP TROMP
CHOOSE, SAMURAI OF OROCHI!!
WILL YOU DIE HERE LIKE YOUR LIEGE?!
DO OM!!
OR WILL YOU CONQUER THE WORLD WITH US?!!

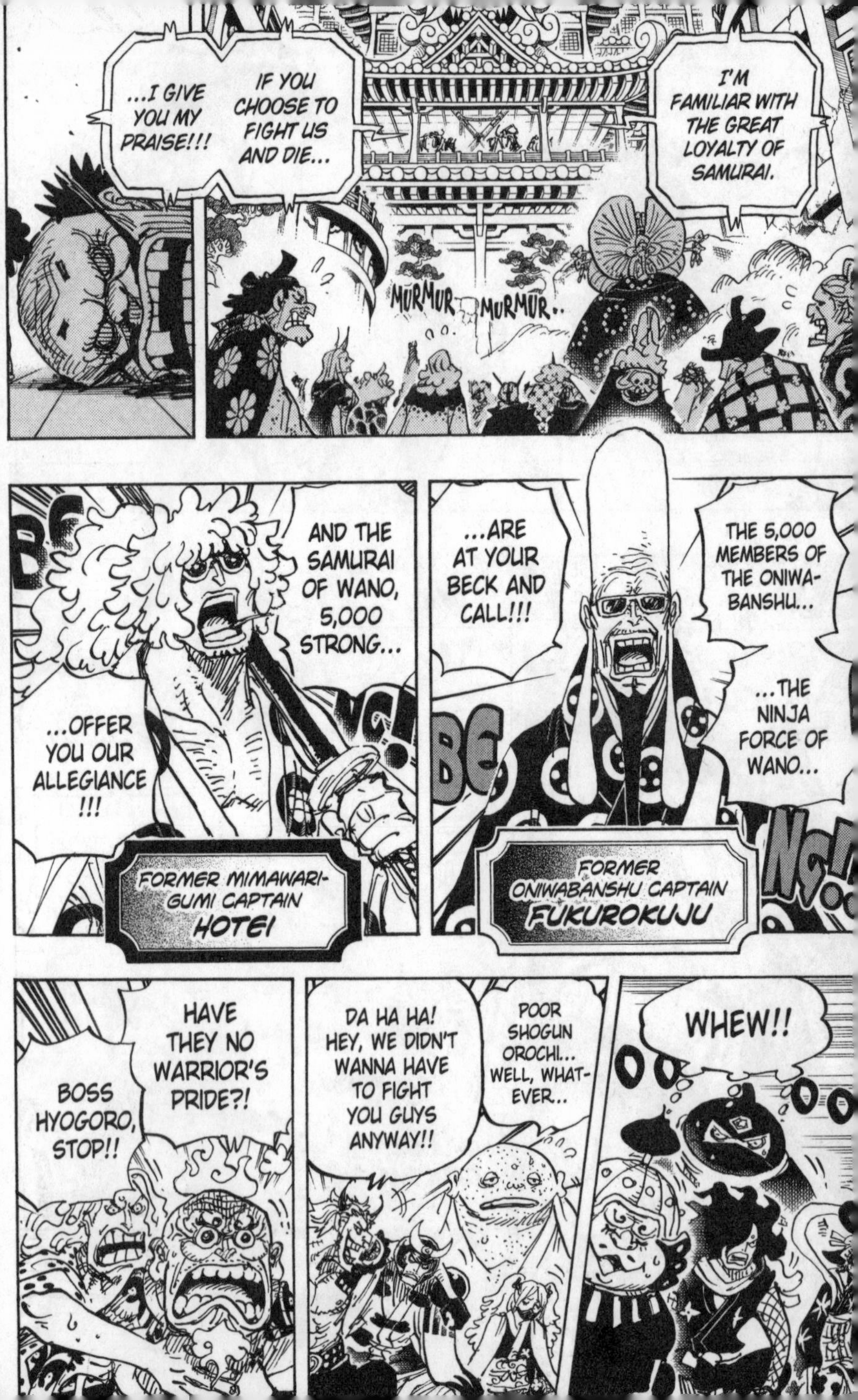
I'M FAMILIAR WITH THE GREAT LOYALTY OF SAMURAI.
IF YOU CHOOSE TO FIGHT US AND DIE...
...I GIVE YOU MY PRAISE!!!
MURMUR MURMUR...
THE 5,000 MEMBERS OF THE ONIWA-BANSHU...
...THE NINJA FORCE OF WANO...
...ARE AT YOUR BECK AND CALL!!!
FORMER ONIWABANSHU CAPTAIN FUKUROKUJU
AND THE SAMURAI OF WANO, 5,000 STRONG...
...OFFER YOU OUR ALLEGIANCE!!!
FORMER MIMAWARI-GUMI CAPTAIN HOTEI
WHEW!!
POOR SHOGUN OROCHI... WELL, WHAT-EVER...
DA HA HA! HEY, WE DIDN'T WANNA HAVE TO FIGHT YOU GUYS ANYWAY!!
HAVE THEY NO WARRIOR'S PRIDE?!
BOSS HYOGORO, STOP!!

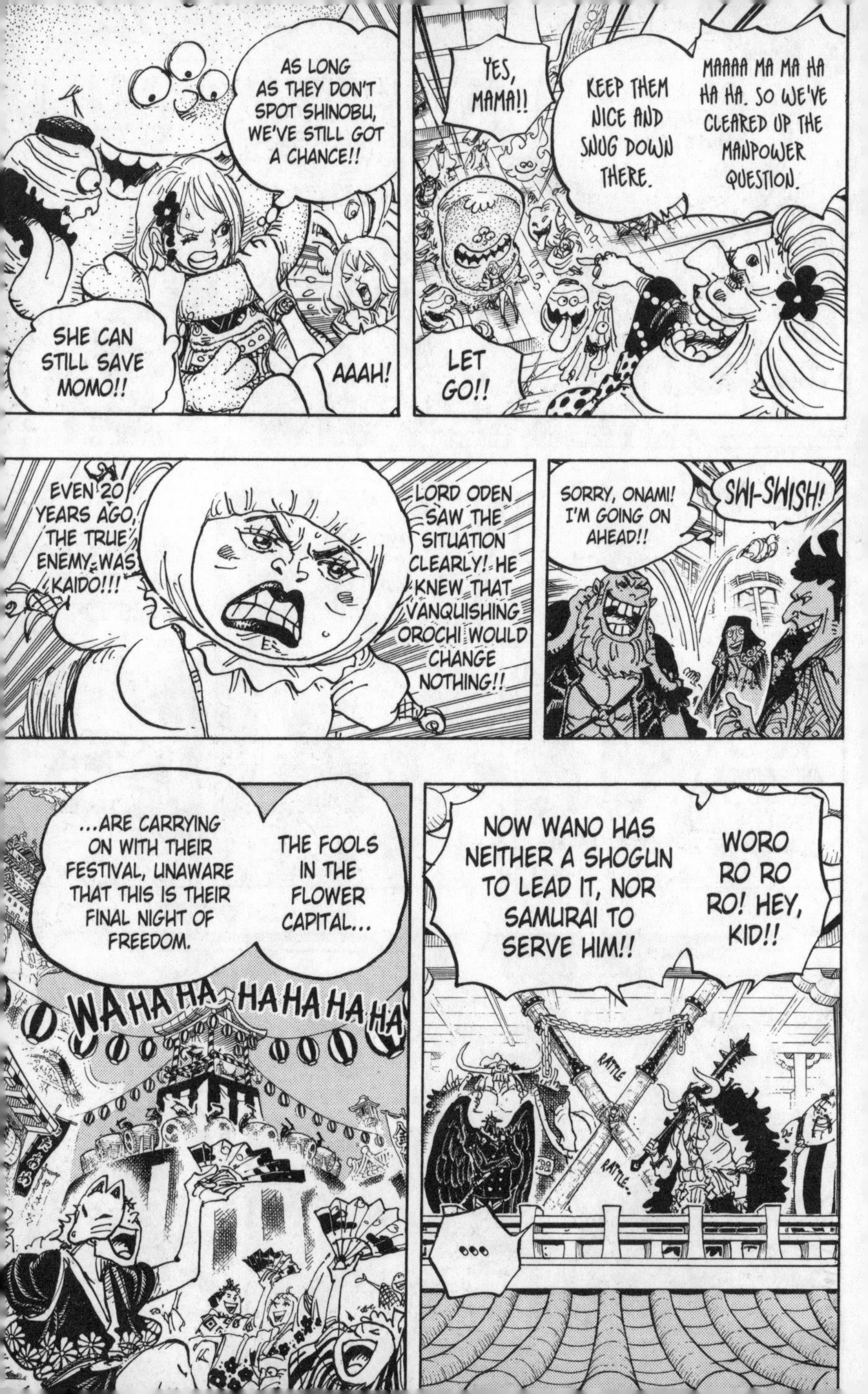
MAAAA MA MA HA HA HA. SO WE'VE CLEARED UP THE MANPOWER QUESTION.
KEEP THEM NICE AND SNUG DOWN THERE.
YES, MAMA!!
LET GO!!
AS LONG AS THEY DON'T SPOT SHINOBU, WE'VE STILL GOT A CHANCE!!
AAAH!
SHE CAN STILL SAVE MOMO!!
SWI-SWISH!
SORRY, ONAMI! I'M GOING ON AHEAD!!
LORD ODEN SAW THE SITUATION CLEARLY! HE KNEW THAT VANQUISHING OROCHI WOULD CHANGE NOTHING!!
EVEN 20 YEARS AGO, THE TRUE ENEMY WAS KAIDO!!!
WORO RO RO RO! HEY, KID!!
NOW WANO HAS NEITHER A SHOGUN TO LEAD IT, NOR SAMURAI TO SERVE HIM!!
RATTLE
RATTLE...
...
THE FOOLS IN THE FLOWER CAPITAL...
...ARE CARRYING ON WITH THEIR FESTIVAL, UNAWARE THAT THIS IS THEIR FINAL NIGHT OF FREEDOM.
WAHAHA HAHAHAHAHA

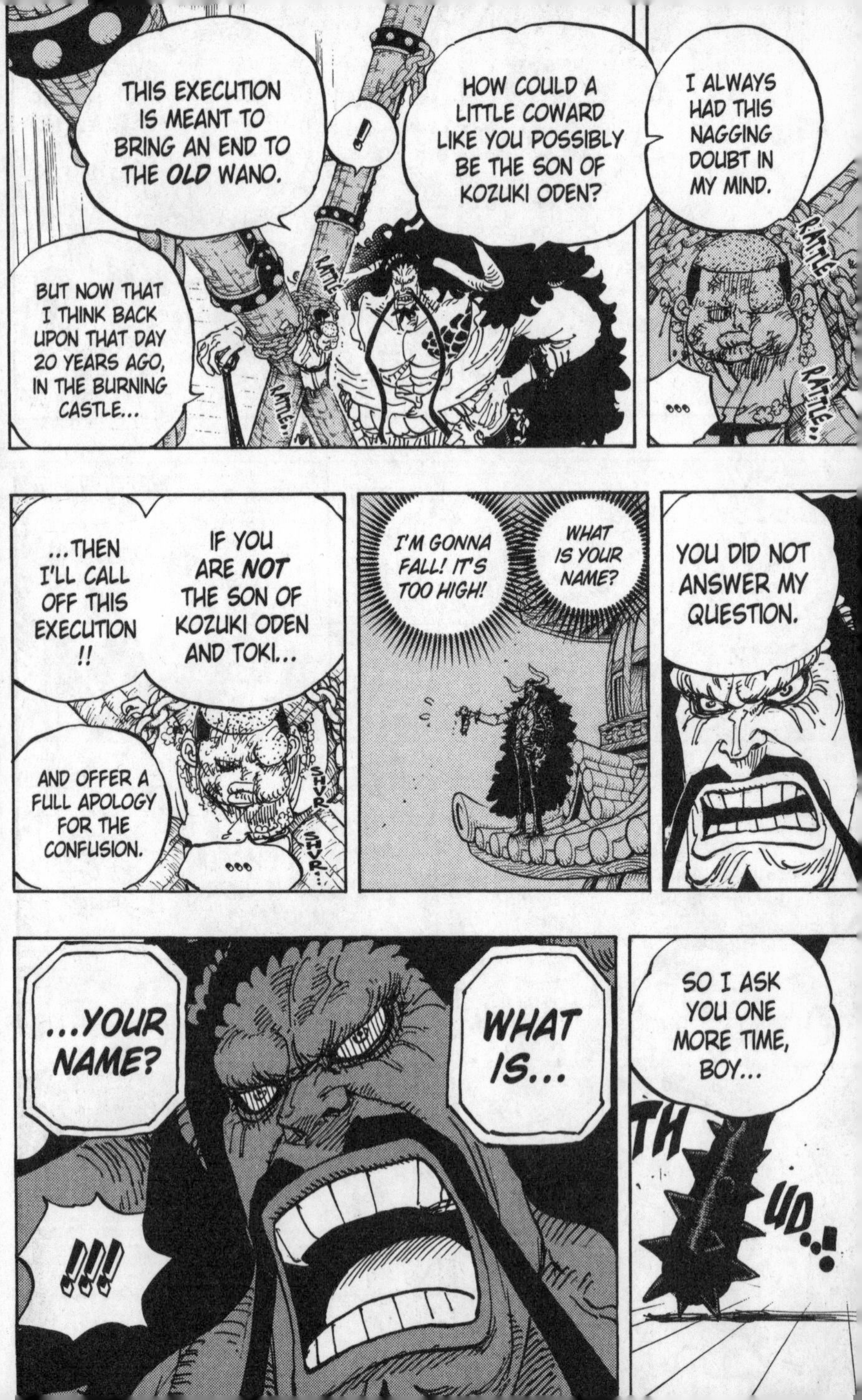
I ALWAYS HAD THIS NAGGING DOUBT IN MY MIND.
RATTLE
RATTLE...
...
HOW COULD A LITTLE COWARD LIKE YOU POSSIBLY BE THE SON OF KOZUKI ODEN?
!
THIS EXECUTION IS MEANT TO BRING AN END TO THE *OLD* WANO.
RATTLE
BUT NOW THAT I THINK BACK UPON THAT DAY 20 YEARS AGO, IN THE BURNING CASTLE...
RATTLE...
YOU DID NOT ANSWER MY QUESTION.
WHAT IS YOUR NAME?
I'M GONNA FALL! IT'S TOO HIGH!
IF YOU ARE *NOT* THE SON OF KOZUKI ODEN AND TOKI...
...THEN I'LL CALL OFF THIS EXECUTION !!
SHVR
SHVR...
AND OFFER A FULL APOLOGY FOR THE CONFUSION.
...
SO I ASK YOU ONE MORE TIME, BOY...
THUD..!
WHAT IS...
...YOUR NAME?
!!!

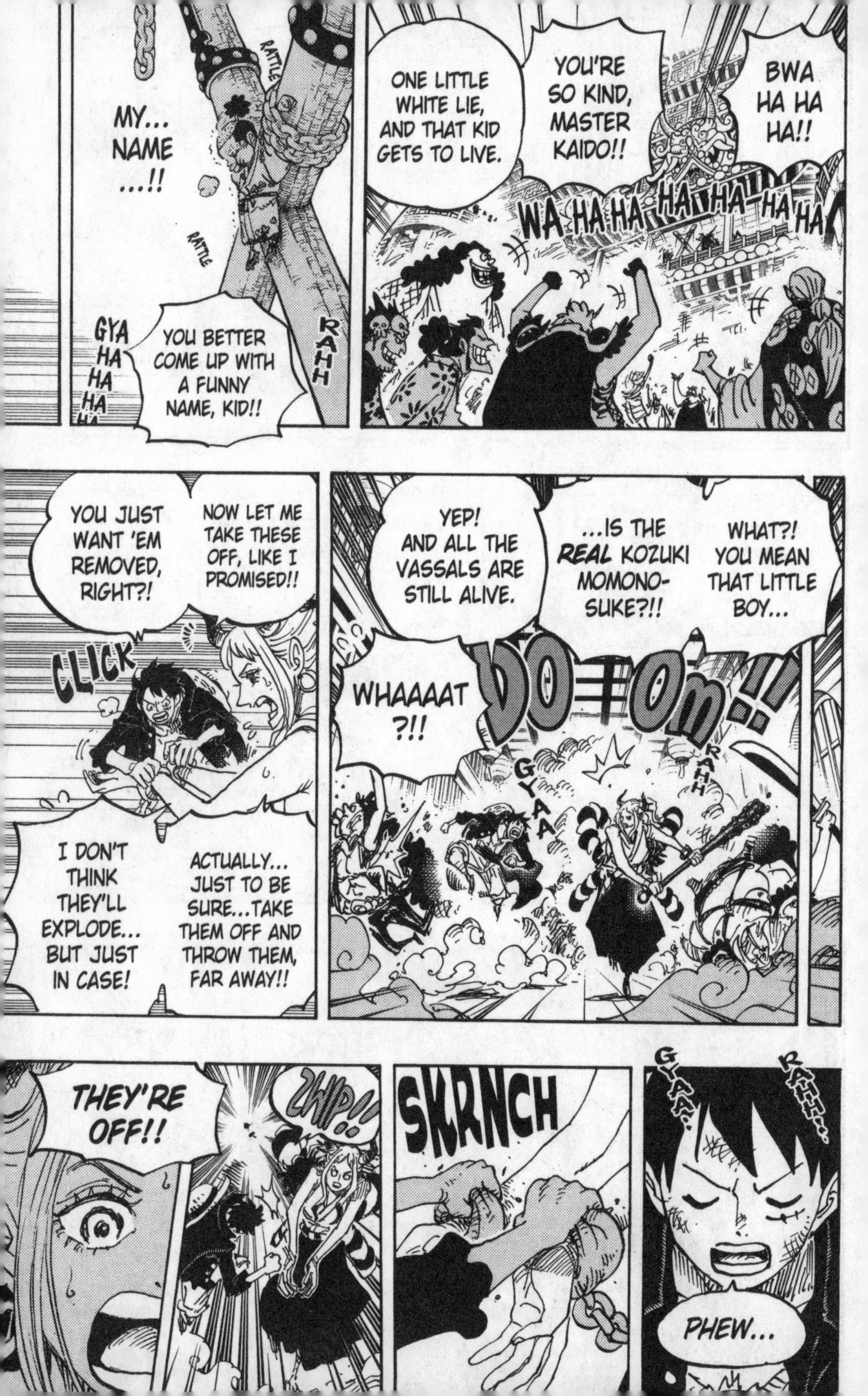
BWA HA HA HA!!
YOU'RE SO KIND, MASTER KAIDO!!
ONE LITTLE WHITE LIE, AND THAT KID GETS TO LIVE.
WA HA HA HA HA HA HA
RATTLE
MY... NAME ...!!
RATTLE
RAHH
YOU BETTER COME UP WITH A FUNNY NAME, KID!!
GYA HA HA HA
WHAT?! YOU MEAN THAT LITTLE BOY...
...IS THE *REAL* KOZUKI MOMONOSUKE?!!
YEP! AND ALL THE VASSALS ARE STILL ALIVE.
WHAAAAT?!!
DOOM!!
RAHH
GYAA
NOW LET ME TAKE THESE OFF, LIKE I PROMISED!!
YOU JUST WANT 'EM REMOVED, RIGHT?!
CLICK
ACTUALLY... JUST TO BE SURE...TAKE THEM OFF AND THROW THEM, FAR AWAY!!
I DON'T THINK THEY'LL EXPLODE... BUT JUST IN CASE!
RAHH...
GYAA
PHEW...
SKRNCH
ZWIP!!
THEY'RE OFF!!

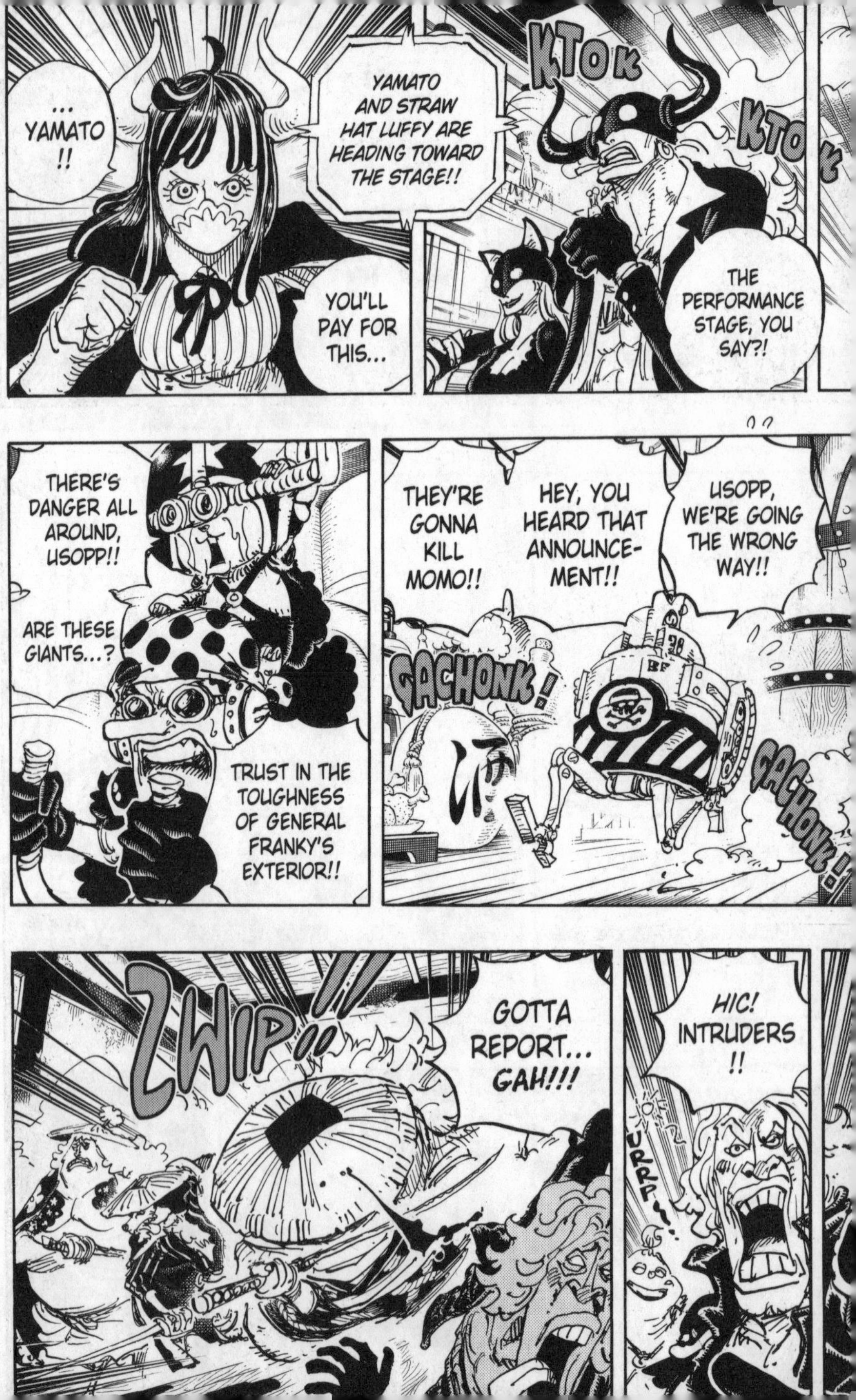
KTOK
KTOK
THE PERFORMANCE STAGE, YOU SAY?!
YAMATO AND STRAW HAT LUFFY ARE HEADING TOWARD THE STAGE!!
... YAMATO !!
YOU'LL PAY FOR THIS...
USOPP, WE'RE GOING THE WRONG WAY!!
HEY, YOU HEARD THAT ANNOUNCEMENT!!
THEY'RE GONNA KILL MOMO!!
GACHONK!!
GACHONK!
THERE'S DANGER ALL AROUND, USOPP!!
ARE THESE GIANTS...?
TRUST IN THE TOUGHNESS OF GENERAL FRANKY'S EXTERIOR!!
HIC! INTRUDERS !!
URRP...
GOTTA REPORT... GAH!!!
ZWIP!!

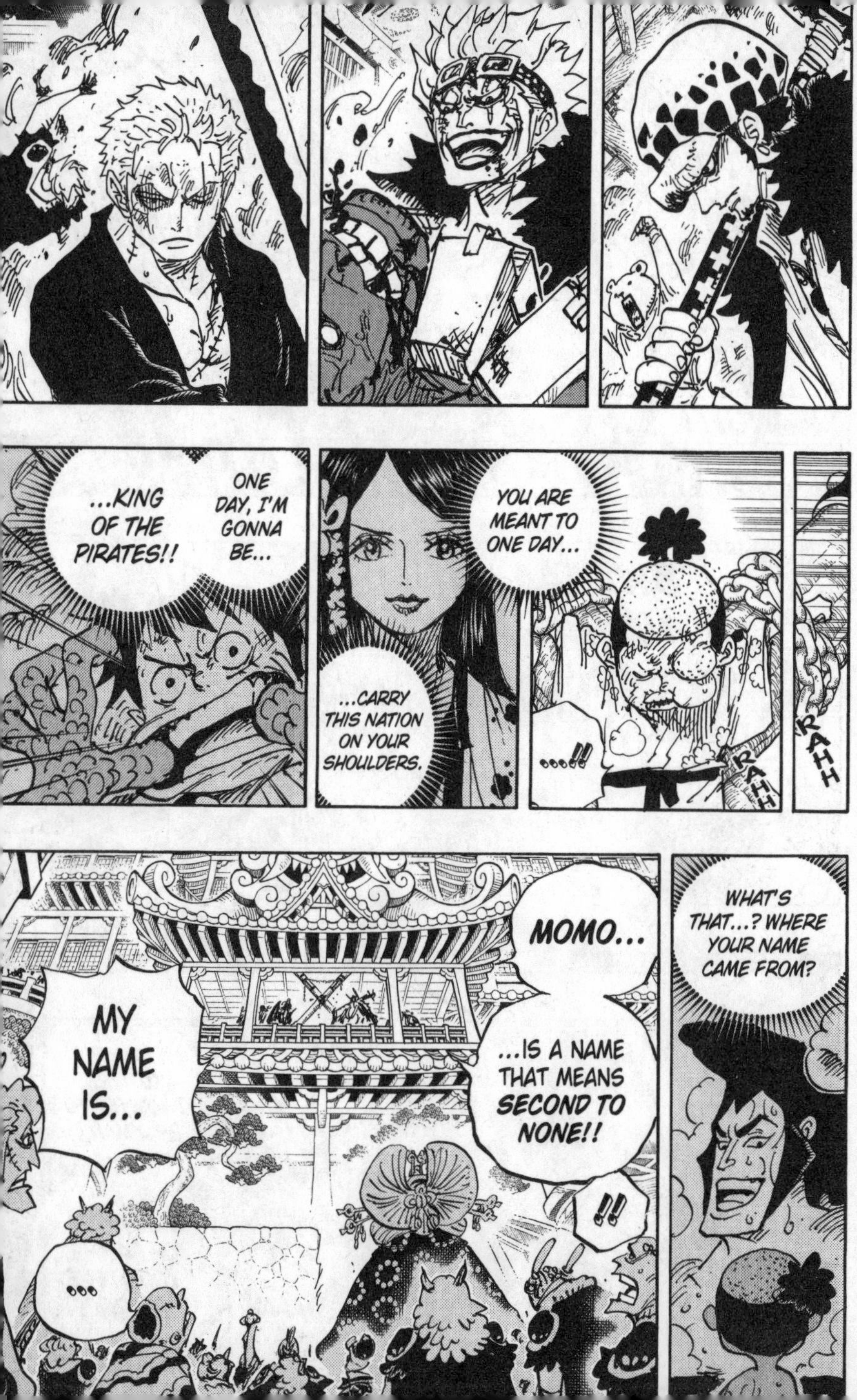

RAHH
RAHH
...!!
YOU ARE MEANT TO ONE DAY...
...CARRY THIS NATION ON YOUR SHOULDERS.
ONE DAY, I'M GONNA BE...
...KING OF THE PIRATES!!
WHAT'S THAT...? WHERE YOUR NAME CAME FROM?
MOMO...
...IS A NAME THAT MEANS SECOND TO NONE!!
!!
MY NAME IS...
...

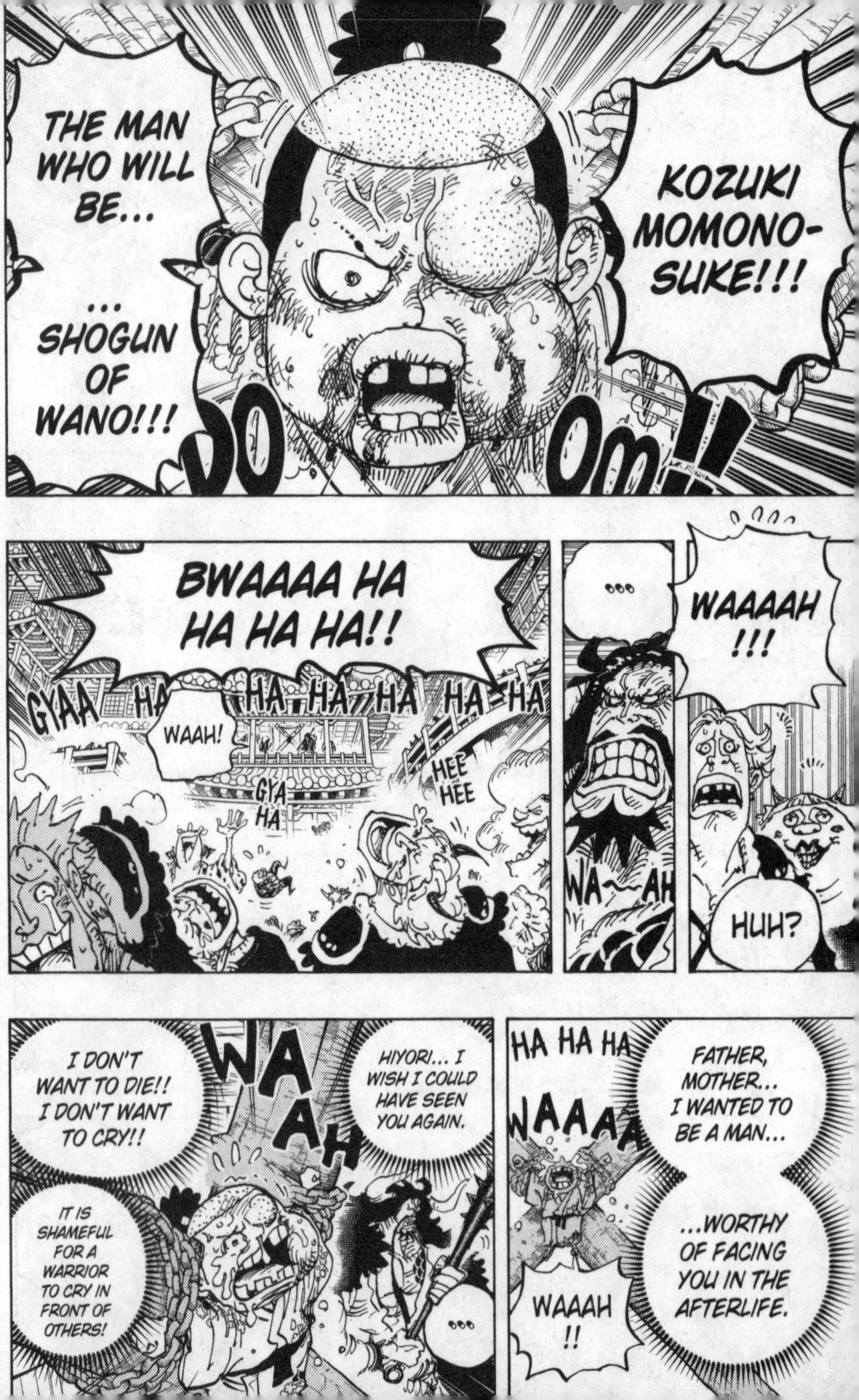
KOZUKI MOMONOSUKE!!!
THE MAN WHO WILL BE...
...SHOGUN OF WANO!!!
DOOOM!!
WAAAAH!!!
HUH?
...
WA~AH
BWAAAA HA HA HA HA!!
GYAA HA HA HA HA HA HA
WAAH!
HEE HEE
GYA HA
HA HA HA
FATHER, MOTHER... I WANTED TO BE A MAN...
...WORTHY OF FACING YOU IN THE AFTERLIFE.
WAAAA
WAAAH!!
HIYORI... I WISH I COULD HAVE SEEN YOU AGAIN.
WAAH
I DON'T WANT TO DIE!! I DON'T WANT TO CRY!!
IT IS SHAMEFUL FOR A WARRIOR TO CRY IN FRONT OF OTHERS!
...

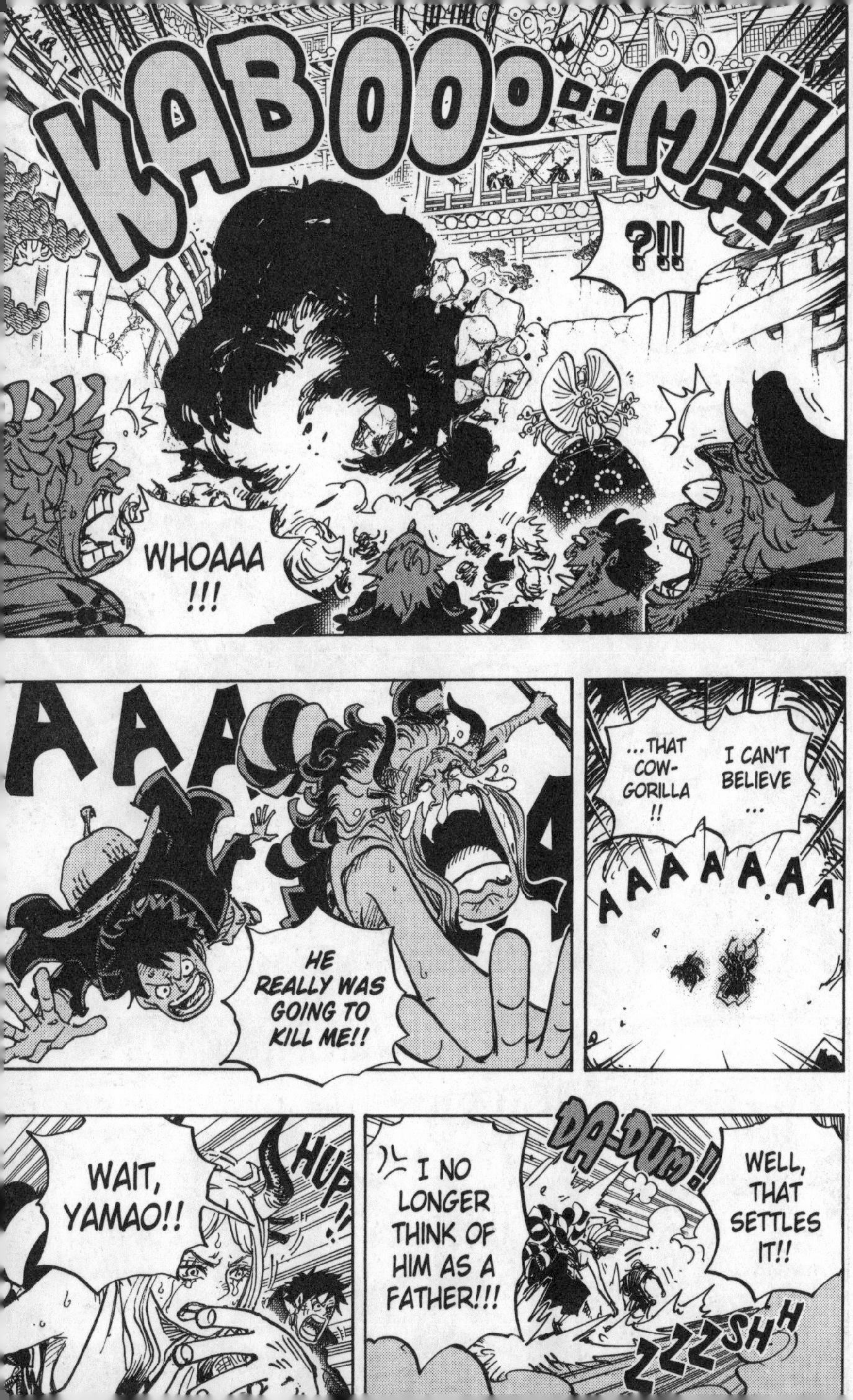
KABOOO--M!!!
?!!
WHOAAA!!!
I CAN'T BELIEVE ...
...THAT COW-GORILLA!!
AAAAAAAA
AAAA
HE REALLY WAS GOING TO KILL ME!!
WELL, THAT SETTLES IT!!
DA-DUM!
I NO LONGER THINK OF HIM AS A FATHER!!!
ZZZSHH
WAIT, YAMAO!!
HUP!!

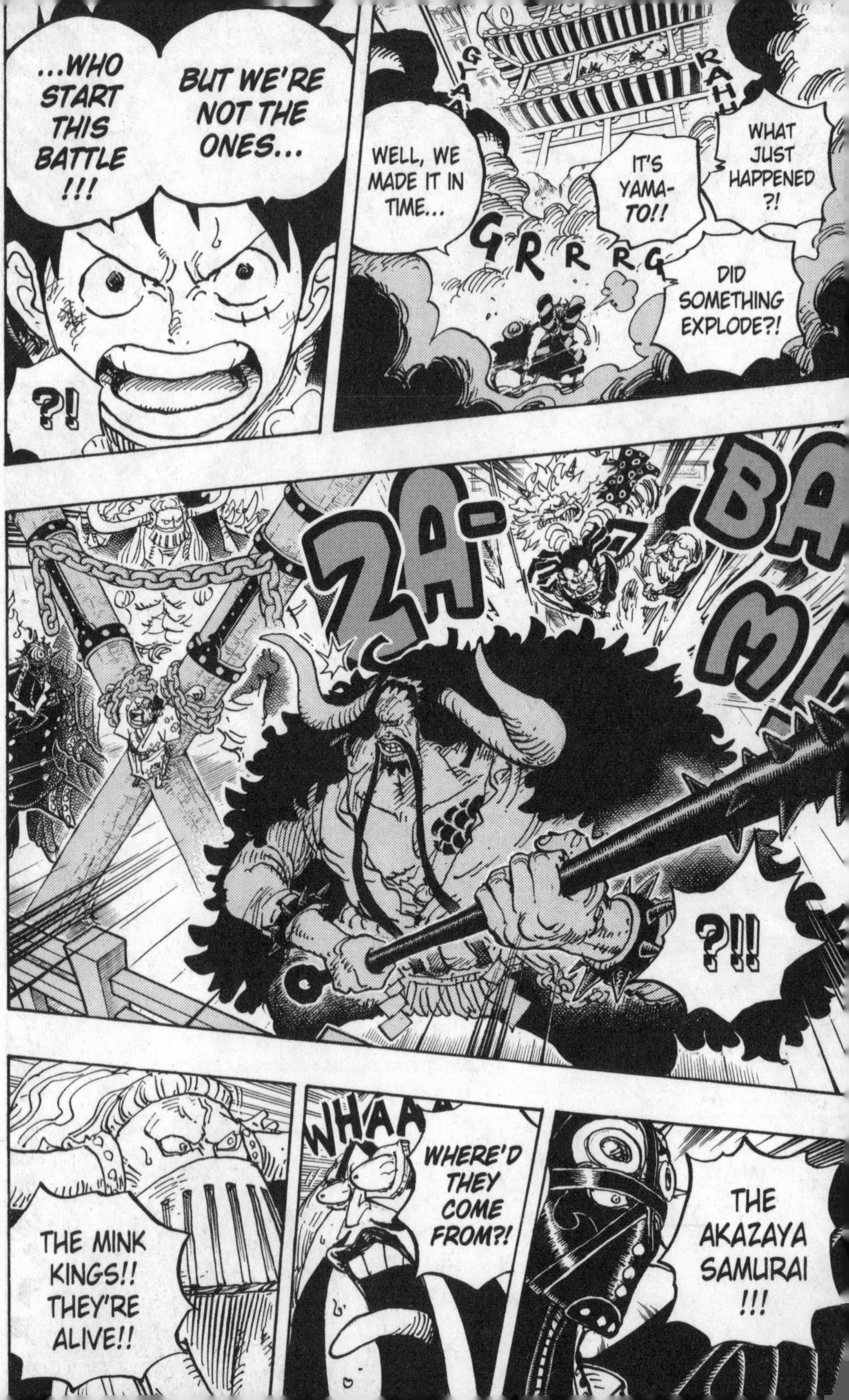

WHAT JUST HAPPENED?!
RAHH
IT'S YAMATO!!
GYAA
WELL, WE MADE IT IN TIME...
DID SOMETHING EXPLODE?!
GRRRRG
BUT WE'RE NOT THE ONES...
...WHO START THIS BATTLE!!!
?!
BA
M!
ZA-
?!!
THE AKAZAYA SAMURAI!!!
WHAA
WHERE'D THEY COME FROM?!
THE MINK KINGS!! THEY'RE ALIVE!!

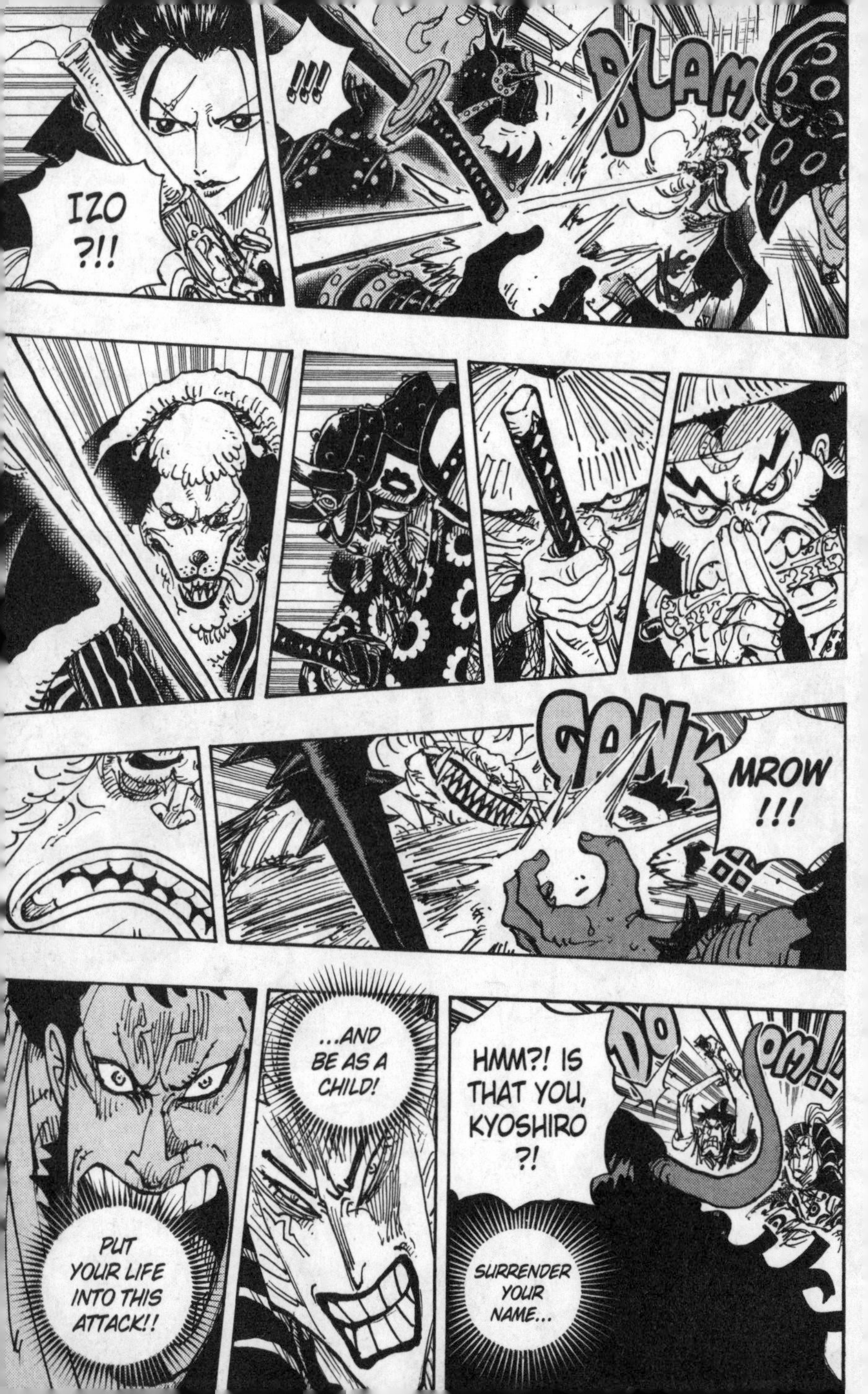
BLAM
!!!
IZO ?!!
GONK
MROW !!!
DO OM!!
HMM?! IS THAT YOU, KYOSHIRO ?!
SURRENDER YOUR NAME...
...AND BE AS A CHILD!
PUT YOUR LIFE INTO THIS ATTACK!!

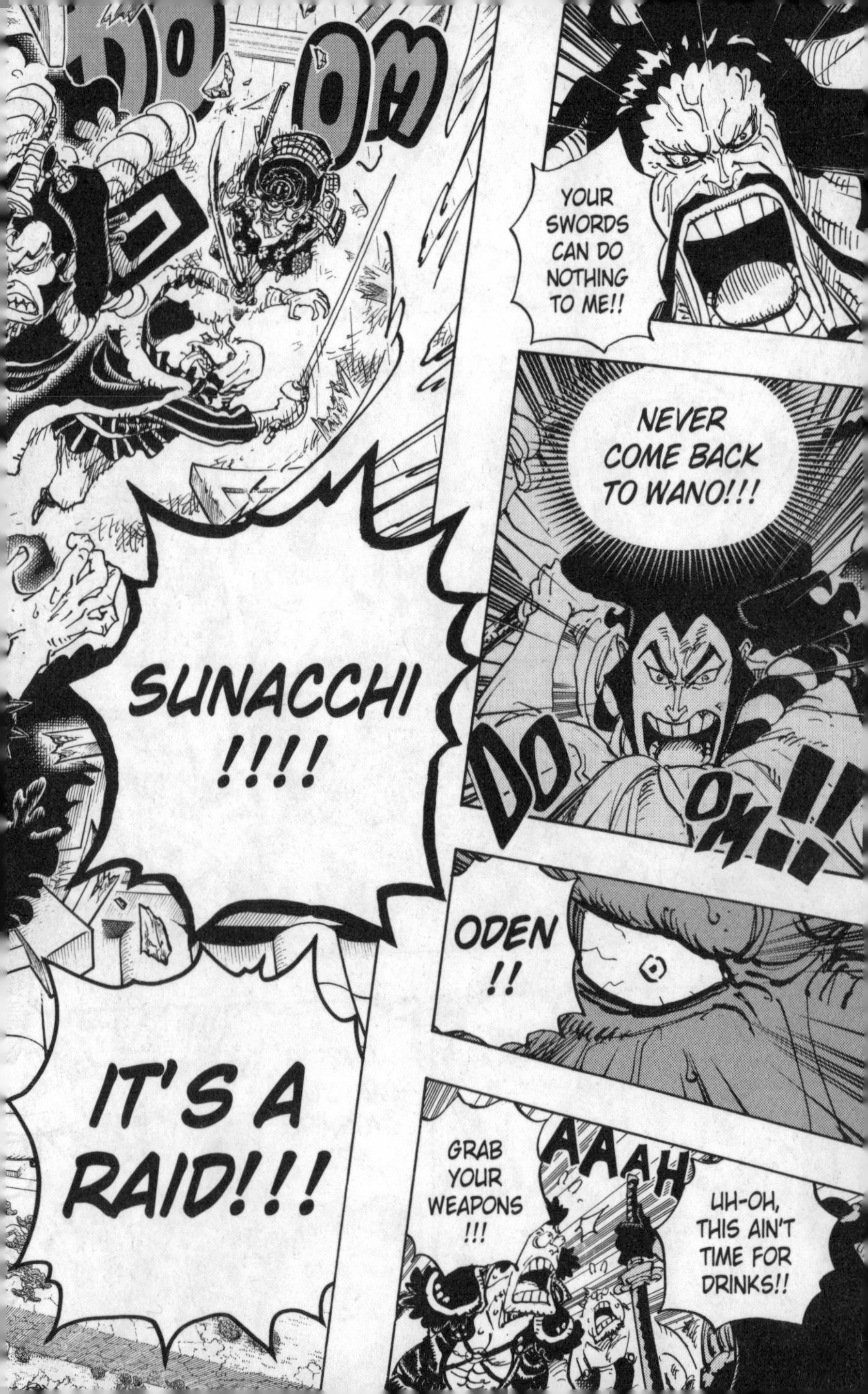
YOUR SWORDS CAN DO NOTHING TO ME!!
NEVER COME BACK TO WANO!!!
DOOM!!
ODEN !!
UH-OH, THIS AIN'T TIME FOR DRINKS!!
AAAAH
GRAB YOUR WEAPONS !!!
DOOM
SUNACCHI !!!!
IT'S A RAID!!!

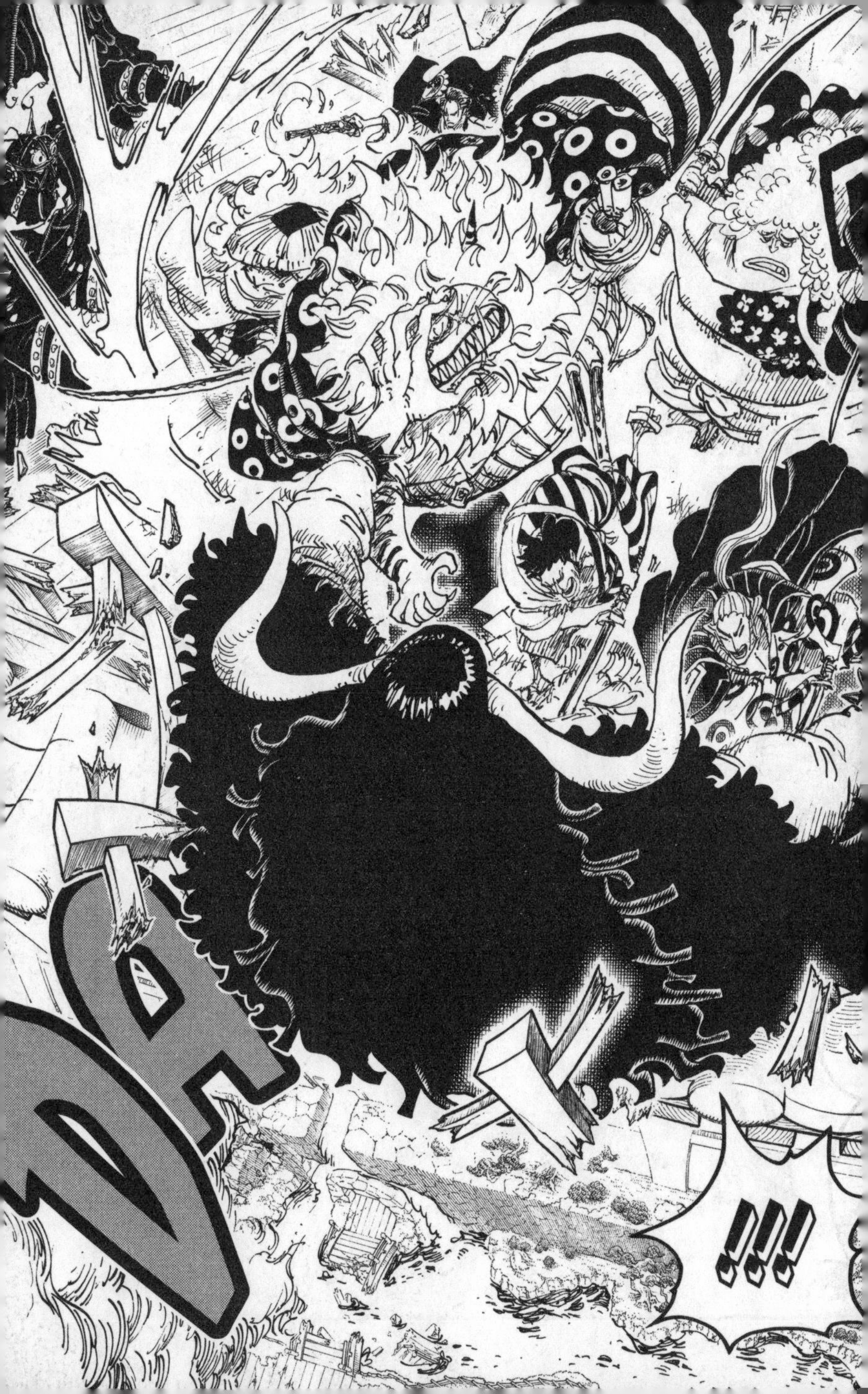
!!!

Chapter 987: VASSALS OF GLORY

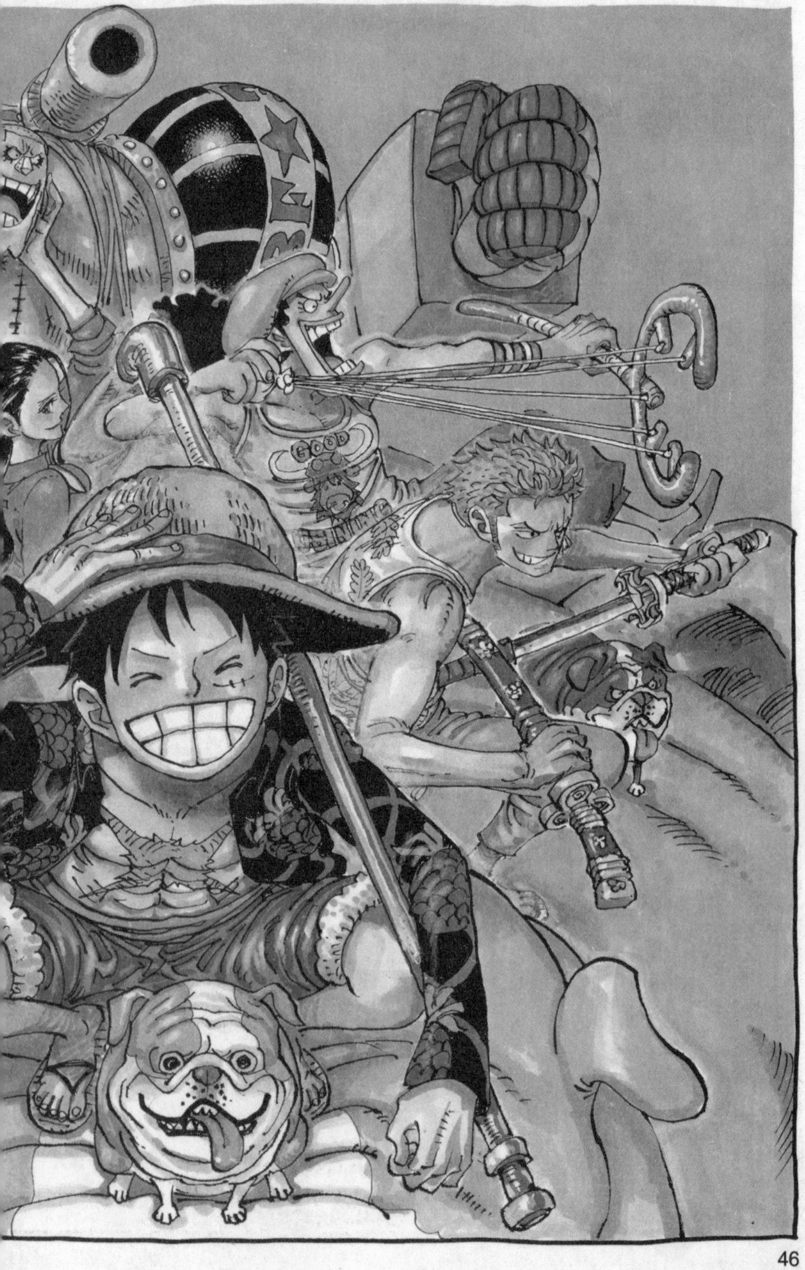
GOOD

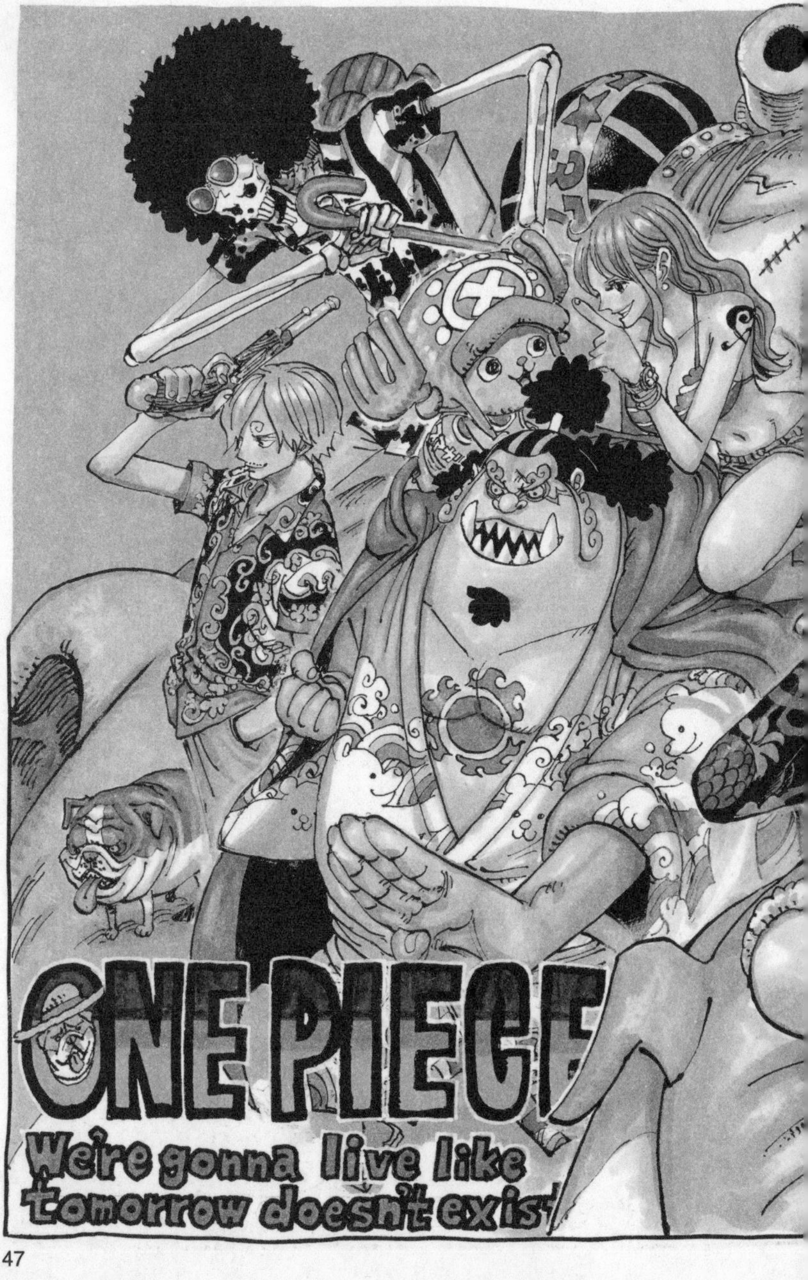
ONE PIECE
We're gonna live like tomorrow doesn't exist

vol.98
ONE PIECE

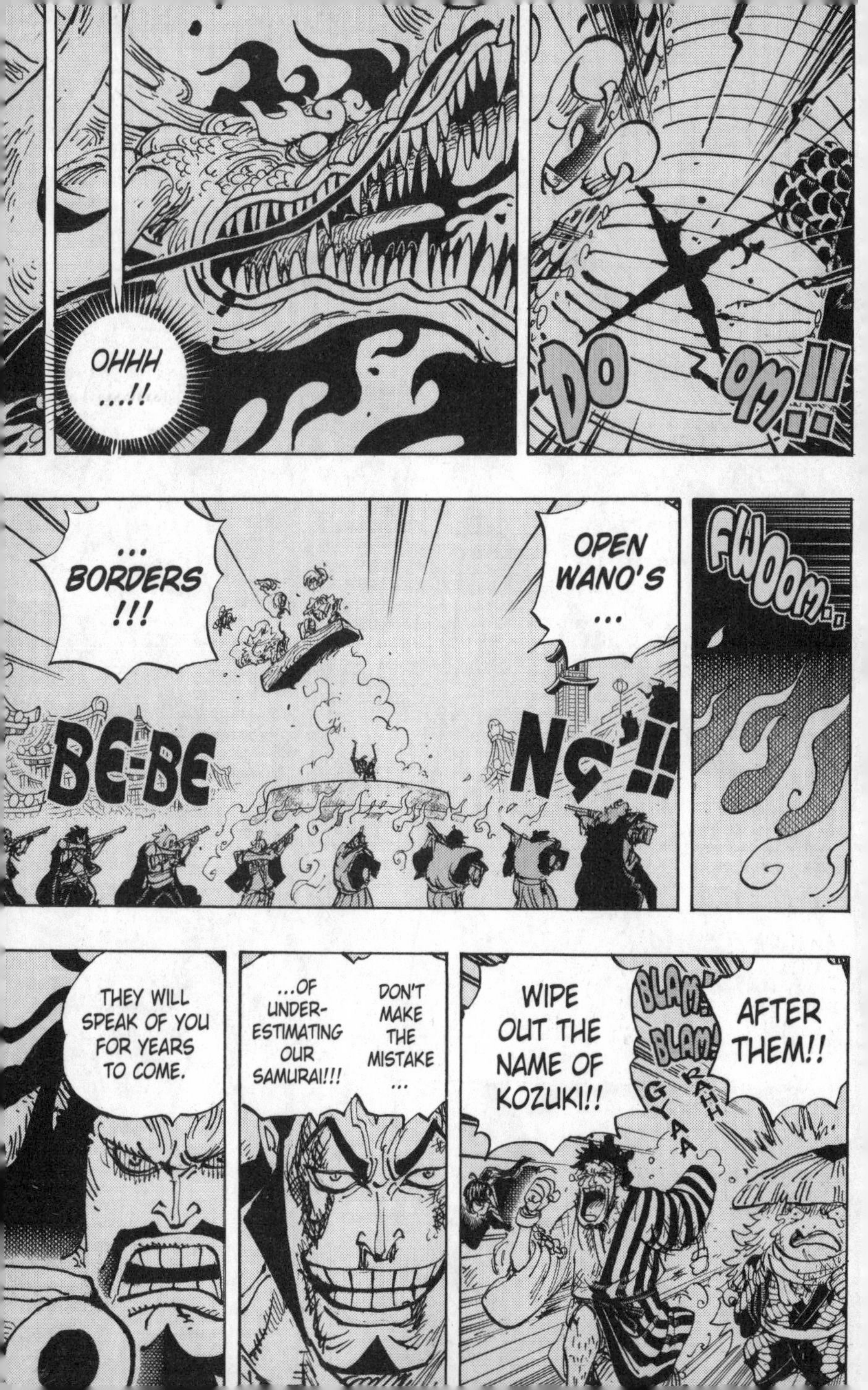
DO
OM!!
OHHH ...!!
FWOOM..
OPEN WANO'S ...
... BORDERS!!!
BE-BE
NG!!
AFTER THEM!!
BLAM! BLAM!
GYAA
RAHH
WIPE OUT THE NAME OF KOZUKI!!
DON'T MAKE THE MISTAKE ...
...OF UNDER-ESTIMATING OUR SAMURAI!!!
THEY WILL SPEAK OF YOU FOR YEARS TO COME.

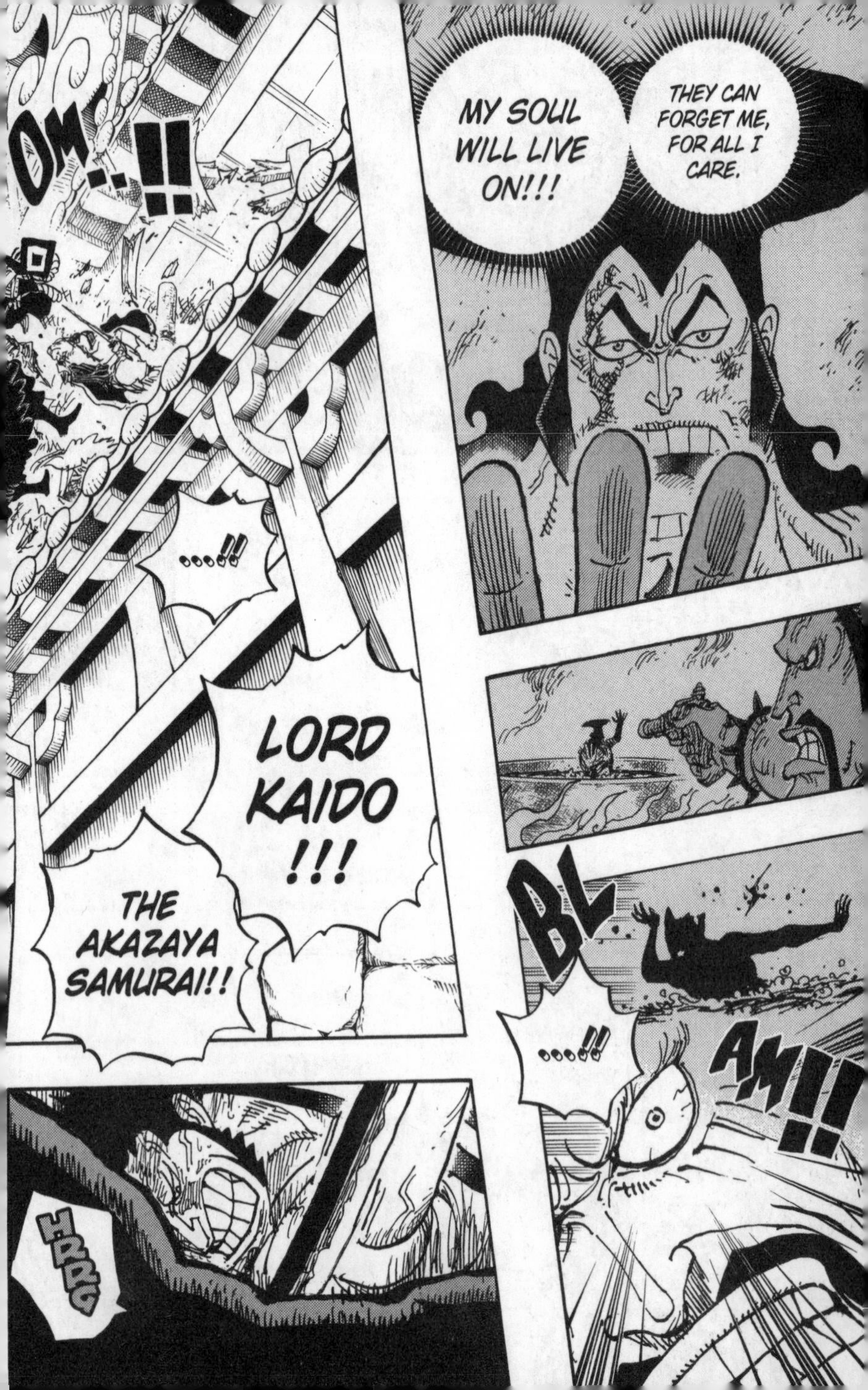
THEY CAN FORGET ME, FOR ALL I CARE.
MY SOUL WILL LIVE ON!!!
BL
AM!!
...!!
OM...!!
...!!
LORD KAIDO!!!
THE AKAZAYA SAMURAI!!
HRRG

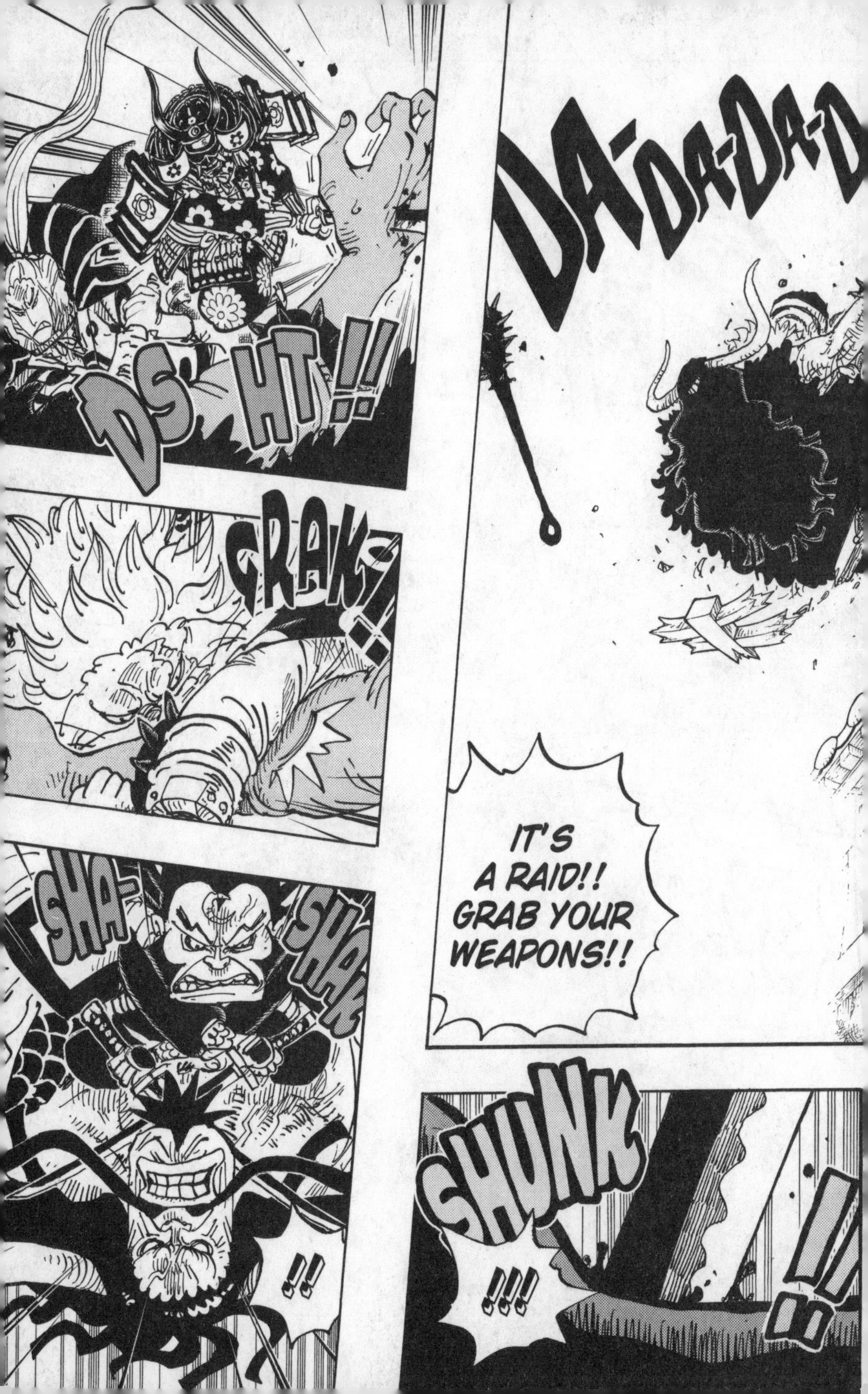
DA-DA-DA-D
IT'S A RAID!! GRAB YOUR WEAPONS!!
SHUNK
!!
!!!
DS-HT!!!
GRAK!!
SHA-
SHAK
!!

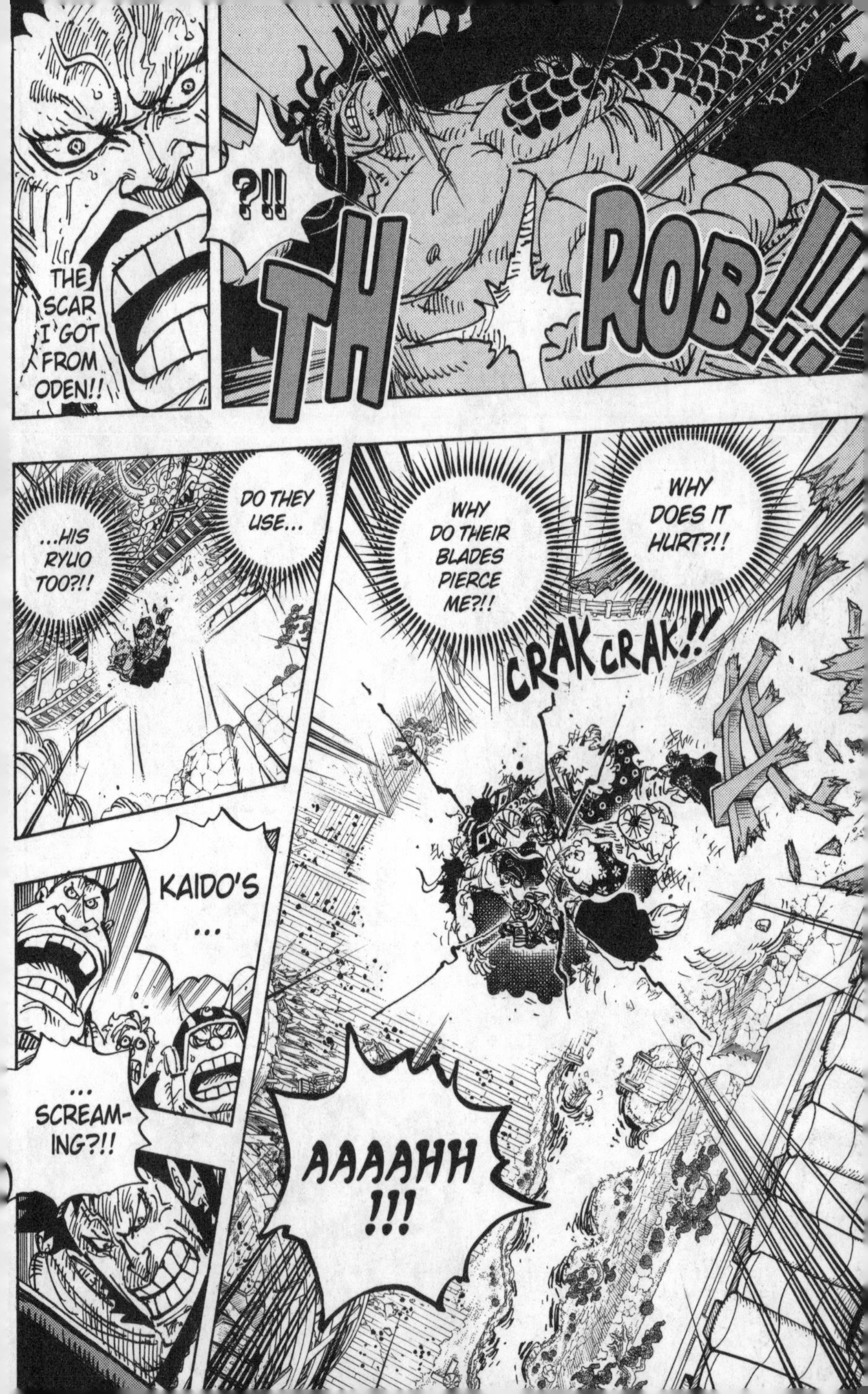
THROB!!!
?!!
THE SCAR I GOT FROM ODEN!!
WHY DOES IT HURT?!!
WHY DO THEIR BLADES PIERCE ME?!!
CRAK CRAK!!
AAAAHH!!!
DO THEY USE...
...HIS RYUO TOO?!!
KAIDO'S ...
... SCREAM-ING?!!

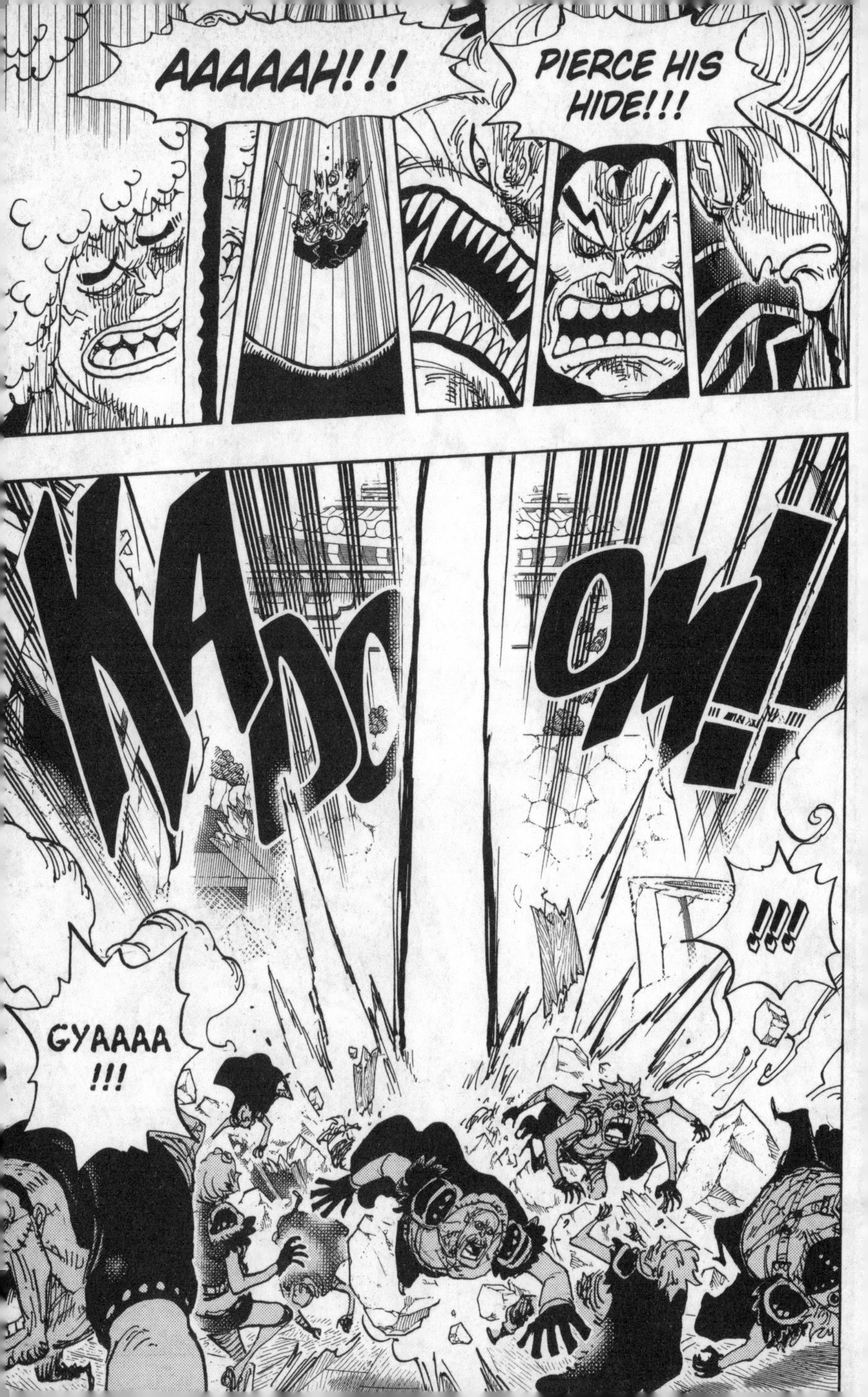
PIERCE HIS HIDE!!!
AAAAAH!!!
KA-DOOM!!
!!!
GYAAAA !!!

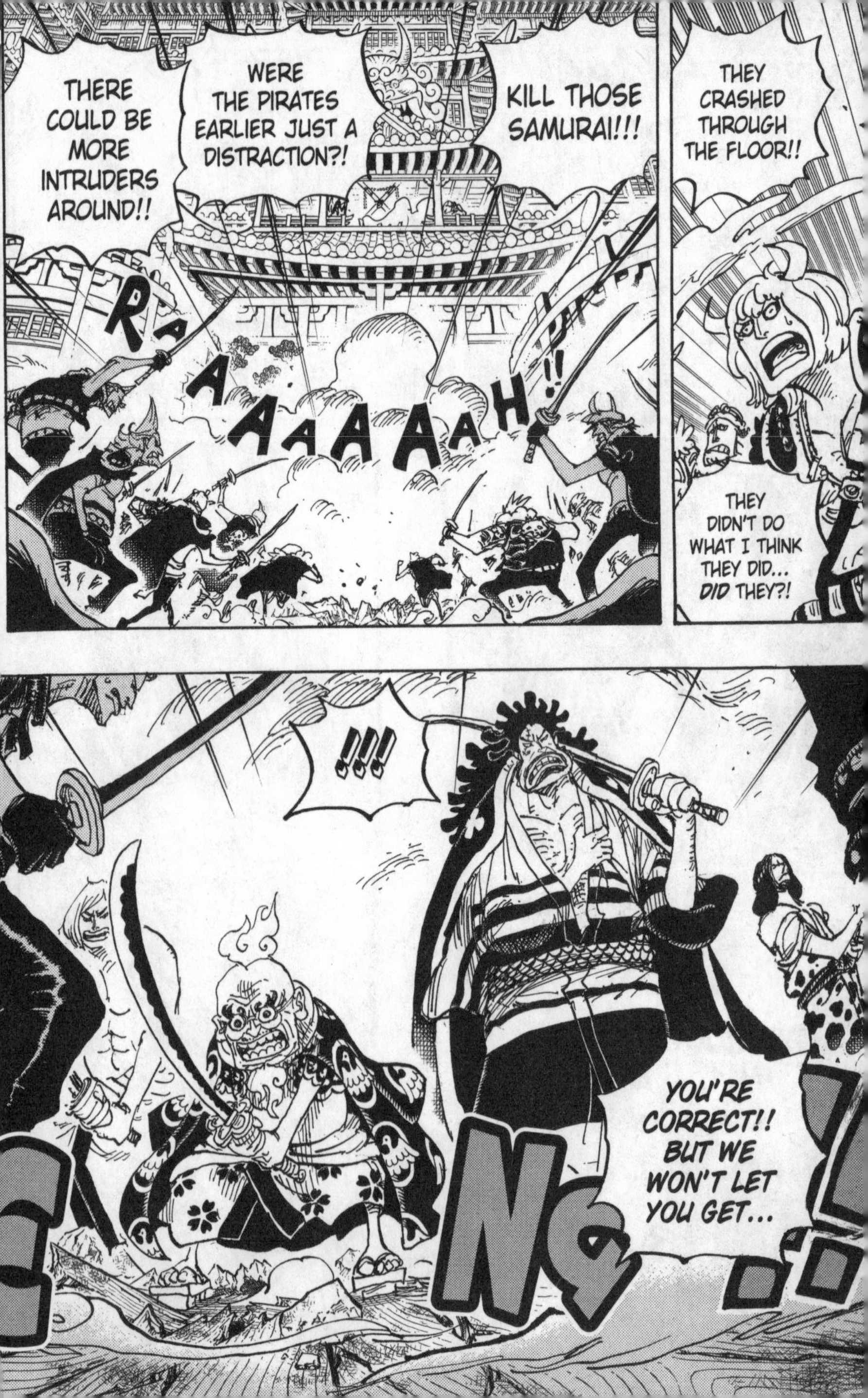
THEY CRASHED THROUGH THE FLOOR!!
THEY DIDN'T DO WHAT I THINK THEY DID... DID THEY?!
KILL THOSE SAMURAI!!!
WERE THE PIRATES EARLIER JUST A DISTRACTION?!
THERE COULD BE MORE INTRUDERS AROUND!!
RAAAAAAAAAH!!
!!!
YOU'RE CORRECT!! BUT WE WON'T LET YOU GET...
No...

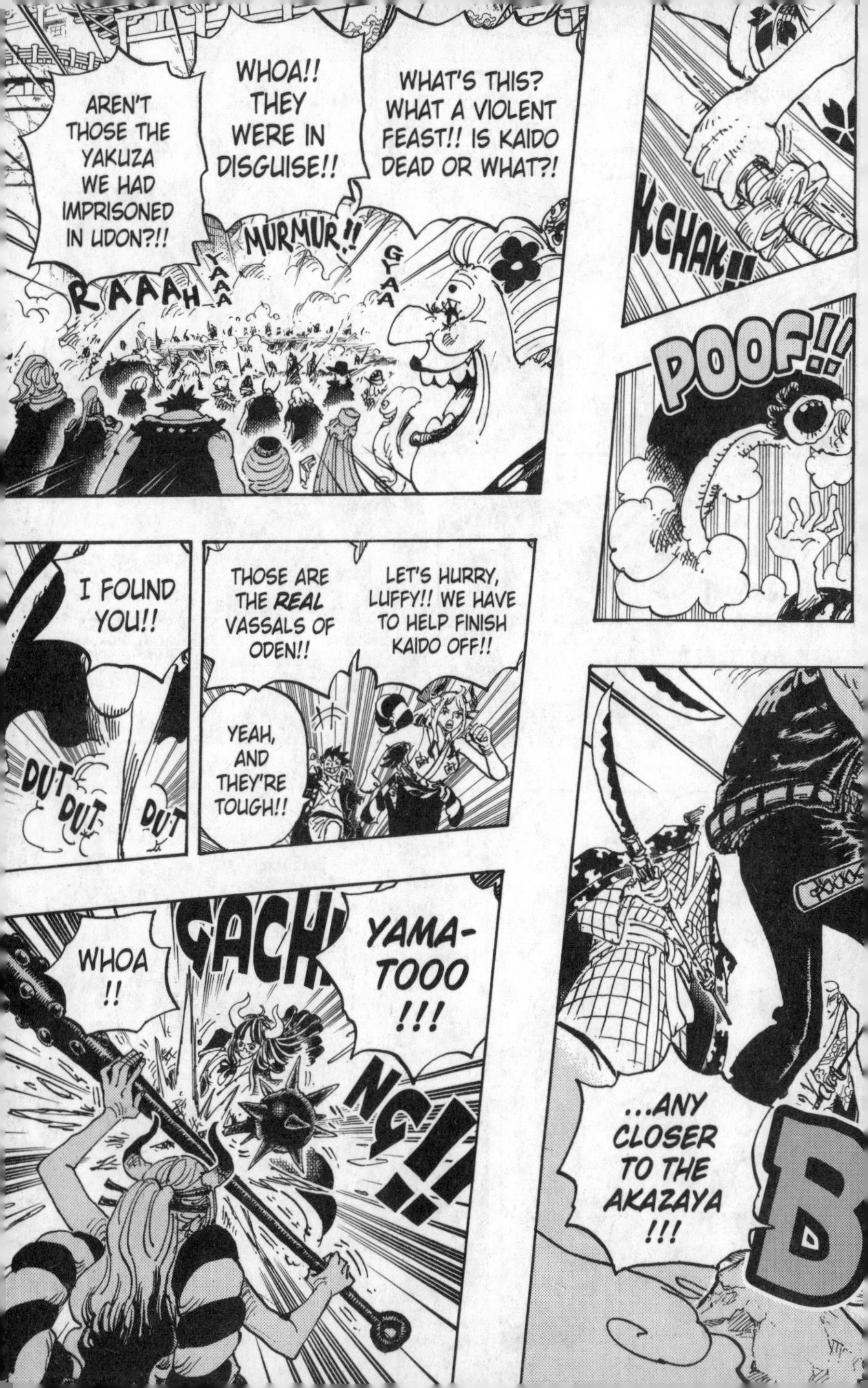
KCHAK!!
POOF!!!
WHAT'S THIS? WHAT A VIOLENT FEAST!! IS KAIDO DEAD OR WHAT?!
WHOA!! THEY WERE IN DISGUISE!!
AREN'T THOSE THE YAKUZA WE HAD IMPRISONED IN UDON?!!
MURMUR!!
GYAA
YAAA
RAAAH
LET'S HURRY, LUFFY!! WE HAVE TO HELP FINISH KAIDO OFF!!
THOSE ARE THE *REAL* VASSALS OF ODEN!!
YEAH, AND THEY'RE TOUGH!!
I FOUND YOU!!
DUT DUT DUT
YAMA-TOOO!!!
GACHINNG!!
WHOA!!
...ANY CLOSER TO THE AKAZAYA!!!
B

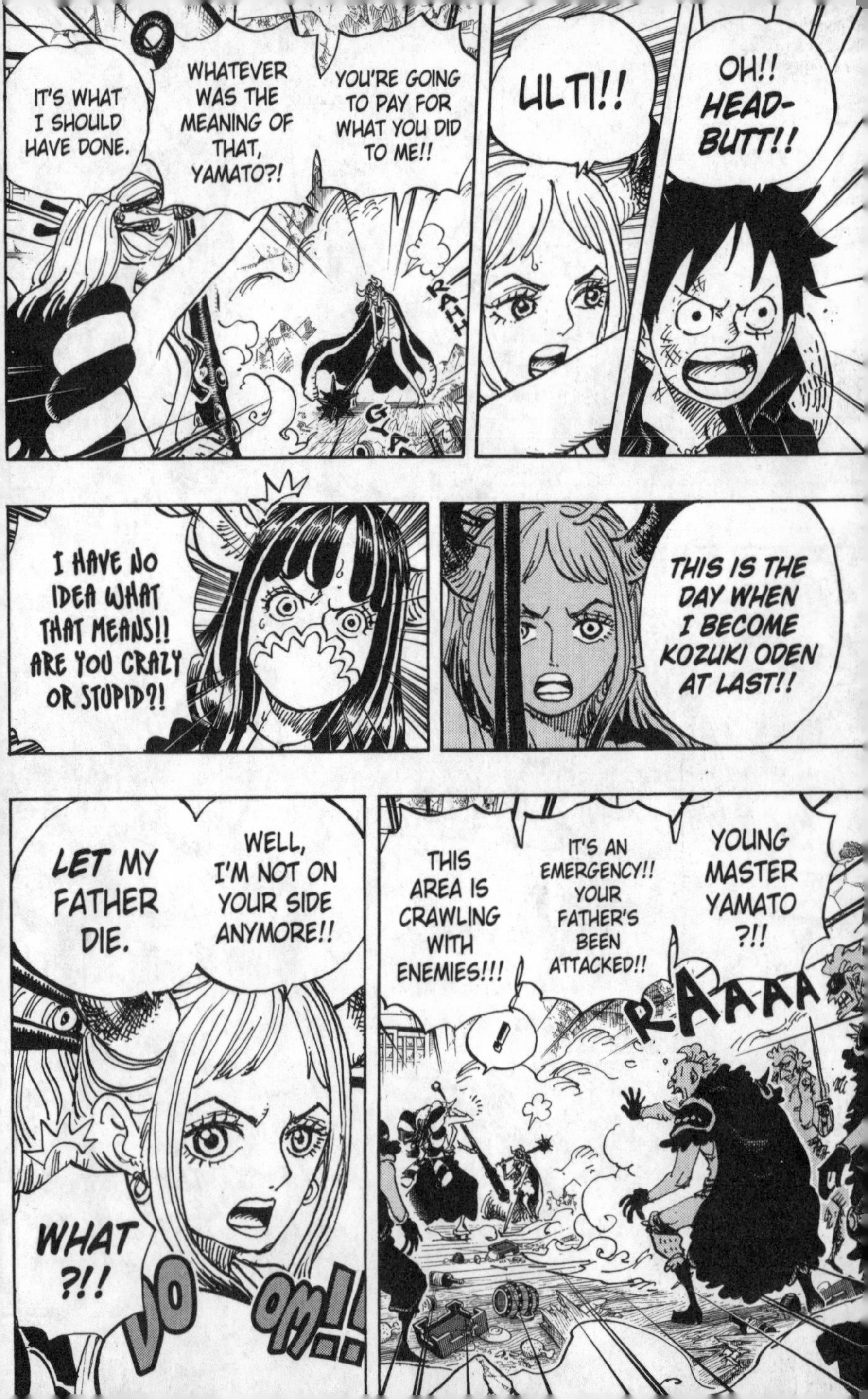
OH!! HEAD-BUTT!!
ULTI!!
YOU'RE GOING TO PAY FOR WHAT YOU DID TO ME!!
WHATEVER WAS THE MEANING OF THAT, YAMATO?!
IT'S WHAT I SHOULD HAVE DONE.
RAHH
THIS IS THE DAY WHEN I BECOME KOZUKI ODEN AT LAST!!
I HAVE NO IDEA WHAT THAT MEANS!! ARE YOU CRAZY OR STUPID?!
YOUNG MASTER YAMATO ?!!
IT'S AN EMERGENCY!! YOUR FATHER'S BEEN ATTACKED!!
THIS AREA IS CRAWLING WITH ENEMIES!!!
RAAAA
!
WELL, I'M NOT ON YOUR SIDE ANYMORE!!
LET MY FATHER DIE.
WHAT ?!!
VOOM!!

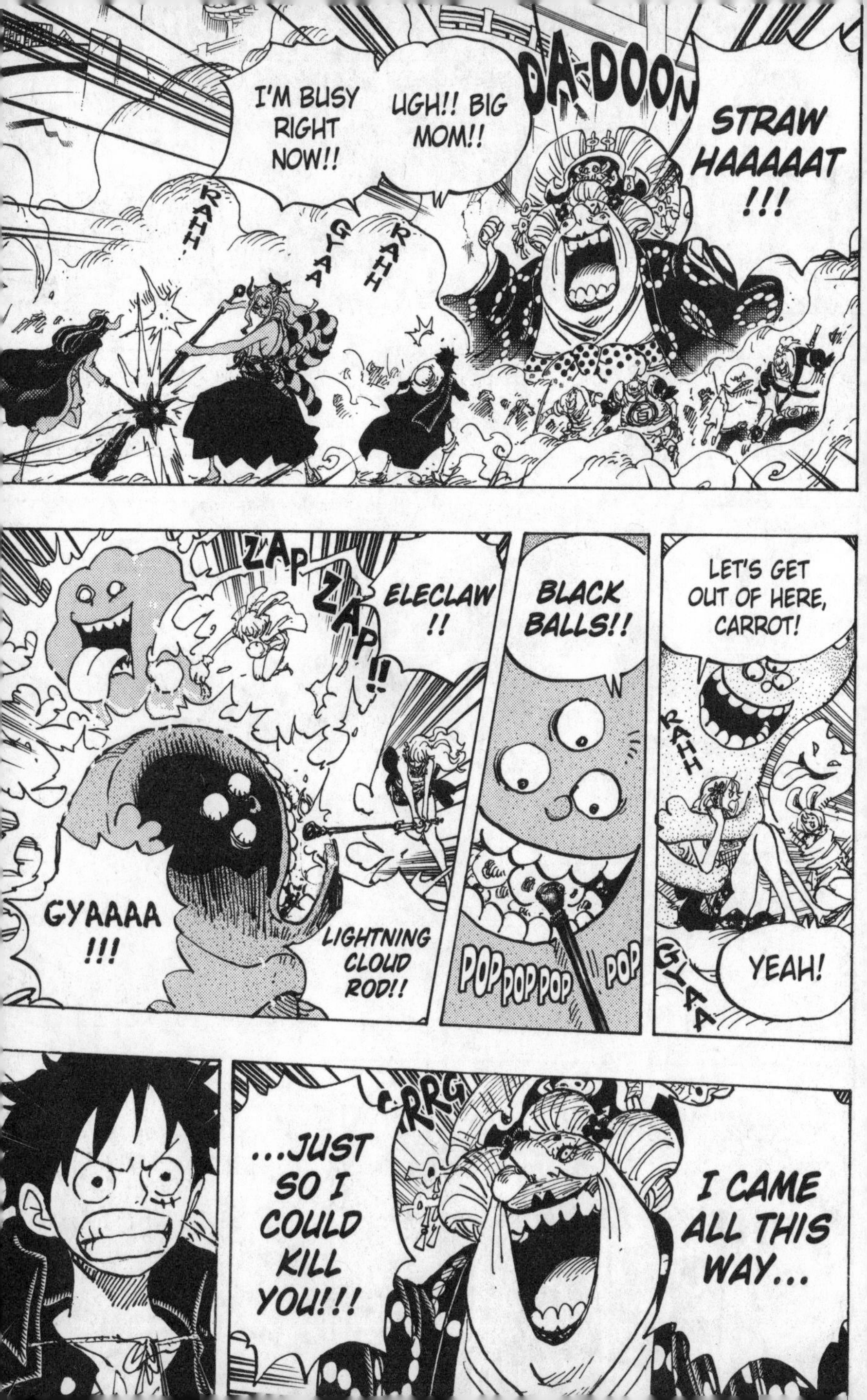

STRAW HAAAAAT!!!
DA-DOON
UGH!! BIG MOM!!
I'M BUSY RIGHT NOW!!
RAHH
GYAA
RAHH
LET'S GET OUT OF HERE, CARROT!
RAHH
YEAH!
GYAA
BLACK BALLS!!
POP POP POP POP
ELECLAW!!
ZAP
ZAP!!
LIGHTNING CLOUD ROD!!
GYAAAA!!!
I CAME ALL THIS WAY...
CRRG
...JUST SO I COULD KILL YOU!!!

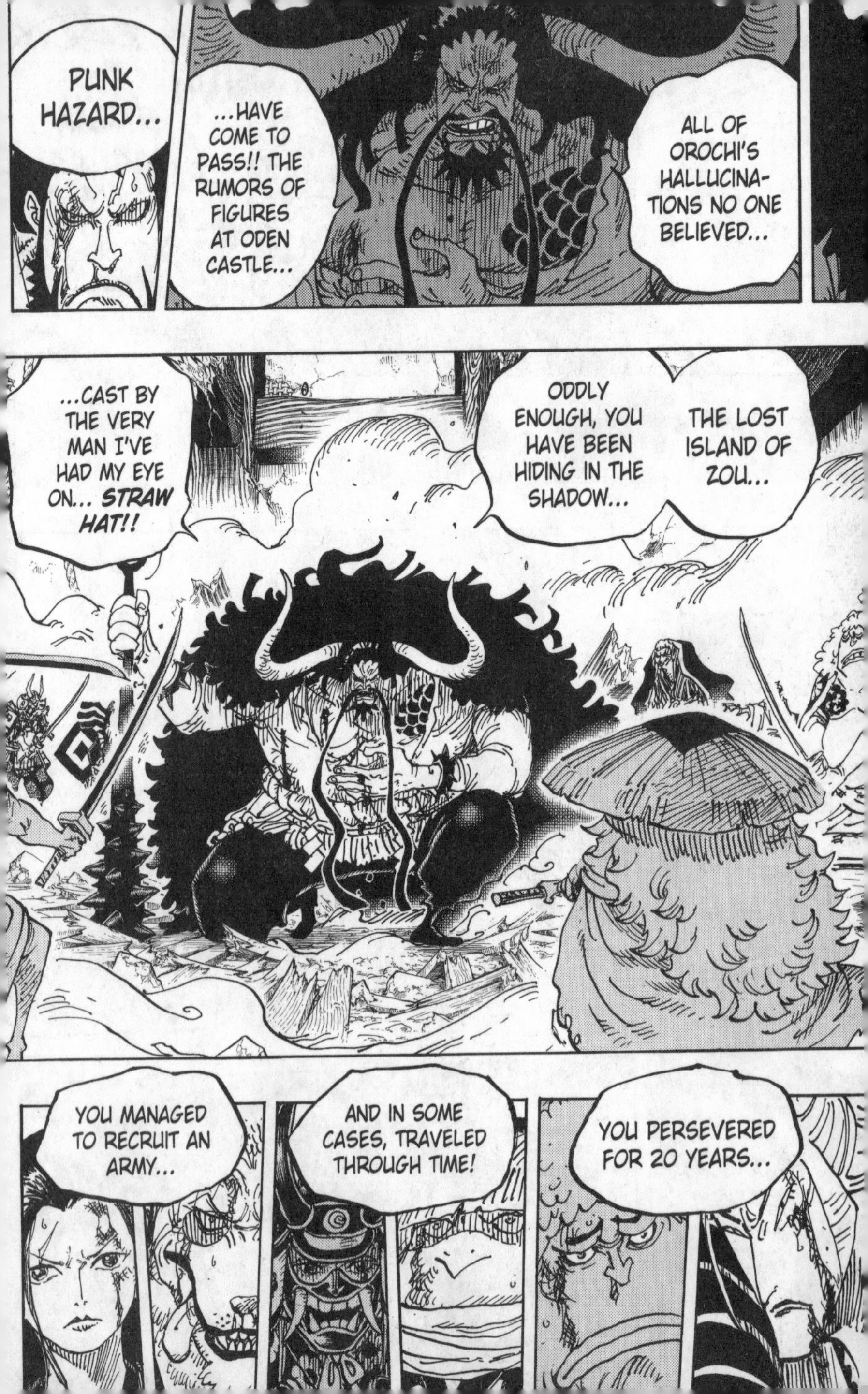
ALL OF OROCHI'S HALLUCINATIONS NO ONE BELIEVED...
...HAVE COME TO PASS!! THE RUMORS OF FIGURES AT ODEN CASTLE...
PUNK HAZARD...
THE LOST ISLAND OF ZOU...
ODDLY ENOUGH, YOU HAVE BEEN HIDING IN THE SHADOW...
...CAST BY THE VERY MAN I'VE HAD MY EYE ON... STRAW HAT!!
YOU PERSEVERED FOR 20 YEARS...
AND IN SOME CASES, TRAVELED THROUGH TIME!
YOU MANAGED TO RECRUIT AN ARMY...

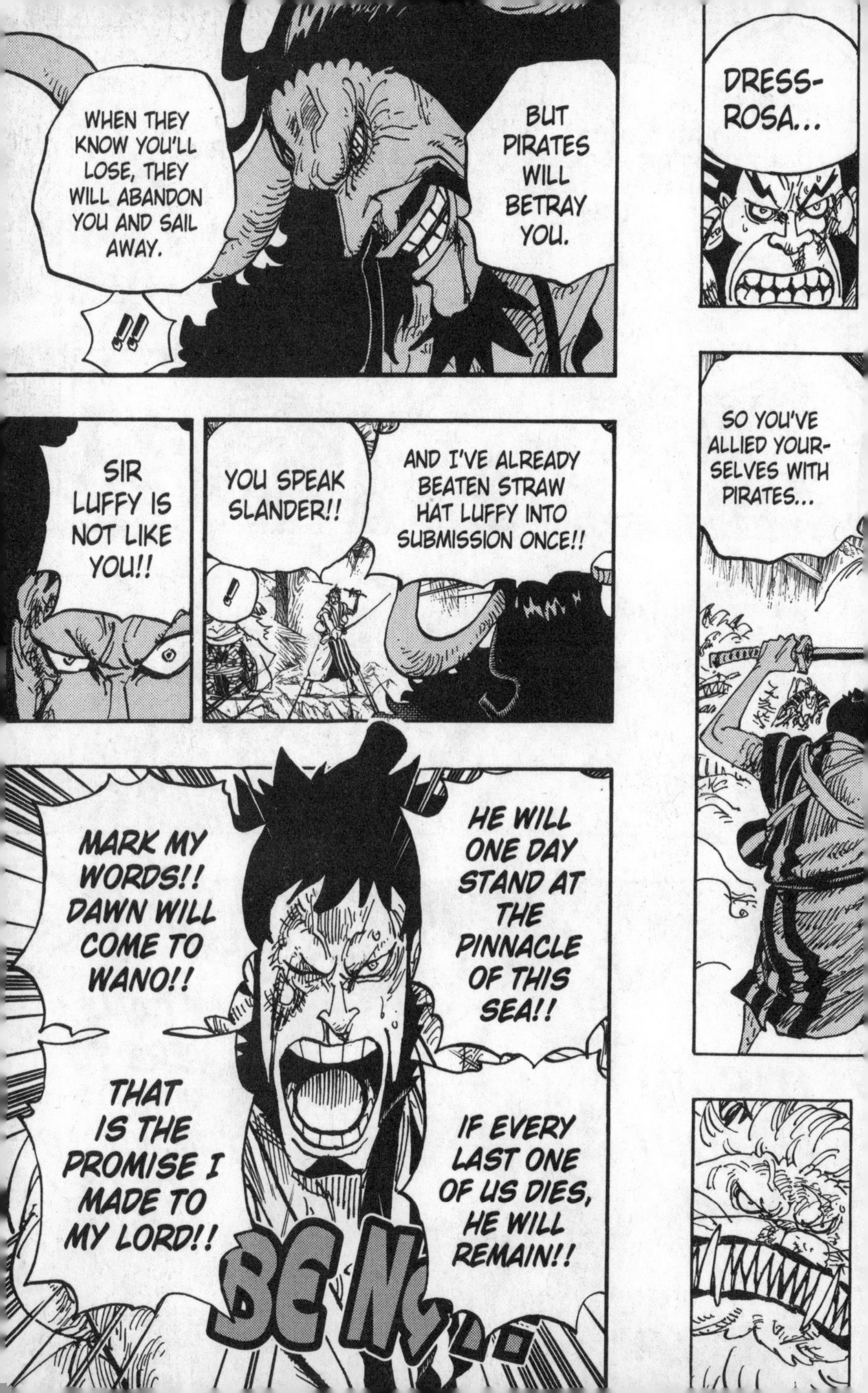
DRESS-ROSA...
SO YOU'VE ALLIED YOUR-SELVES WITH PIRATES...
BUT PIRATES WILL BETRAY YOU.
WHEN THEY KNOW YOU'LL LOSE, THEY WILL ABANDON YOU AND SAIL AWAY.
!!
AND I'VE ALREADY BEATEN STRAW HAT LUFFY INTO SUBMISSION ONCE!!
YOU SPEAK SLANDER!!
!
SIR LUFFY IS NOT LIKE YOU!!
HE WILL ONE DAY STAND AT THE PINNACLE OF THIS SEA!!
MARK MY WORDS!! DAWN WILL COME TO WANO!!
IF EVERY LAST ONE OF US DIES, HE WILL REMAIN!!
THAT IS THE PROMISE I MADE TO MY LORD!!
BE N...

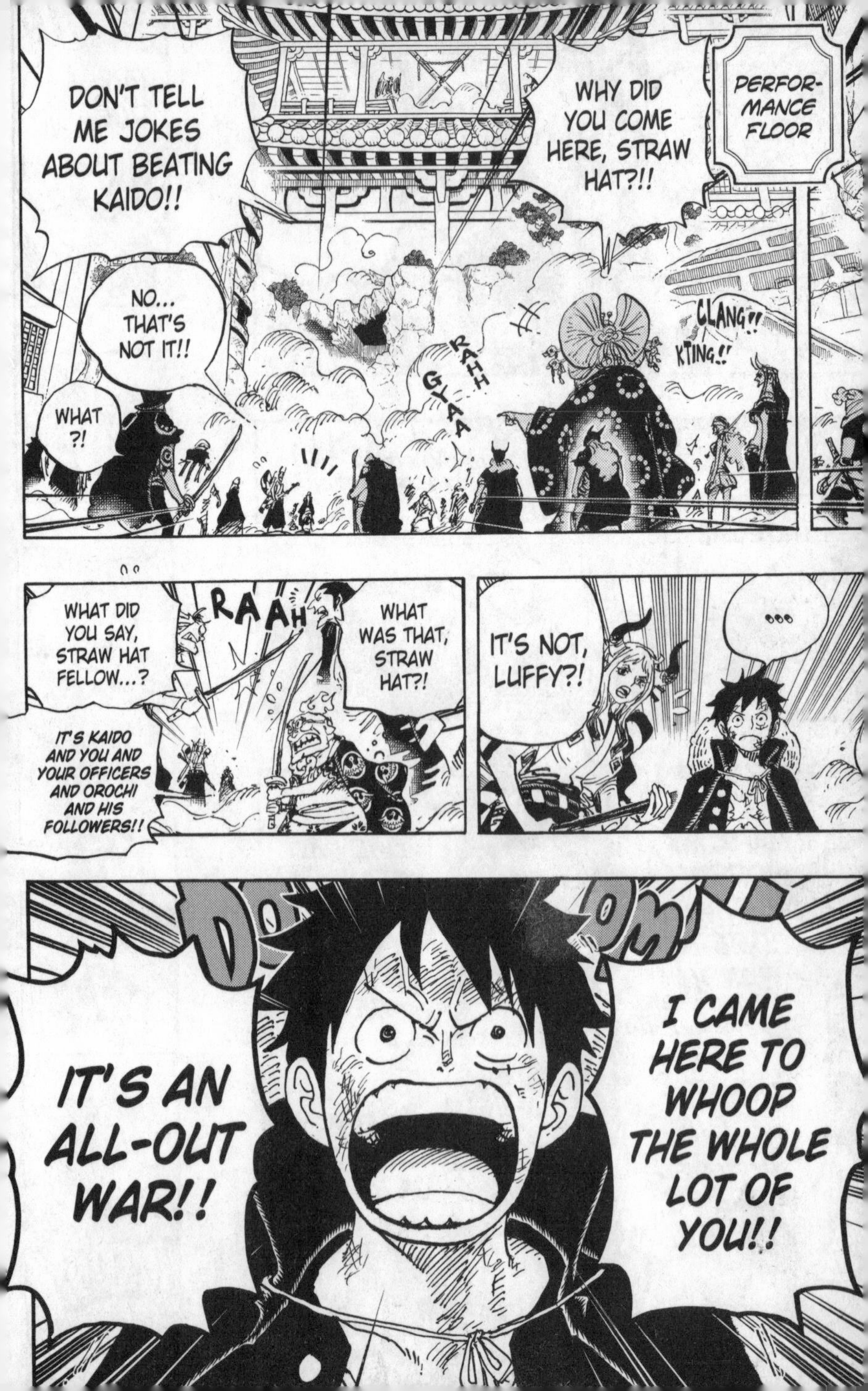
PERFOR-MANCE FLOOR
WHY DID YOU COME HERE, STRAW HAT?!!
DON'T TELL ME JOKES ABOUT BEATING KAIDO!!
CLANG!!
KTING!!
RAHH
GYAA
NO... THAT'S NOT IT!!
WHAT ?!
...
IT'S NOT, LUFFY?!
WHAT WAS THAT, STRAW HAT?!
RAAAH
WHAT DID YOU SAY, STRAW HAT FELLOW...?
IT'S KAIDO AND YOU AND YOUR OFFICERS AND OROCHI AND HIS FOLLOWERS!!
I CAME HERE TO WHOOP THE WHOLE LOT OF YOU!!
IT'S AN ALL-OUT WAR!!

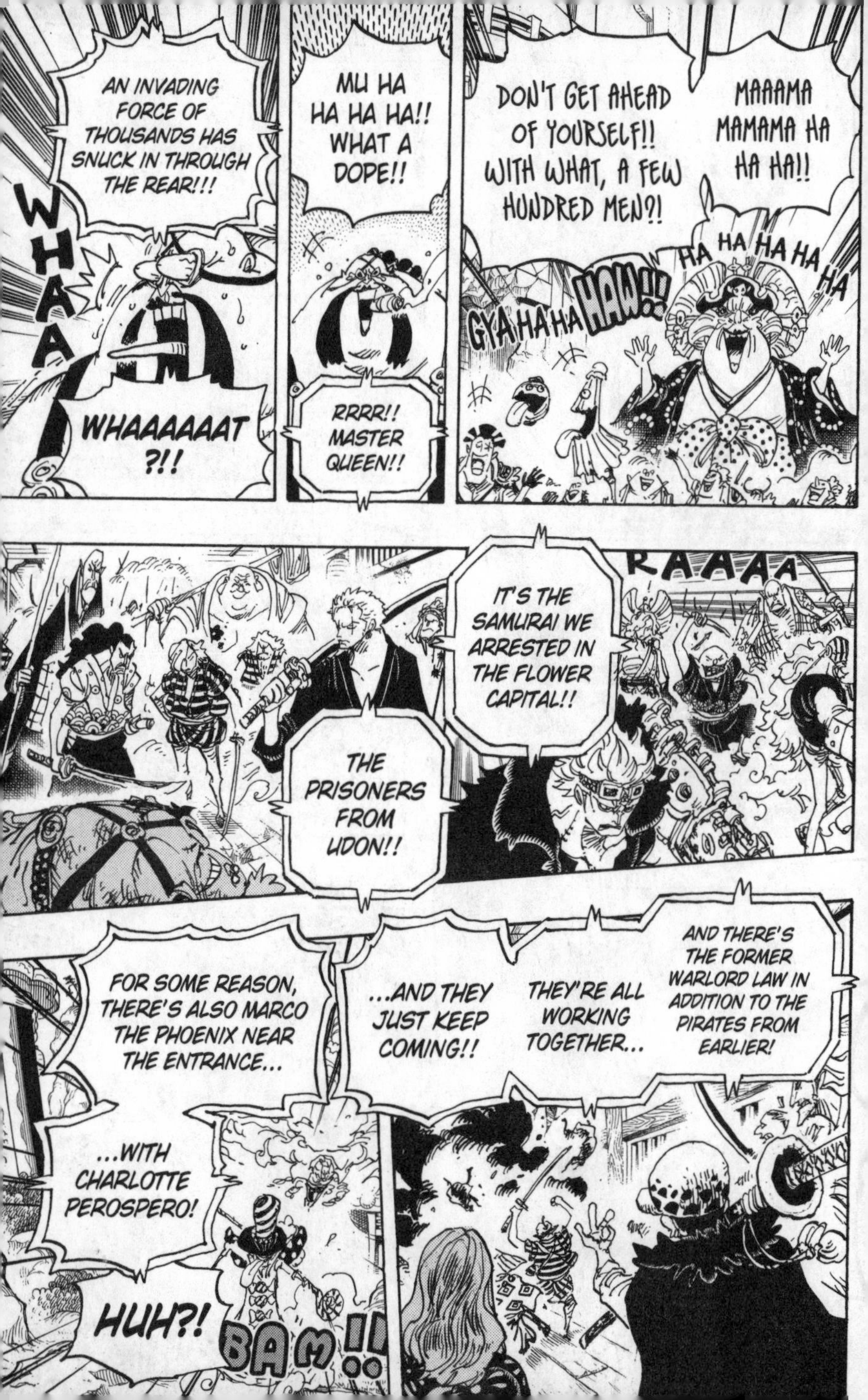
MAAAMA MAMAMA HA HA HA!!
DON'T GET AHEAD OF YOURSELF!! WITH WHAT, A FEW HUNDRED MEN?!
HA HA HA HA HA HA
GYAHAHA HAW!!
MU HA HA HA HA!! WHAT A DOPE!!
RRRR!! MASTER QUEEN!!
AN INVADING FORCE OF THOUSANDS HAS SNUCK IN THROUGH THE REAR!!!
WHAA
WHAAAAAAT ?!!
RAAAA
IT'S THE SAMURAI WE ARRESTED IN THE FLOWER CAPITAL!!
THE PRISONERS FROM UDON!!
AND THERE'S THE FORMER WARLORD LAW IN ADDITION TO THE PIRATES FROM EARLIER!
THEY'RE ALL WORKING TOGETHER...
...AND THEY JUST KEEP COMING!!
FOR SOME REASON, THERE'S ALSO MARCO THE PHOENIX NEAR THE ENTRANCE...
...WITH CHARLOTTE PEROSPERO!
HUH?!
BAM!!

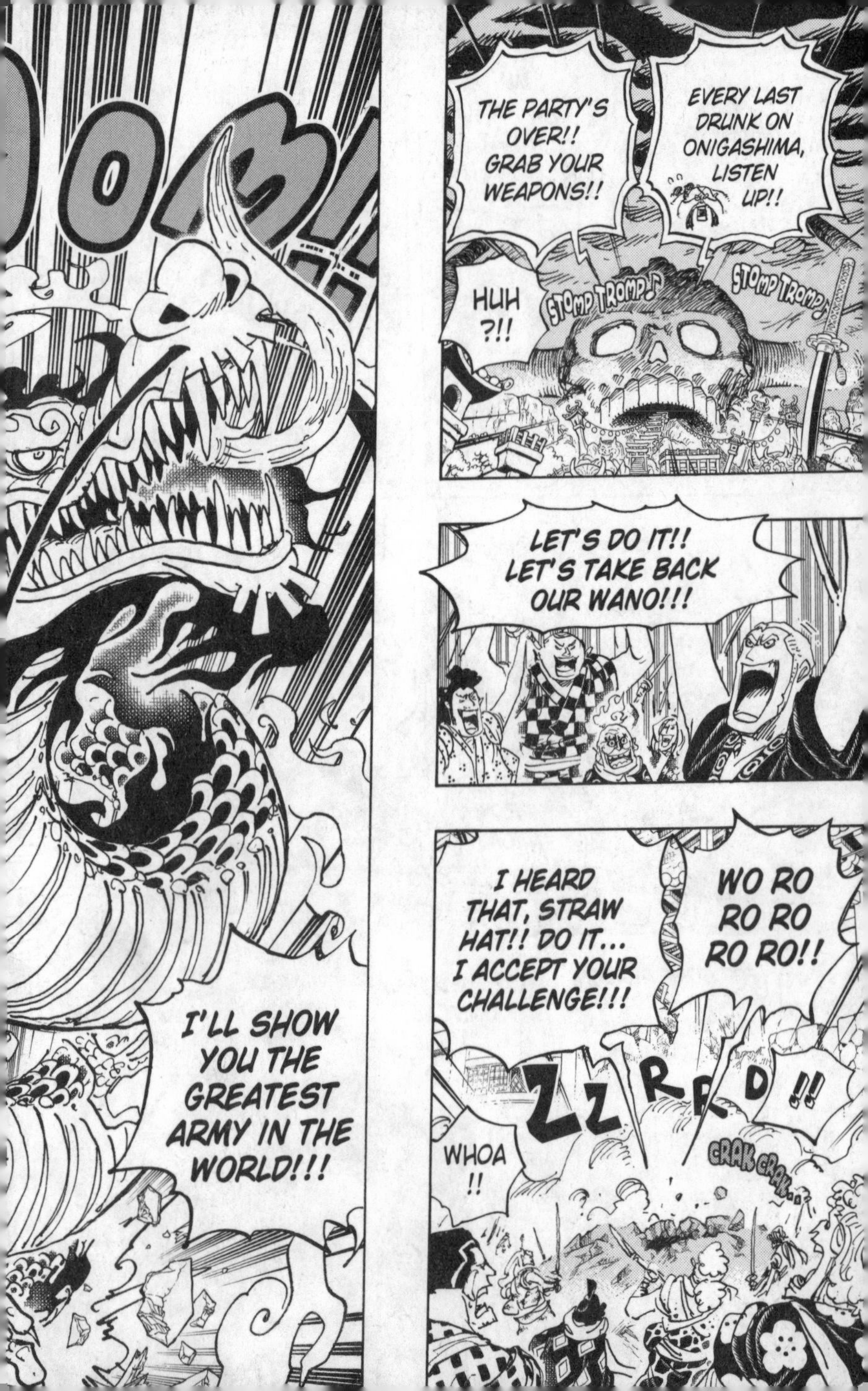
EVERY LAST DRUNK ON ONIGASHIMA, LISTEN UP!!
THE PARTY'S OVER!! GRAB YOUR WEAPONS!!
STOMP TROMP♪
STOMP TROMP♪
HUH ?!!
LET'S DO IT!! LET'S TAKE BACK OUR WANO!!!
WO RO RO RO RO RO!!
I HEARD THAT, STRAW HAT!! DO IT... I ACCEPT YOUR CHALLENGE!!!
ZZRRD!!
CRAK CRAK...
WHOA !!
I'LL SHOW YOU THE GREATEST ARMY IN THE WORLD!!!

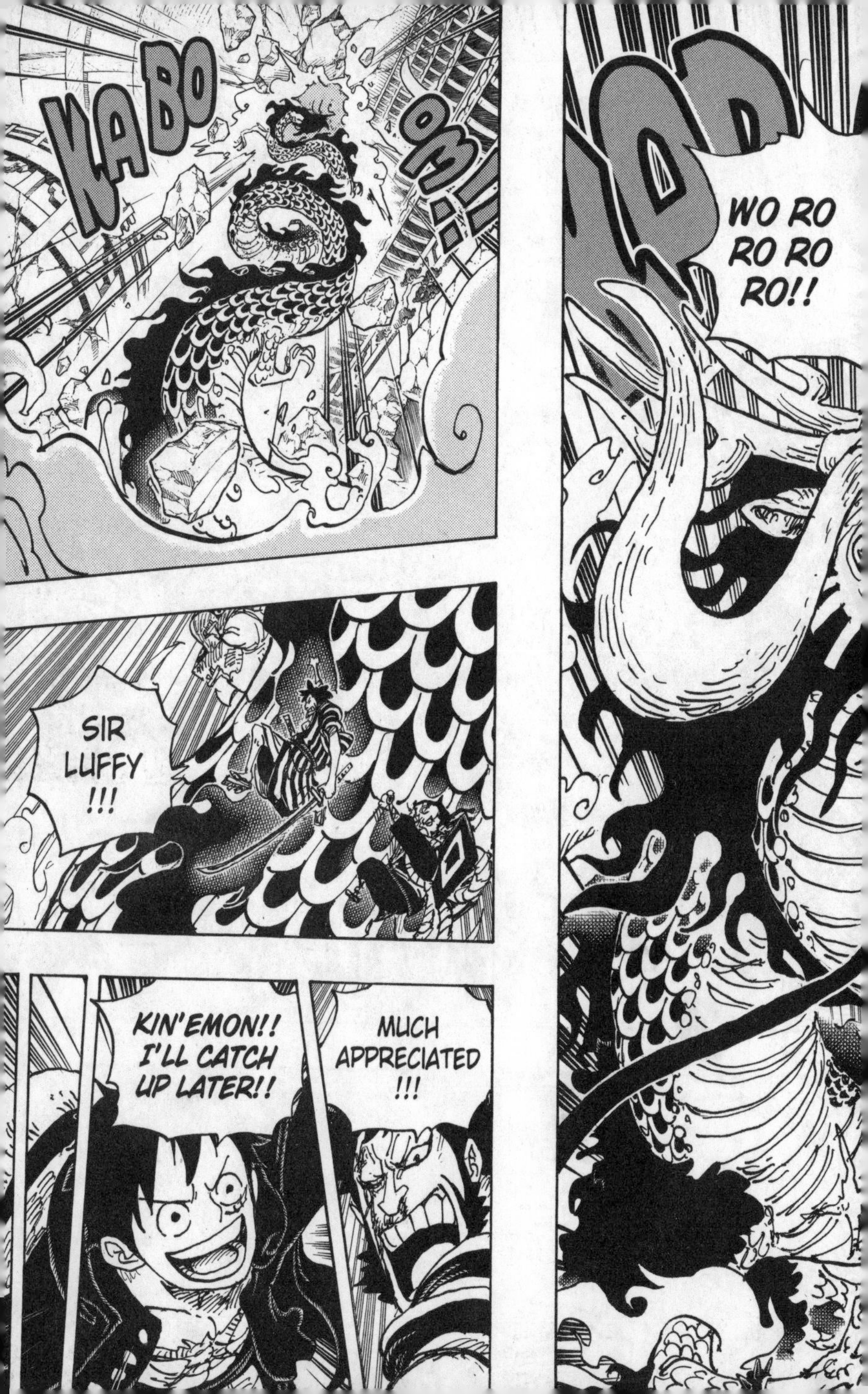
WO RO RO RO RO!!
KABOOM!!
SIR LUFFY!!!
MUCH APPRECIATED!!!
KIN'EMON!! I'LL CATCH UP LATER!!

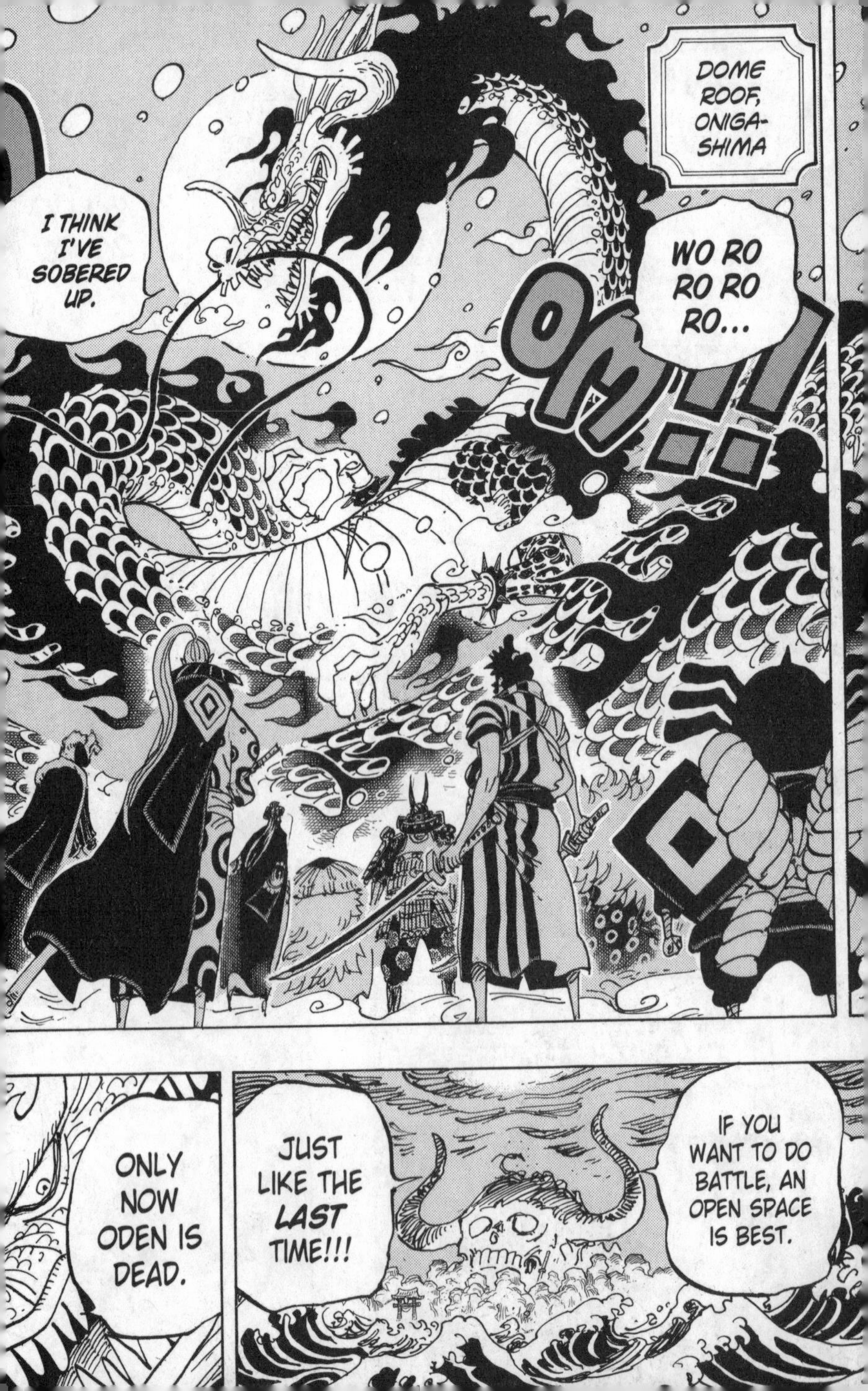
DOME ROOF, ONIGA-SHIMA
WO RO RO RO RO...
I THINK I'VE SOBERED UP.
IF YOU WANT TO DO BATTLE, AN OPEN SPACE IS BEST.
JUST LIKE THE LAST TIME!!!
ONLY NOW ODEN IS DEAD.

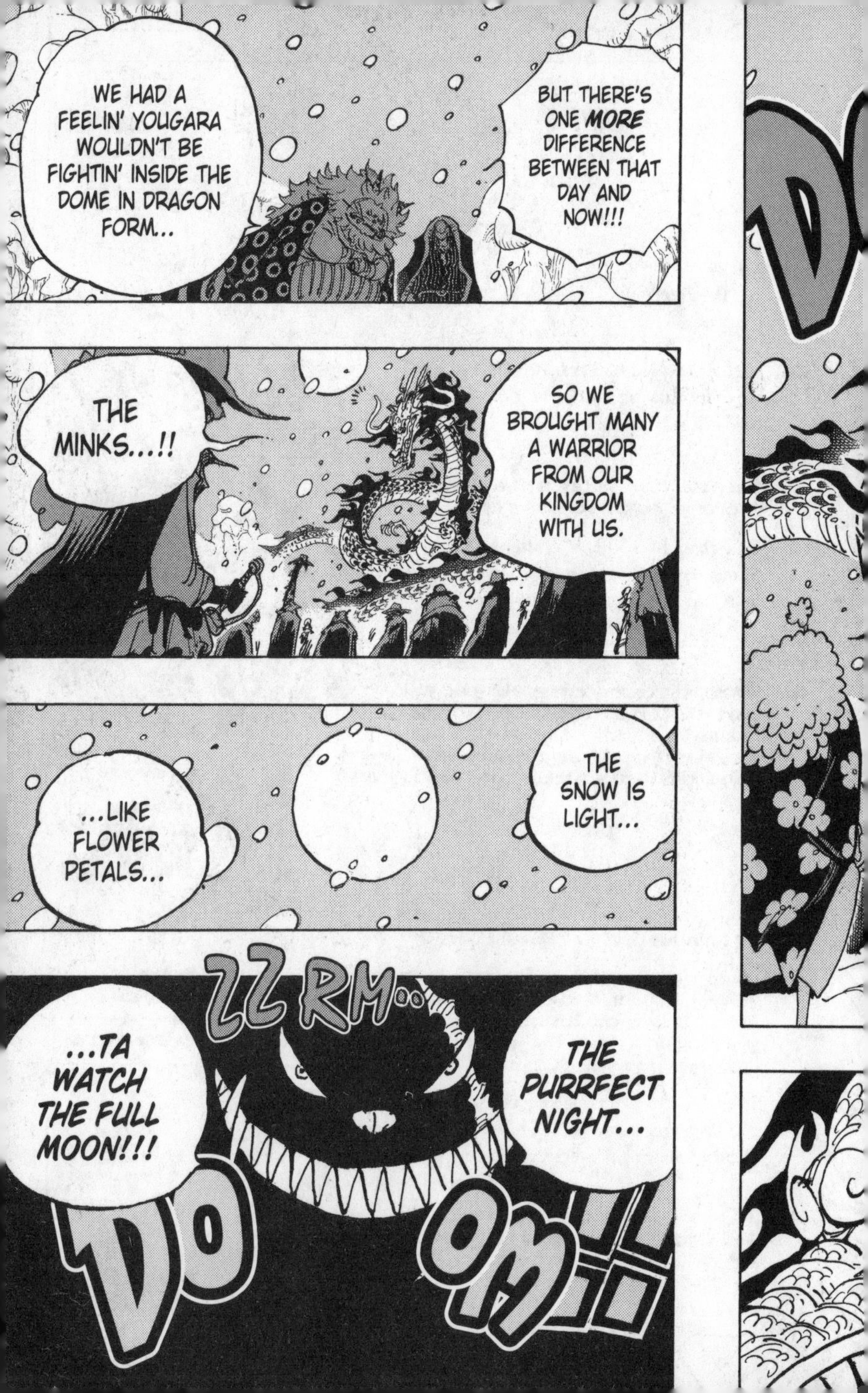
BUT THERE'S ONE MORE DIFFERENCE BETWEEN THAT DAY AND NOW!!!
WE HAD A FEELIN' YOUGARA WOULDN'T BE FIGHTIN' INSIDE THE DOME IN DRAGON FORM...
SO WE BROUGHT MANY A WARRIOR FROM OUR KINGDOM WITH US.
THE MINKS...!!
THE SNOW IS LIGHT...
...LIKE FLOWER PETALS...
ZZRM..
THE PURRFECT NIGHT...
...TA WATCH THE FULL MOON!!!
DOOM!!

SBS Question Corner

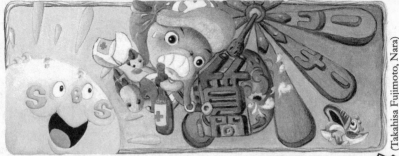

(Takahisa Fujimoto, Nara)

RAH!!

Q: Hi, Oda Sensei!! Earlier I used Haki of the Supreme King on my one-year-old sister, and she laughed. Why?

--Yucchi

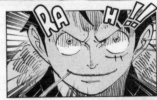

A: Because your sister is the one who has the true disposition of a king.

AND HAVING A BIG SEND-OFF...
THAT!

Q: Odacchiii!! In chapter 977, after Nami gives Jimbei that big hug, I spotted Sanji in the corner biting his handkerchief out of sheer frustration!!

--A purehearted middle schooler who wanted to meet Odacchi on Tanabata

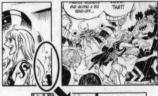

A: Wow, that's incredible. How did you spot that? It's cut off on the side of the panel, so you really have to use your imagination to figure it out. Yes, Sanji is doing this in the background. Good job!

Q: ルフィのギア4があるなら
ギア5はきますか!?

--Aoi Y.

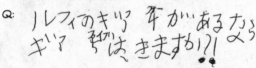

*If Luffy has Gear 4 will there be Gear 5?!

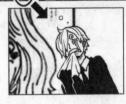

A: I liked the power in your writing, so I printed it directly in the book. Hmm, I wonder if there will be Gear Five! I mean, the enemy Luffy has to beat now is supposedly the strongest in the world. And if you look around in the world today, there's 4G and 5G everywhere. I assume G stands for "Gear," right?

HE JUST CALLED THE TOBI ROPPO ARROGANT PUNKS! WHY, THE NERVE OF THAT BEASTLY MAN!!
IS THIS ANOTHER ONE OF YOUR WEIRD TRENDS? STOP TALKING LIKE THAT, IT'S EMBARRASSING.

Q: In chapter 978, Ulti is talking like an "ever so fancy" lady, and Page One says, "Is this another one of your weird trends?" So what was her trend before that?!

--EtoYotsuya

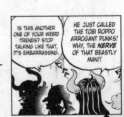

A: Ah, yes. Before that, she talked even more old-fashioned. She would say, "Pay-Pay, pity thy poor wretched sister!" But currently she seems to have settled on talking like a fancy lady.

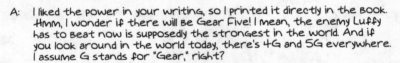

Chapter 988:
SORRY FOR THE WAIT

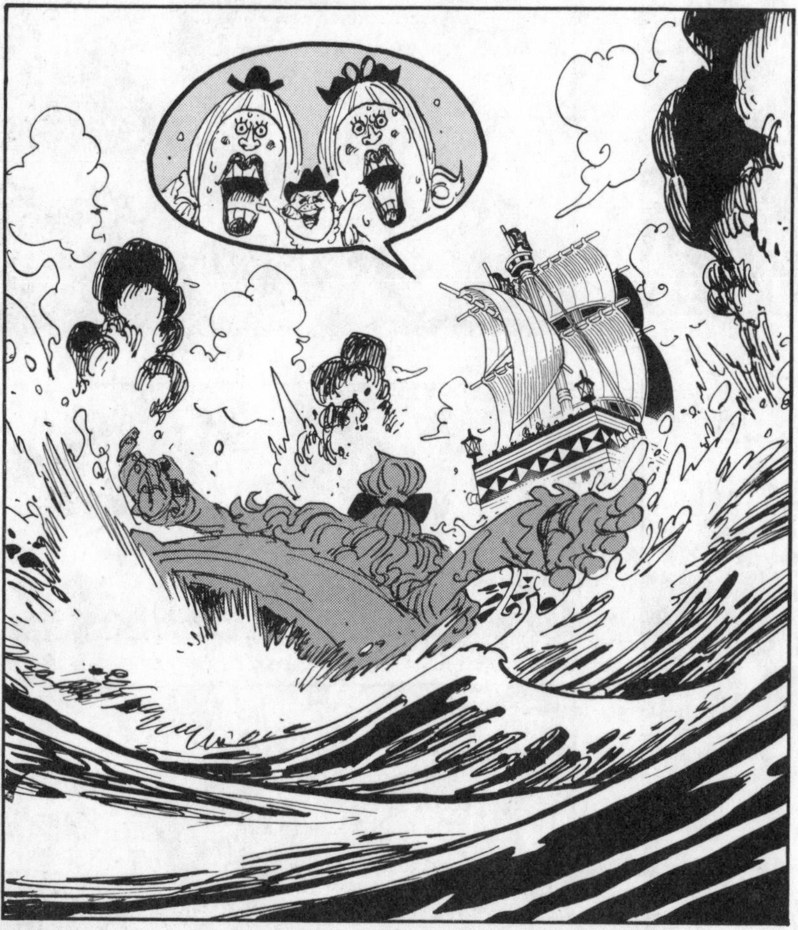

GANG BEGE'S OH MY FAMILY
VOL. 32: "DESPITE THE NAVY BOMBARDMENT, I'M STILL, LIKE, YOUR FATHER!!"

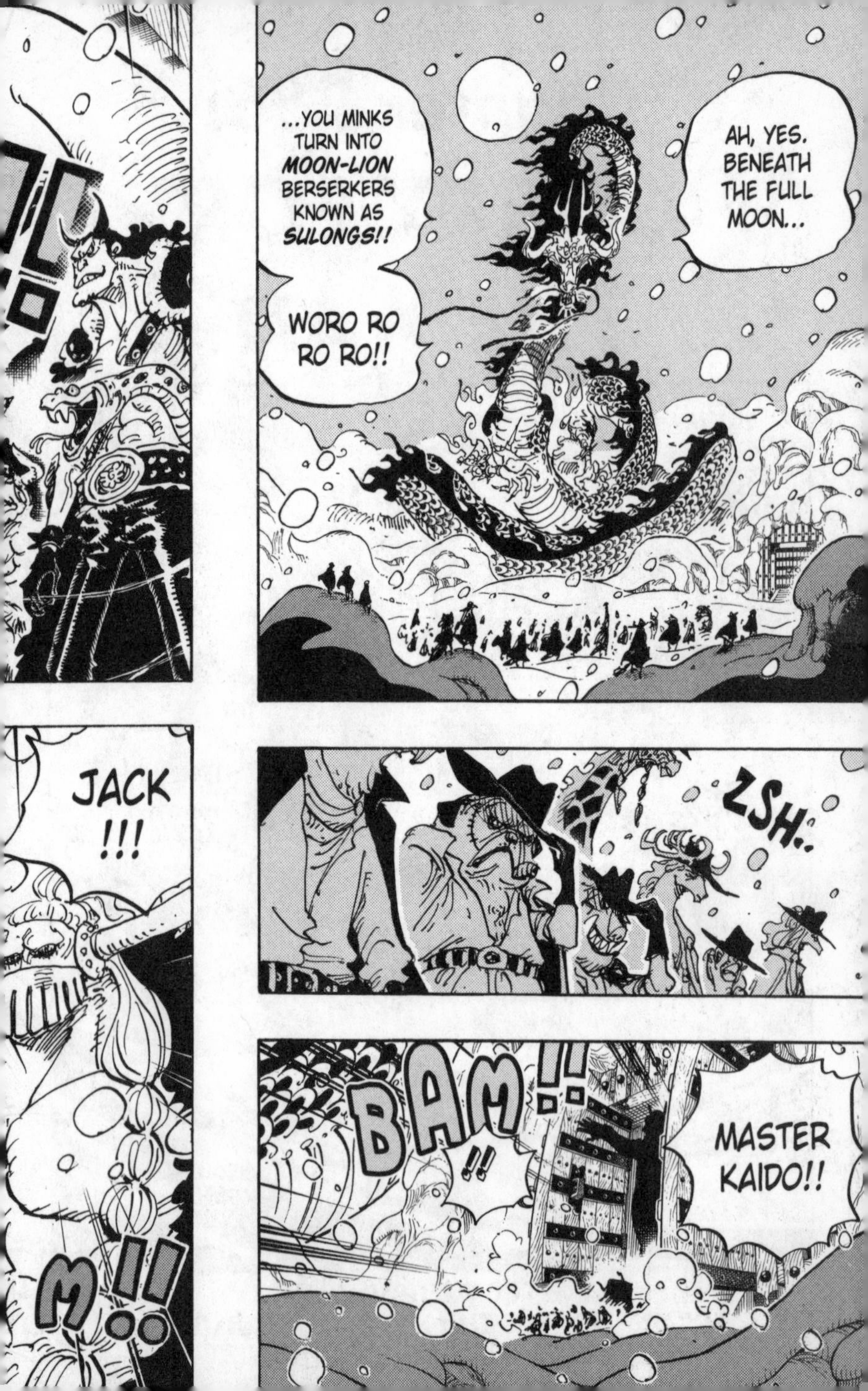

AH, YES. BENEATH THE FULL MOON...
...YOU MINKS TURN INTO MOON-LION BERSERKERS KNOWN AS SULONGS!!
WORO RO RO RO!!
ZSH..
BAM!!
!!
MASTER KAIDO!!
JACK !!!
M!!

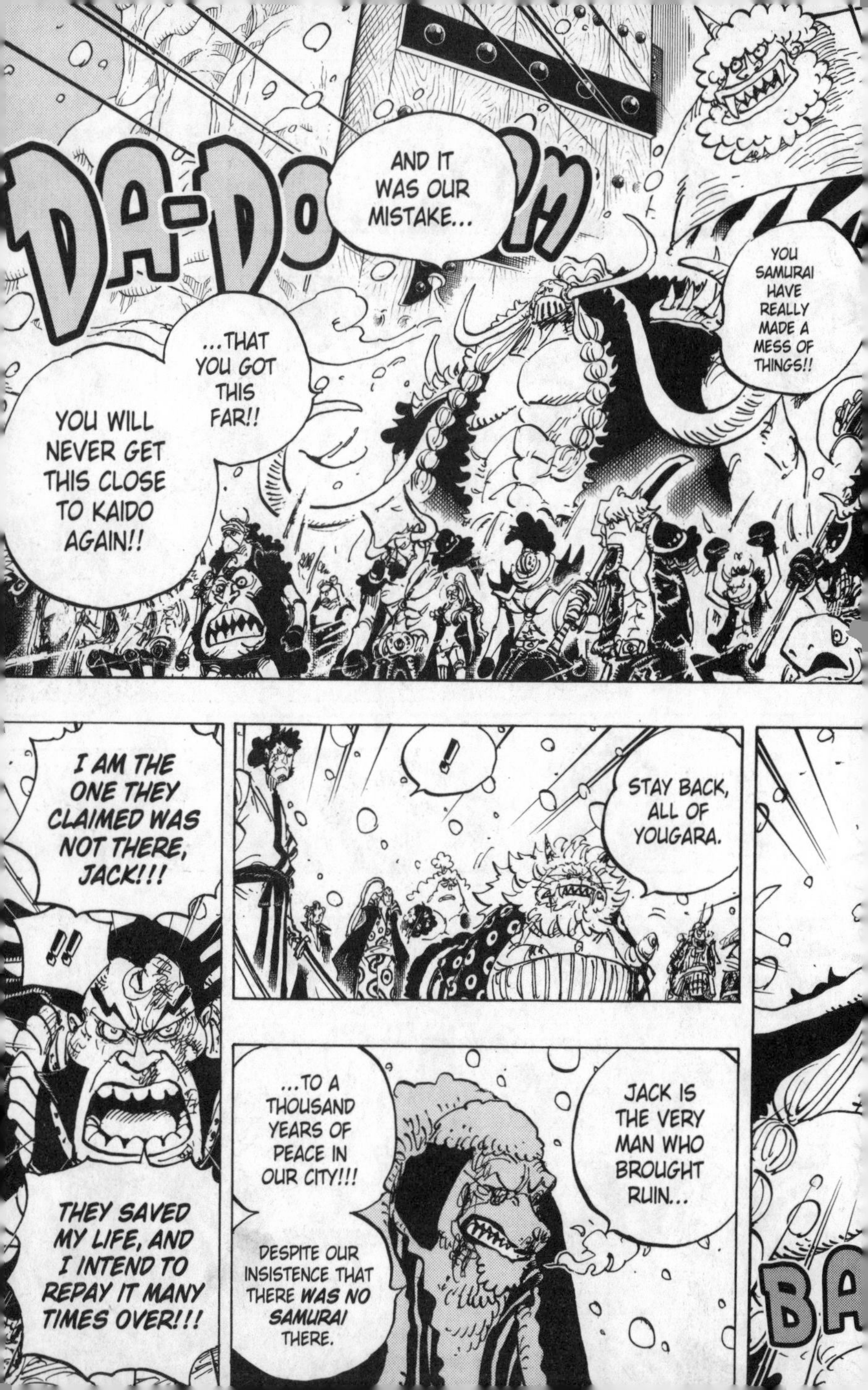
YOU SAMURAI HAVE REALLY MADE A MESS OF THINGS!!
AND IT WAS OUR MISTAKE...
DA-DO
...THAT YOU GOT THIS FAR!!
YOU WILL NEVER GET THIS CLOSE TO KAIDO AGAIN!!
BA
STAY BACK, ALL OF YOUGARA.
!
JACK IS THE VERY MAN WHO BROUGHT RUIN...
...TO A THOUSAND YEARS OF PEACE IN OUR CITY!!!
DESPITE OUR INSISTENCE THAT THERE WAS NO SAMURAI THERE.
I AM THE ONE THEY CLAIMED WAS NOT THERE, JACK!!!
!!
THEY SAVED MY LIFE, AND I INTEND TO REPAY IT MANY TIMES OVER!!!

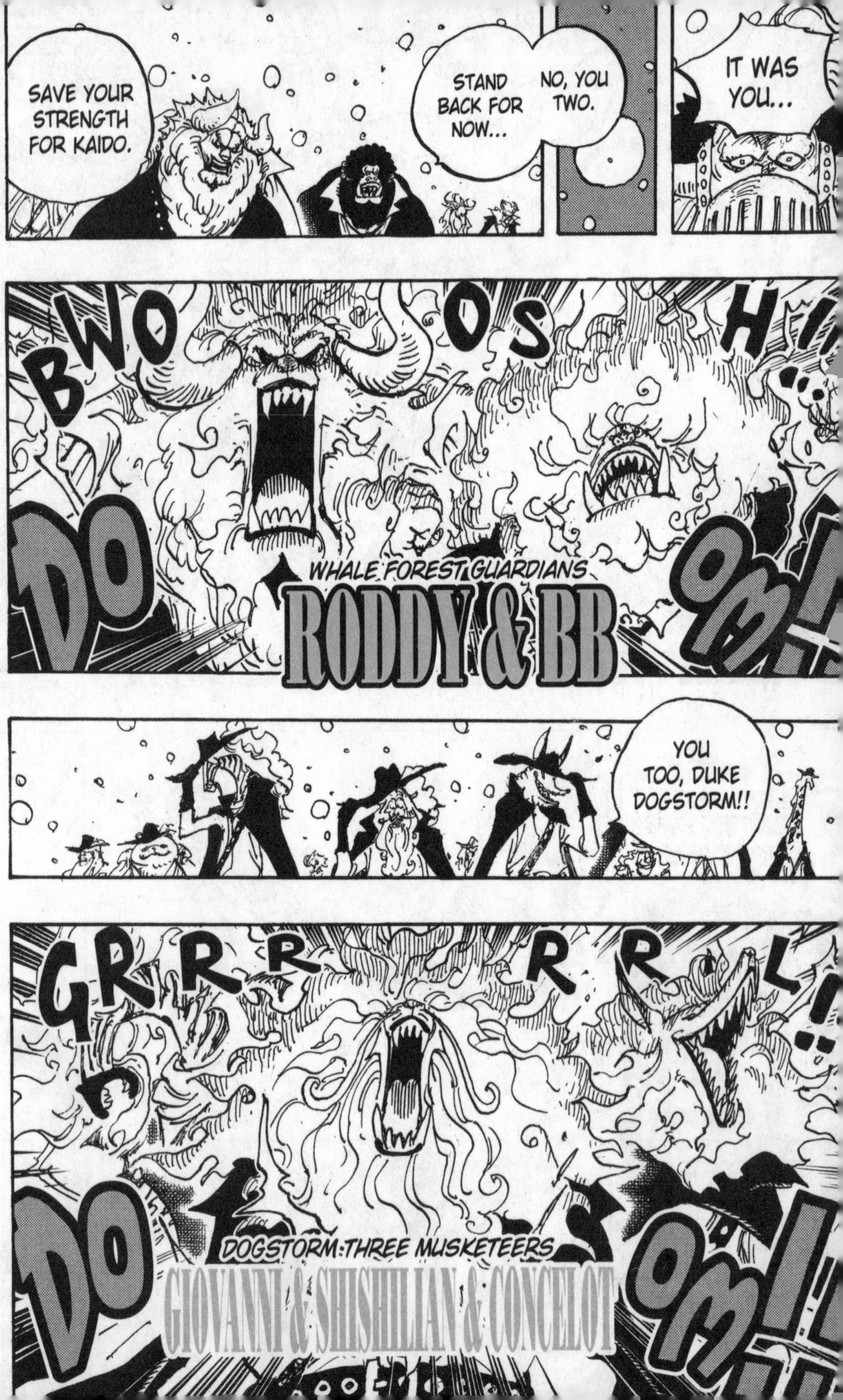
IT WAS YOU...
NO, YOU TWO.
STAND BACK FOR NOW...
SAVE YOUR STRENGTH FOR KAIDO.
BWOOSH!!
DOOM!!
WHALE FOREST GUARDIANS
RODDY & BB
YOU TOO, DUKE DOGSTORM!!
GRRRRRL!!
DOOM!!
DOGSTORM THREE MUSKETEERS
GIOVANNI & SHISHILIAN & CONCELOT

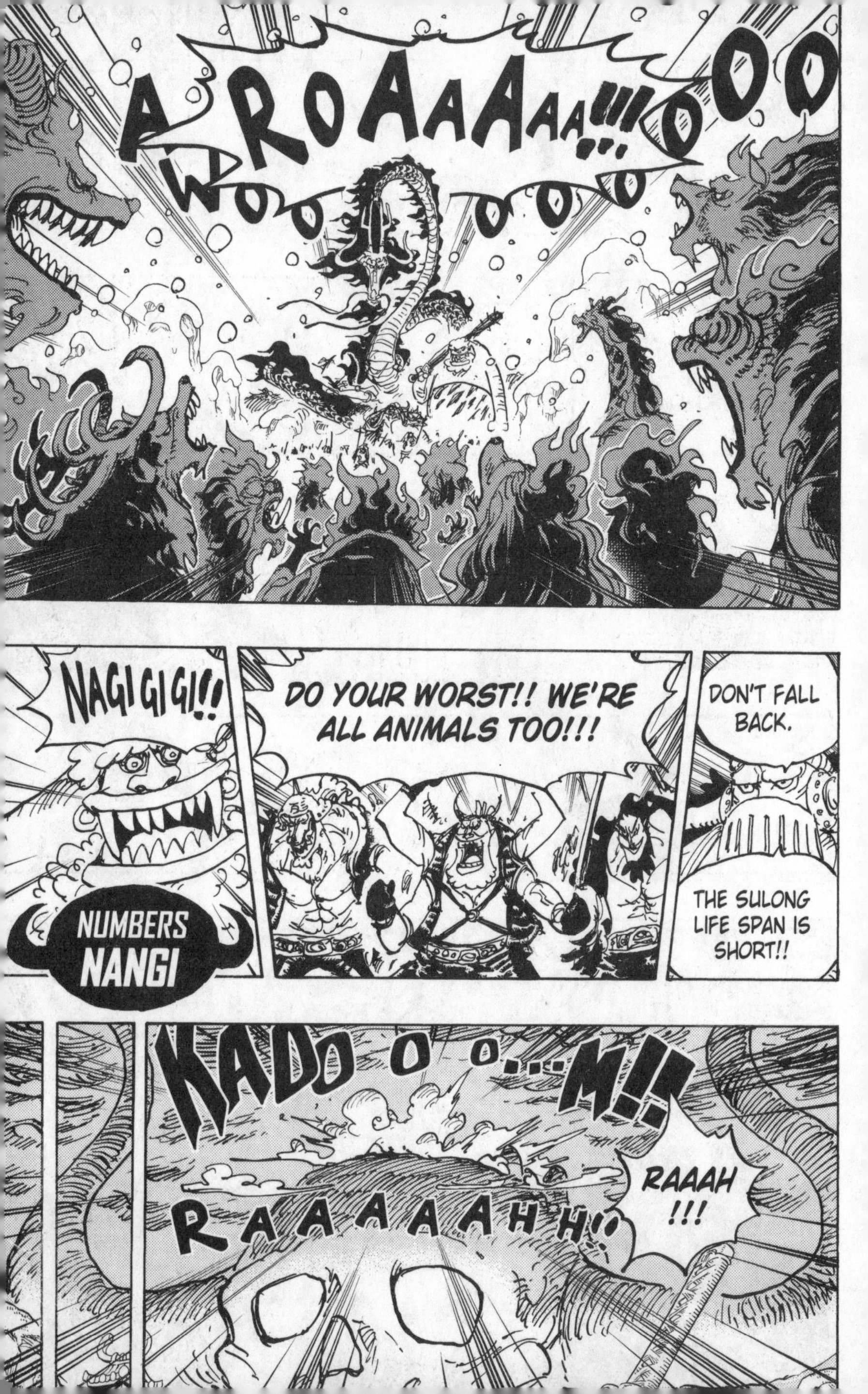
AROAAAAA!!!
WOOOOOOOO
DON'T FALL BACK.
THE SULONG LIFE SPAN IS SHORT!!
DO YOUR WORST!! WE'RE ALL ANIMALS TOO!!!
NAGIGIGI!!
NUMBERS NANGI
KADOOO...M!!
RAAAH!!!
RAAAAAHH!!

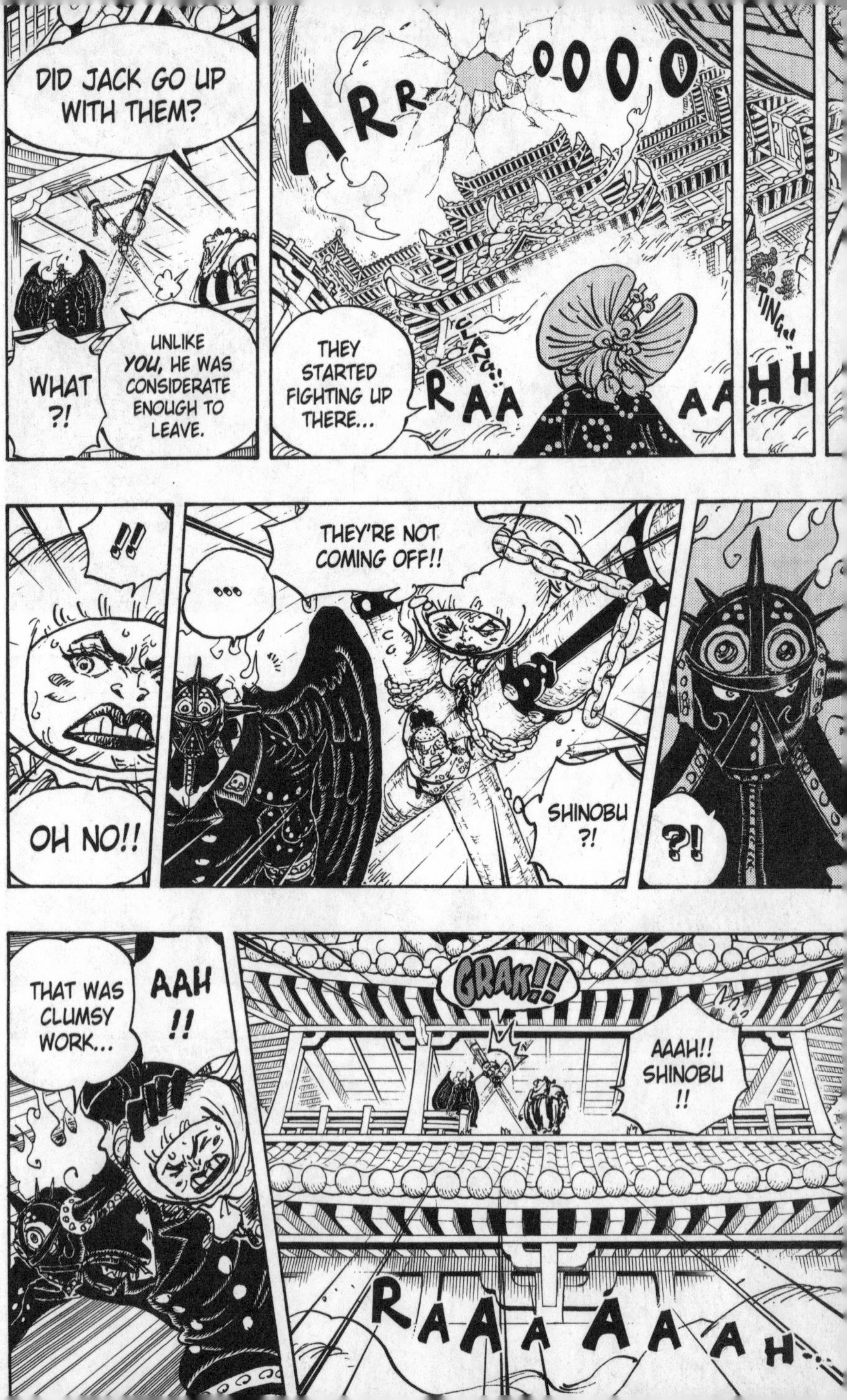
TING!!
ARROOOO
CLANG!!
THEY STARTED FIGHTING UP THERE...
RAAAAHH
DID JACK GO UP WITH THEM?
UNLIKE YOU, HE WAS CONSIDERATE ENOUGH TO LEAVE.
WHAT?!
?!
THEY'RE NOT COMING OFF!!
SHINOBU ?!
...
!!
OH NO!!
GRAK!!
AAAH!! SHINOBU !!
RAAAAAAAH...!
AAH !!
THAT WAS CLUMSY WORK...

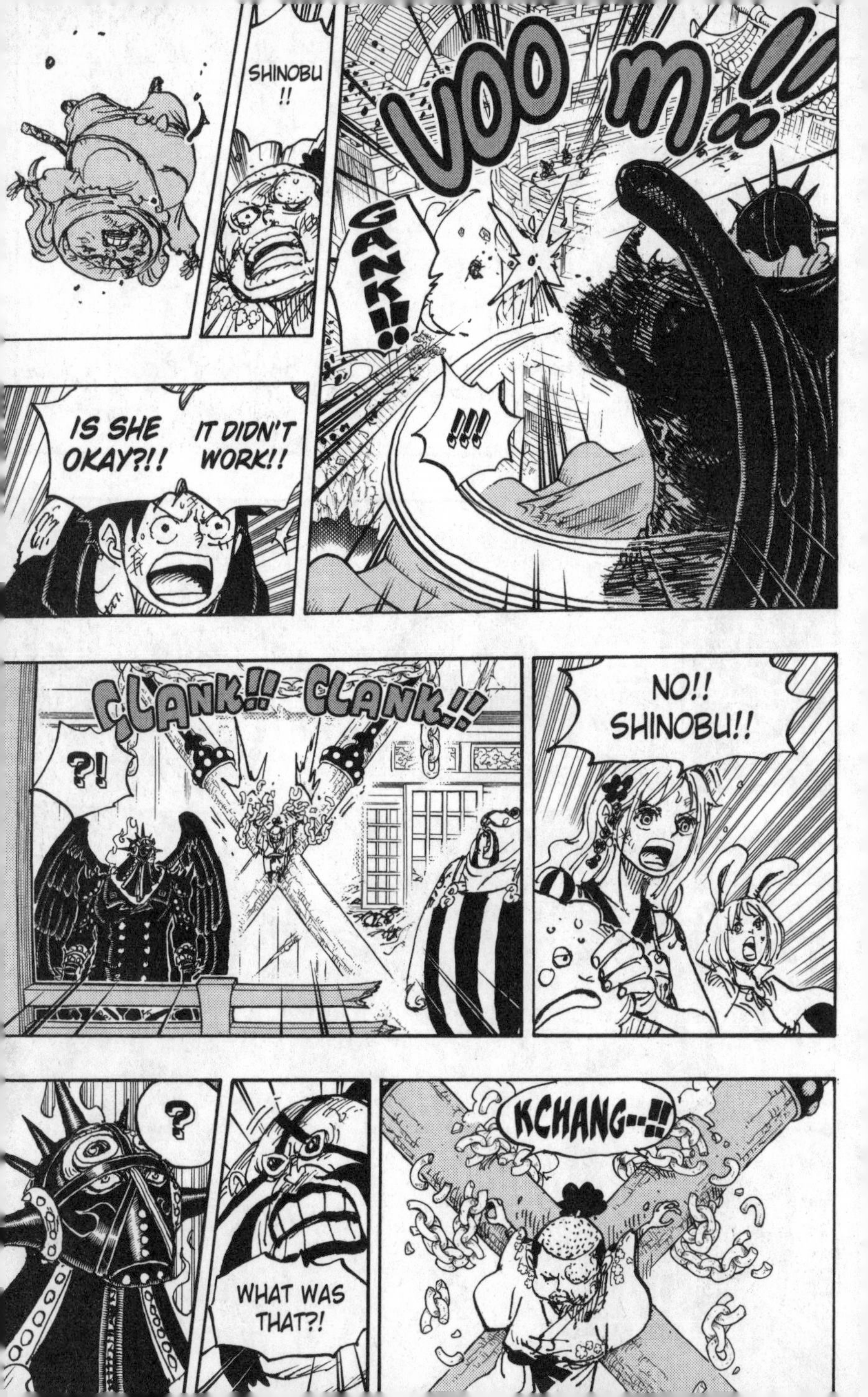
VOOM..!!
GANK!!
!!!
SHINOBU!!
IT DIDN'T WORK!!
IS SHE OKAY?!!
NO!! SHINOBU!!
CLANK!! CLANK!!
?!
KCHANG--!!
WHAT WAS THAT?!
?

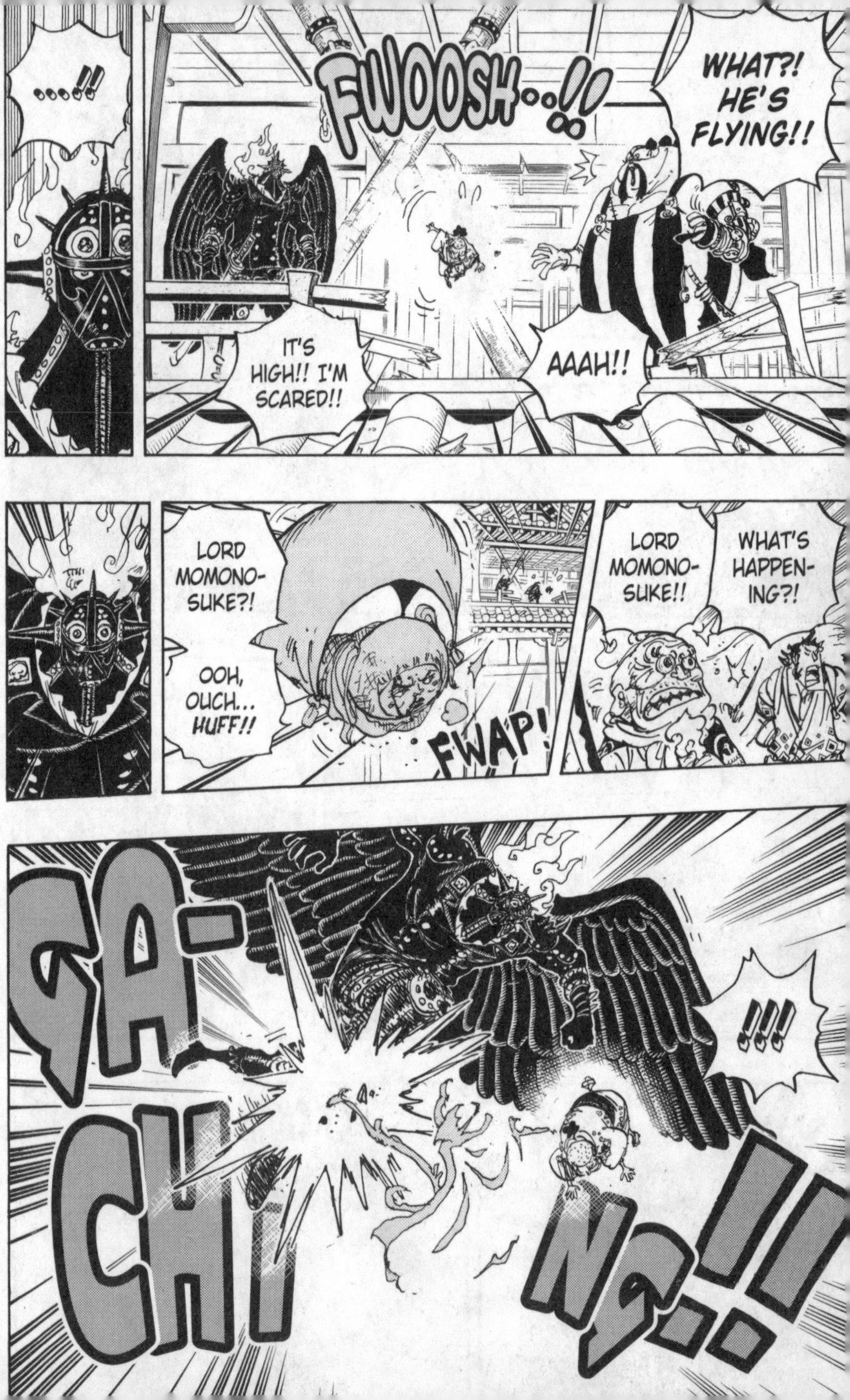
WHAT?! HE'S FLYING!!
FWOOSH..!!
AAAH!!
IT'S HIGH!! I'M SCARED!!
...!!
WHAT'S HAPPEN-ING?!
LORD MOMONO-SUKE!!
LORD MOMONO-SUKE?!
OOH, OUCH... HUFF!!
FWAP!
!!!
GA-CHI NG..!!

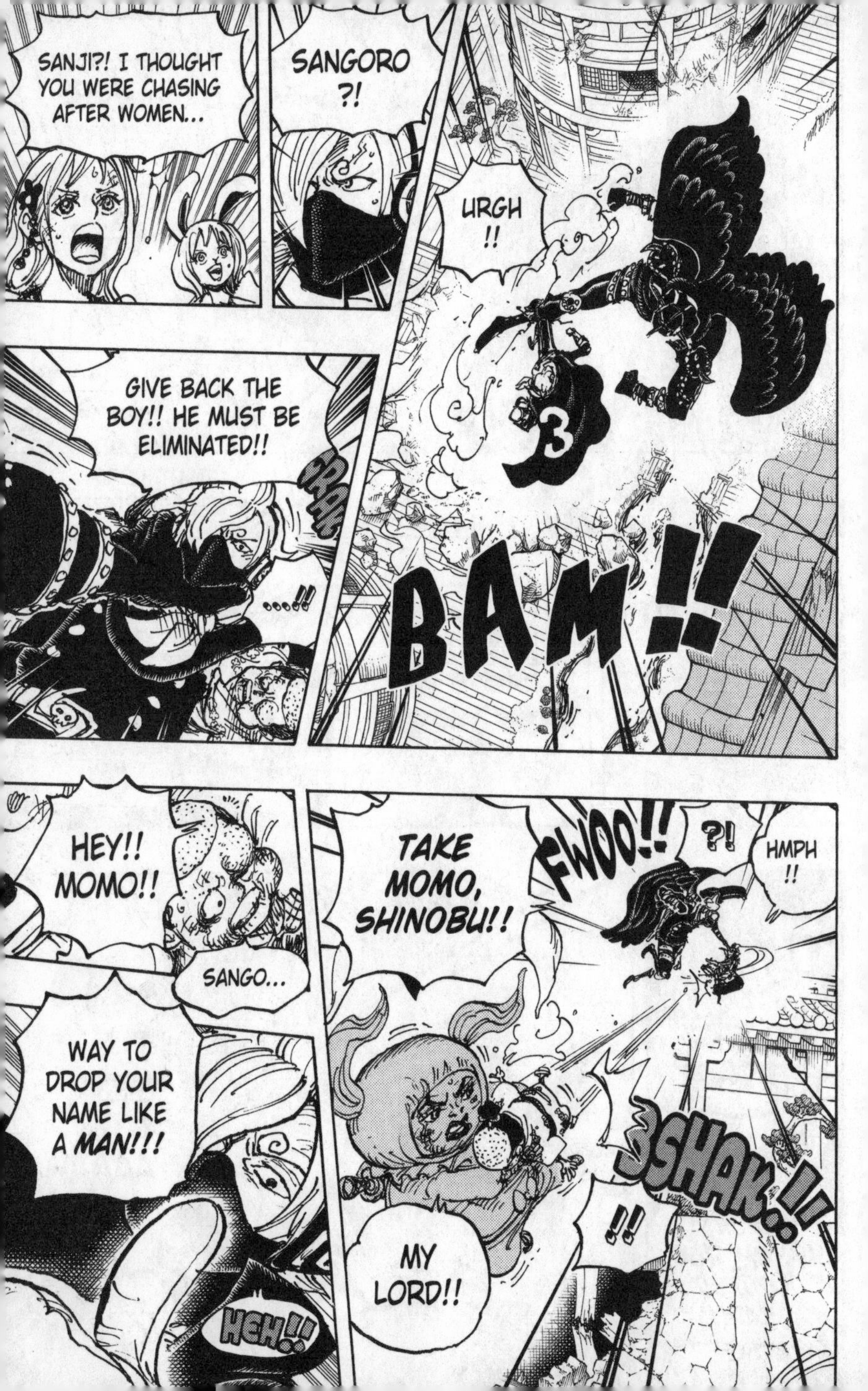
URGH!!
BAM!!
SANGORO?!
SANJI?! I THOUGHT YOU WERE CHASING AFTER WOMEN...
GIVE BACK THE BOY!! HE MUST BE ELIMINATED!!
CRAK
....!!
HMPH!!
?!
FWOO!!
TAKE MOMO, SHINOBU!!
SHAK...!!!
!!
MY LORD!!
HEY!! MOMO!!
SANGO...
WAY TO DROP YOUR NAME LIKE A *MAN*!!!
HEH!!

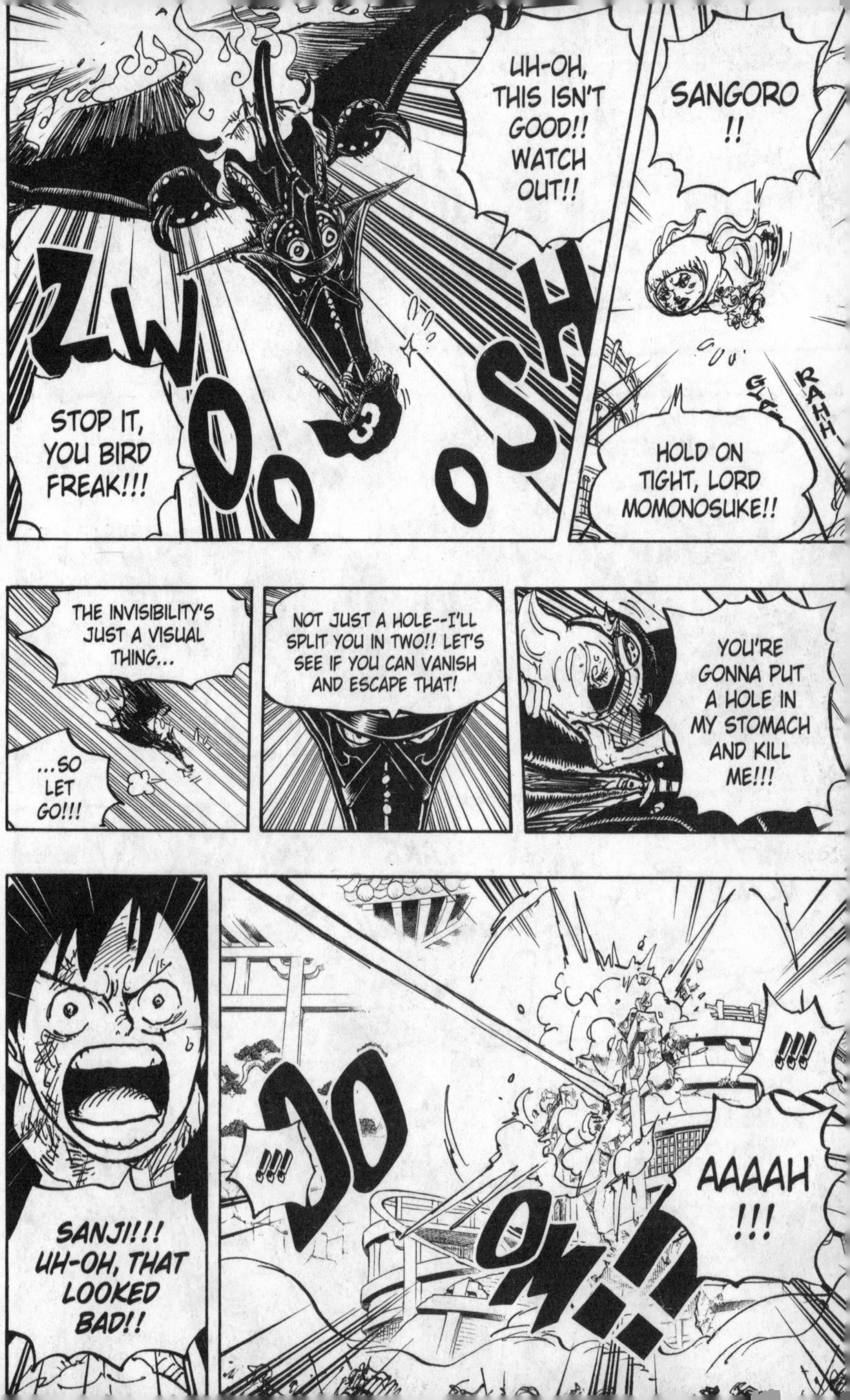
SANGORO !!
GYARAHH
HOLD ON TIGHT, LORD MOMONOSUKE!!
UH-OH, THIS ISN'T GOOD!! WATCH OUT!!
ZWOOOSH
STOP IT, YOU BIRD FREAK!!!
YOU'RE GONNA PUT A HOLE IN MY STOMACH AND KILL ME!!!
NOT JUST A HOLE--I'LL SPLIT YOU IN TWO!! LET'S SEE IF YOU CAN VANISH AND ESCAPE THAT!
THE INVISIBILITY'S JUST A VISUAL THING...
...SO LET GO!!!
!!!
AAAAH !!!
DOOM!!
!!!
SANJI!!! UH-OH, THAT LOOKED BAD!!

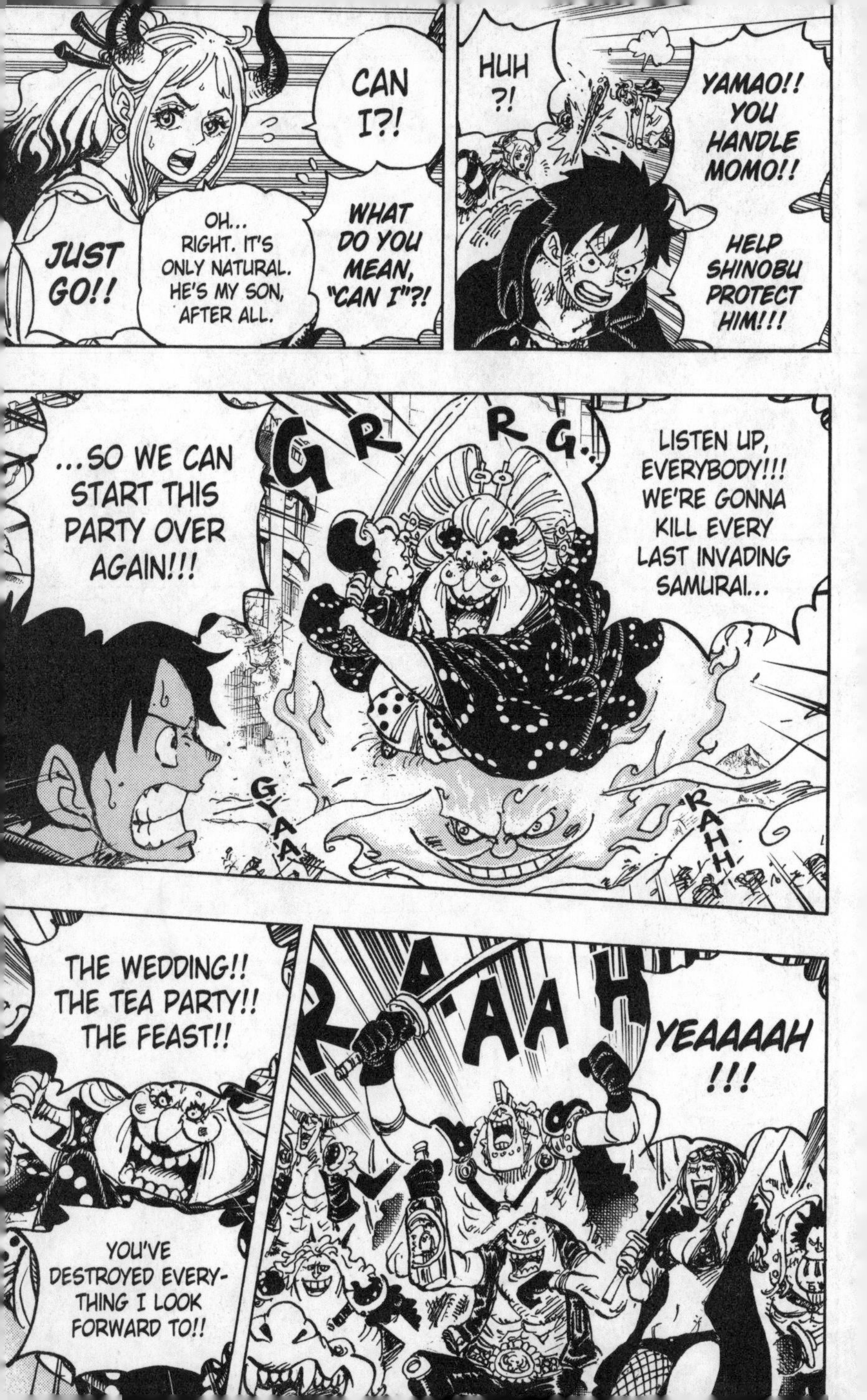
YAMAO!! YOU HANDLE MOMO!!
HUH ?!
HELP SHINOBU PROTECT HIM!!!
CAN I?!
WHAT DO YOU MEAN, "CAN I"?!
OH... RIGHT. IT'S ONLY NATURAL. HE'S MY SON, AFTER ALL.
JUST GO!!
LISTEN UP, EVERYBODY!!! WE'RE GONNA KILL EVERY LAST INVADING SAMURAI...
GRRG.
...SO WE CAN START THIS PARTY OVER AGAIN!!!
RAHH
GYAA
RAAAH
YEAAAAH !!!
THE WEDDING!! THE TEA PARTY!! THE FEAST!!
YOU'VE DESTROYED EVERY-THING I LOOK FORWARD TO!!

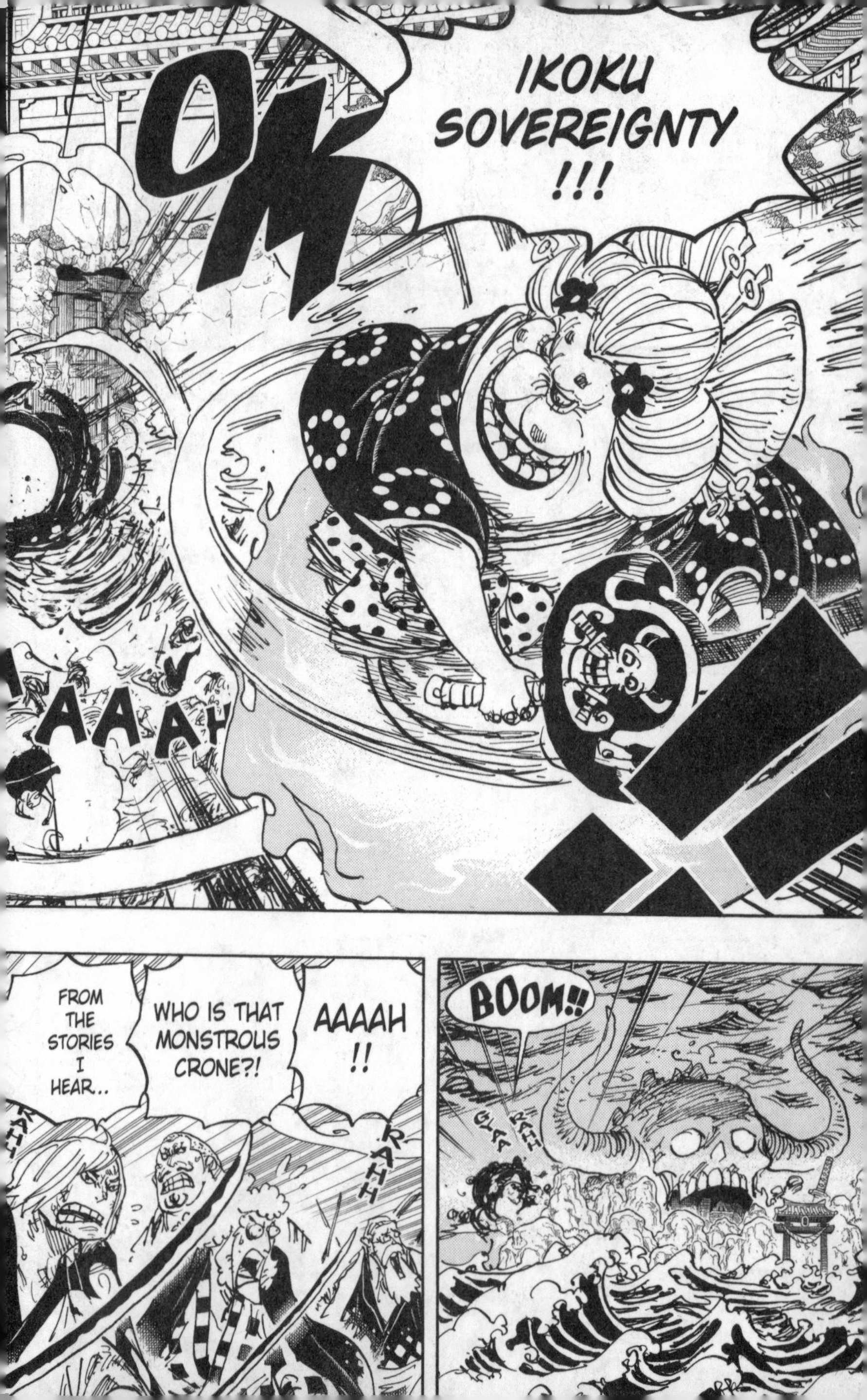

IKOKU SOVEREIGNTY !!!
OM
AAAAH
BOOM!!
RAHH
GYAA
AAAAH !!
WHO IS THAT MONSTROUS CRONE?!
FROM THE STORIES I HEAR...
RAHH

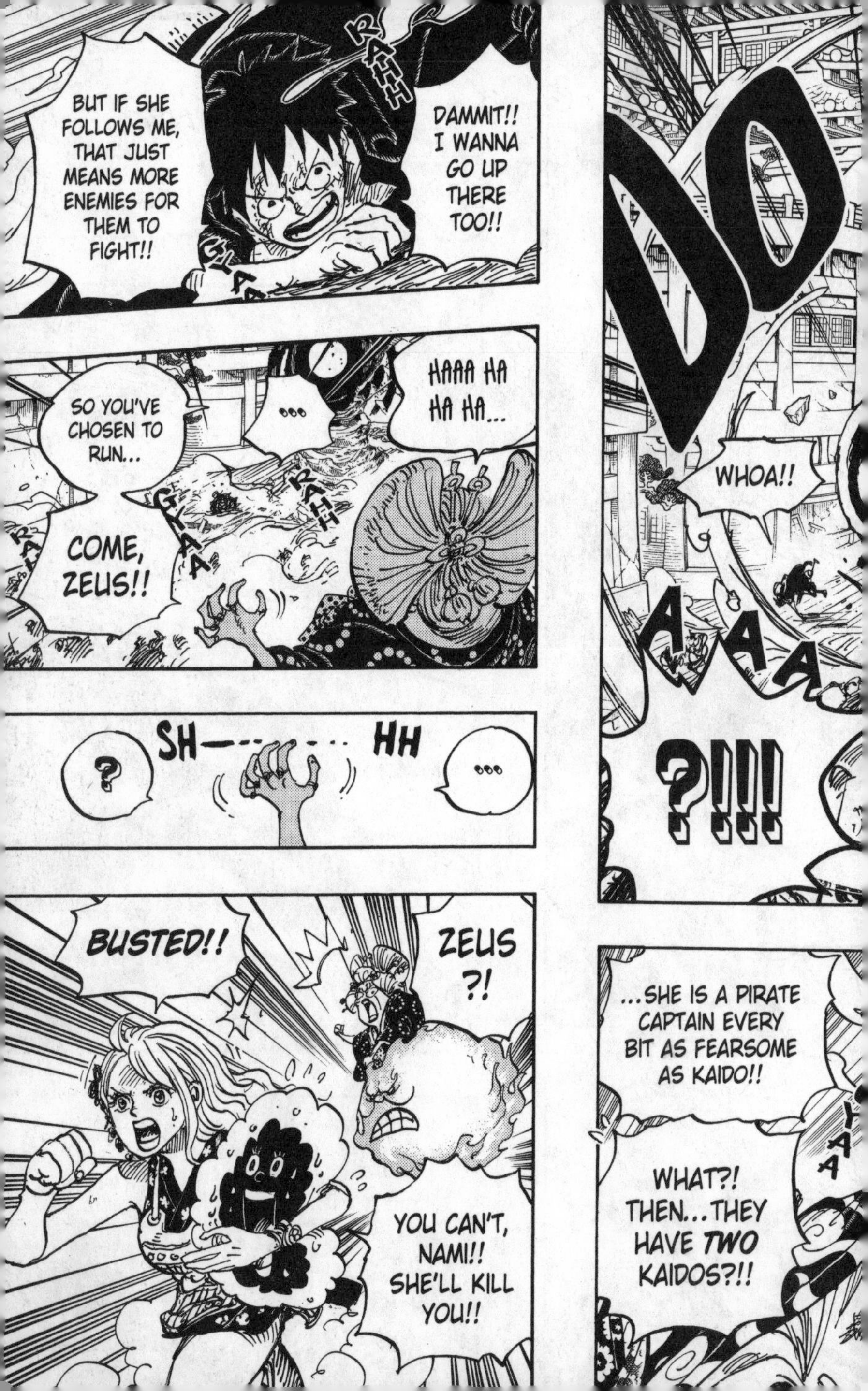
DO
WHOA!!
AAA
?!!!
...SHE IS A PIRATE CAPTAIN EVERY BIT AS FEARSOME AS KAIDO!!
YAA
WHAT?! THEN...THEY HAVE TWO KAIDOS?!!
DAMMIT!! I WANNA GO UP THERE TOO!!
RAHHH
BUT IF SHE FOLLOWS ME, THAT JUST MEANS MORE ENEMIES FOR THEM TO FIGHT!!
GYAA
HAAA HA HA HA...
...
SO YOU'VE CHOSEN TO RUN...
COME, ZEUS!!
RAHH
GYAA
...
SH—... HH
?
ZEUS ?!
BUSTED!!
YOU CAN'T, NAMI!! SHE'LL KILL YOU!!

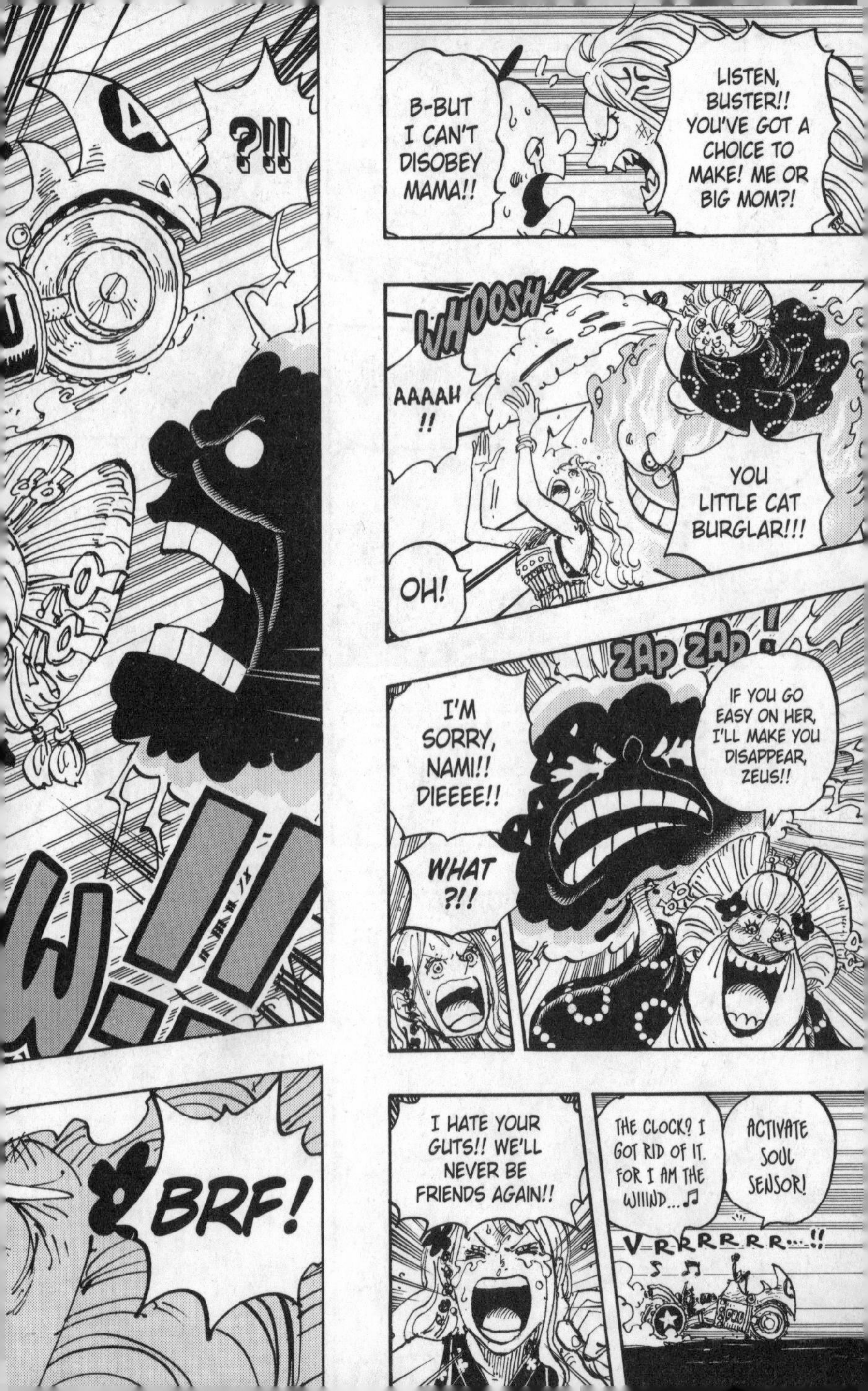
LISTEN, BUSTER!! YOU'VE GOT A CHOICE TO MAKE! ME OR BIG MOM?!
B-BUT I CAN'T DISOBEY MAMA!!
YOU LITTLE CAT BURGLAR!!!
WHOOSH!!
AAAAH!!
OH!
ZAP ZAP!
IF YOU GO EASY ON HER, I'LL MAKE YOU DISAPPEAR, ZEUS!!
I'M SORRY, NAMI!! DIEEEE!!
WHAT?!!
?!!
ACTIVATE SOUL SENSOR!
THE CLOCK? I GOT RID OF IT. FOR I AM THE WIIIND...♫
VRRRRRRR...!!
I HATE YOUR GUTS!! WE'LL NEVER BE FRIENDS AGAIN!!
BRF!

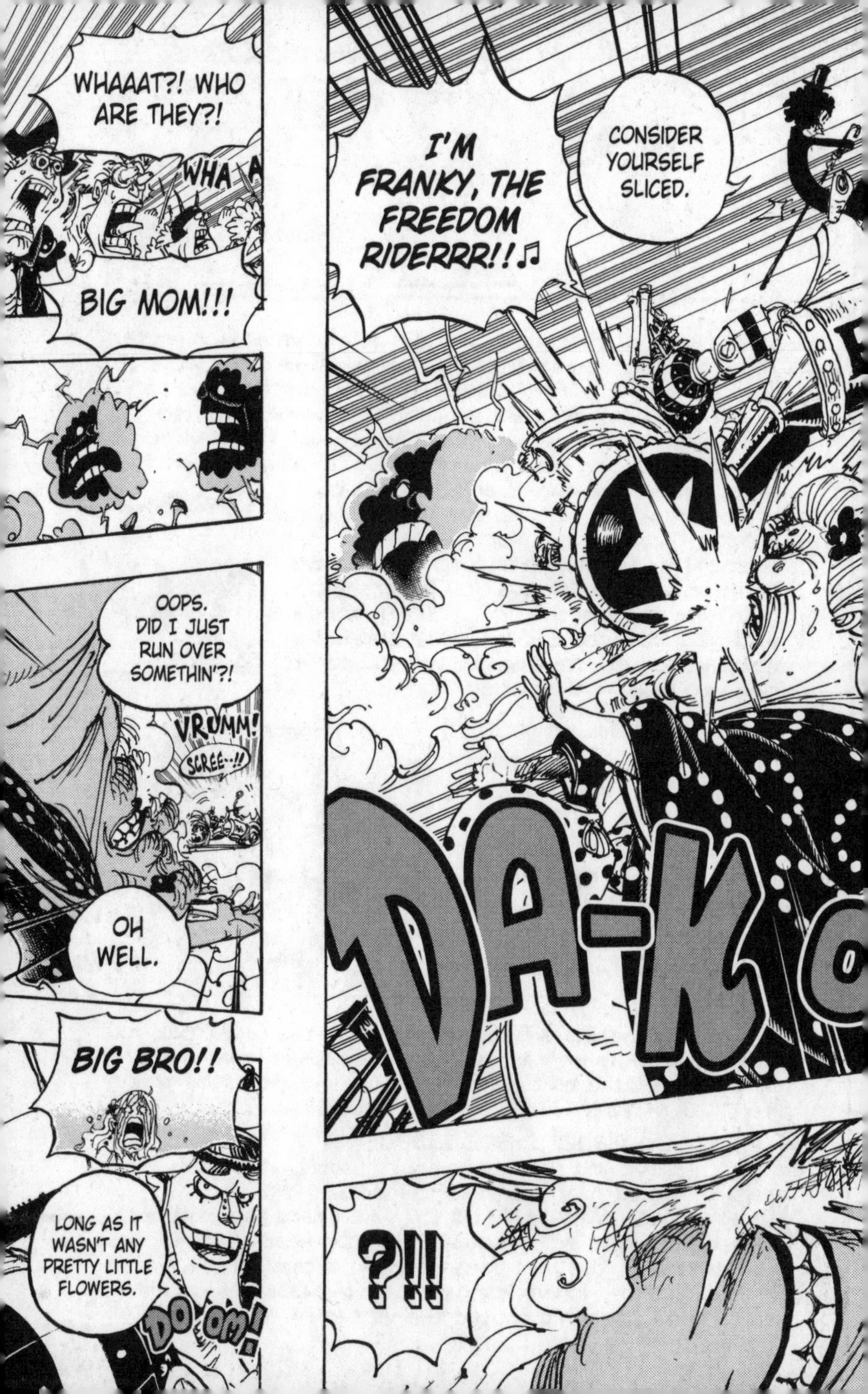
CONSIDER YOURSELF SLICED.
I'M FRANKY, THE FREEDOM RIDERRR!! ♫
DA-K
?!!
WHAAAT?! WHO ARE THEY?!
WHA
BIG MOM!!!
OOPS. DID I JUST RUN OVER SOMETHIN'?!
VRUMM!
SCREE--!!
OH WELL.
BIG BRO!!
LONG AS IT WASN'T ANY PRETTY LITTLE FLOWERS.
DOOM!

SBS Question Corner

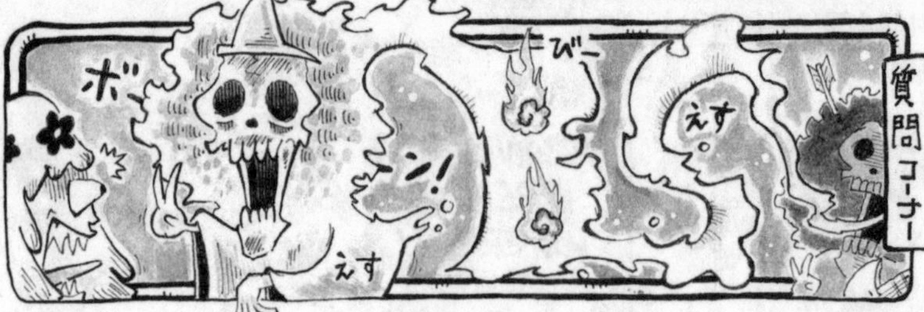
ボ
ン!
びー
えす
えす
質問コーナー
(Hayato Asami, Kanagawa)

A: Okay, I have an apology to make! I had a postcard (or letter?) from a reader that I've lost somehow. But don't worry, because I remember the content. It was from a person whose pen name was "Eeyan," and they wanted me to check out their YouTube page. And it was full of videos of homemade figure construction! Huh? Strange, that figure looks familiar, I thought...and it turns out it was from the very person whose figure photos they'd sent in for the fan art section! It's so fascinating to see readers of mine become famous YouTubers! Go to YouTube and search for "EEYAN." Good luck with your figures! Oh, he said he also has a collab video with Sanadacchi, but you don't need to look at that one!

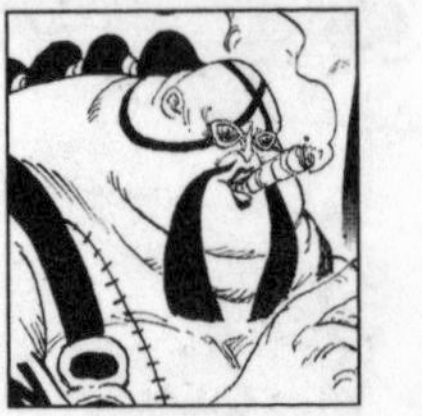

Q: I was doing some research on the culture of mixed bathing. Apparently, even in the past, when a young woman would come to the bath, perverts like Odacchi would flock to her, so the older women and grannies would keep her safe. Ugh, the nerve of those perverts! Anyway, I've decided to live out of a bathhouse.

--Sanadacchi

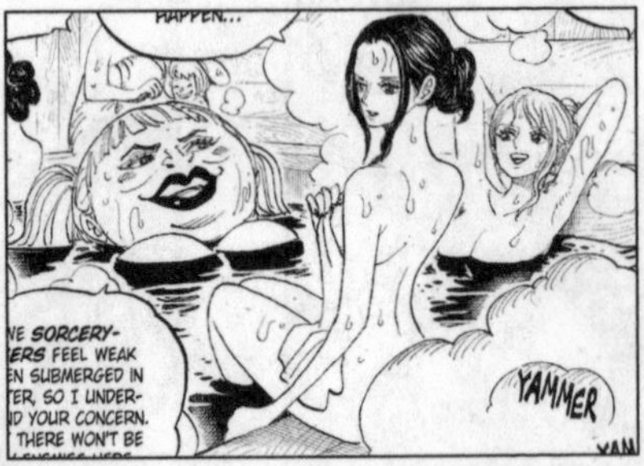
HAPPEN...
NE SORCERY-
ERS FEEL WEAK
EN SUBMERGED IN
TER, SO I UNDER-
D YOUR CONCERN.
THERE WON'T BE
YAMMER

A: Uh, excuse me, ma'am! You're kind of in the way! Could you please scooch over a little? I can't see what I came here to see! I oppose this culture of yours!! Ouch!! Hey, stop trying to crush my balls!! Ow!! Stop...ow! Stop!! The SBS... is...

A sacred place! Sanadaaaa!!

I can't believe you showed up again!! Ladies, go and crush his balls now!! Ow!! No, not mine!! Sanadaaaa...
Okay, enough of that. All of you who heard about mixed bathing and got dirty thoughts in your heads, just because it was long in the past doesn't mean people didn't have shame. So now you've learned something about how the culture of Japan protected the virtue of young ladies!

Chapter 989:
I CAN'T IMAGINE LOSING

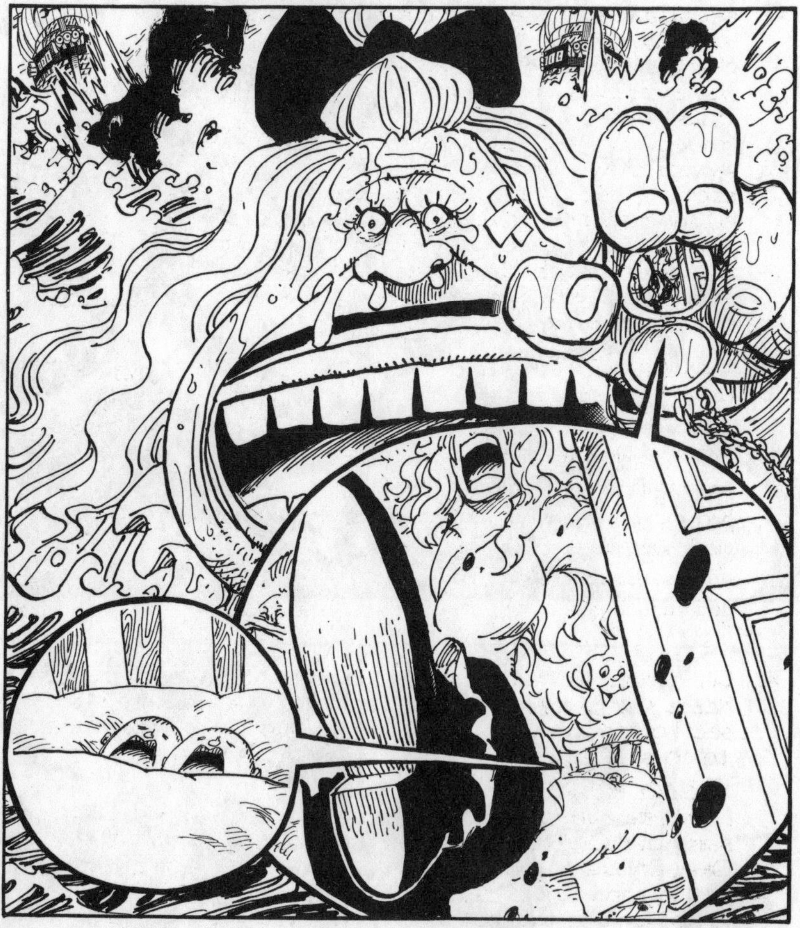

GANG BEGE'S OH MY FAMILY
VOL. 33: "LIKE, I HAVE PROOF!!"

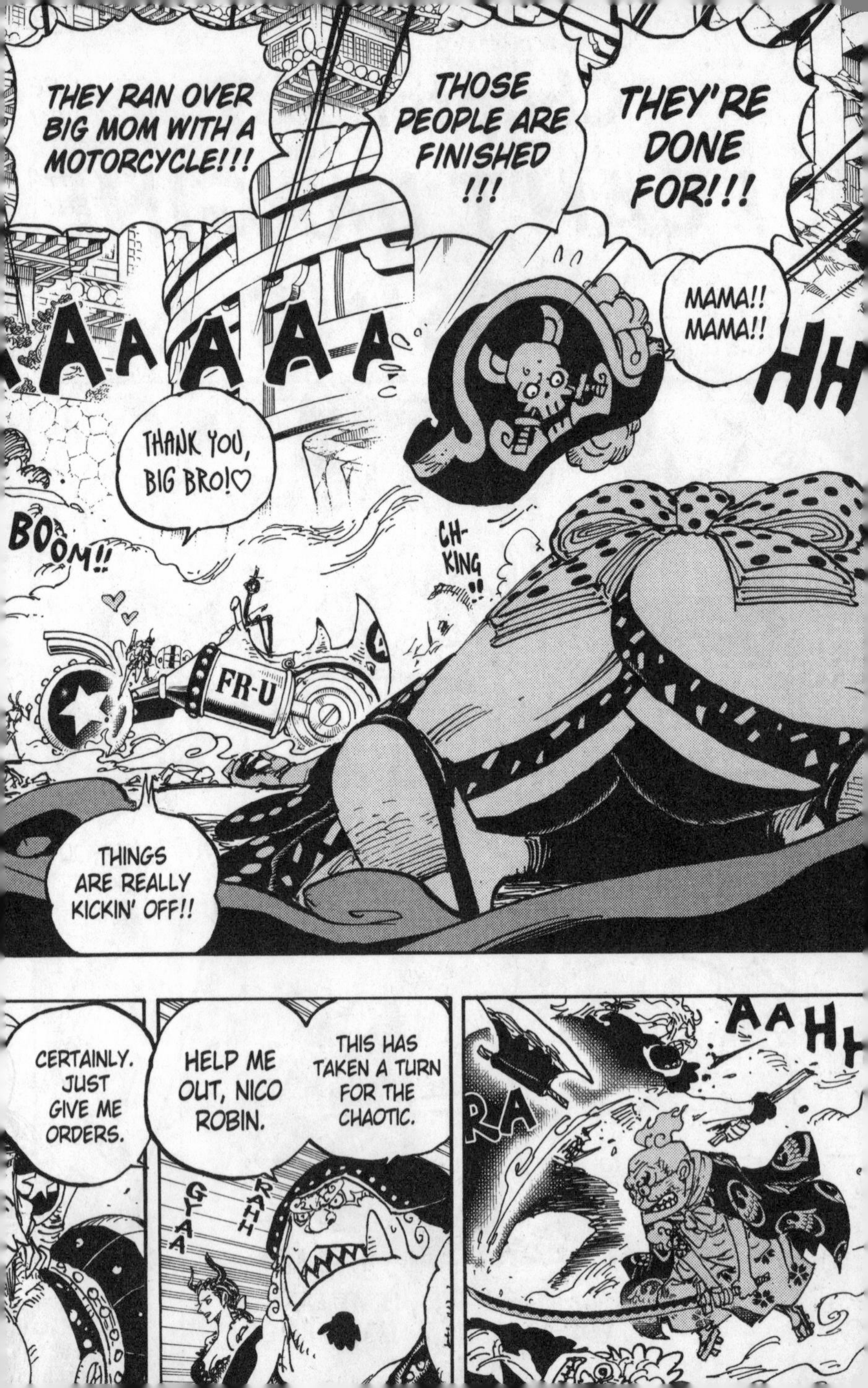

THEY'RE DONE FOR!!!
THOSE PEOPLE ARE FINISHED !!!
THEY RAN OVER BIG MOM WITH A MOTORCYCLE!!!
MAMA!! MAMA!!
HH
AAAAA
THANK YOU, BIG BRO!♡
CH-KING!!
BOOM!!
FR-U
THINGS ARE REALLY KICKIN' OFF!!
AAHH
RA
THIS HAS TAKEN A TURN FOR THE CHAOTIC.
HELP ME OUT, NICO ROBIN.
RAHH
GYAA
CERTAINLY. JUST GIVE ME ORDERS.

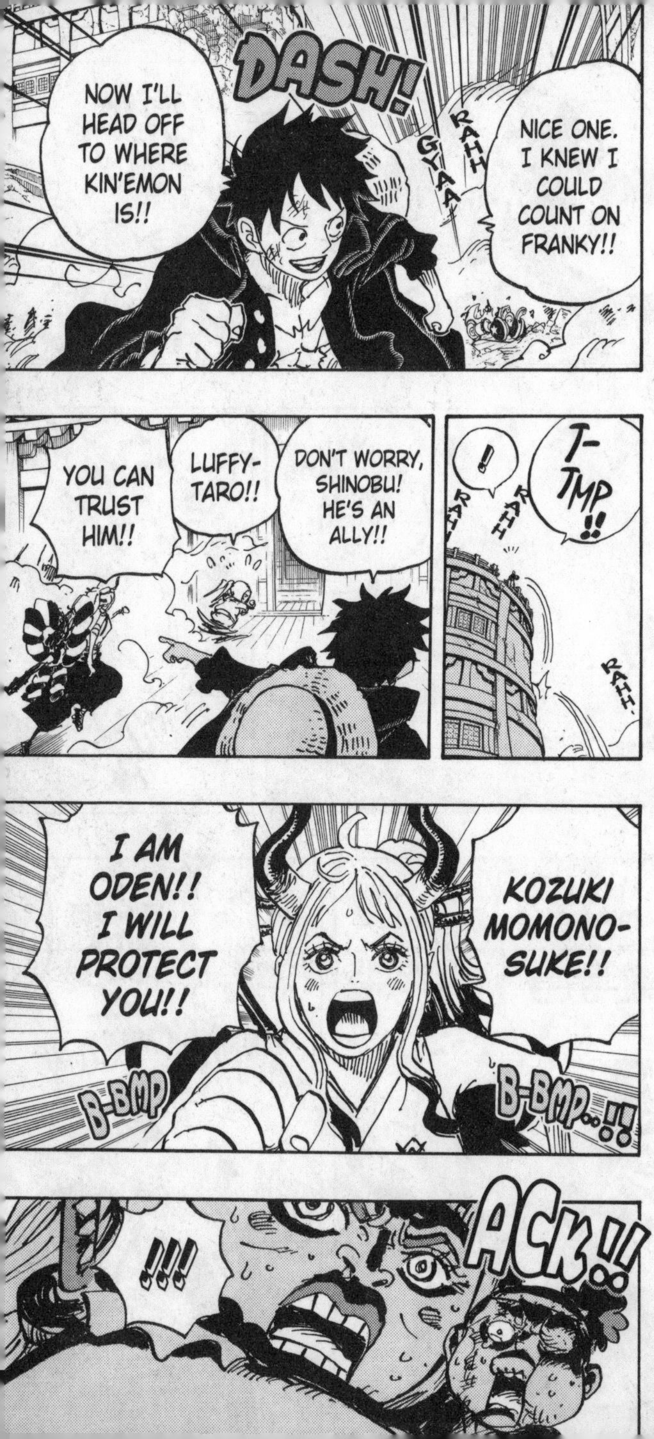
DASH!
GYAA
RAHH
NICE ONE. I KNEW I COULD COUNT ON FRANKY!!
NOW I'LL HEAD OFF TO WHERE KIN'EMON IS!!
T-TMP!!
!
RAHH
RAHH
DON'T WORRY, SHINOBU! HE'S AN ALLY!!
LUFFY-TARO!!
YOU CAN TRUST HIM!!
RAHH.
KOZUKI MOMONO-SUKE!!
I AM ODEN!! I WILL PROTECT YOU!!
B-BMP..!!
B-BMP
ACK!!
!!!
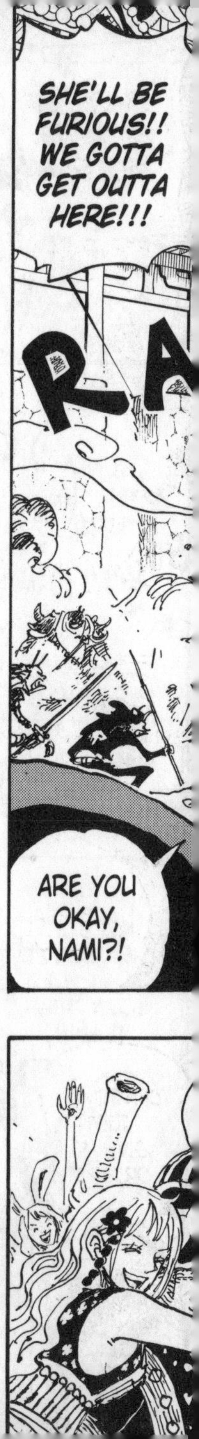
SHE'LL BE FURIOUS!! WE GOTTA GET OUTTA HERE!!!
RA
ARE YOU OKAY, NAMI?!

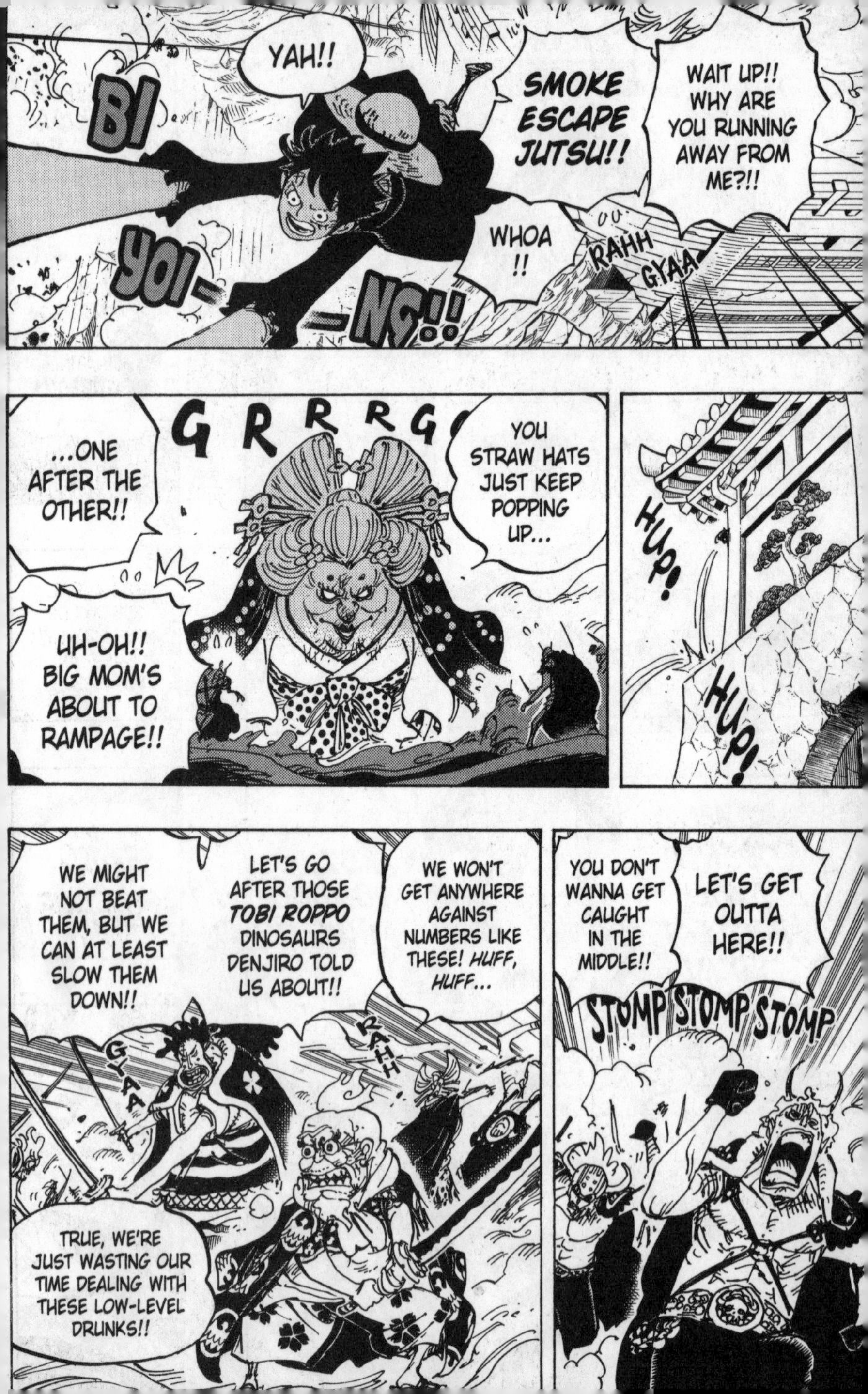
WAIT UP!! WHY ARE YOU RUNNING AWAY FROM ME?!!
SMOKE ESCAPE JUTSU!!
YAH!!
RAHH
GYAA
WHOA!!
BIYOI--NG!!
HUP!
HUP!
YOU STRAW HATS JUST KEEP POPPING UP...
GRRRG
...ONE AFTER THE OTHER!!
UH-OH!! BIG MOM'S ABOUT TO RAMPAGE!!
LET'S GET OUTTA HERE!!
YOU DON'T WANNA GET CAUGHT IN THE MIDDLE!!
STOMP STOMP STOMP
WE WON'T GET ANYWHERE AGAINST NUMBERS LIKE THESE! *HUFF, HUFF...*
LET'S GO AFTER THOSE *TOBI ROPPO* DINOSAURS DENJIRO TOLD US ABOUT!!
WE MIGHT NOT BEAT THEM, BUT WE CAN AT LEAST SLOW THEM DOWN!!
RAHH
GYAA
TRUE, WE'RE JUST WASTING OUR TIME DEALING WITH THESE LOW-LEVEL DRUNKS!!

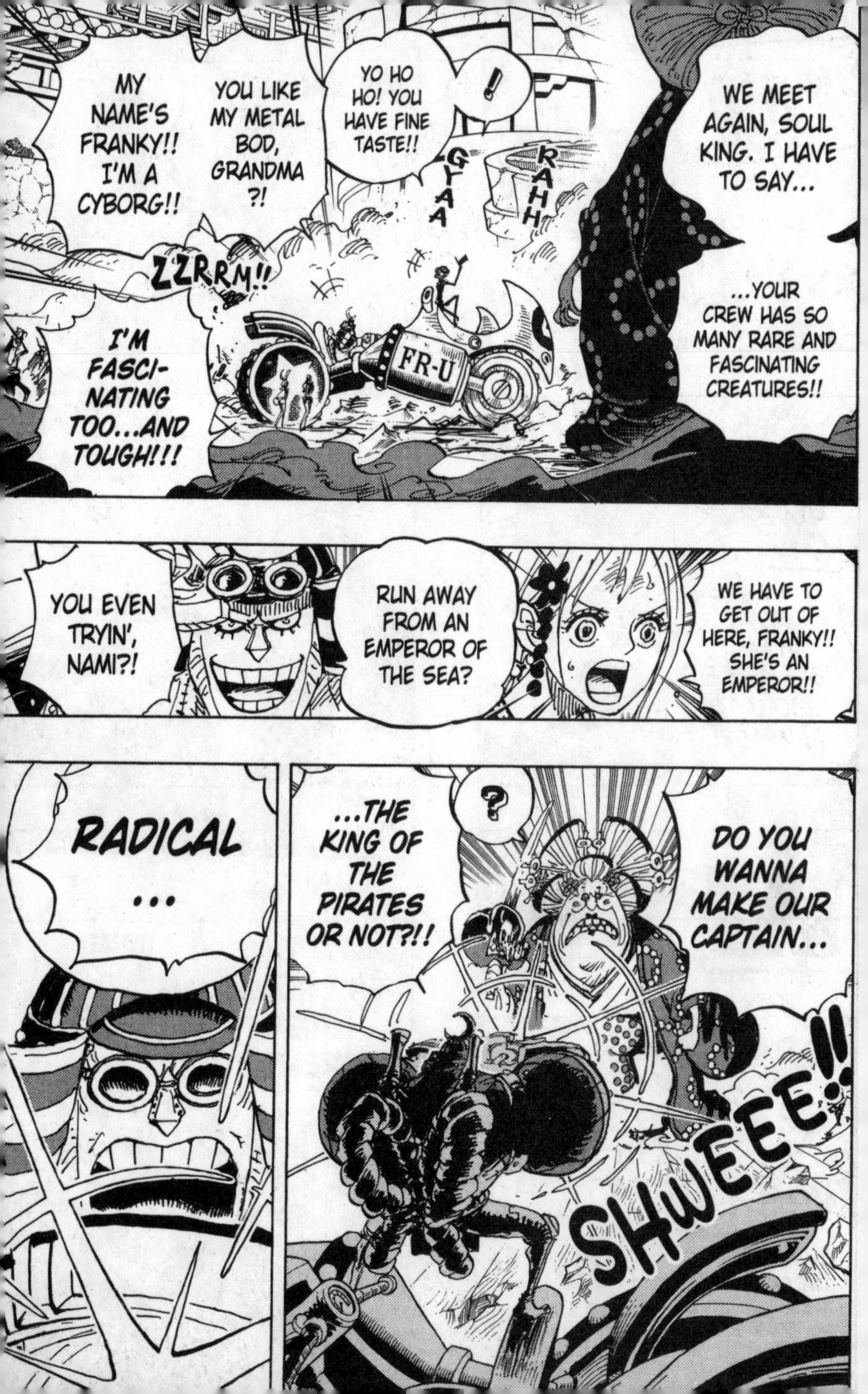
WE MEET AGAIN, SOUL KING. I HAVE TO SAY...
...YOUR CREW HAS SO MANY RARE AND FASCINATING CREATURES!!
!
YO HO HO! YOU HAVE FINE TASTE!!
RAHHH
GYAA
YOU LIKE MY METAL BOD, GRANDMA?!
MY NAME'S FRANKY!! I'M A CYBORG!!
ZZRRRM!!
FR-U
I'M FASCINATING TOO...AND TOUGH!!!
WE HAVE TO GET OUT OF HERE, FRANKY!! SHE'S AN EMPEROR!!
RUN AWAY FROM AN EMPEROR OF THE SEA?
YOU EVEN TRYIN', NAMI?!
DO YOU WANNA MAKE OUR CAPTAIN...
?
...THE KING OF THE PIRATES OR NOT?!!
SHWEEE!!
RADICAL ...

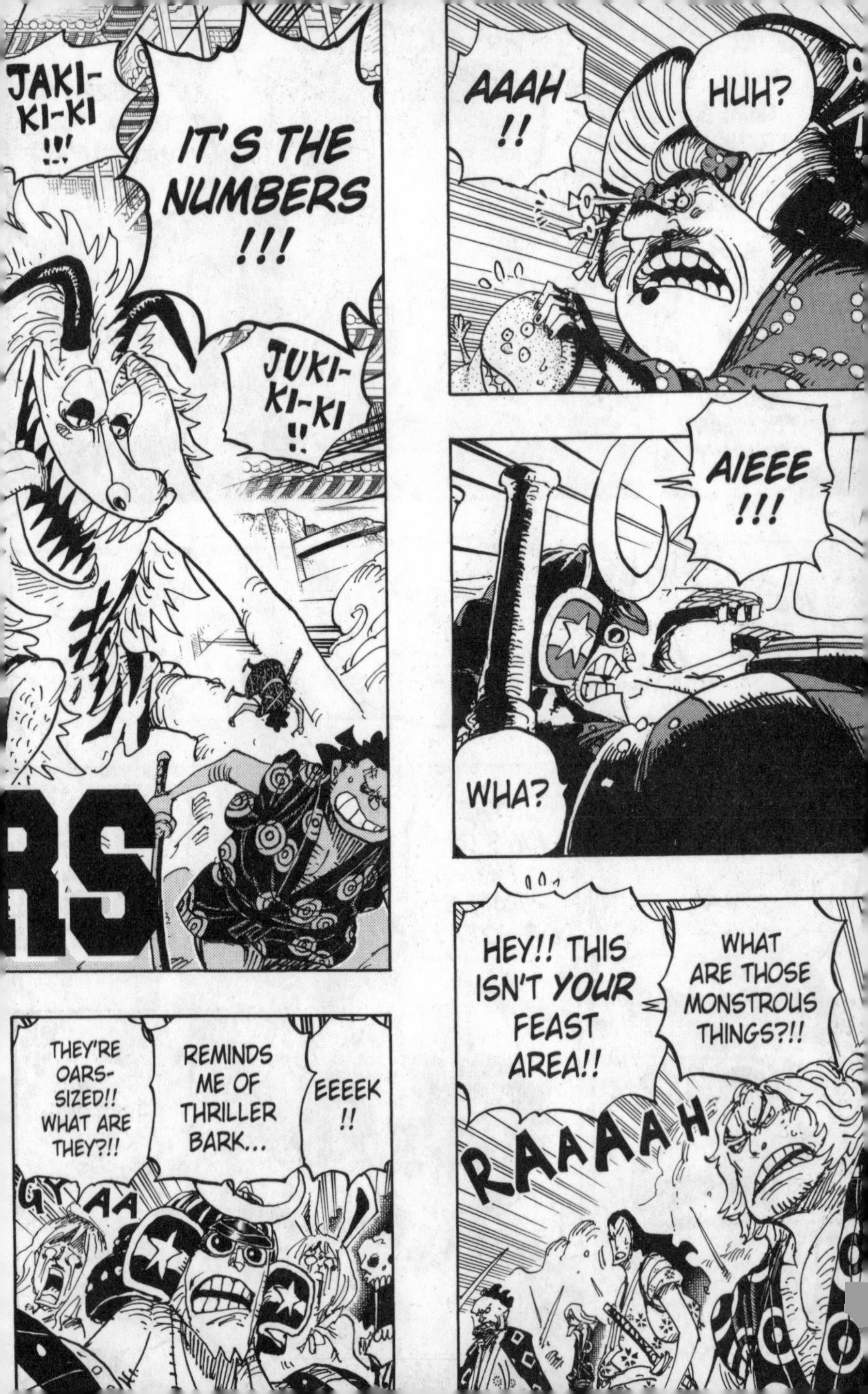
HUH?
AAAH!!
AIEEE!!!
WHA?
WHAT ARE THOSE MONSTROUS THINGS?!!
HEY!! THIS ISN'T YOUR FEAST AREA!!
RAAAAH
IT'S THE NUMBERS!!!
JAKI-KI-KI!!!
JUKI-KI-KI!!
RS
EEEEK!!
REMINDS ME OF THRILLER BARK...
THEY'RE OARS-SIZED!! WHAT ARE THEY?!!
GYAA

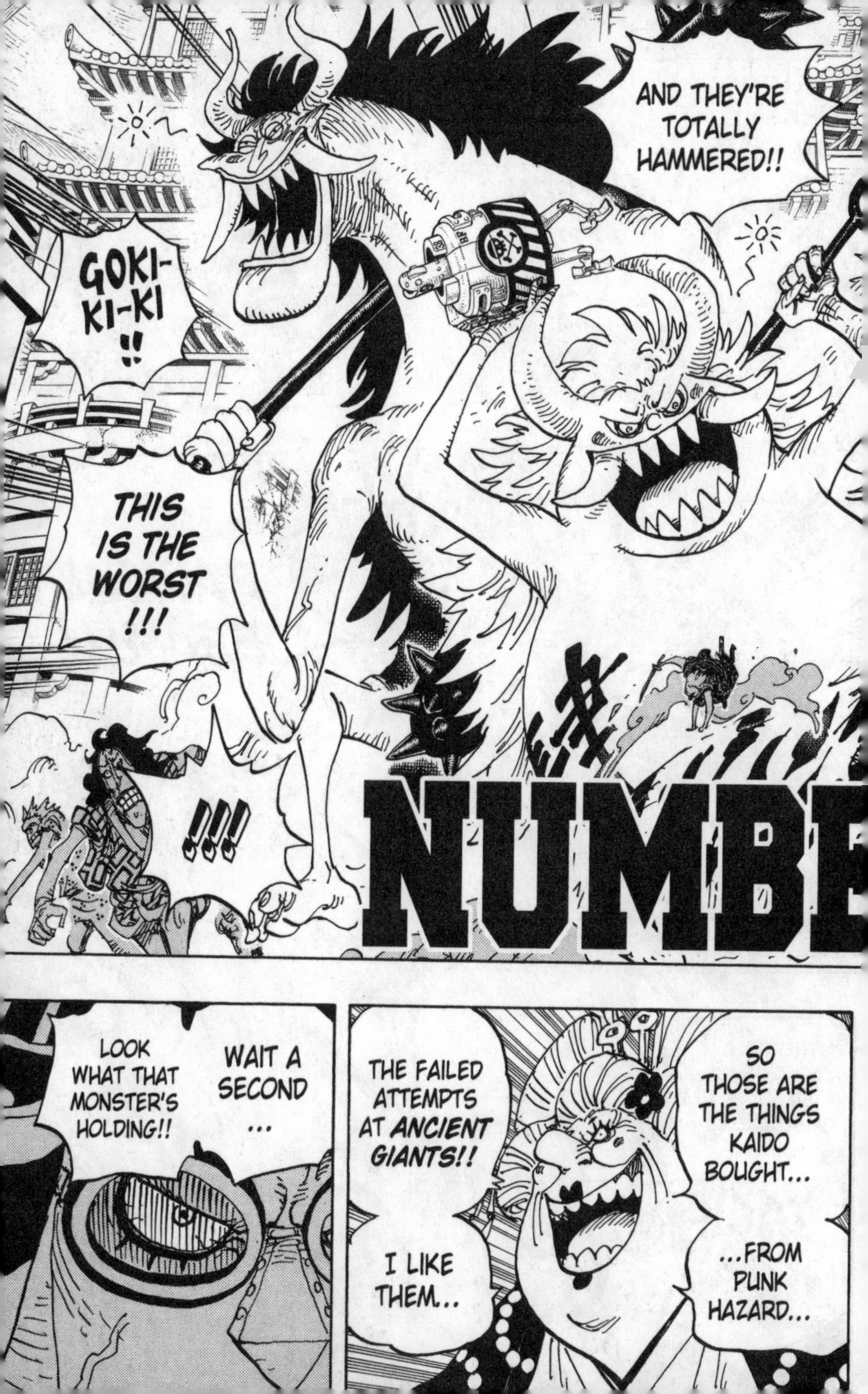
AND THEY'RE TOTALLY HAMMERED!!
GOKI-KI-KI!!
THIS IS THE WORST!!!
!!!
NUMBE
SO THOSE ARE THE THINGS KAIDO BOUGHT...
THE FAILED ATTEMPTS AT ANCIENT GIANTS!!
...FROM PUNK HAZARD...
I LIKE THEM...
WAIT A SECOND ...
LOOK WHAT THAT MONSTER'S HOLDING!!

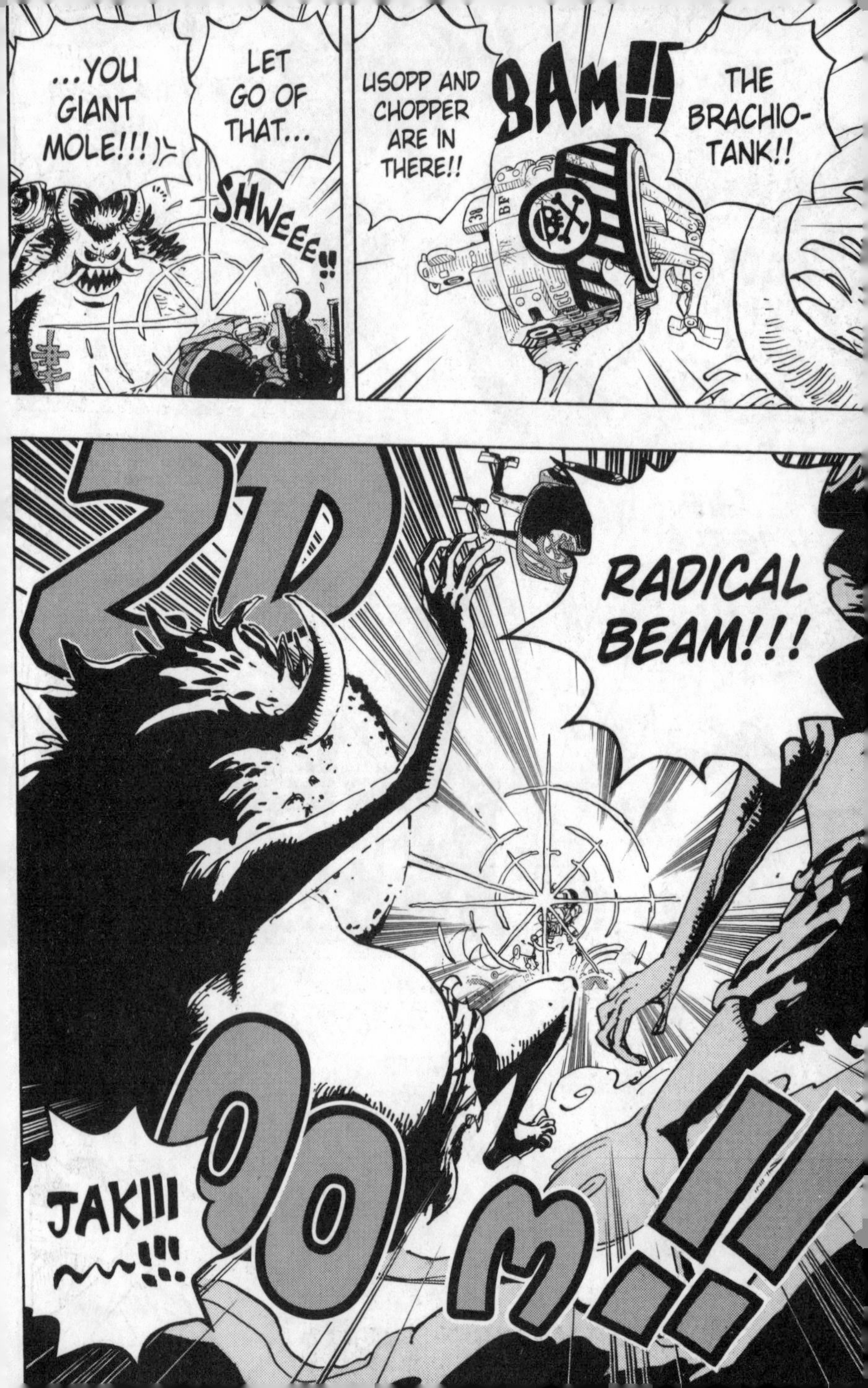
THE BRACHIO-TANK!!
BAM!!
USOPP AND CHOPPER ARE IN THERE!!
LET GO OF THAT...
...YOU GIANT MOLE!!!
SHWEEEE!!
RADICAL BEAM!!!
ZDOOOM..!!
JAKIIII ~~!!!

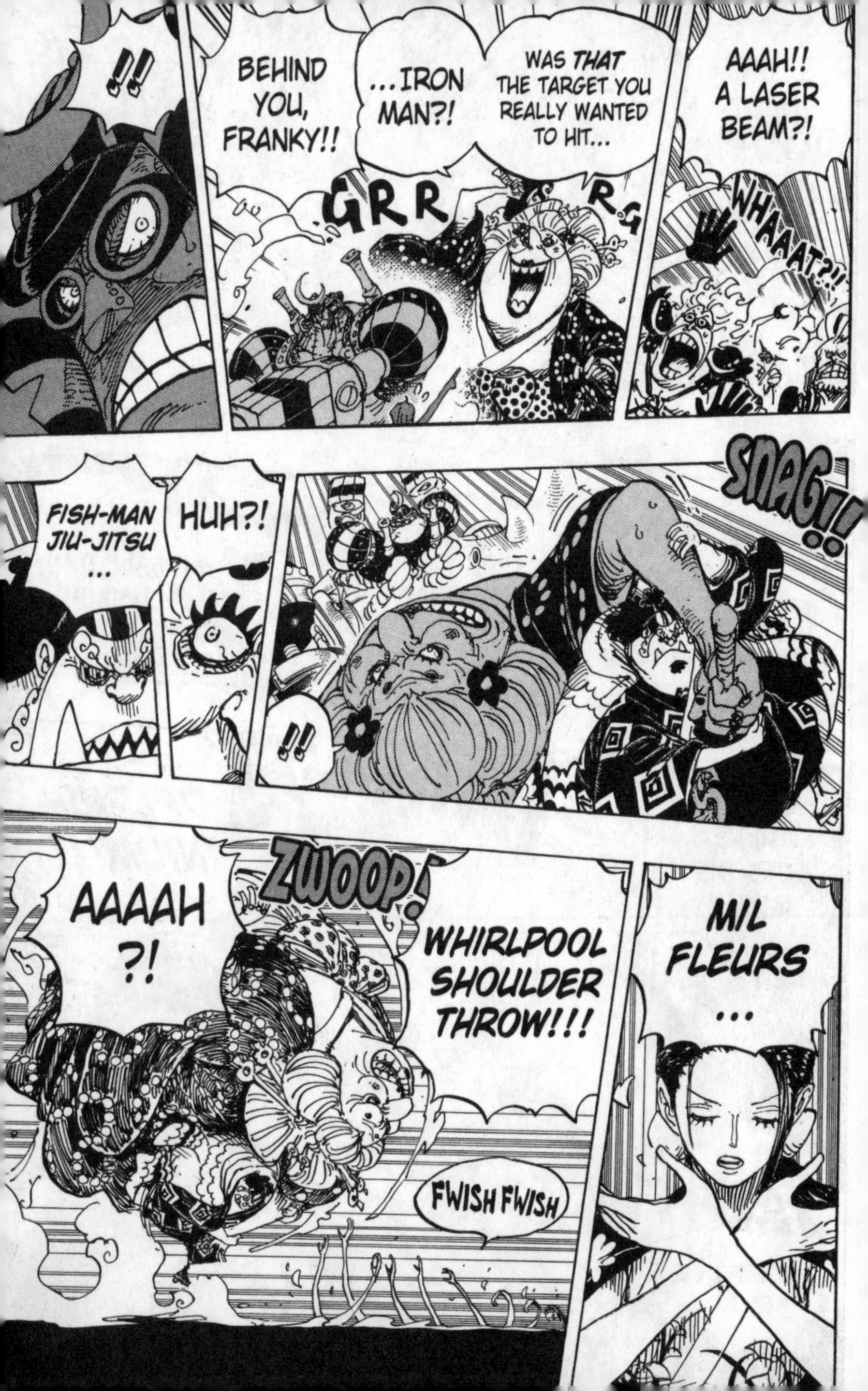
AAAH!! A LASER BEAM?!
WHAAAAT?!!
WAS THAT THE TARGET YOU REALLY WANTED TO HIT...
...IRON MAN?!
BEHIND YOU, FRANKY!!
GRR
RG
!!
SNAG!!
!!
HUH?!
FISH-MAN JIU-JITSU ...
MIL FLEURS ...
ZWOOP!
WHIRLPOOL SHOULDER THROW!!!
AAAAH ?!
FWISH FWISH

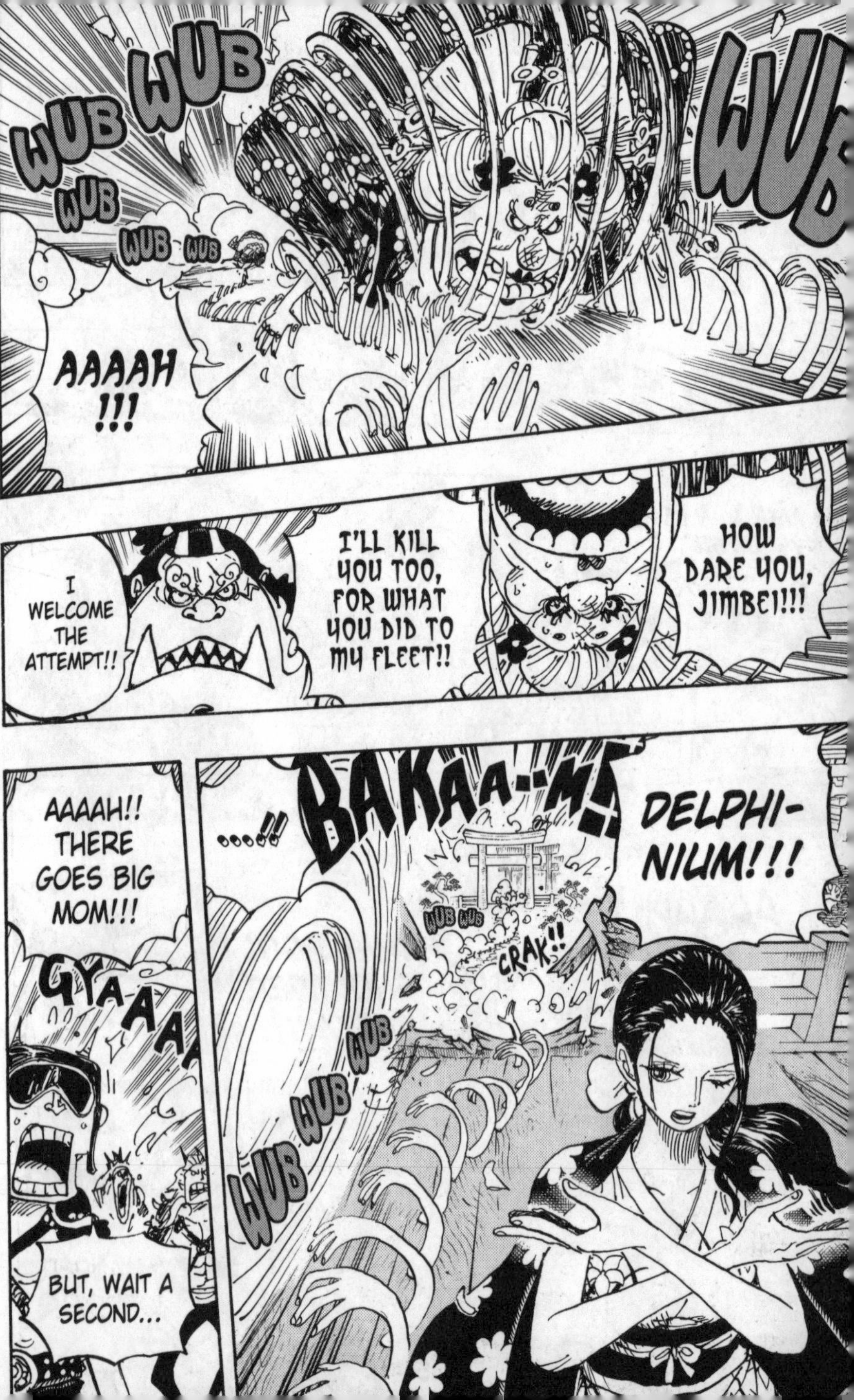
WUB
WUB WUB
WUB
WUB WUB
AAAAH!!!
HOW DARE YOU, JIMBEI!!!!
I'LL KILL YOU TOO, FOR WHAT YOU DID TO MY FLEET!!
I WELCOME THE ATTEMPT!!
BAKAA--M!!
DELPHI-NIUM!!!
...!!
WUB WUB
CRAK!!
WUB WUB WUB
AAAAH!! THERE GOES BIG MOM!!!
GYAAAA
BUT, WAIT A SECOND...

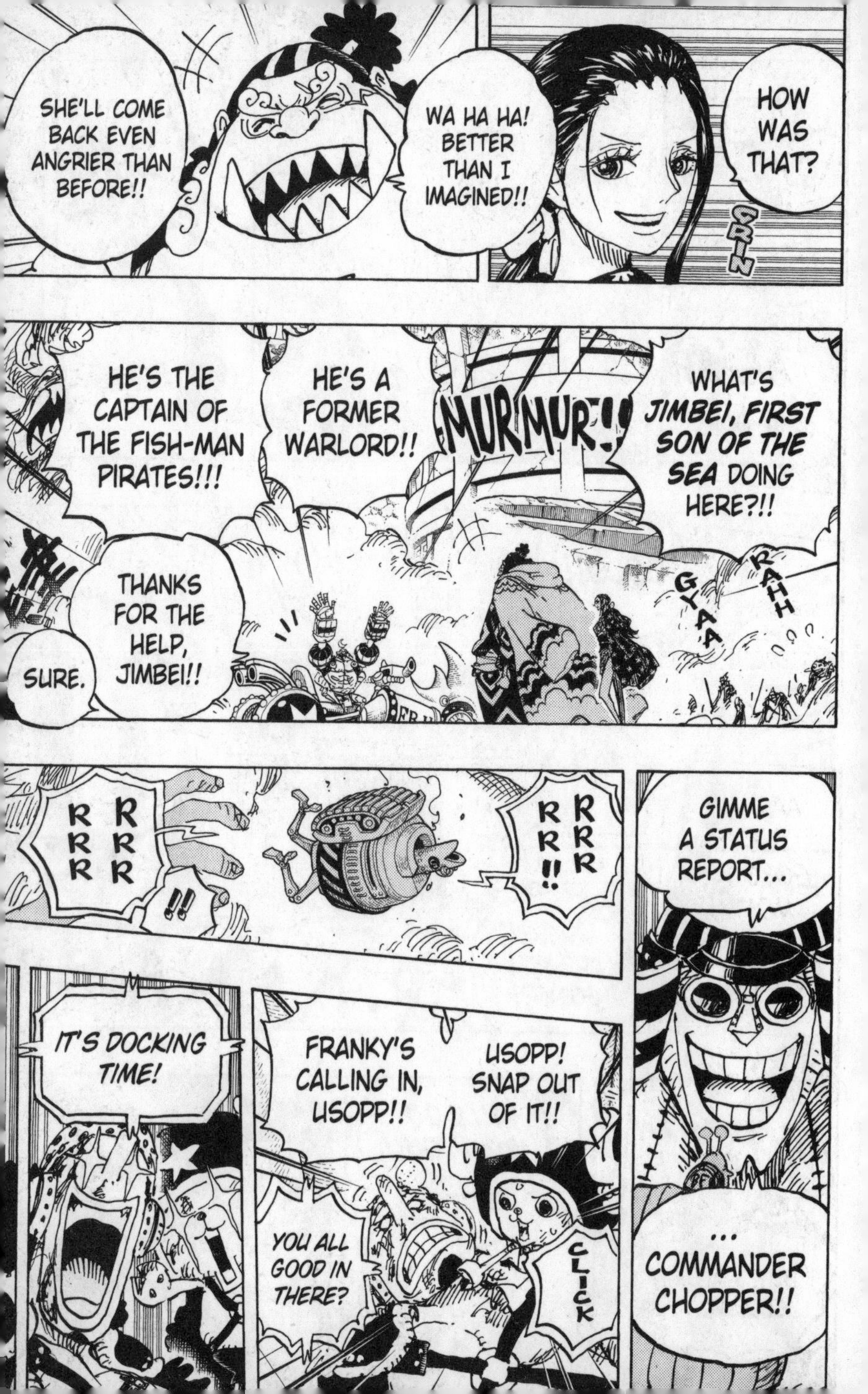
HOW WAS THAT?
GRIN
WA HA HA! BETTER THAN I IMAGINED!!
SHE'LL COME BACK EVEN ANGRIER THAN BEFORE!!
WHAT'S JIMBEI, FIRST SON OF THE SEA DOING HERE?!!
MURMUR!!
HE'S A FORMER WARLORD!!
HE'S THE CAPTAIN OF THE FISH-MAN PIRATES!!!
RAHH
GYAA
THANKS FOR THE HELP, JIMBEI!!
SURE.
GIMME A STATUS REPORT...
...COMMANDER CHOPPER!!
RRRR RR!!
RRRR RRR
!!
USOPP! SNAP OUT OF IT!!
FRANKY'S CALLING IN, USOPP!!
YOU ALL GOOD IN THERE?
CLICK
IT'S DOCKING TIME!

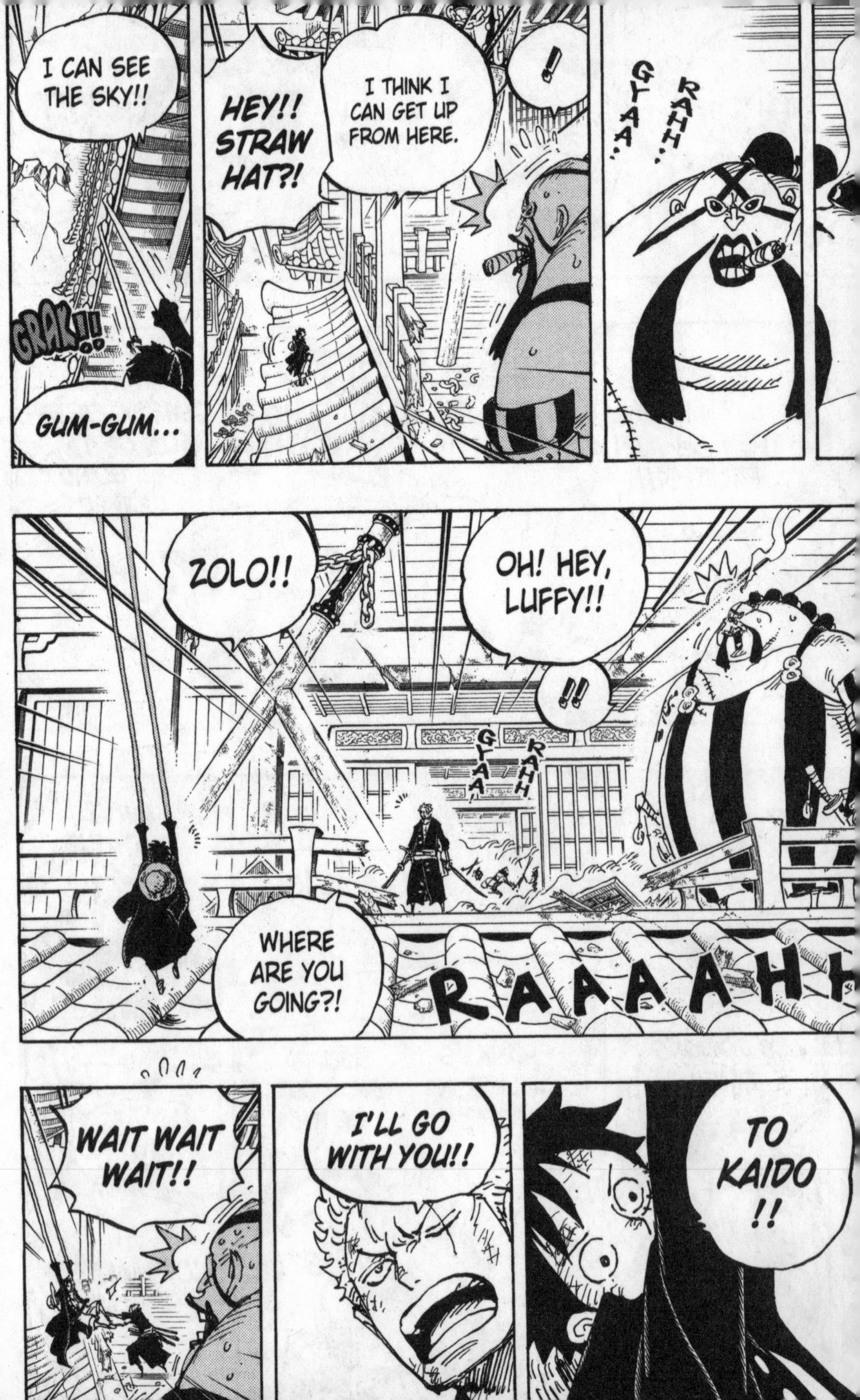
RAHH..
GYAA..
!
I THINK I CAN GET UP FROM HERE.
HEY!! STRAW HAT?!
I CAN SEE THE SKY!!
GRAK!!
GUM-GUM...
OH! HEY, LUFFY!!
ZOLO!!
!!
RAHH
GYAA
RAAAAH
WHERE ARE YOU GOING?!
TO KAIDO!!
I'LL GO WITH YOU!!
WAIT WAIT WAIT!!

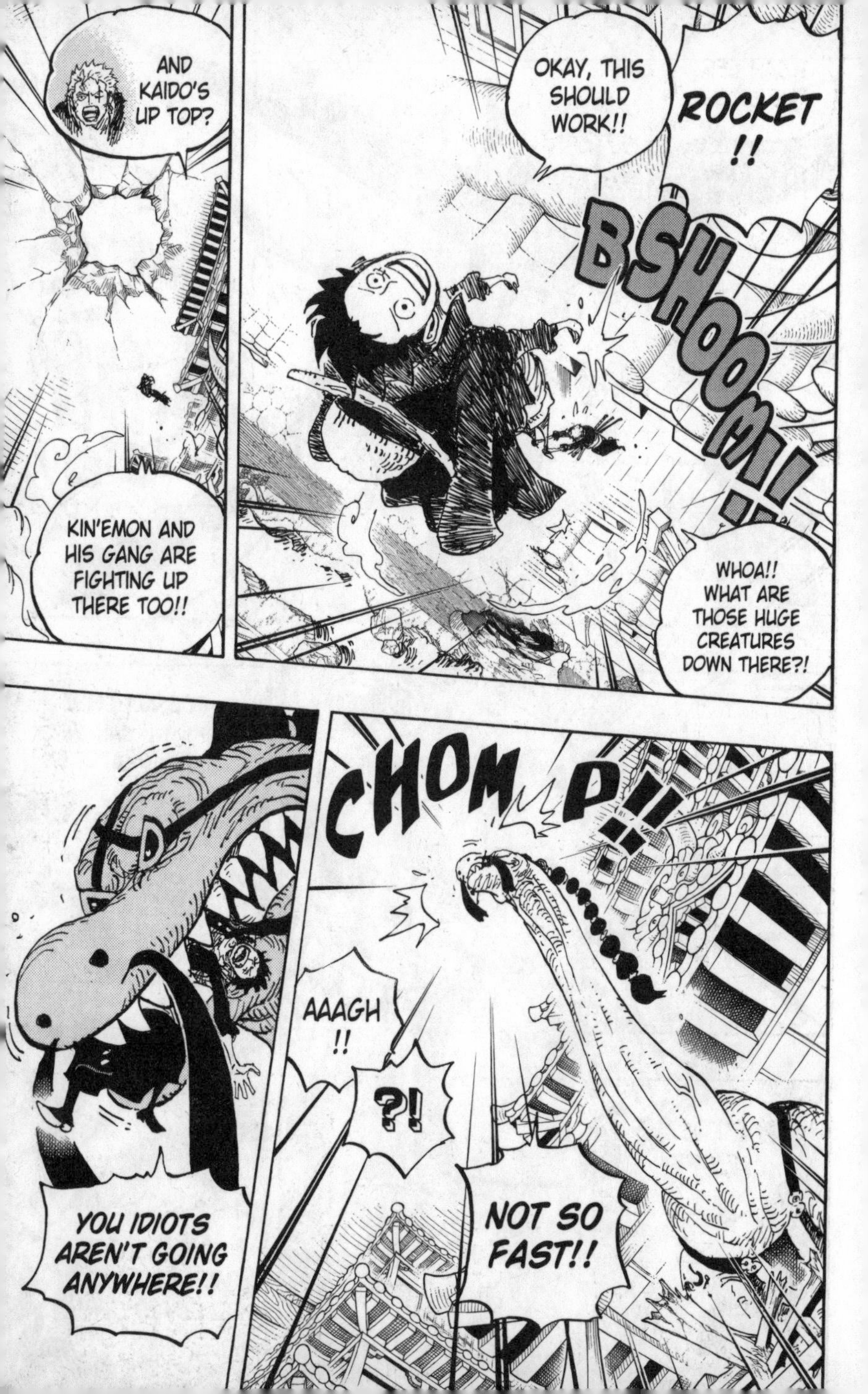
OKAY, THIS SHOULD WORK!!
ROCKET !!
BSHOOOM!!
WHOA!! WHAT ARE THOSE HUGE CREATURES DOWN THERE?!
AND KAIDO'S UP TOP?
KIN'EMON AND HIS GANG ARE FIGHTING UP THERE TOO!!
CHOMP!!
AAAGH !!
?!
NOT SO FAST!!
YOU IDIOTS AREN'T GOING ANYWHERE!!

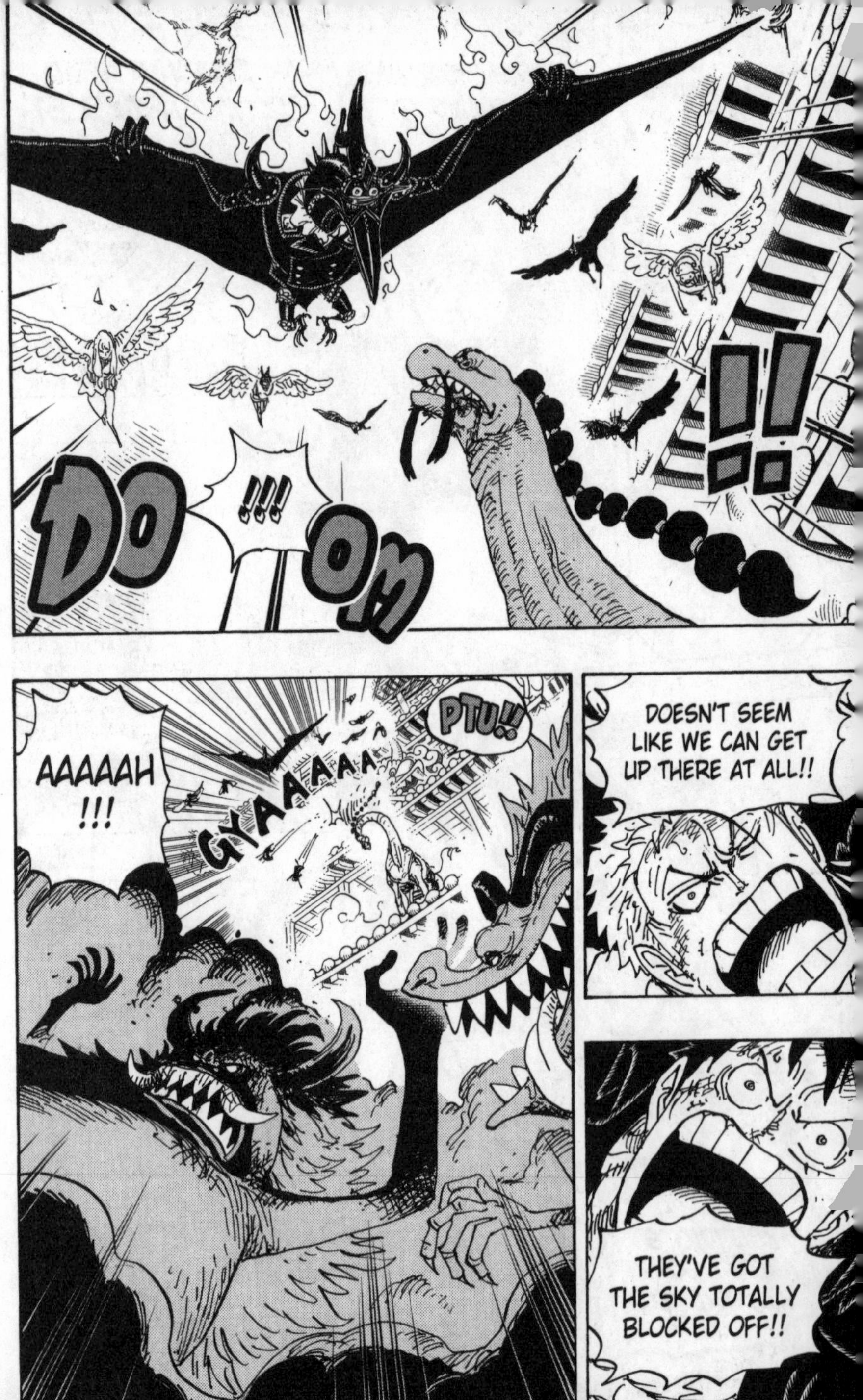
!!
DO !!! OM
DOESN'T SEEM LIKE WE CAN GET UP THERE AT ALL!!
THEY'VE GOT THE SKY TOTALLY BLOCKED OFF!!
PTU!!
GYAAAAAA
AAAAAH !!!

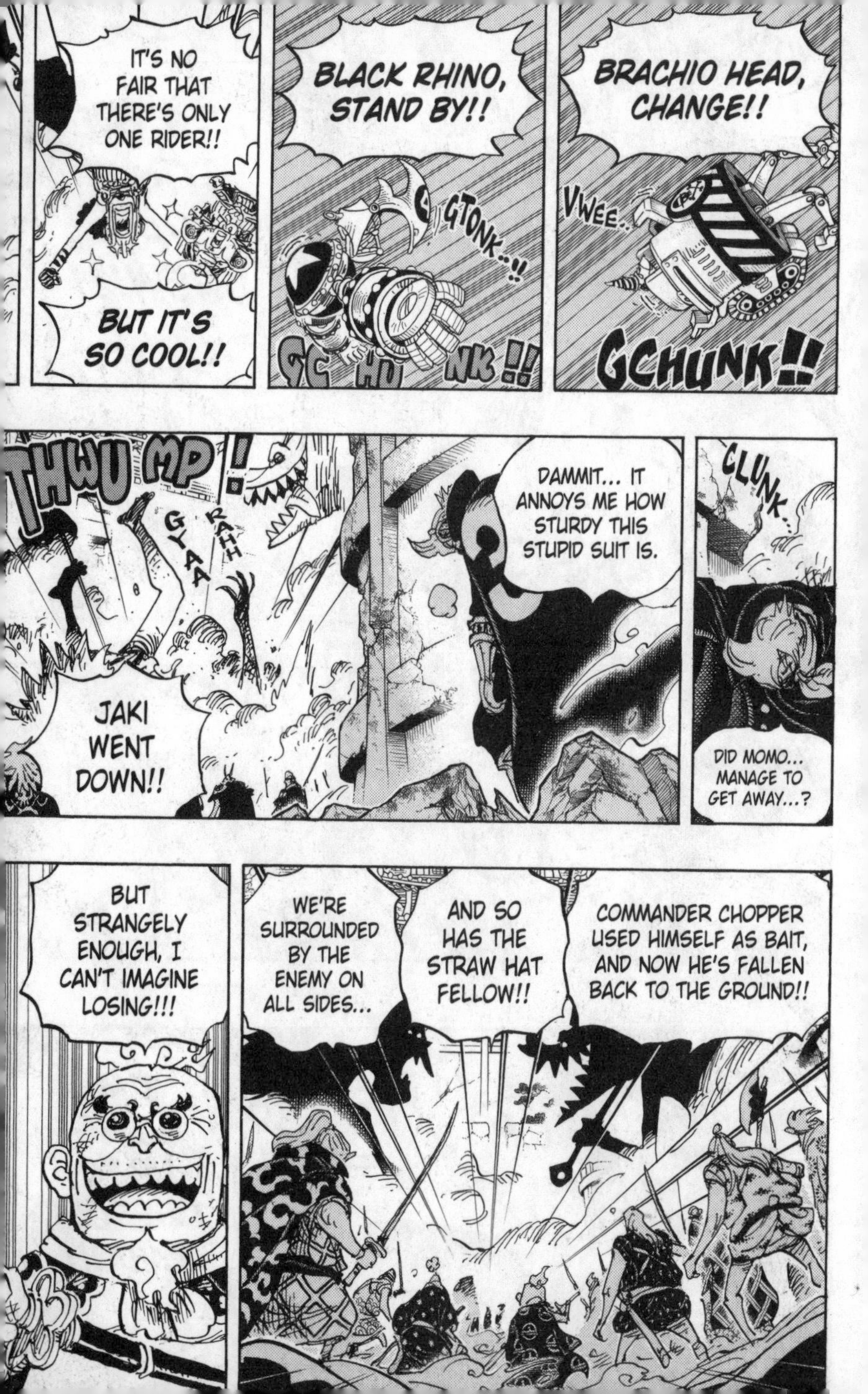
BRACHIO HEAD, CHANGE!!
VWEE..
GCHUNK!!
BLACK RHINO, STAND BY!!
GTONK..!!
GCHUNK!!
IT'S NO FAIR THAT THERE'S ONLY ONE RIDER!!
BUT IT'S SO COOL!!
CLUNK...
DID MOMO... MANAGE TO GET AWAY...?
DAMMIT... IT ANNOYS ME HOW STURDY THIS STUPID SUIT IS.
THWUMP!!
RAHH
GYAA
JAKI WENT DOWN!!
COMMANDER CHOPPER USED HIMSELF AS BAIT, AND NOW HE'S FALLEN BACK TO THE GROUND!!
AND SO HAS THE STRAW HAT FELLOW!!
WE'RE SURROUNDED BY THE ENEMY ON ALL SIDES...
BUT STRANGELY ENOUGH, I CAN'T IMAGINE LOSING!!!

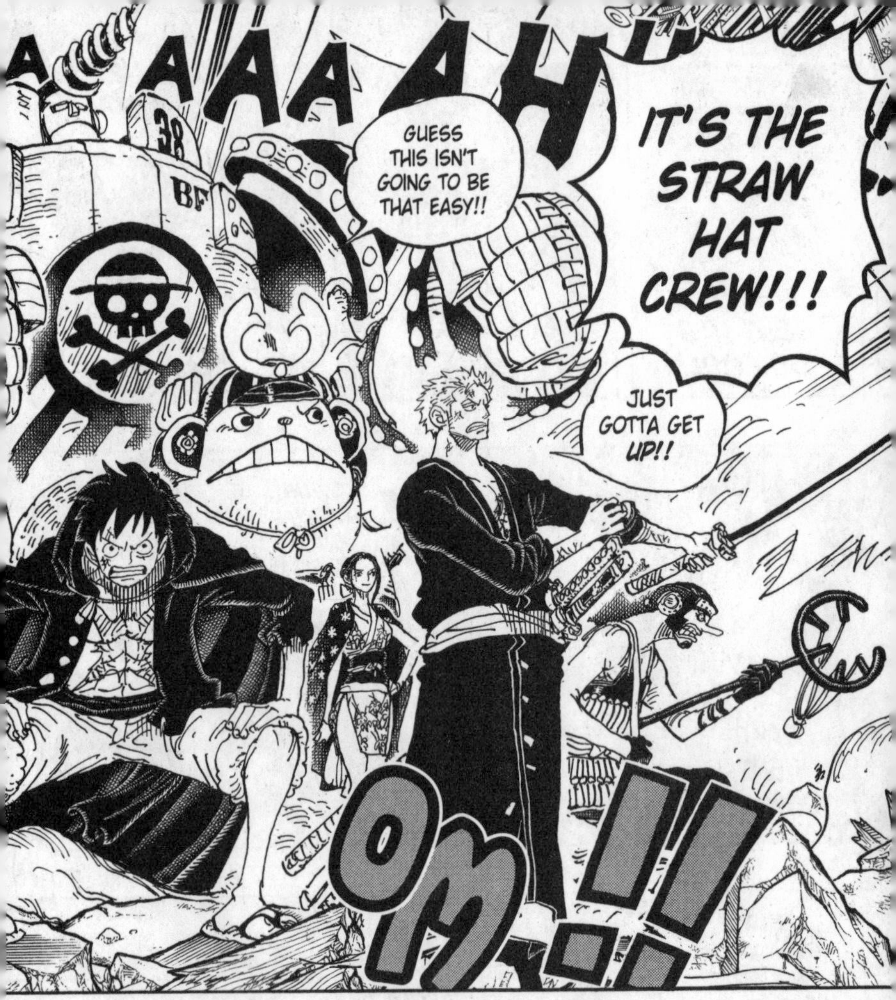
AAAAH!!
IT'S THE STRAW HAT CREW!!!
GUESS THIS ISN'T GOING TO BE THAT EASY!!
JUST GOTTA GET UP!!
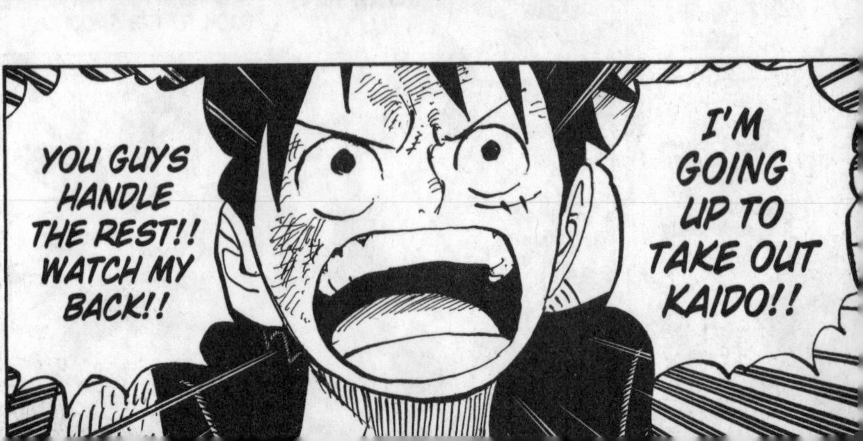
I'M GOING UP TO TAKE OUT KAIDO!!
YOU GUYS HANDLE THE REST!! WATCH MY BACK!!

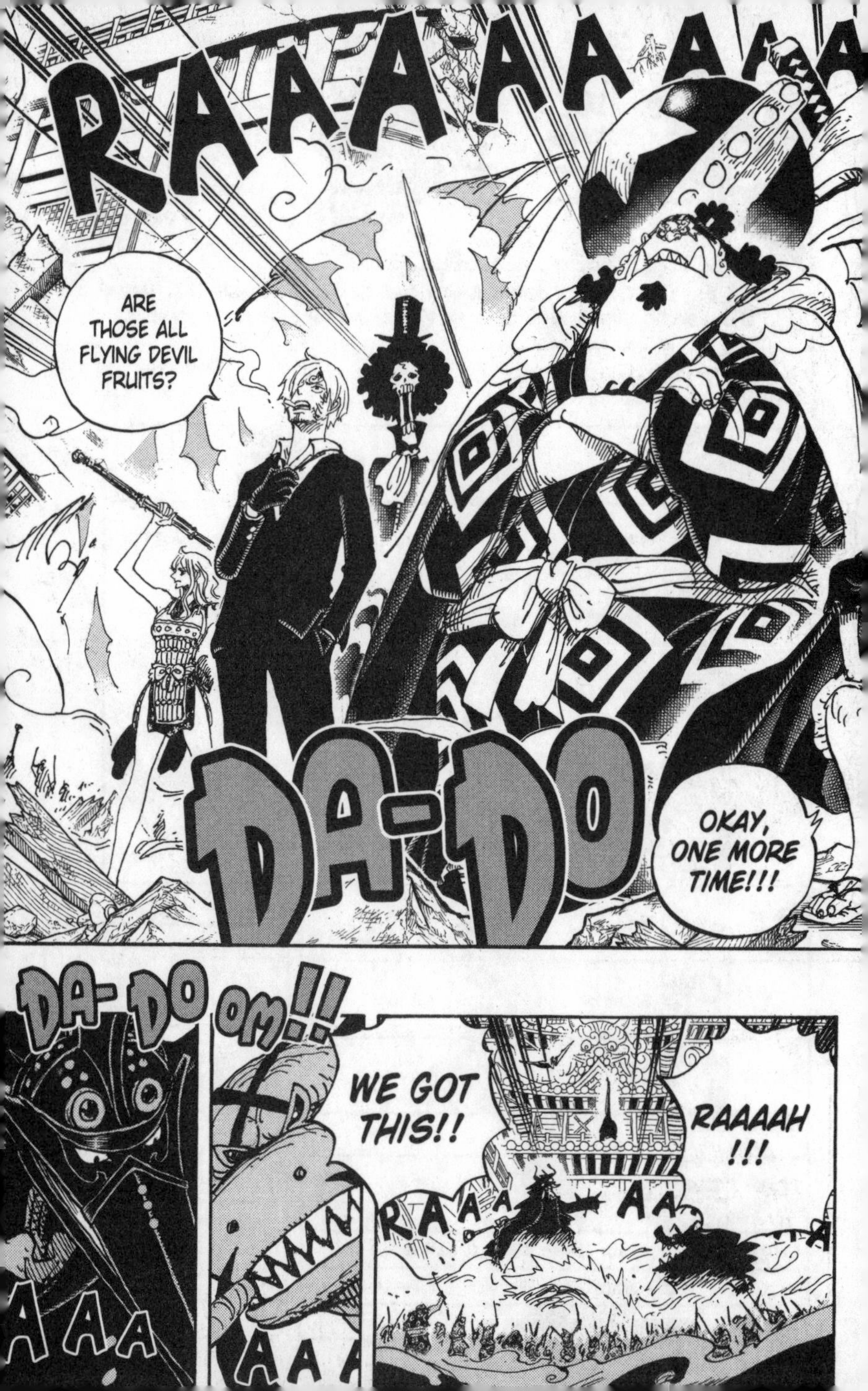
RAAAAAAAA
ARE THOSE ALL FLYING DEVIL FRUITS?
OKAY, ONE MORE TIME!!!
DA-DO
RAAAAH!!!
WE GOT THIS!!
RAAAAA
AAA
DA-DOOM!!
AAA

SBS Question Corner

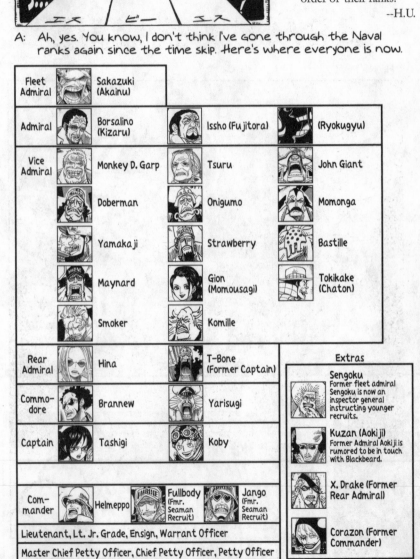

(Anonymous, Tokyo)

"Bone" S... Right all Wrong answers!

Q: I know the Navy has admirals, vice admirals, captains, and so on. I guess the fleet admiral is on the top? What's the order of their ranks?
--H.U.

A: Ah, yes. You know, I don't think I've gone through the Naval ranks again since the time skip. Here's where everyone is now.

Rank					
Fleet Admiral	Sakazuki (Akainu)				
Admiral	Borsalino (Kizaru)	Issho (Fujitora)	(Ryokugyu)		
Vice Admiral	Monkey D. Garp	Tsuru	John Giant		
	Doberman	Onigumo	Momonga		
	Yamakaji	Strawberry	Bastille		
	Maynard	Gion (Momousagi)	Tokikake (Chaton)		
	Smoker	Komille			
Rear Admiral	Hina	T-Bone (Former Captain)			
Commodore	Brannew	Yarisugi			
Captain	Tashigi	Koby			
Commander	Helmeppo	Fullbody (Fmr. Seaman Recruit)	Jango (Fmr. Seaman Recruit)		

Lieutenant, Lt. Jr. Grade, Ensign, Warrant Officer

Master Chief Petty Officer, Chief Petty Officer, Petty Officer

Seaman, Seaman Apprentice, Seaman Recruit, Chore Boy

Extras

Sengoku
Former fleet admiral Sengoku is now an inspector general instructing younger recruits.

Kuzan (Aokiji)
Former Admiral Aokiji is rumored to be in touch with Blackbeard.

X. Drake (Former Rear Admiral)

Corazon (Former Commander)

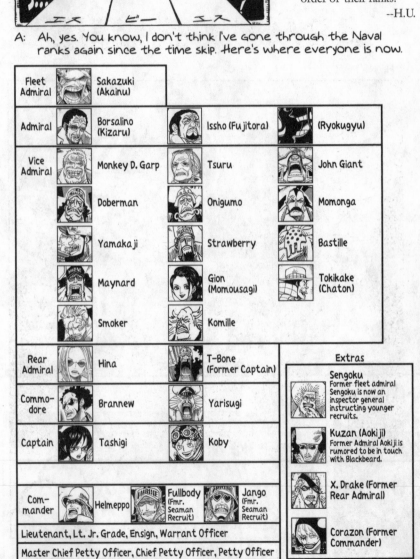

100

Chapter 990:
ARMY OF ONE

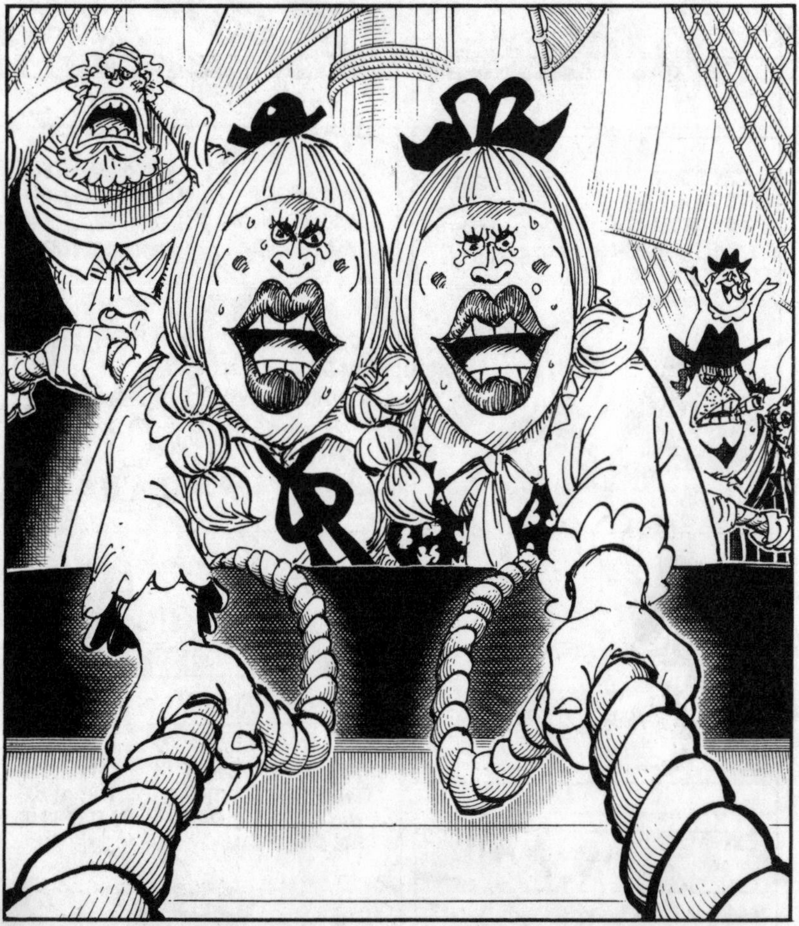

GANG BEGE'S OH MY FAMILY, VOL. 34: "HANG ON TIGHT!! MAMA TOLD US OUR FATHER IS A CLINGY MAN WHO NEVER GIVES UP, NO MATTER HOW MANY TIMES HE'S KICKED!!"

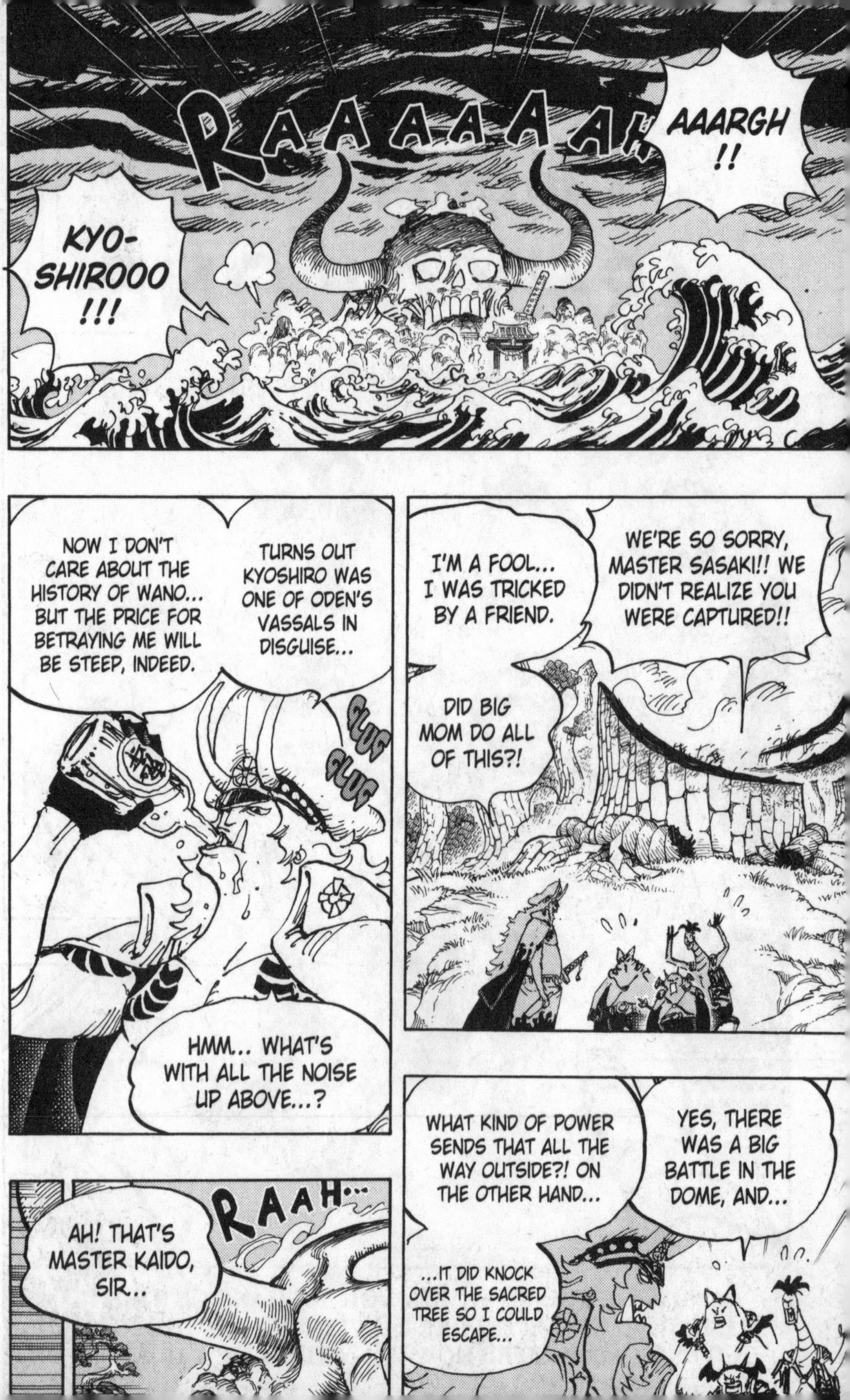
AAARGH!!
RAAAAAAH
KYO-SHIROOO!!!
WE'RE SO SORRY, MASTER SASAKI!! WE DIDN'T REALIZE YOU WERE CAPTURED!!
I'M A FOOL... I WAS TRICKED BY A FRIEND.
DID BIG MOM DO ALL OF THIS?!
TURNS OUT KYOSHIRO WAS ONE OF ODEN'S VASSALS IN DISGUISE...
NOW I DON'T CARE ABOUT THE HISTORY OF WANO... BUT THE PRICE FOR BETRAYING ME WILL BE STEEP, INDEED.
GLUG GLUG
HMM... WHAT'S WITH ALL THE NOISE UP ABOVE...?
YES, THERE WAS A BIG BATTLE IN THE DOME, AND...
WHAT KIND OF POWER SENDS THAT ALL THE WAY OUTSIDE?! ON THE OTHER HAND...
...IT DID KNOCK OVER THE SACRED TREE SO I COULD ESCAPE...
RAAH...
AH! THAT'S MASTER KAIDO, SIR...

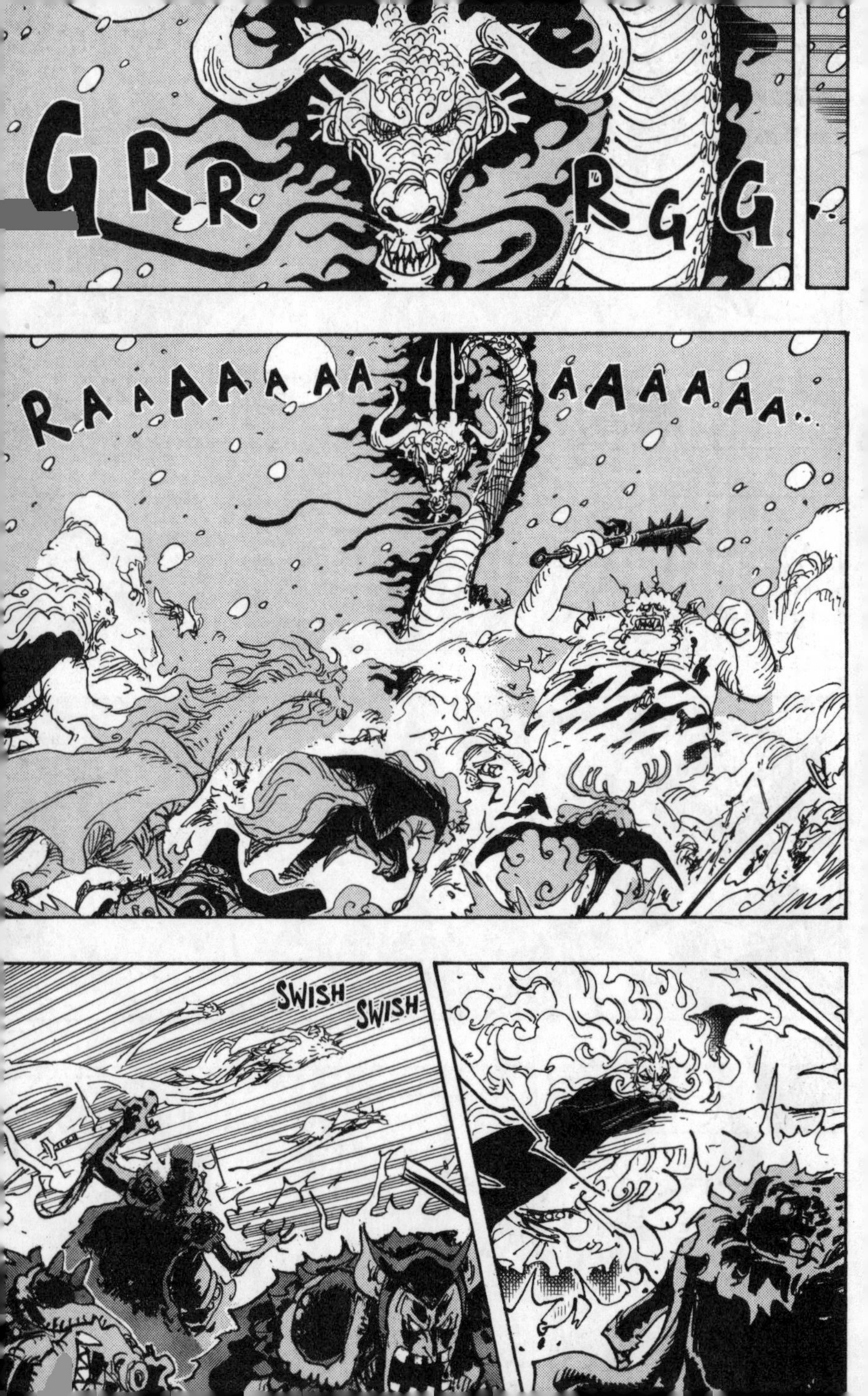
GRRRGG
RAAAAAAAAAAAAAA...
SWISH SWISH

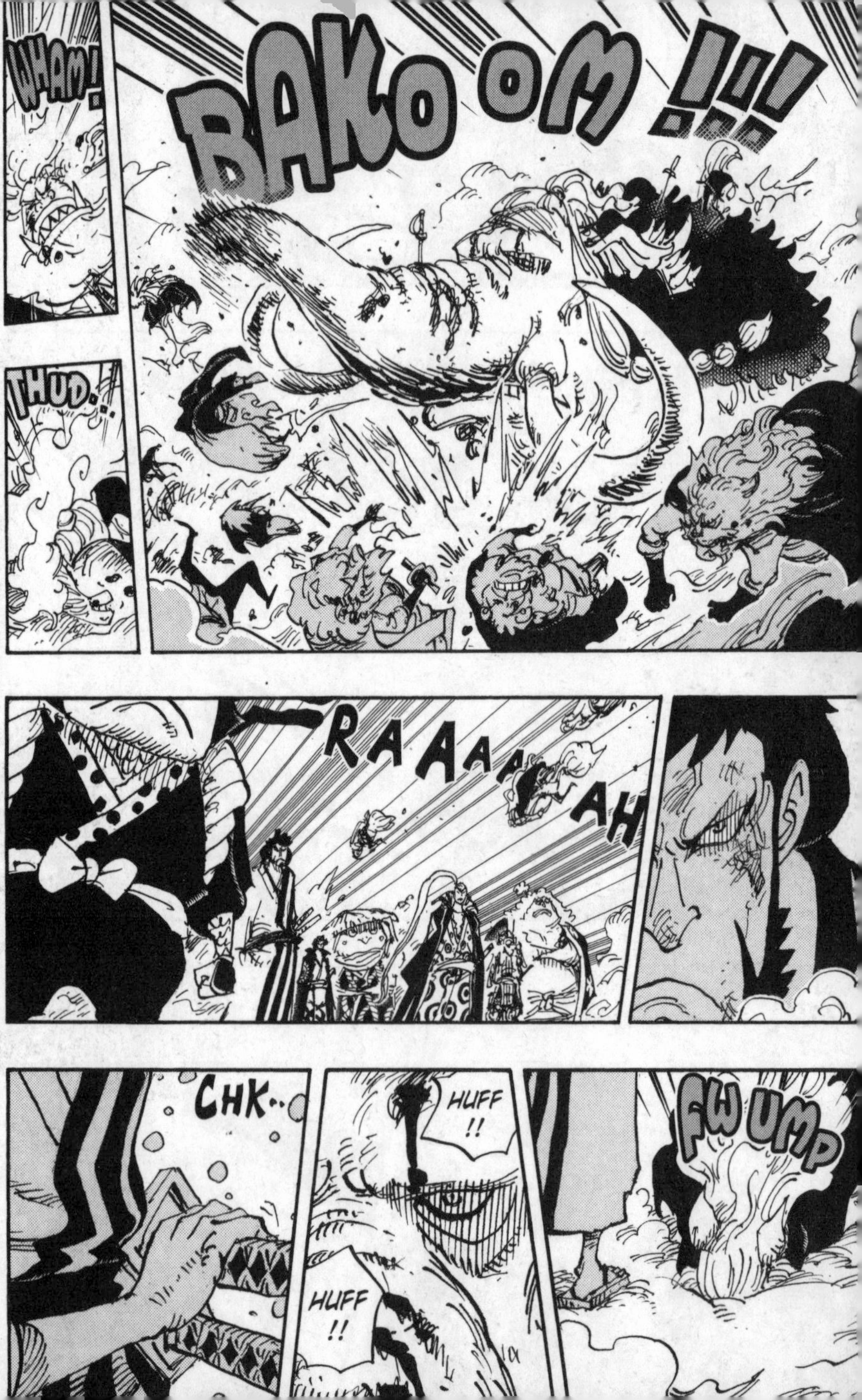
BAKOOM!!!
WHAM!!
THUD...
RAAAAAAH
FWUMP
HUFF!!
HUFF!!
CHK...

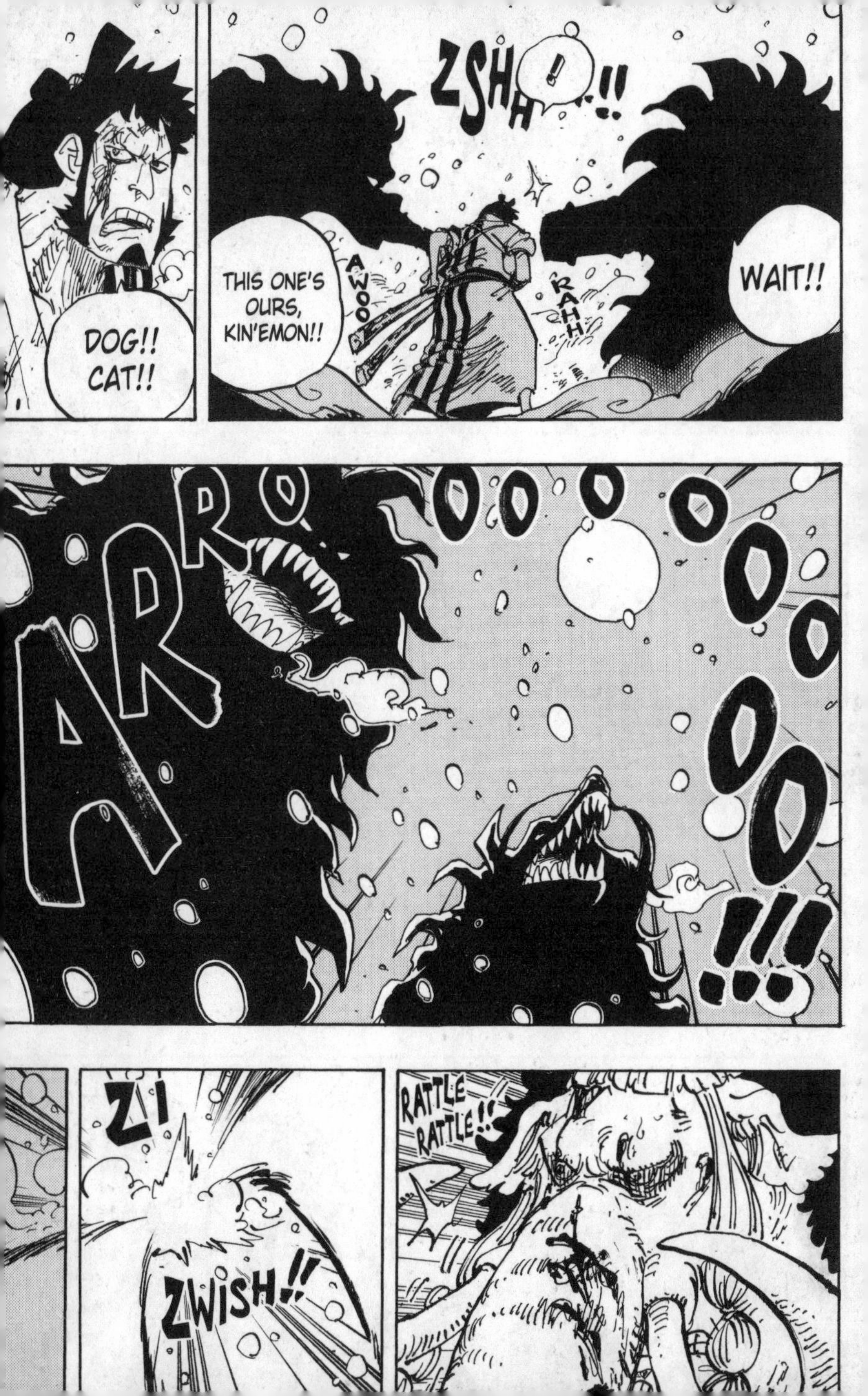
ZSHH!!
!
WAIT!!
RAHH
AWOO
THIS ONE'S OURS, KIN'EMON!!
DOG!! CAT!!
ARROOOOOOOOOOO!!!
RATTLE RATTLE!!
ZI
ZWISH!!

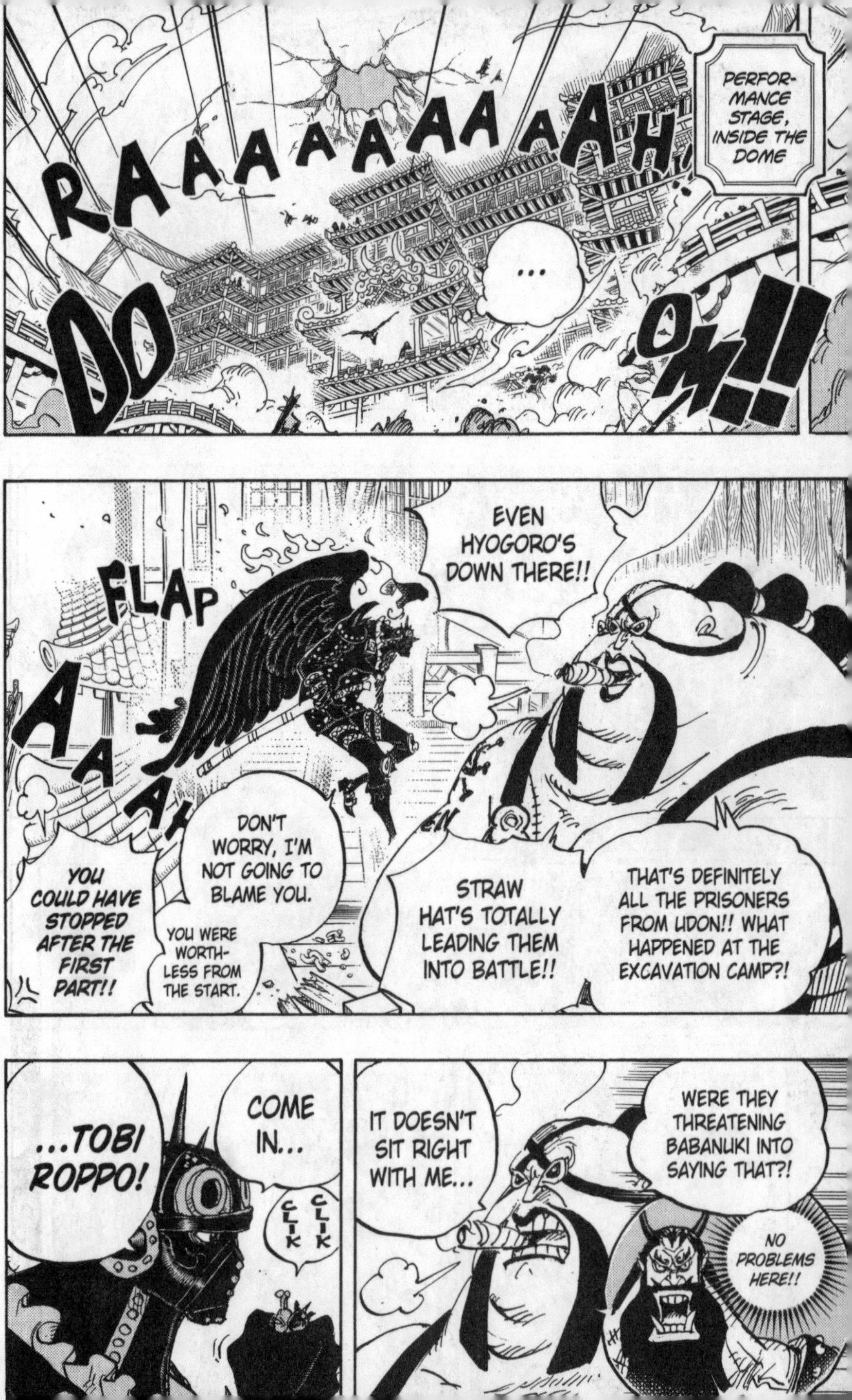
PERFORMANCE STAGE, INSIDE THE DOME
RAAAAAAAAAH
...
DOOM!!
EVEN HYOGORO'S DOWN THERE!!
THAT'S DEFINITELY ALL THE PRISONERS FROM UDON!! WHAT HAPPENED AT THE EXCAVATION CAMP?!
STRAW HAT'S TOTALLY LEADING THEM INTO BATTLE!!
FLAP
DON'T WORRY, I'M NOT GOING TO BLAME YOU.
YOU WERE WORTHLESS FROM THE START.
AAAH
YOU COULD HAVE STOPPED AFTER THE FIRST PART!!
WERE THEY THREATENING BABANUKI INTO SAYING THAT?!
IT DOESN'T SIT RIGHT WITH ME...
NO PROBLEMS HERE!!
COME IN...
CLIK CLIK
...TOBI ROPPO!

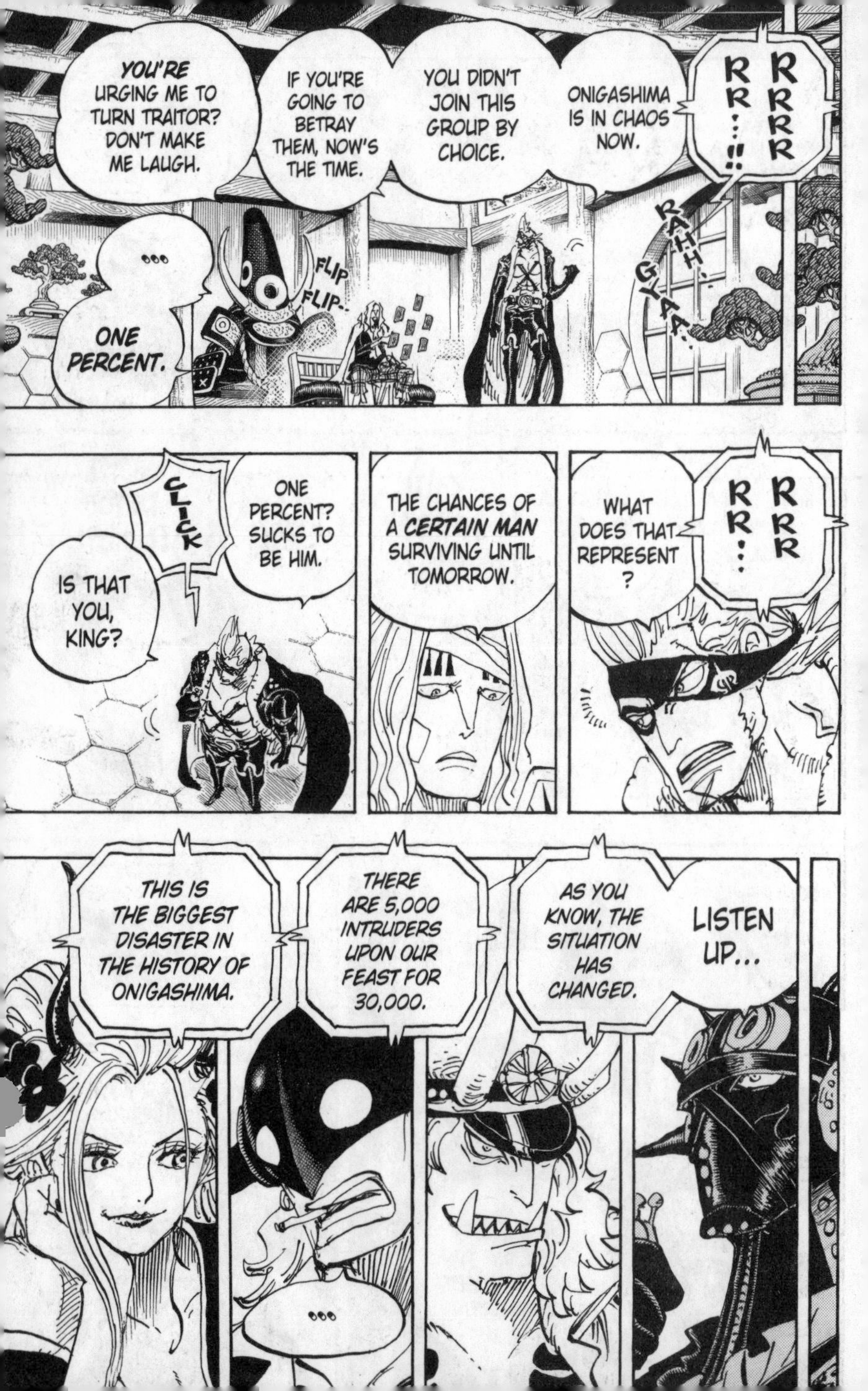
RRRR RR...!!
ONIGASHIMA IS IN CHAOS NOW.
YOU DIDN'T JOIN THIS GROUP BY CHOICE.
IF YOU'RE GOING TO BETRAY THEM, NOW'S THE TIME.
YOU'RE URGING ME TO TURN TRAITOR? DON'T MAKE ME LAUGH.
RAHH GYAA..
FLIP FLIP..
...
ONE PERCENT.
RRR RR...
WHAT DOES THAT REPRESENT?
THE CHANCES OF A CERTAIN MAN SURVIVING UNTIL TOMORROW.
ONE PERCENT? SUCKS TO BE HIM.
CLICK
IS THAT YOU, KING?
LISTEN UP...
AS YOU KNOW, THE SITUATION HAS CHANGED.
THERE ARE 5,000 INTRUDERS UPON OUR FEAST FOR 30,000.
THIS IS THE BIGGEST DISASTER IN THE HISTORY OF ONIGASHIMA.
...

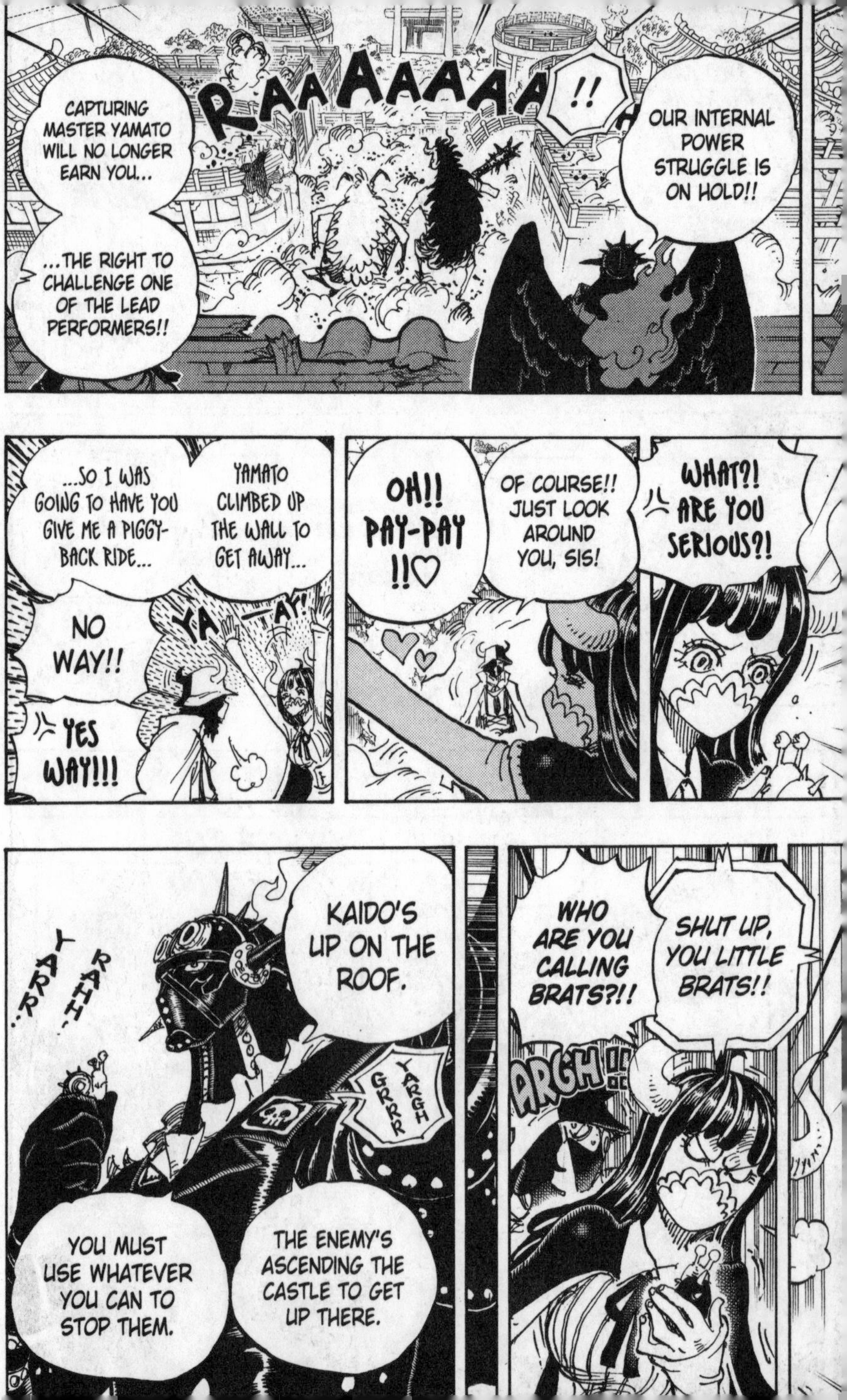
OUR INTERNAL POWER STRUGGLE IS ON HOLD!!
RAAAAAAH!!
CAPTURING MASTER YAMATO WILL NO LONGER EARN YOU...
...THE RIGHT TO CHALLENGE ONE OF THE LEAD PERFORMERS!!
WHAT?! ARE YOU SERIOUS?!
OF COURSE!! JUST LOOK AROUND YOU, SIS!
OH!! PAY-PAY!!♡
YAMATO CLIMBED UP THE WALL TO GET AWAY...
...SO I WAS GOING TO HAVE YOU GIVE ME A PIGGY-BACK RIDE...
YA—AY!
NO WAY!!
YES WAY!!!
SHUT UP, YOU LITTLE BRATS!!
WHO ARE YOU CALLING BRATS?!!
ARGH!!
KAIDO'S UP ON THE ROOF.
YARGH GRRR
YARRR... RAHH...
THE ENEMY'S ASCENDING THE CASTLE TO GET UP THERE.
YOU MUST USE WHATEVER YOU CAN TO STOP THEM.

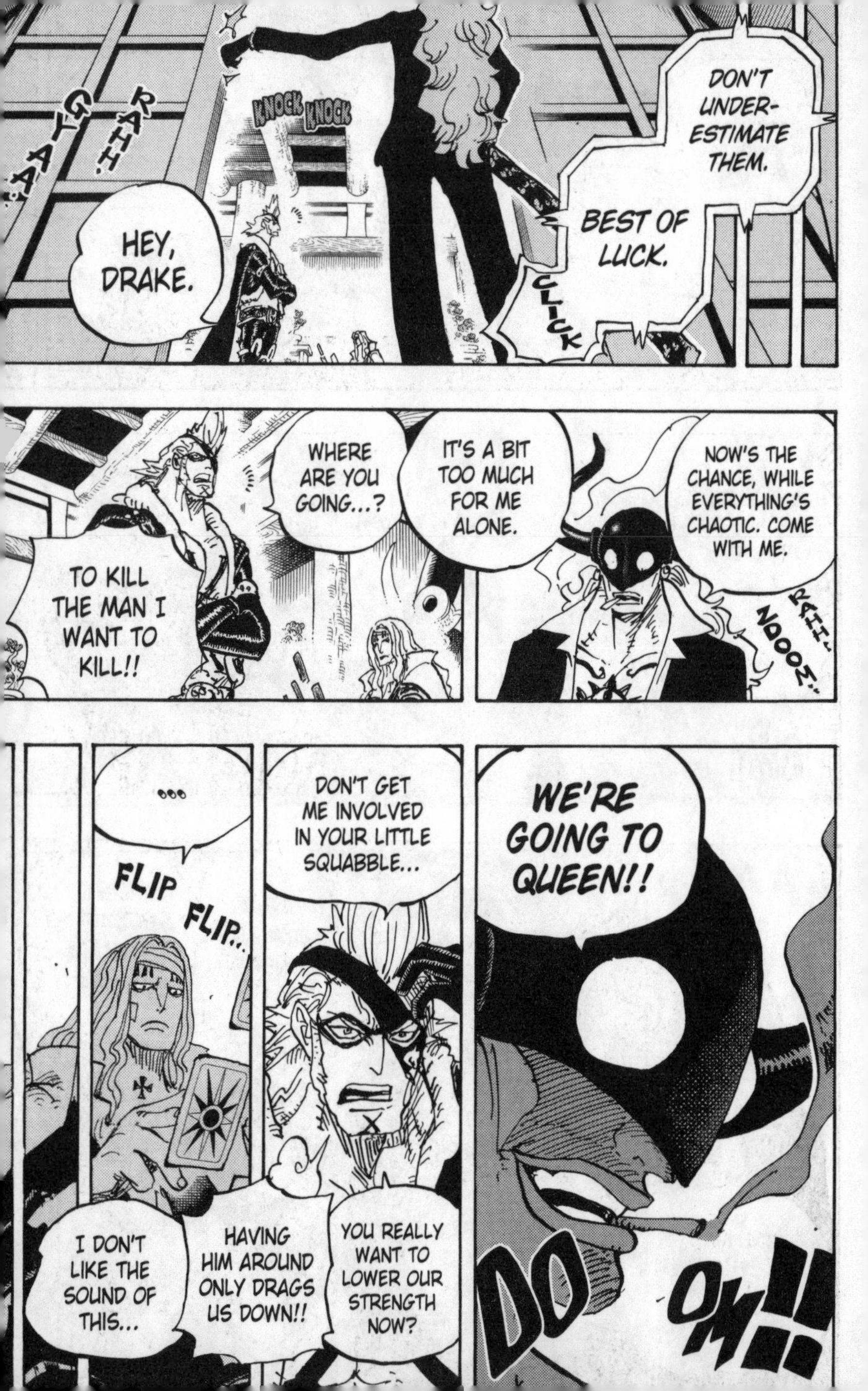
DON'T UNDER-ESTIMATE THEM.
BEST OF LUCK.
CLICK
KNOCK KNOCK
RAHH!
GYAAA
HEY, DRAKE.
NOW'S THE CHANCE, WHILE EVERYTHING'S CHAOTIC. COME WITH ME.
RAHH!
ZDOOOM!!
IT'S A BIT TOO MUCH FOR ME ALONE.
WHERE ARE YOU GOING...?
TO KILL THE MAN I WANT TO KILL!!
WE'RE GOING TO QUEEN!!
DOOM!!
DON'T GET ME INVOLVED IN YOUR LITTLE SQUABBLE...
YOU REALLY WANT TO LOWER OUR STRENGTH NOW?
HAVING HIM AROUND ONLY DRAGS US DOWN!!
...
FLIP
FLIP...
I DON'T LIKE THE SOUND OF THIS...

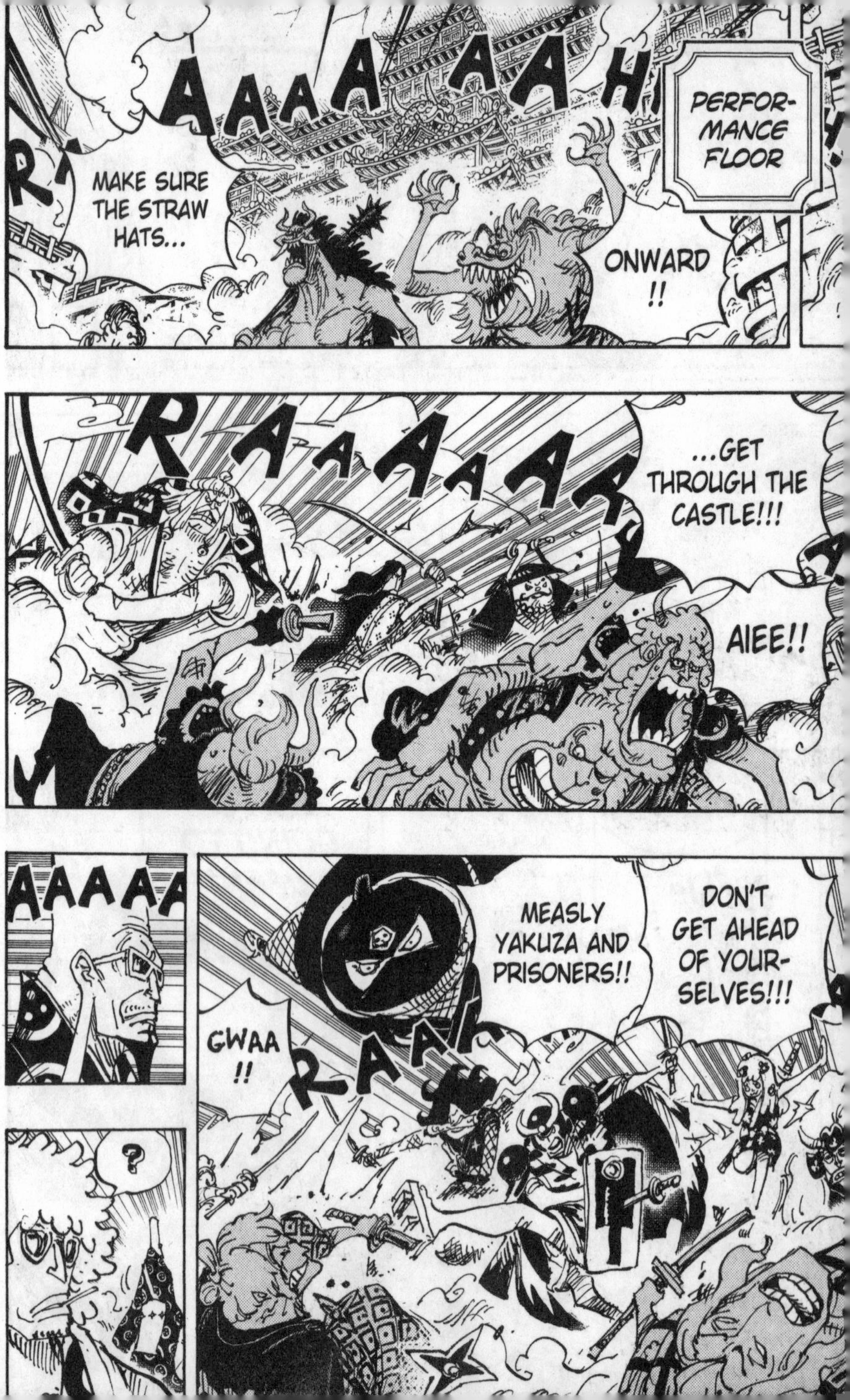
PERFORMANCE FLOOR
ONWARD!!
AAAAAH
MAKE SURE THE STRAW HATS...
...GET THROUGH THE CASTLE!!!
RAAAAAAR
AIEE!!
DON'T GET AHEAD OF YOURSELVES!!!
MEASLY YAKUZA AND PRISONERS!!
GWAA!!
RAA
AAAAA
?

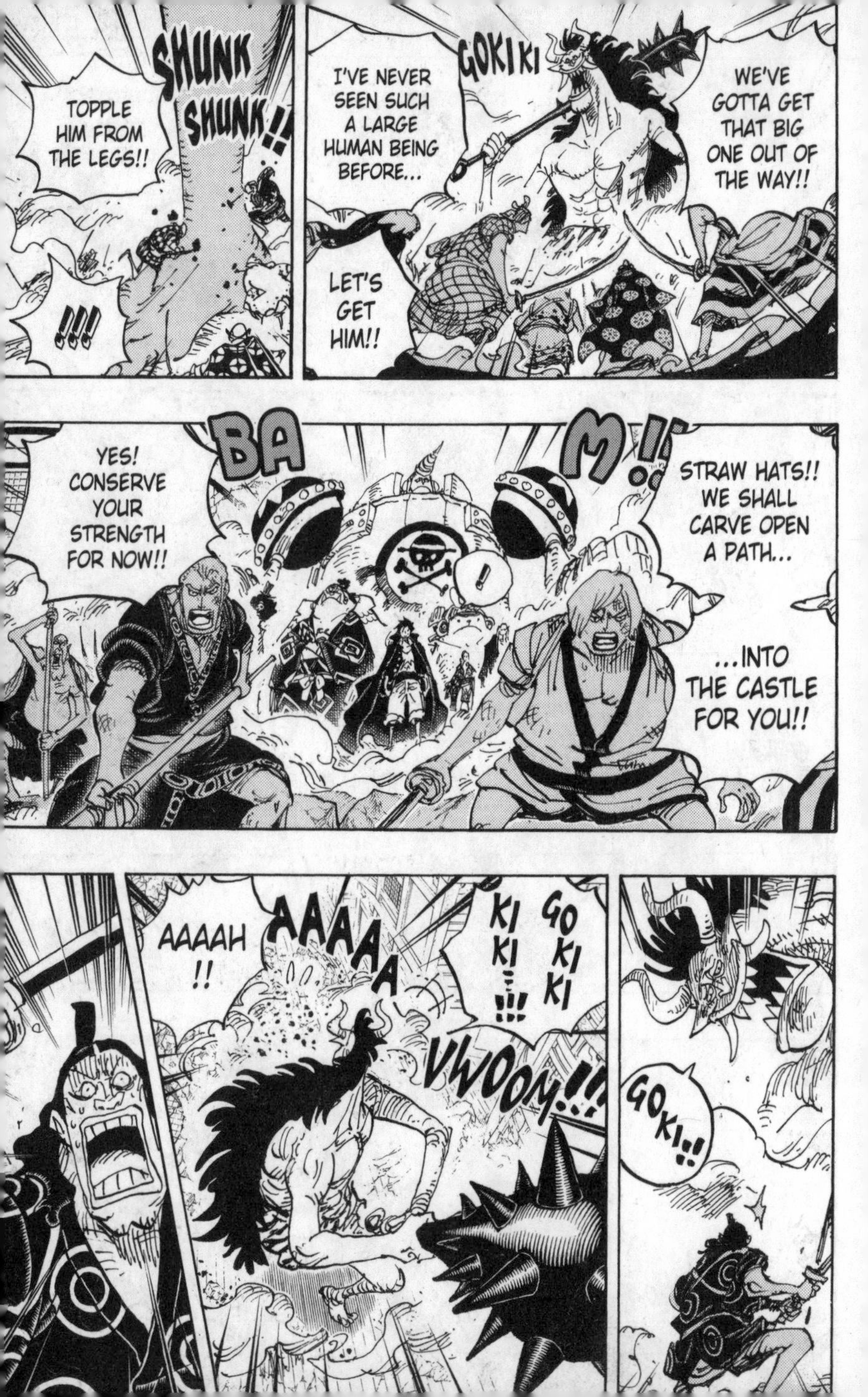
WE'VE GOTTA GET THAT BIG ONE OUT OF THE WAY!!
GOKIKI
I'VE NEVER SEEN SUCH A LARGE HUMAN BEING BEFORE...
LET'S GET HIM!!
SHUNK
SHUNK!!
TOPPLE HIM FROM THE LEGS!!
!!!
BAM!!
STRAW HATS!! WE SHALL CARVE OPEN A PATH...
...INTO THE CASTLE FOR YOU!!
!
YES! CONSERVE YOUR STRENGTH FOR NOW!!
GOKI!!
GOKIKI
KIKI...!!!
VWOOM!!!
AAAAA
AAAAH!!

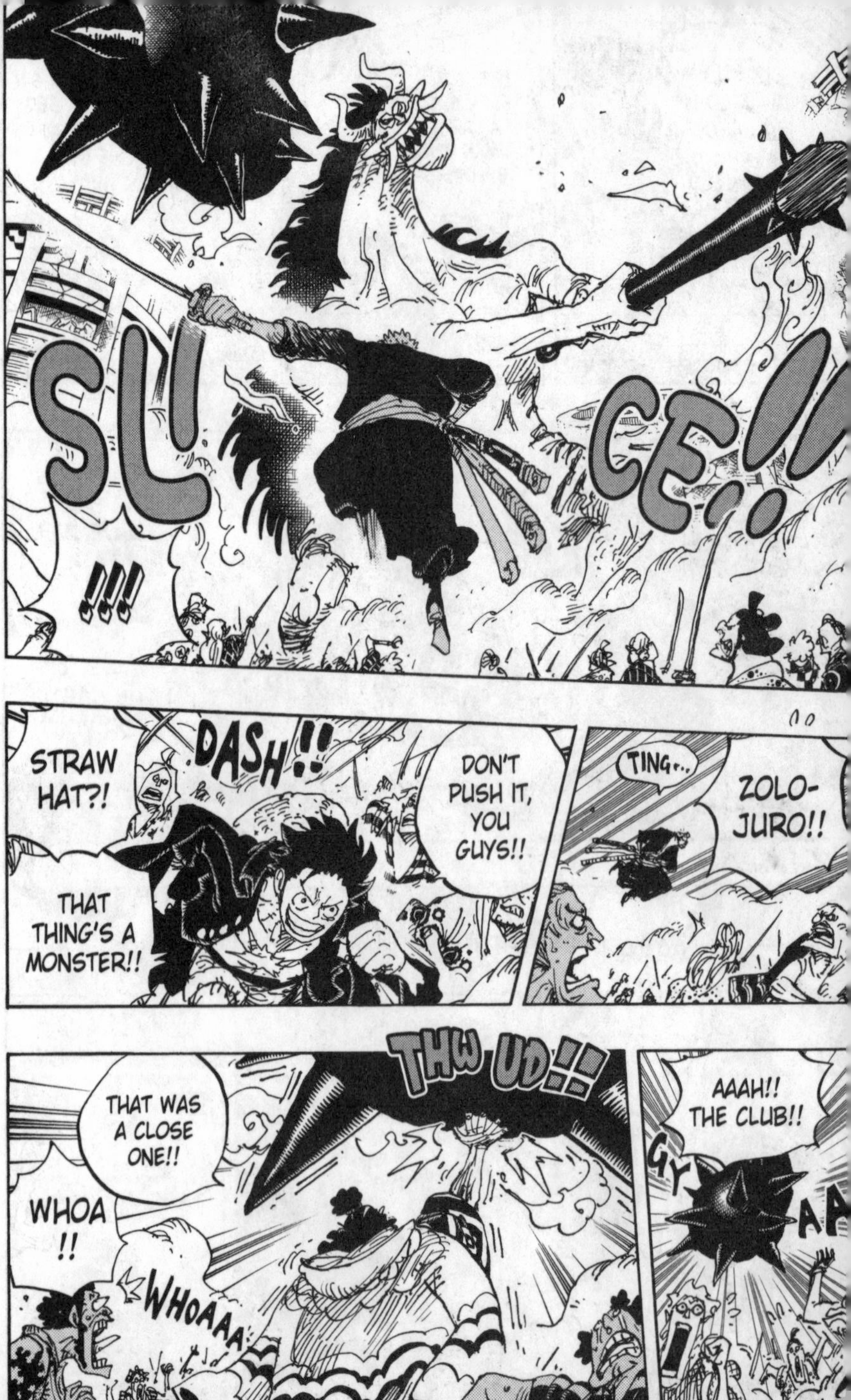
SLICE!!
!!!
TING..
ZOLO-JURO!!
DON'T PUSH IT, YOU GUYS!!
DASH!!
STRAW HAT?!
THAT THING'S A MONSTER!!
AAAH!! THE CLUB!!
GYAA
THWUD!!
THAT WAS A CLOSE ONE!!
WHOA!!
WHOAAA

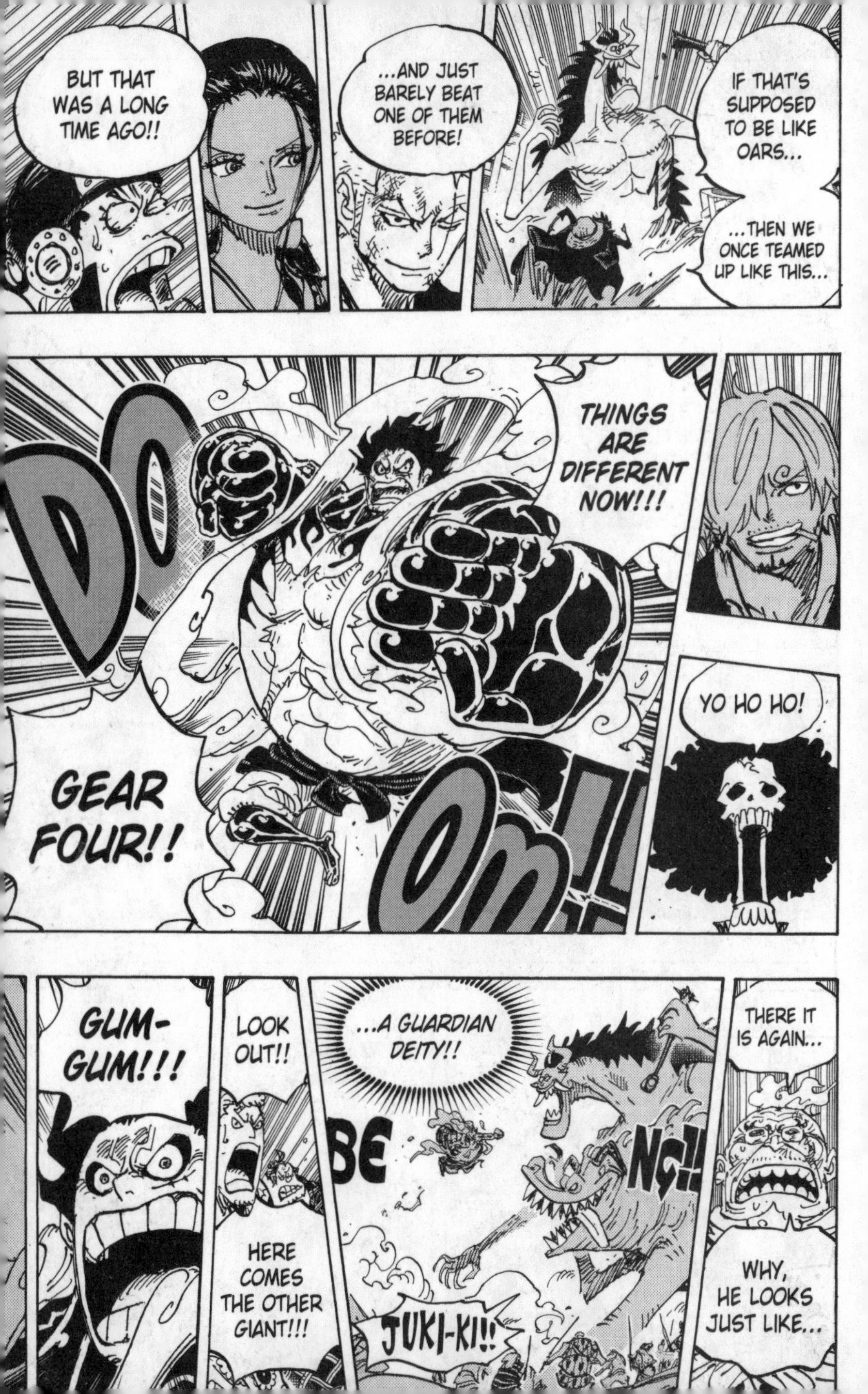
IF THAT'S SUPPOSED TO BE LIKE OARS...
...THEN WE ONCE TEAMED UP LIKE THIS...
...AND JUST BARELY BEAT ONE OF THEM BEFORE!
BUT THAT WAS A LONG TIME AGO!!
YO HO HO!
THINGS ARE DIFFERENT NOW!!!
DOOM!!
GEAR FOUR!!
THERE IT IS AGAIN...
WHY, HE LOOKS JUST LIKE...
...A GUARDIAN DEITY!!
BENG!!
JUKI-KI!!
LOOK OUT!!
HERE COMES THE OTHER GIANT!!!
GUM-GUM!!!

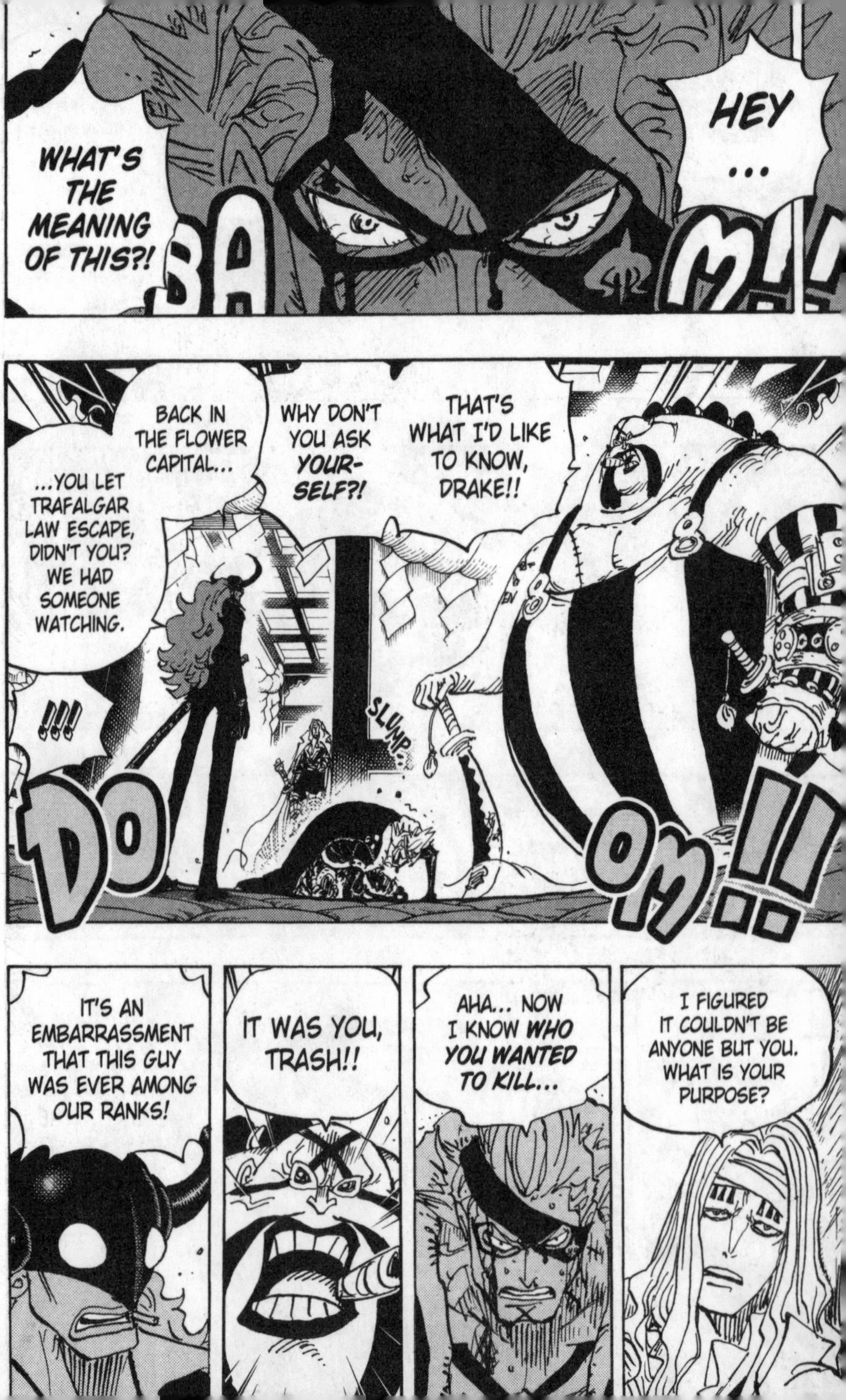
HEY ...
WHAT'S THE MEANING OF THIS?!
BAM!!
THAT'S WHAT I'D LIKE TO KNOW, DRAKE!!
WHY DON'T YOU ASK YOURSELF?!
BACK IN THE FLOWER CAPITAL...
...YOU LET TRAFALGAR LAW ESCAPE, DIDN'T YOU? WE HAD SOMEONE WATCHING.
!!!
SLUMP
DOOM!!
I FIGURED IT COULDN'T BE ANYONE BUT YOU. WHAT IS YOUR PURPOSE?
AHA... NOW I KNOW WHO YOU WANTED TO KILL...
IT WAS YOU, TRASH!!
IT'S AN EMBARRASSMENT THAT THIS GUY WAS EVER AMONG OUR RANKS!

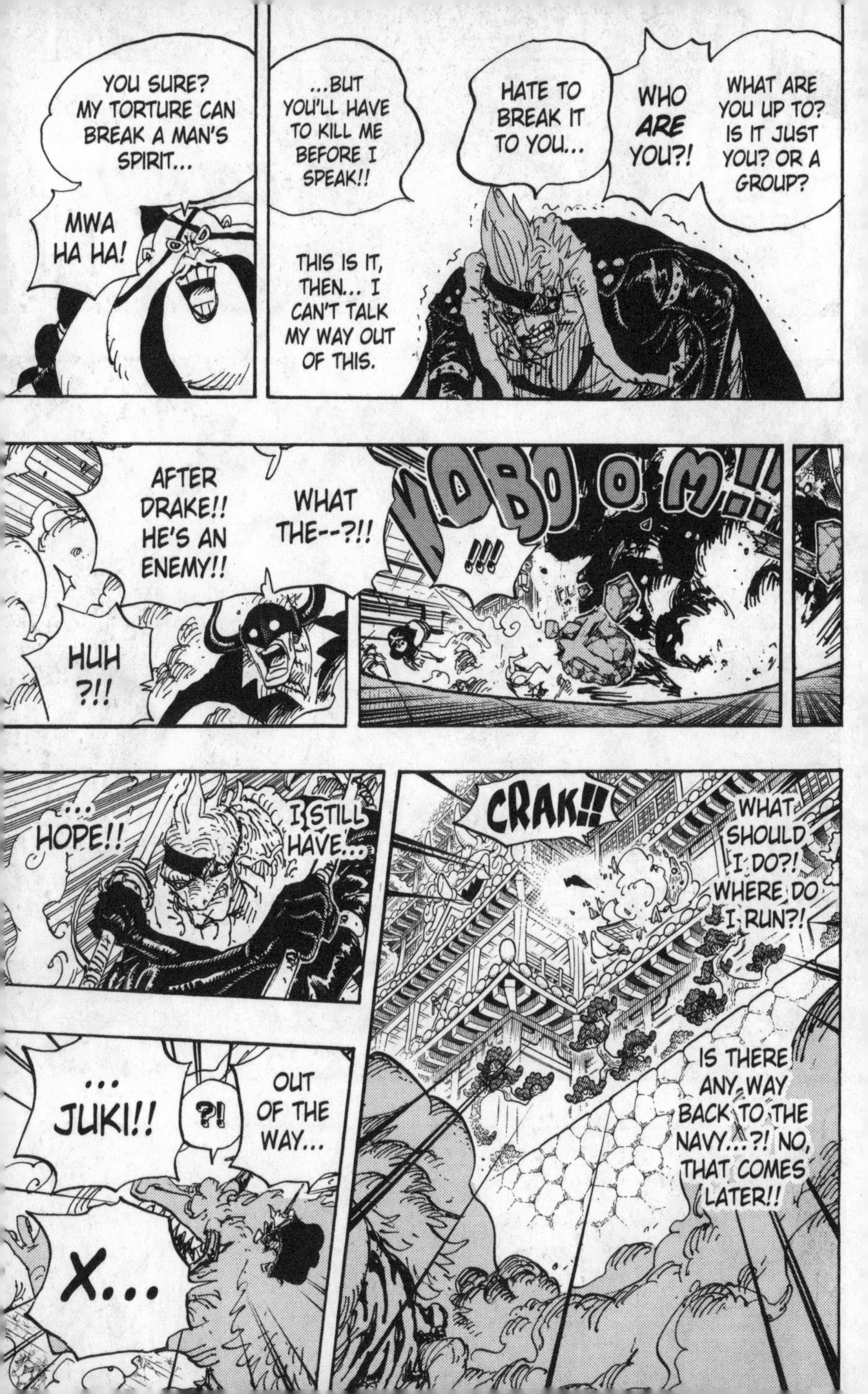
WHAT ARE YOU UP TO? IS IT JUST YOU? OR A GROUP?
WHO ARE YOU?!
HATE TO BREAK IT TO YOU...
...BUT YOU'LL HAVE TO KILL ME BEFORE I SPEAK!!
THIS IS IT, THEN... I CAN'T TALK MY WAY OUT OF THIS.
YOU SURE? MY TORTURE CAN BREAK A MAN'S SPIRIT...
MWA HA HA!
VOBOOM!!
!!!
WHAT THE--?!!
AFTER DRAKE!! HE'S AN ENEMY!!
HUH ?!!
CRAK!!
WHAT SHOULD I DO?! WHERE DO I RUN?!
IS THERE ANY WAY BACK TO THE NAVY...?! NO, THAT COMES LATER!!
I STILL HAVE...
...HOPE!!
OUT OF THE WAY...
?!
...JUKI!!
X...

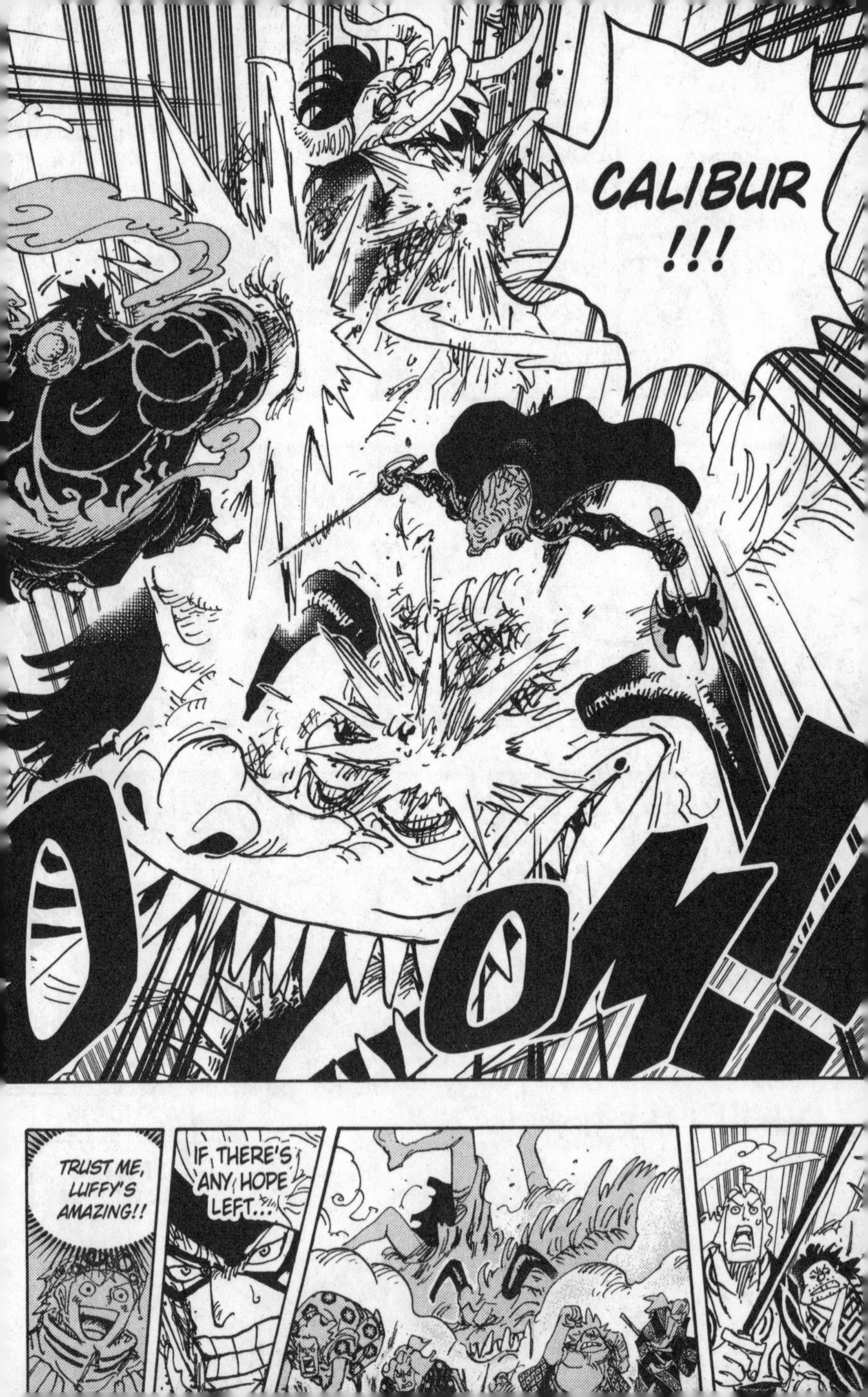
CALIBUR !!!
IF THERE'S ANY HOPE LEFT...
TRUST ME, LUFFY'S AMAZING!!

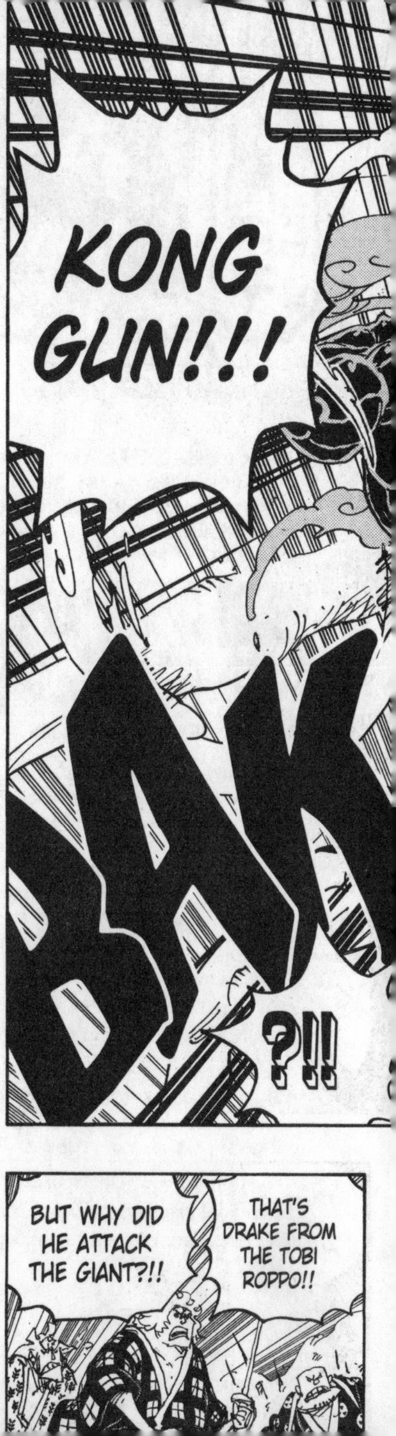
KONG GUN!!!
BAK
?!!
THAT'S DRAKE FROM THE TOBI ROPPO!!
BUT WHY DID HE ATTACK THE GIANT?!!
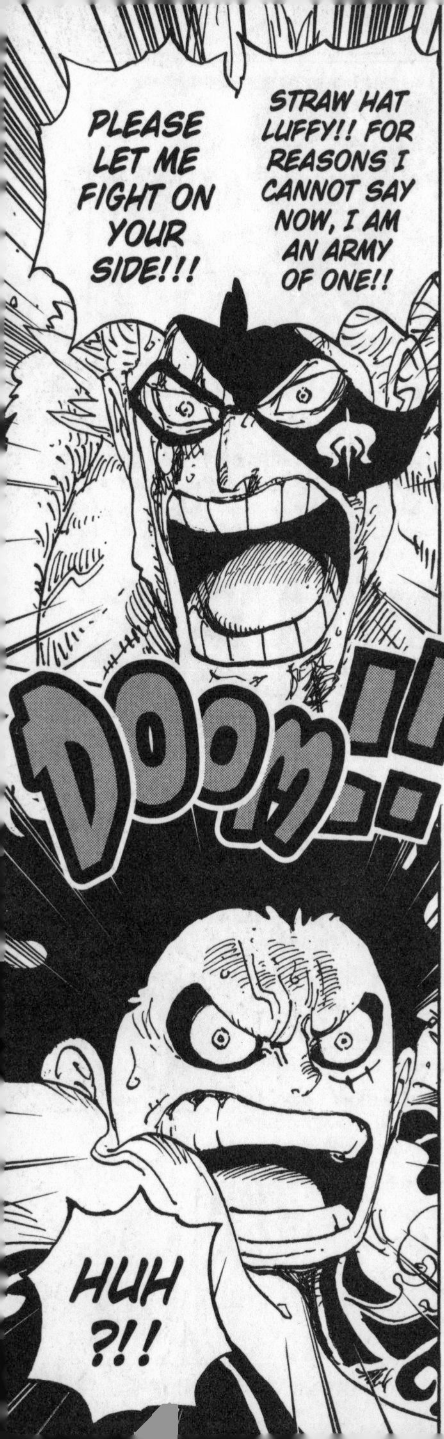
STRAW HAT LUFFY!! FOR REASONS I CANNOT SAY NOW, I AM AN ARMY OF ONE!!
PLEASE LET ME FIGHT ON YOUR SIDE!!!
DOOM..!!
HUH ?!!

(Hamane, Kanagawa)

Q: The officers of Kaido's pirate crew are all named after cards and card games, aren't they?

--Akibe

A: That's right. The three Lead Performers are pretty obvious, but in addition to them, the Tobi Roppo, Numbers, and Headliners are all named for card games, or the cards themselves. The exceptions are Drake, Apoo and Hawkins, since they came from outside the organization.

Who's-Who Black Maria Ulti Page One Sasaki Holdem Babanuki

It would fill the entire page if I listed them all. I'm sure for most of these, you're thinking, "I've never heard of that!" Well, it turns out there are tons and tons of card games played all over the world. Incidentally, you may remember that Doflamingo's code name was "Joker" back in Dressrosa. That's because in my initial plans, he was going to show up in Wano as one of Kaido's powerful allies. Good thing he was beaten in Dressrosa first!!

Q: I'm a member of the SBS Board of Morals and Ethics. I think that Sanadacchi has gone too far this time. But putting that aside, I really want to eat your millet dumplings, Odacchi!!

--Sanadacchi Fan

A: Uhh, the kind that pop off of my cheeks? I don't think you want to eat them. They're covered in gross, unshaved stubble. Also, change your pen name.

Q: Question for you, Oda Sensei. The people who've eaten Smile fruits grow horns, right? Why do the Pleasures have only one horn, and the Gifters have two?

--Hadock 10

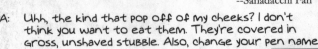

A: Well spotted. That's just fashion, actually! It's not enforced, but the rule is that Pleasures can wear one horn, and Gifters and up can wear two horns, if they want.

Chapter 991:
LET US DIE!!!

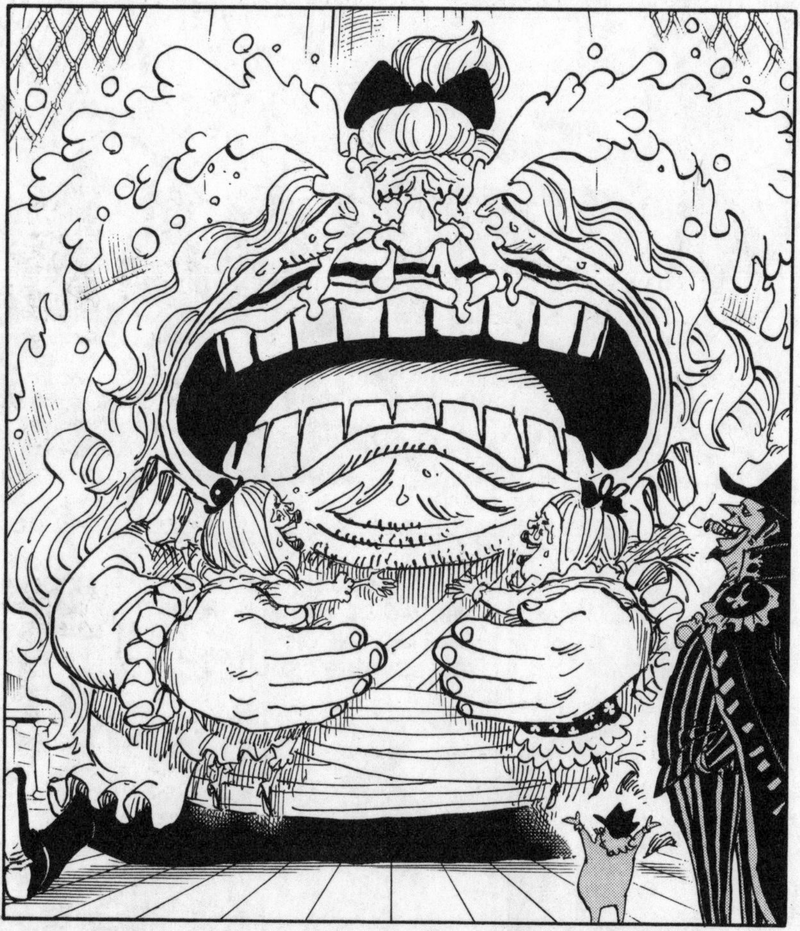

GANG BEGE'S OH MY FAMILY, VOL. 35: "AFTER 26 YEARS OF PLEADING, HIS FIRST HUG AS A FATHER"

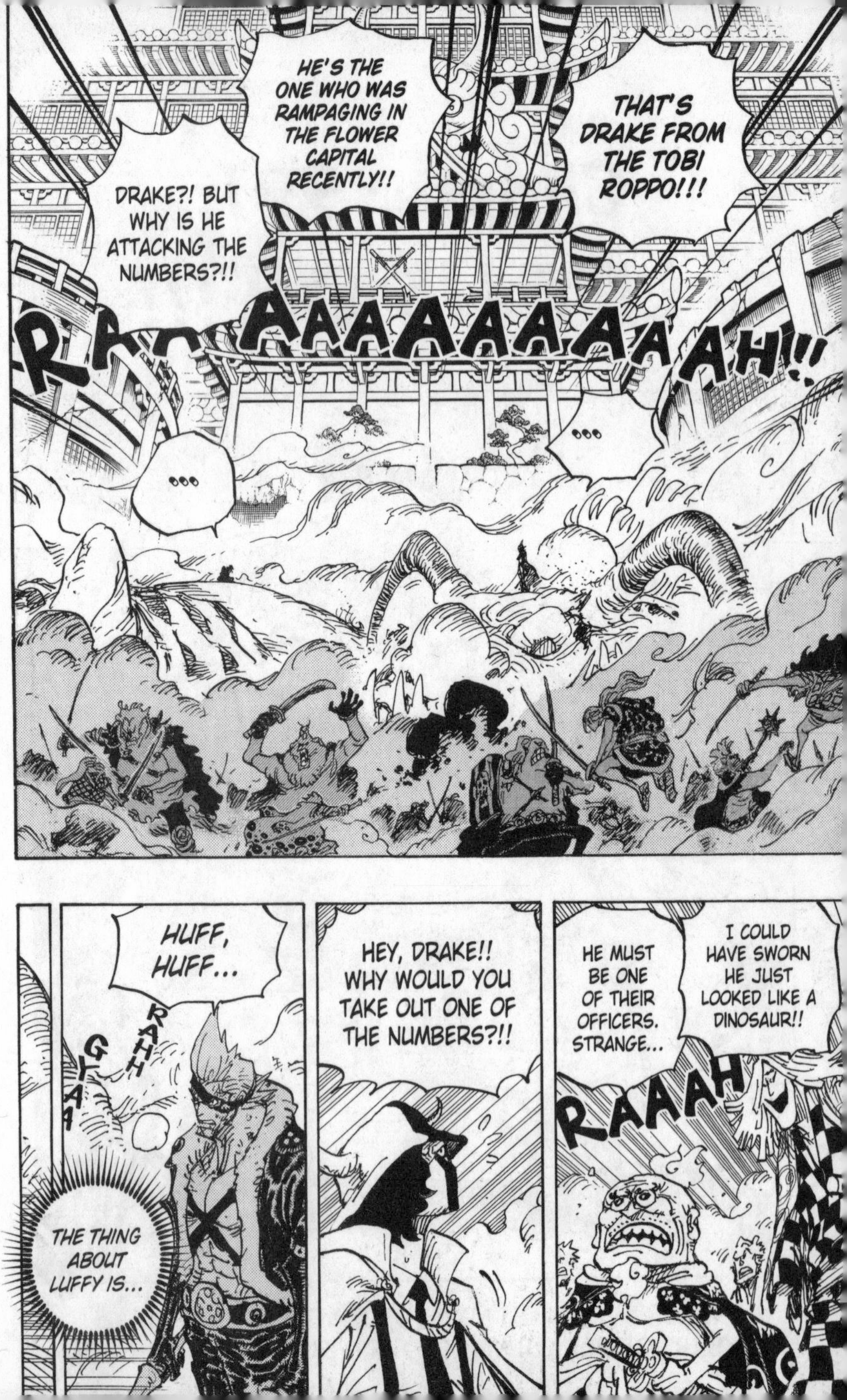
THAT'S DRAKE FROM THE TOBI ROPPO!!!
HE'S THE ONE WHO WAS RAMPAGING IN THE FLOWER CAPITAL RECENTLY!!
DRAKE?! BUT WHY IS HE ATTACKING THE NUMBERS?!!
RAAAAAAAAAAAH!!!
...
...
I COULD HAVE SWORN HE JUST LOOKED LIKE A DINOSAUR!!
HE MUST BE ONE OF THEIR OFFICERS. STRANGE...
RAAAH
HEY, DRAKE!! WHY WOULD YOU TAKE OUT ONE OF THE NUMBERS?!!
HUFF, HUFF...
RAHH
GYAA
THE THING ABOUT LUFFY IS...

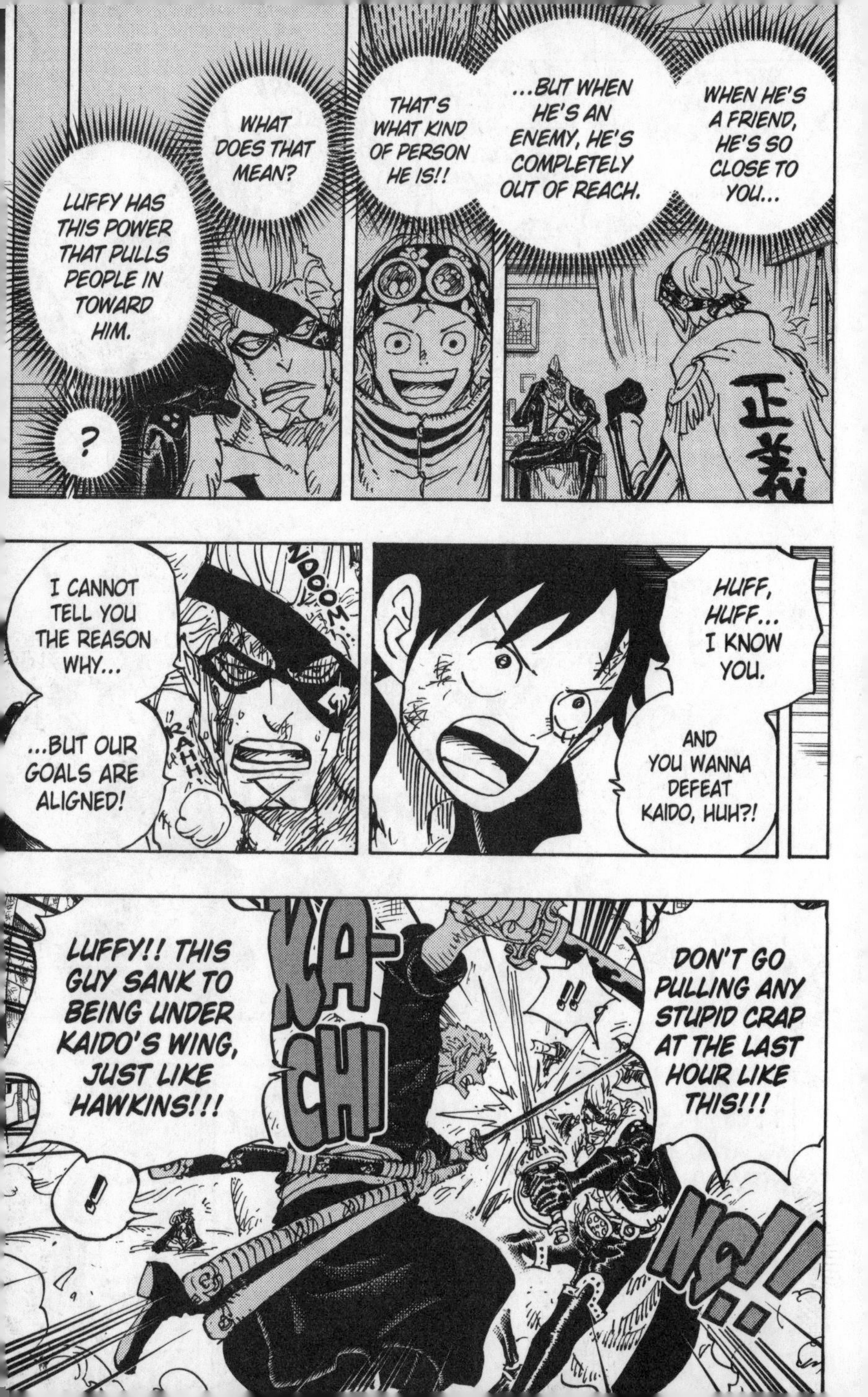
WHEN HE'S A FRIEND, HE'S SO CLOSE TO YOU...
...BUT WHEN HE'S AN ENEMY, HE'S COMPLETELY OUT OF REACH.
THAT'S WHAT KIND OF PERSON HE IS!!
WHAT DOES THAT MEAN?
LUFFY HAS THIS POWER THAT PULLS PEOPLE IN TOWARD HIM.
?
HUFF, HUFF... I KNOW YOU.
AND YOU WANNA DEFEAT KAIDO, HUH?!
I CANNOT TELL YOU THE REASON WHY...
...BUT OUR GOALS ARE ALIGNED!
DON'T GO PULLING ANY STUPID CRAP AT THE LAST HOUR LIKE THIS!!!
!!
LUFFY!! THIS GUY SANK TO BEING UNDER KAIDO'S WING, JUST LIKE HAWKINS!!!
KA-CHI
NG!!
!

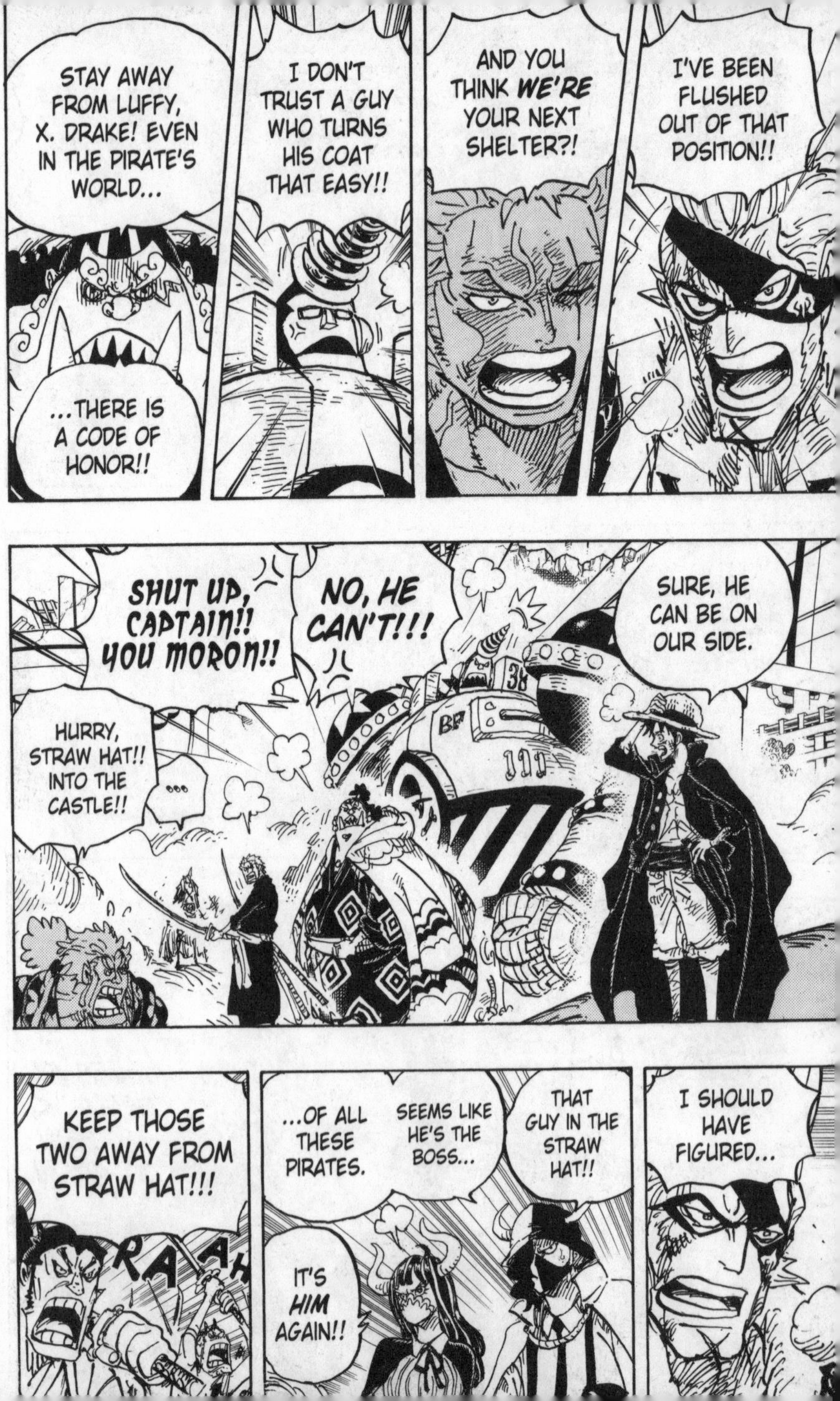
I'VE BEEN FLUSHED OUT OF THAT POSITION!!
AND YOU THINK *WE'RE* YOUR NEXT SHELTER?!
I DON'T TRUST A GUY WHO TURNS HIS COAT THAT EASY!!
STAY AWAY FROM LUFFY, X. DRAKE! EVEN IN THE PIRATE'S WORLD...
...THERE IS A CODE OF HONOR!!
SURE, HE CAN BE ON OUR SIDE.
NO, HE CAN'T!!!
SHUT UP, CAPTAIN!! YOU MORON!!
...
HURRY, STRAW HAT!! INTO THE CASTLE!!
I SHOULD HAVE FIGURED...
THAT GUY IN THE STRAW HAT!!
SEEMS LIKE HE'S THE BOSS...
...OF ALL THESE PIRATES.
IT'S *HIM* AGAIN!!
KEEP THOSE TWO AWAY FROM STRAW HAT!!!
RAAH

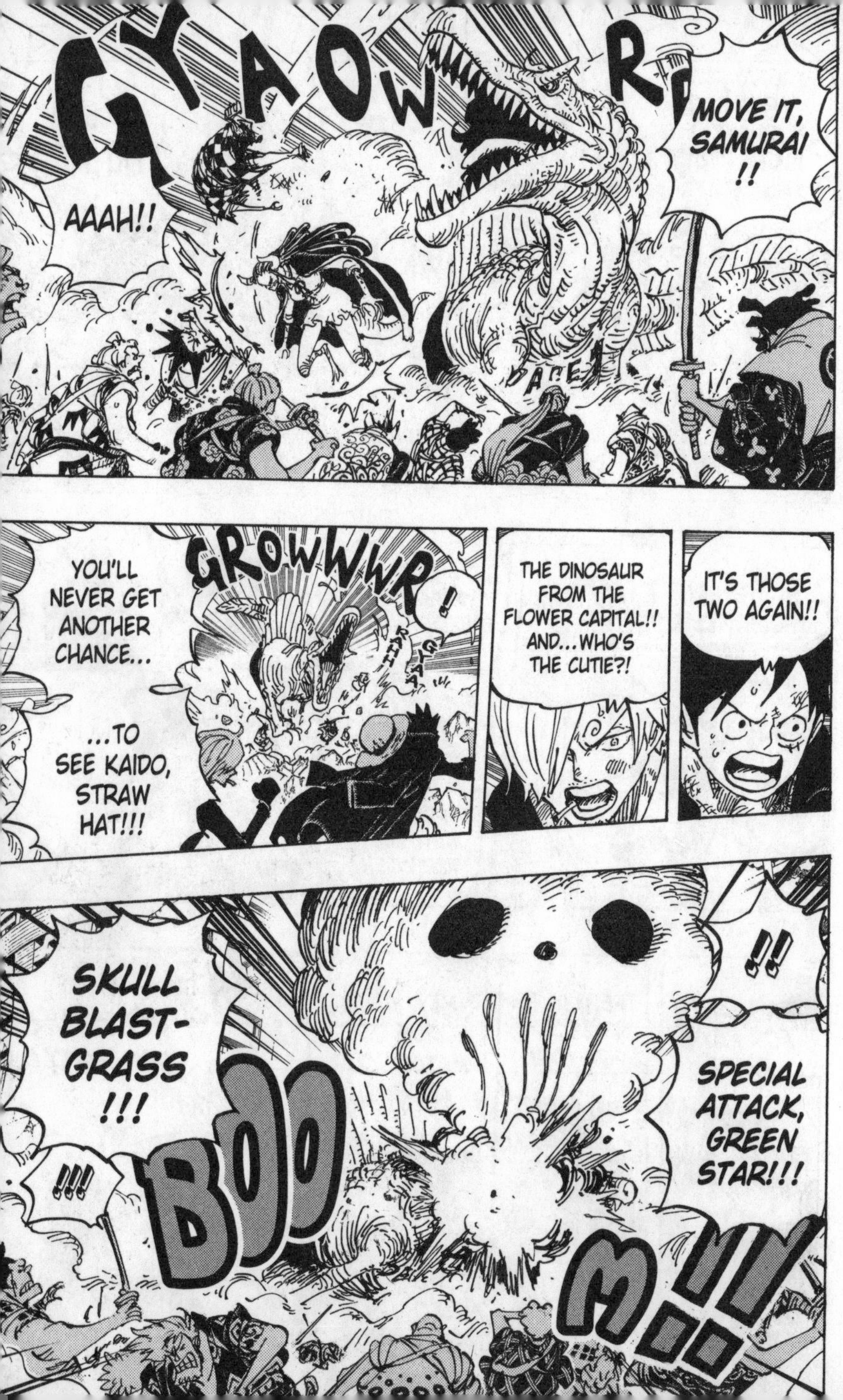
GYAOWR
MOVE IT, SAMURAI!!
AAAH!!
IT'S THOSE TWO AGAIN!!
THE DINOSAUR FROM THE FLOWER CAPITAL!! AND...WHO'S THE CUTIE?!
GROWWWR
!
YOU'LL NEVER GET ANOTHER CHANCE...
...TO SEE KAIDO, STRAW HAT!!!
!!
SPECIAL ATTACK, GREEN STAR!!!
SKULL BLAST-GRASS!!!
BOOOM!!
!!!

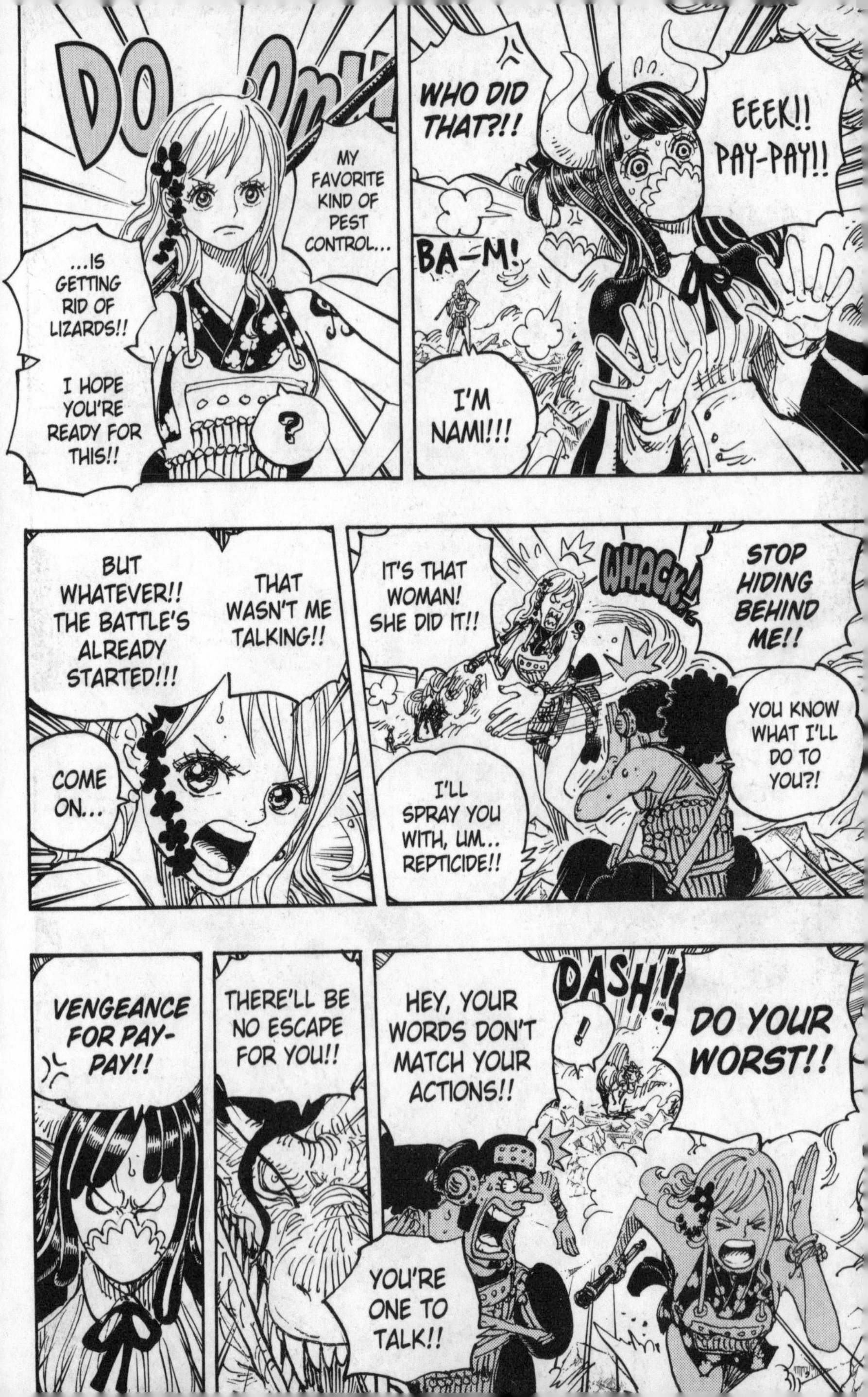
EEEK!! PAY-PAY!!
WHO DID THAT?!!
BA-M!
I'M NAMI!!!
DO-OM!!
MY FAVORITE KIND OF PEST CONTROL...
...IS GETTING RID OF LIZARDS!!
I HOPE YOU'RE READY FOR THIS!!
?
STOP HIDING BEHIND ME!!
WHACK!
IT'S THAT WOMAN! SHE DID IT!!
YOU KNOW WHAT I'LL DO TO YOU?!
I'LL SPRAY YOU WITH, UM... REPTICIDE!!
THAT WASN'T ME TALKING!!
BUT WHATEVER!! THE BATTLE'S ALREADY STARTED!!!
COME ON...
DO YOUR WORST!!
DASH!!
!
HEY, YOUR WORDS DON'T MATCH YOUR ACTIONS!!
YOU'RE ONE TO TALK!!
THERE'LL BE NO ESCAPE FOR YOU!!
VENGEANCE FOR PAY-PAY!!

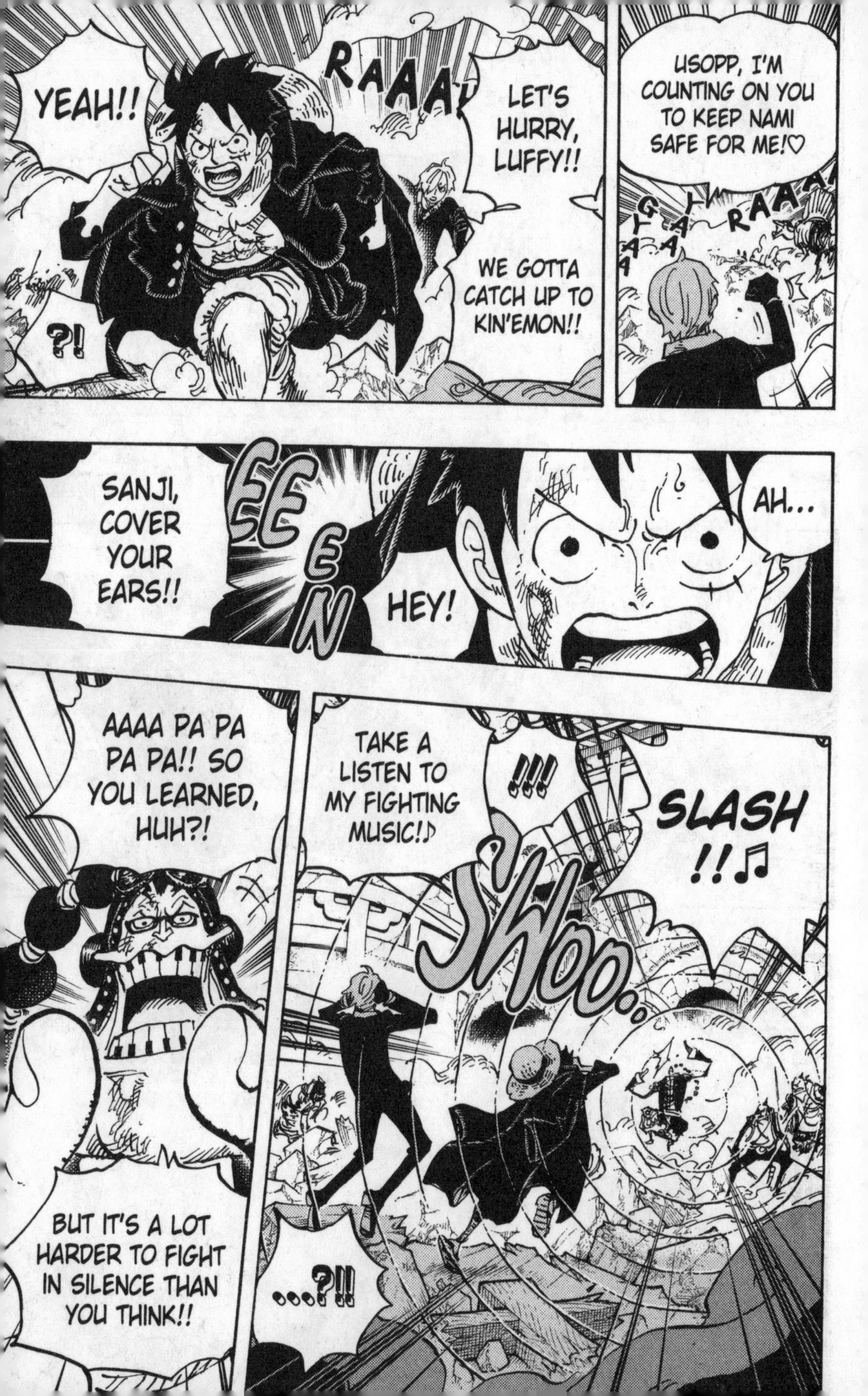
USOPP, I'M COUNTING ON YOU TO KEEP NAMI SAFE FOR ME!♡
RAAAA
RAAAA
LET'S HURRY, LUFFY!!
WE GOTTA CATCH UP TO KIN'EMON!!
YEAH!!
?!
AH...
HEY!
EEEN
SANJI, COVER YOUR EARS!!
SLASH!!♫
!!!
TAKE A LISTEN TO MY FIGHTING MUSIC!♪
SHOO..
...?!!
AAAA PA PA PA PA!! SO YOU LEARNED, HUH?!
BUT IT'S A LOT HARDER TO FIGHT IN SILENCE THAN YOU THINK!!

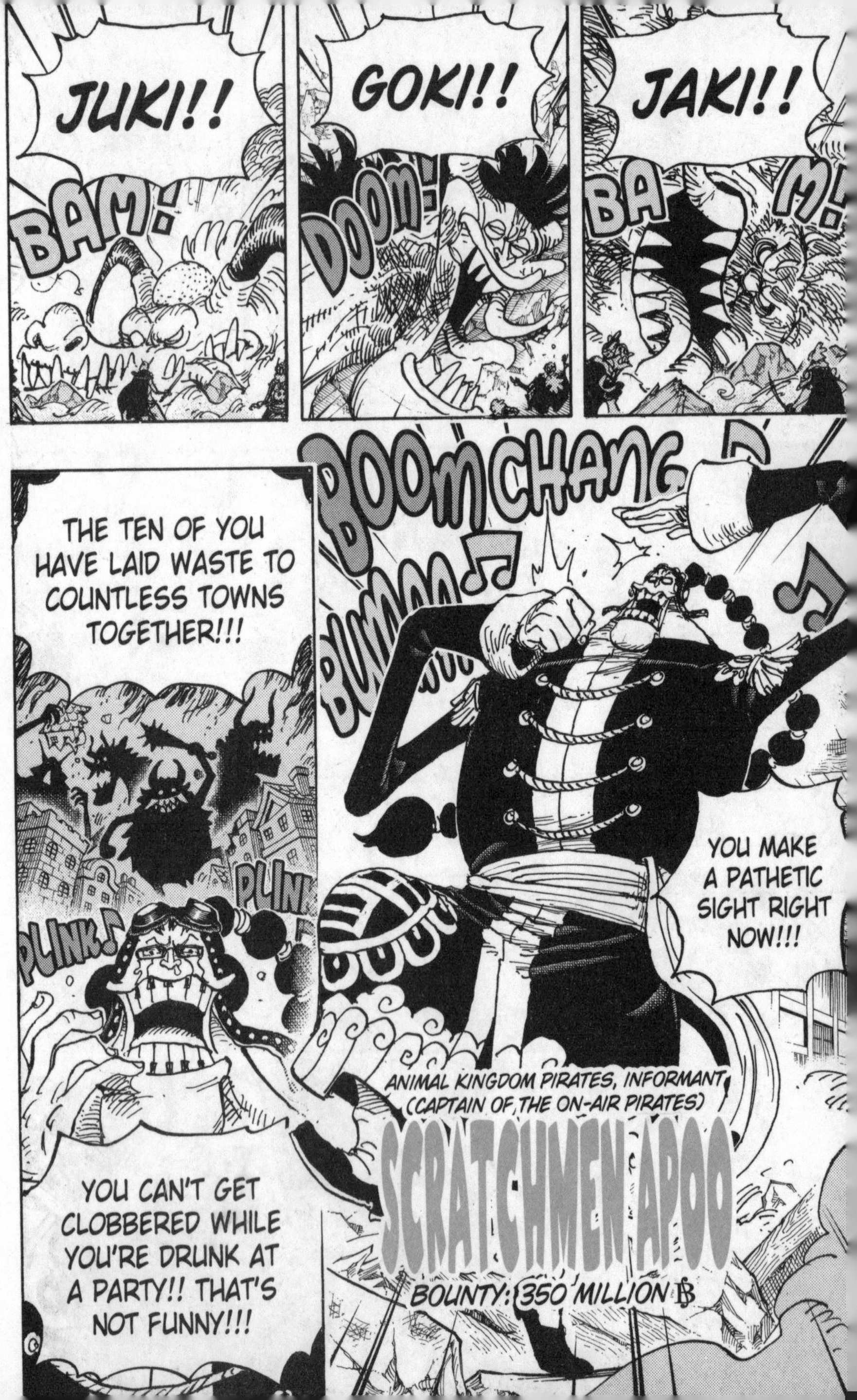
JAKI!!
BAM!
GOKI!!
DOOM!
JUKI!!
BAM!
BOOM CHANG
YOU MAKE A PATHETIC SIGHT RIGHT NOW!!!
ANIMAL KINGDOM PIRATES, INFORMANT (CAPTAIN OF THE ON-AIR PIRATES)
SCRATCHMEN APOO
BOUNTY: 350 MILLION ฿
THE TEN OF YOU HAVE LAID WASTE TO COUNTLESS TOWNS TOGETHER!!!
PLINK♪
YOU CAN'T GET CLOBBERED WHILE YOU'RE DRUNK AT A PARTY!! THAT'S NOT FUNNY!!!

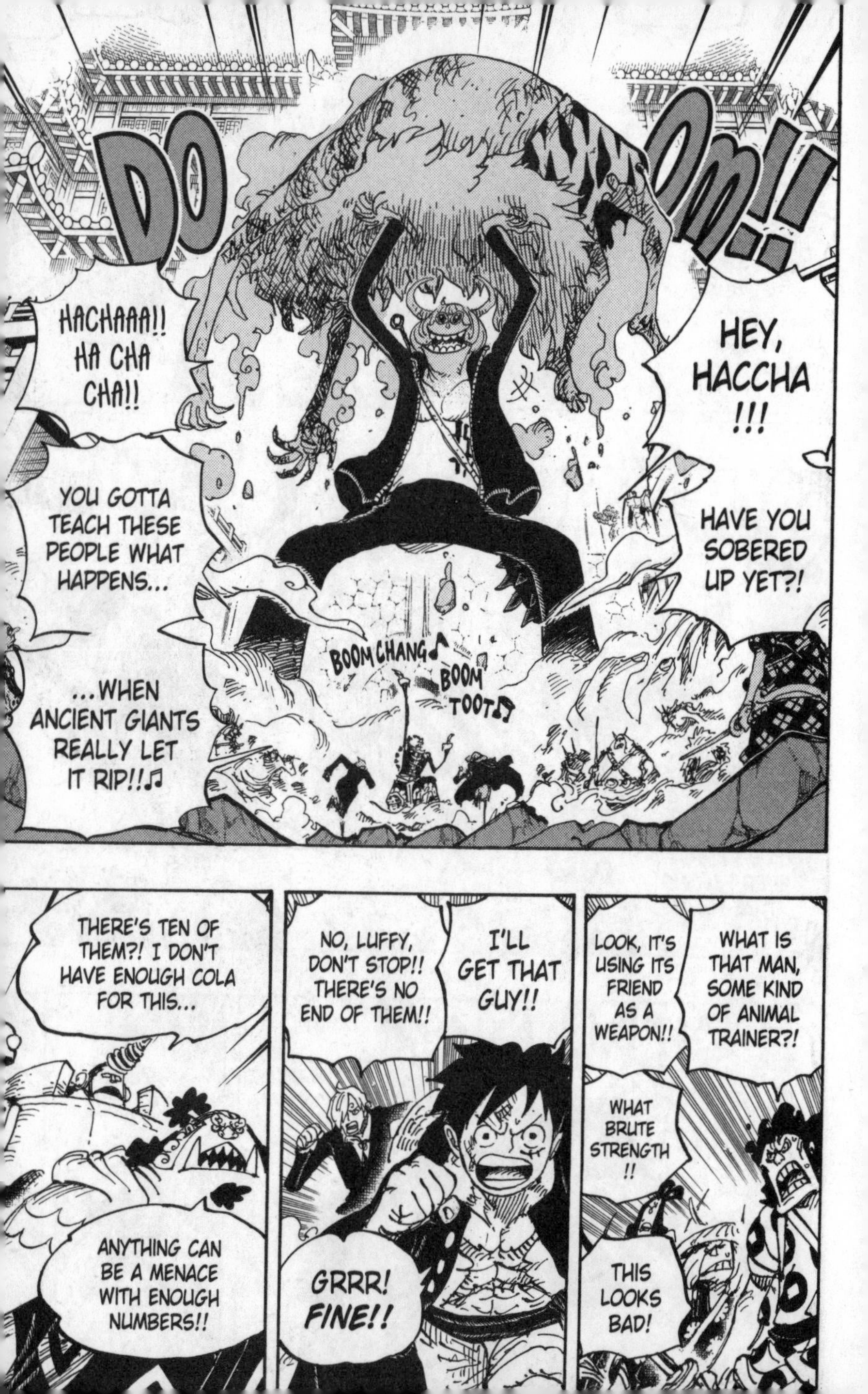
DO
OM!!
HEY, HACCHA!!!
HAVE YOU SOBERED UP YET?!
HACHAAA!! HA CHA CHA!!
YOU GOTTA TEACH THESE PEOPLE WHAT HAPPENS...
...WHEN ANCIENT GIANTS REALLY LET IT RIP!!♫
BOOM CHANG♪
BOOM TOOT♫
WHAT IS THAT MAN, SOME KIND OF ANIMAL TRAINER?!
LOOK, IT'S USING ITS FRIEND AS A WEAPON!!
WHAT BRUTE STRENGTH!!
THIS LOOKS BAD!
I'LL GET THAT GUY!!
NO, LUFFY, DON'T STOP!! THERE'S NO END OF THEM!!
GRRR! FINE!!
THERE'S TEN OF THEM?! I DON'T HAVE ENOUGH COLA FOR THIS...
ANYTHING CAN BE A MENACE WITH ENOUGH NUMBERS!!

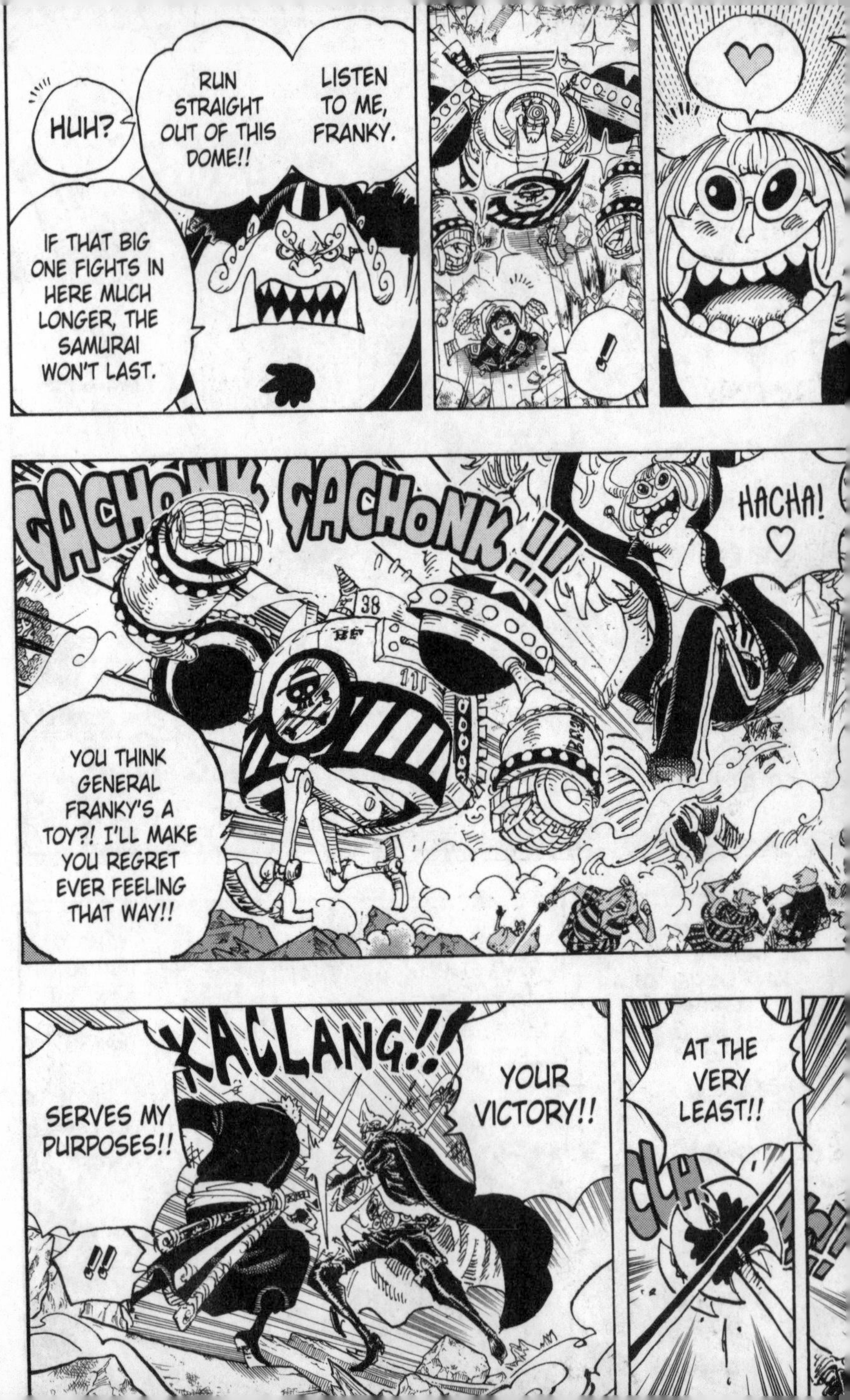
!
LISTEN TO ME, FRANKY.
RUN STRAIGHT OUT OF THIS DOME!!
HUH?
IF THAT BIG ONE FIGHTS IN HERE MUCH LONGER, THE SAMURAI WON'T LAST.
HACHA! ♡
GACHONK GACHONK!!
YOU THINK GENERAL FRANKY'S A TOY?! I'LL MAKE YOU REGRET EVER FEELING THAT WAY!!
AT THE VERY LEAST!!
YOUR VICTORY!!
XACLANG!!
SERVES MY PURPOSES!!
!!

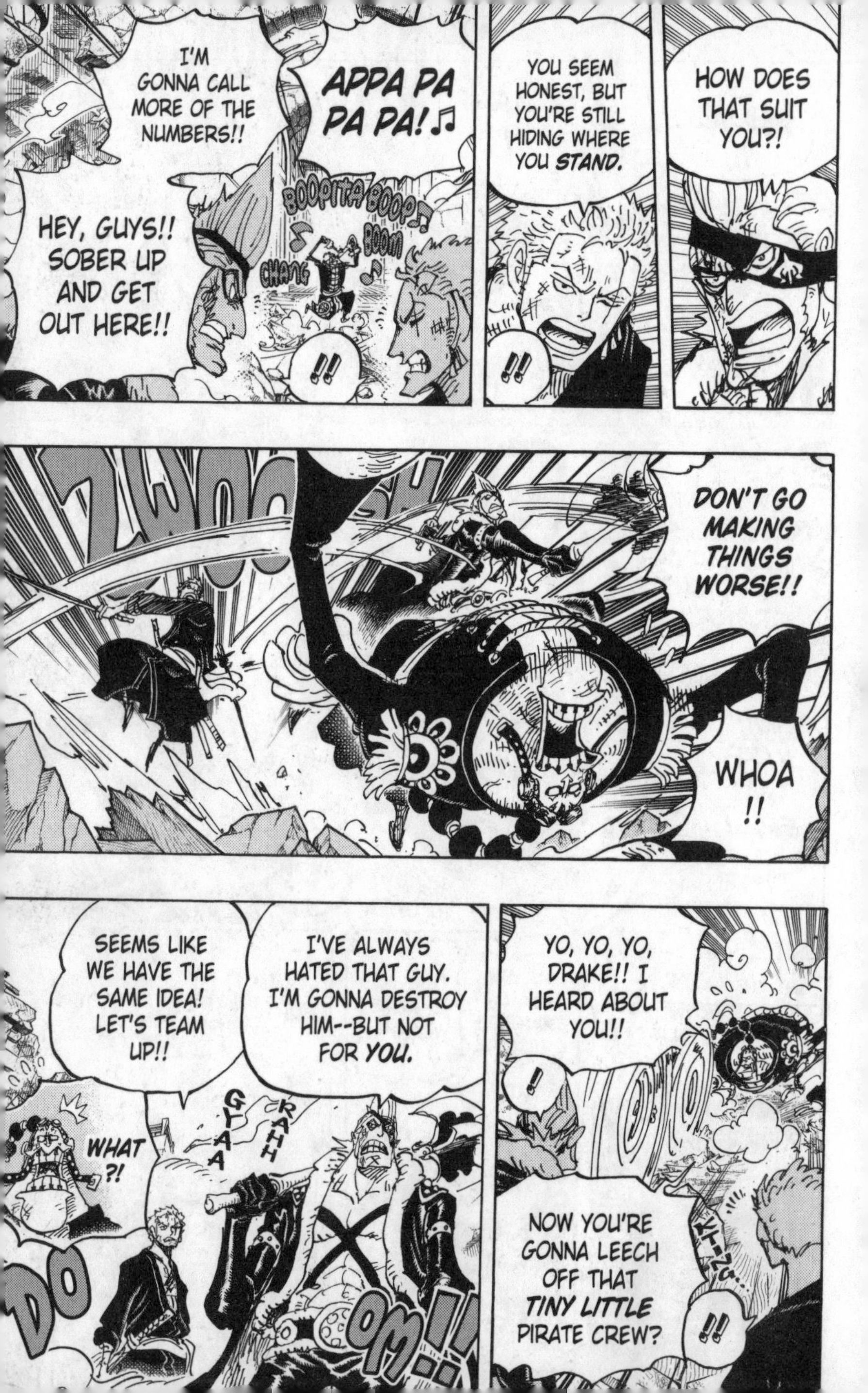
HOW DOES THAT SUIT YOU?!
YOU SEEM HONEST, BUT YOU'RE STILL HIDING WHERE YOU *STAND.*
!!
APPA PA PA PA! ♫
I'M GONNA CALL MORE OF THE NUMBERS!!
HEY, GUYS!! SOBER UP AND GET OUT HERE!!
BOOPITA BOOP♫
BOOM
CHANG
!!
DON'T GO MAKING THINGS WORSE!!
WHOA !!
ZWOO
SH
YO, YO, YO, DRAKE!! I HEARD ABOUT YOU!!
!
NOW YOU'RE GONNA LEECH OFF THAT *TINY LITTLE* PIRATE CREW?
!!
I'VE ALWAYS HATED THAT GUY. I'M GONNA DESTROY HIM--BUT NOT FOR *YOU.*
SEEMS LIKE WE HAVE THE SAME IDEA! LET'S TEAM UP!!
GYAA
RAHH
WHAT ?!
DOOM!!

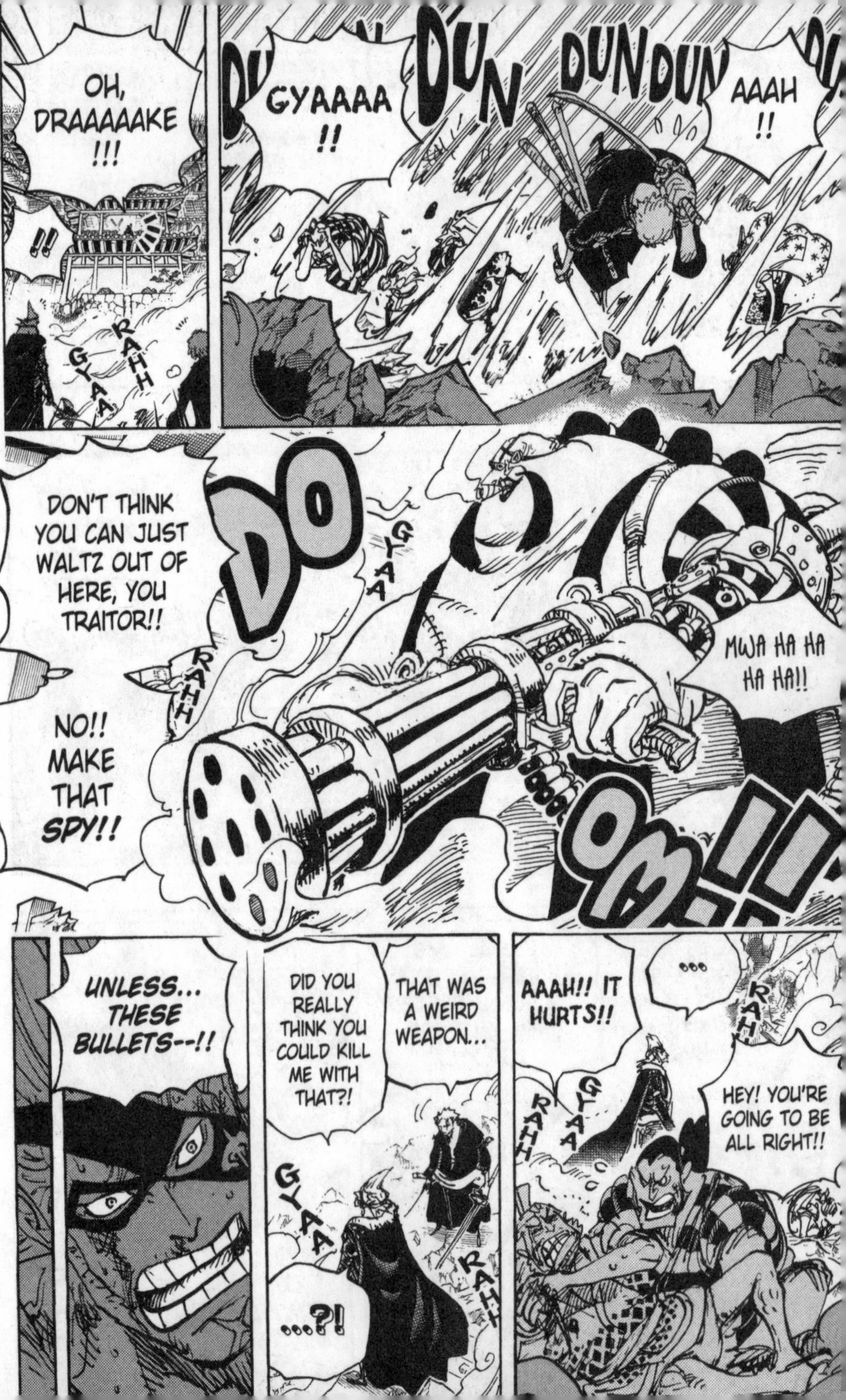
DUN DUN
AAAH !!
DUN
GYAAAA !!
OH, DRAAAAAKE !!!
!!
RAHH
GYAA
MWA HA HA HA HA!!
DO
GYAA
DON'T THINK YOU CAN JUST WALTZ OUT OF HERE, YOU TRAITOR!!
RAHH
NO!! MAKE THAT SPY!!
OM!!
...
RAH
HEY! YOU'RE GOING TO BE ALL RIGHT!!
AAAH!! IT HURTS!!
GYAA
RAHH
THAT WAS A WEIRD WEAPON...
DID YOU REALLY THINK YOU COULD KILL ME WITH THAT?!
GYAA
RAHH
...?!
UNLESS... THESE BULLETS--!!

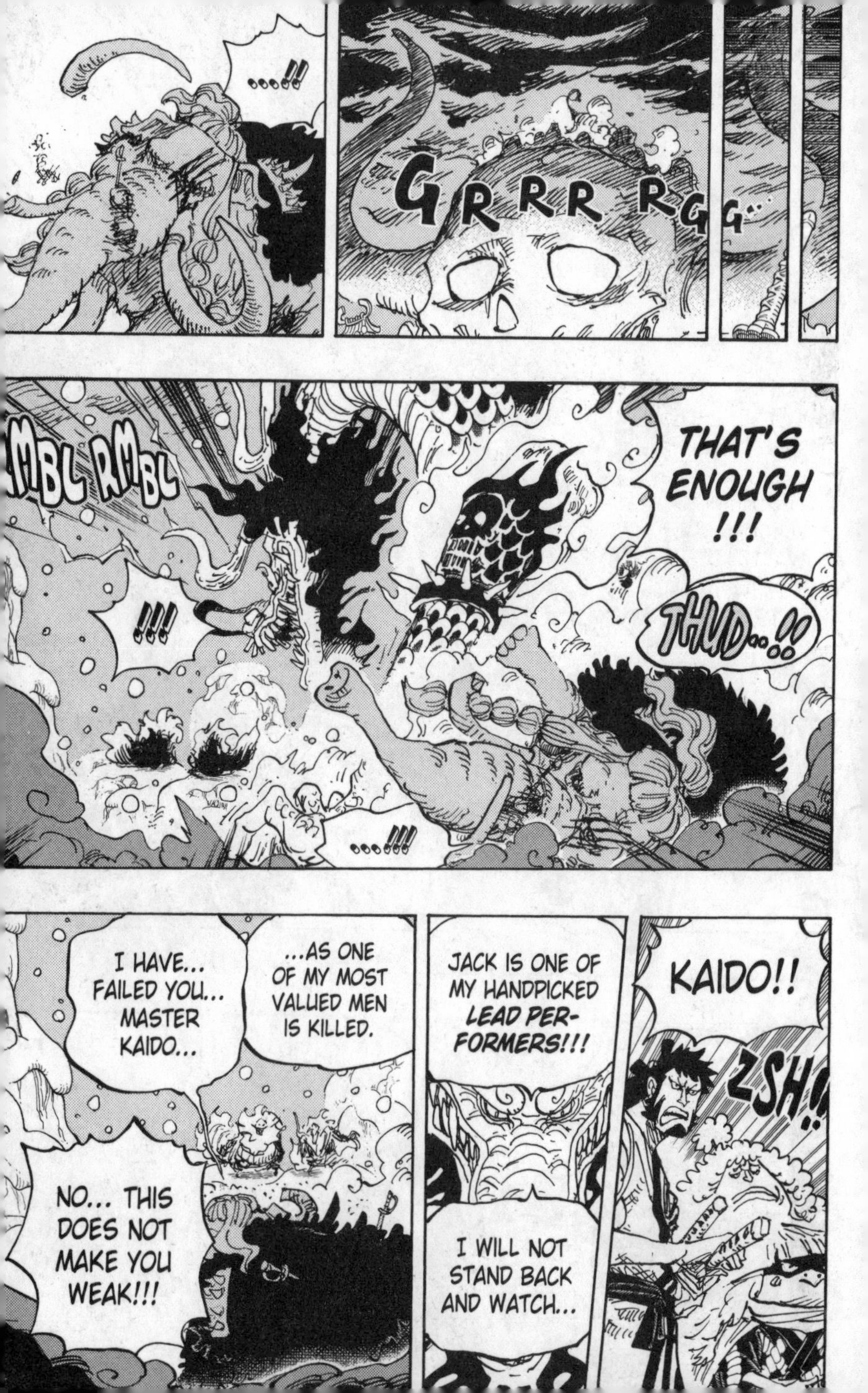
GRRRR RGG...
...!!
THAT'S ENOUGH!!!
THUD...!!
RMBL RMBL
!!!
...!!!
KAIDO!!
ZSH!!
JACK IS ONE OF MY HANDPICKED LEAD PER-FORMERS!!!
I WILL NOT STAND BACK AND WATCH...
...AS ONE OF MY MOST VALUED MEN IS KILLED.
I HAVE... FAILED YOU... MASTER KAIDO...
NO... THIS DOES NOT MAKE YOU WEAK!!!

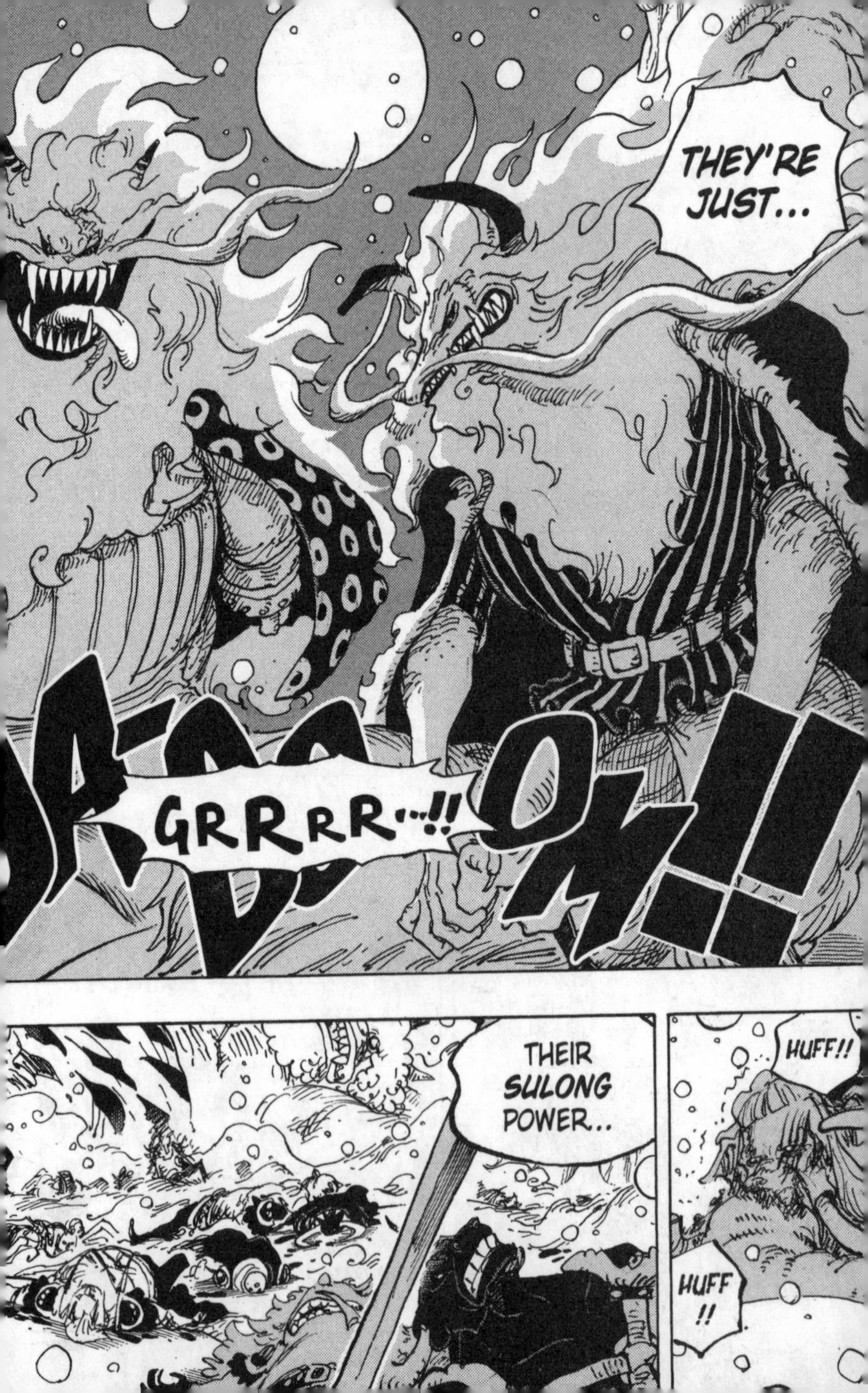
THEY'RE JUST...
GRRRR...!!
HUFF!!
HUFF !!
THEIR SULONG POWER...

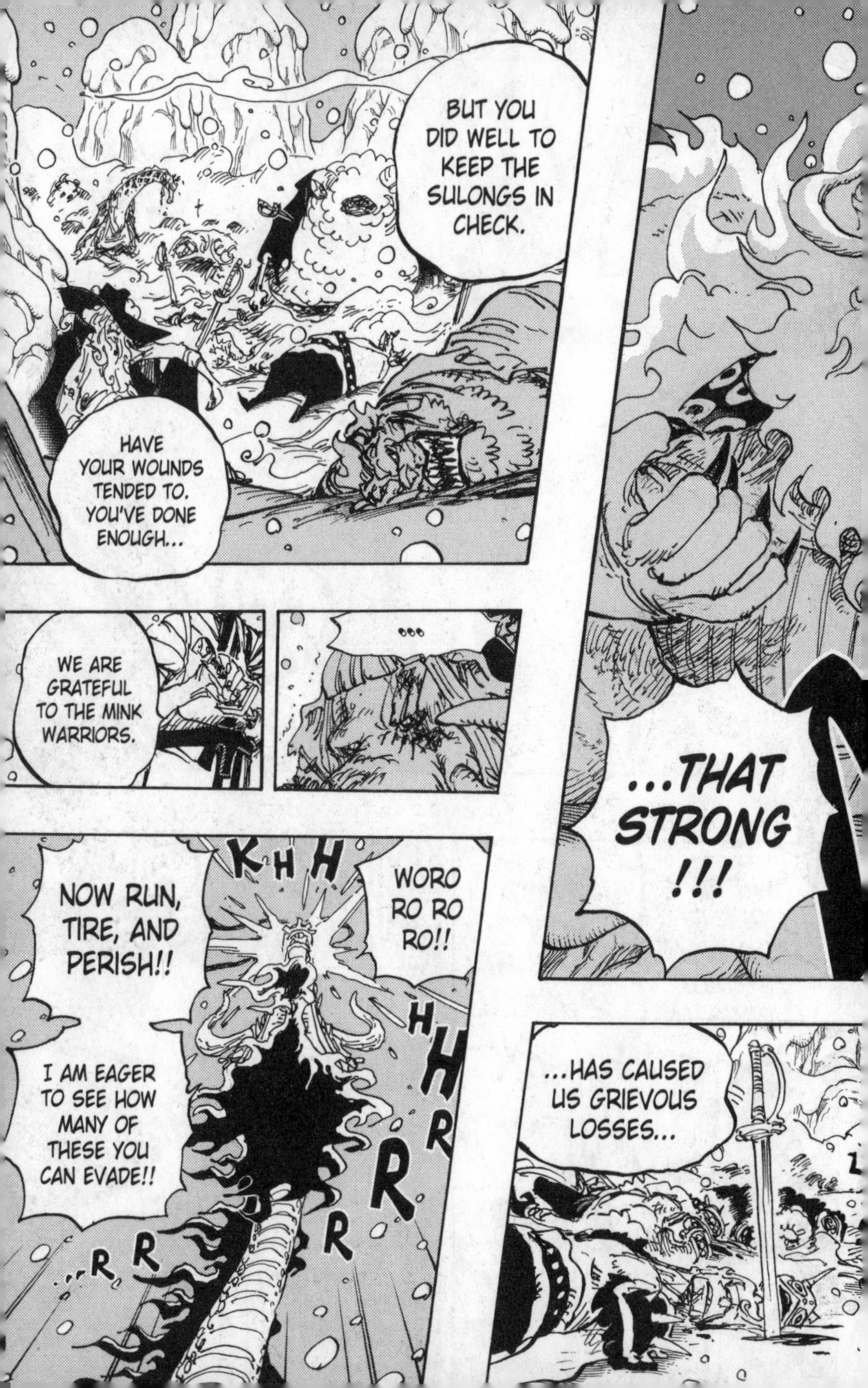
...THAT STRONG !!!
BUT YOU DID WELL TO KEEP THE SULONGS IN CHECK.
HAVE YOUR WOUNDS TENDED TO. YOU'VE DONE ENOUGH...
...
WE ARE GRATEFUL TO THE MINK WARRIORS.
KHH
WORO RO RO RO!!
NOW RUN, TIRE, AND PERISH!!
HHRRR
I AM EAGER TO SEE HOW MANY OF THESE YOU CAN EVADE!!
RRR...
...HAS CAUSED US GRIEVOUS LOSSES...

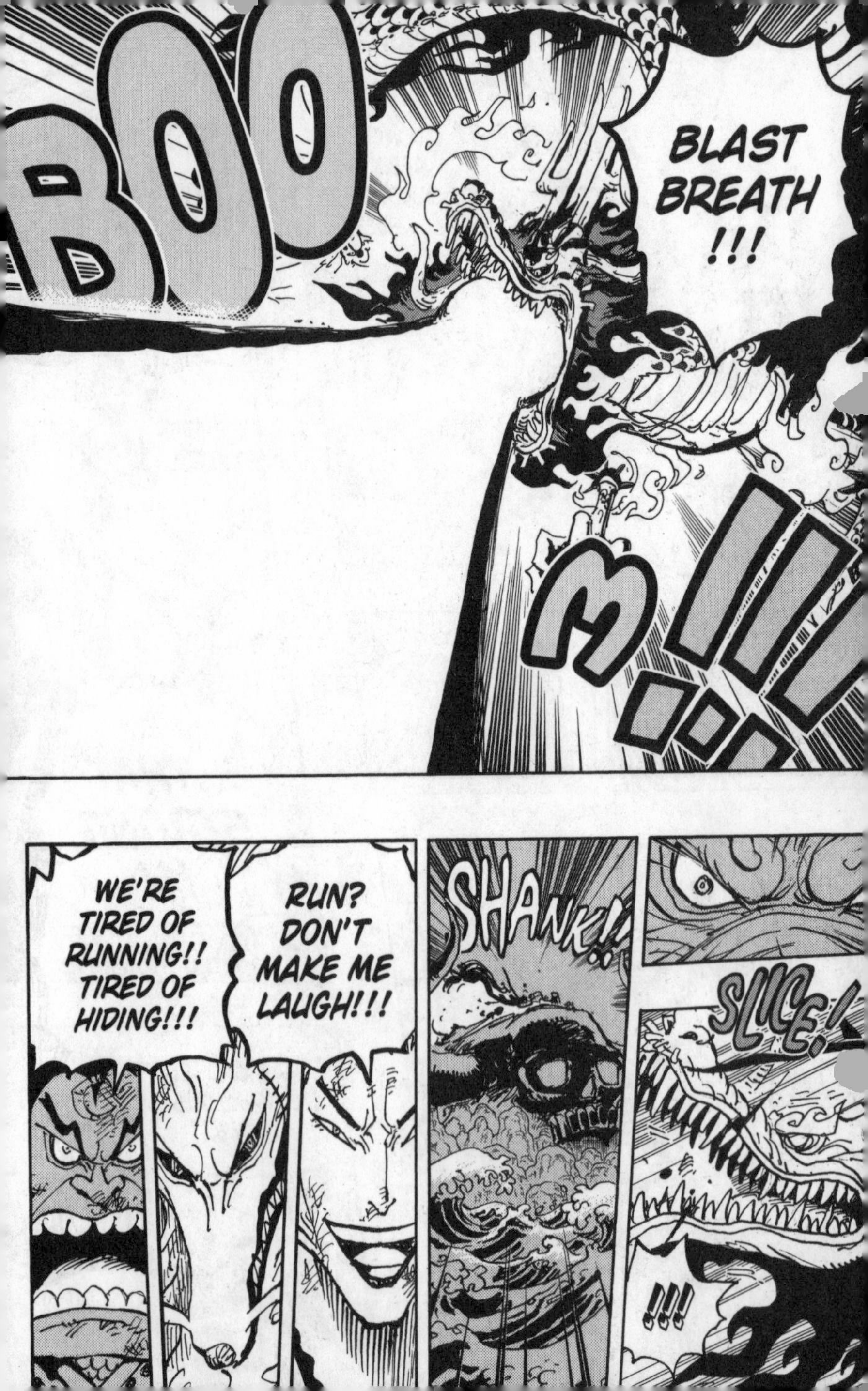
BLAST BREATH!!!
BOOO
M!!
SLICE!!
!!!
SHANK!!
RUN? DON'T MAKE ME LAUGH!!!
WE'RE TIRED OF RUNNING!! TIRED OF HIDING!!!

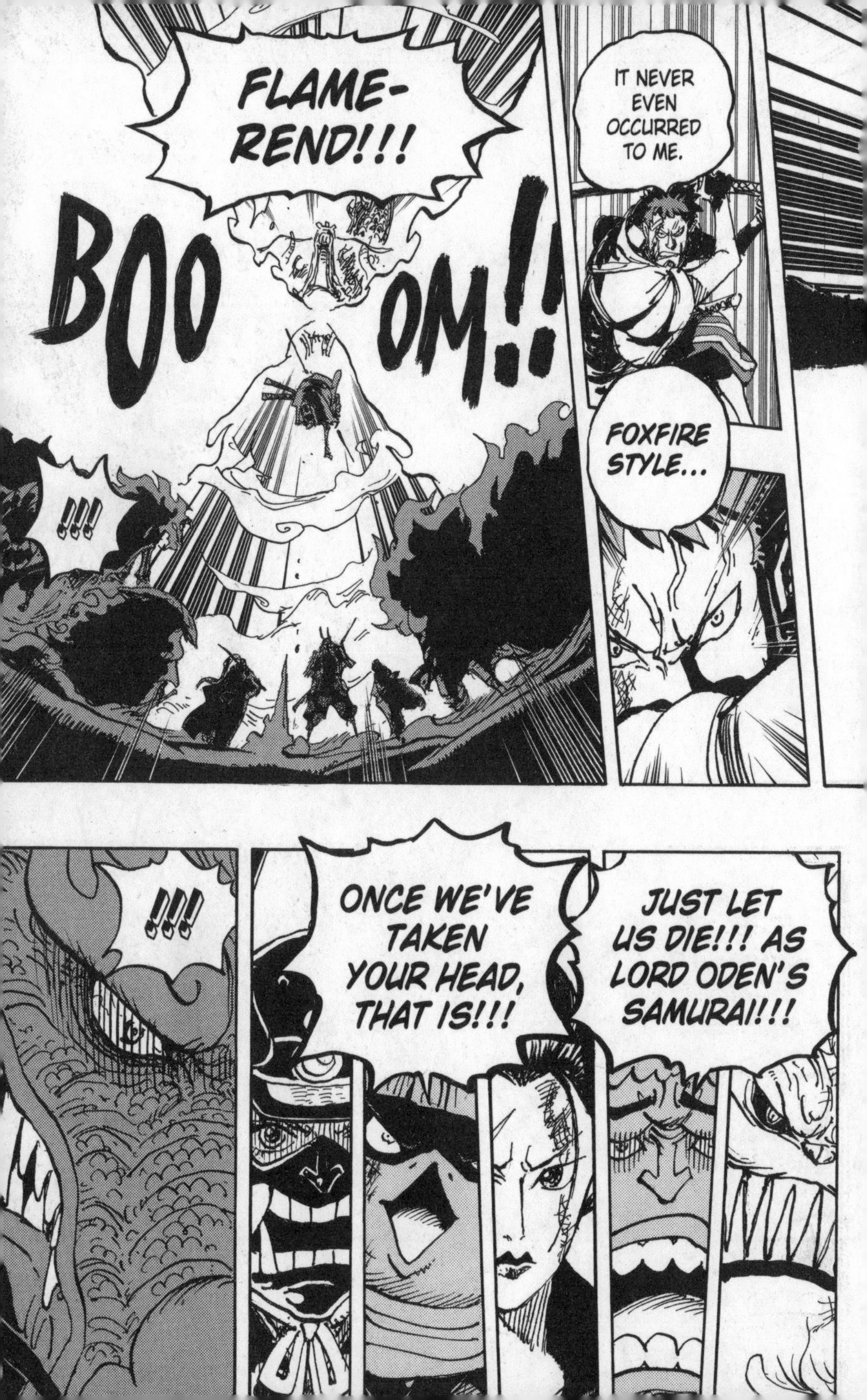
IT NEVER EVEN OCCURRED TO ME.
FOXFIRE STYLE...
FLAME-REND!!!
BOOOM!!
!!!
JUST LET US DIE!!! AS LORD ODEN'S SAMURAI!!!
ONCE WE'VE TAKEN YOUR HEAD, THAT IS!!!
!!!

Chapter 992: REMNANTS

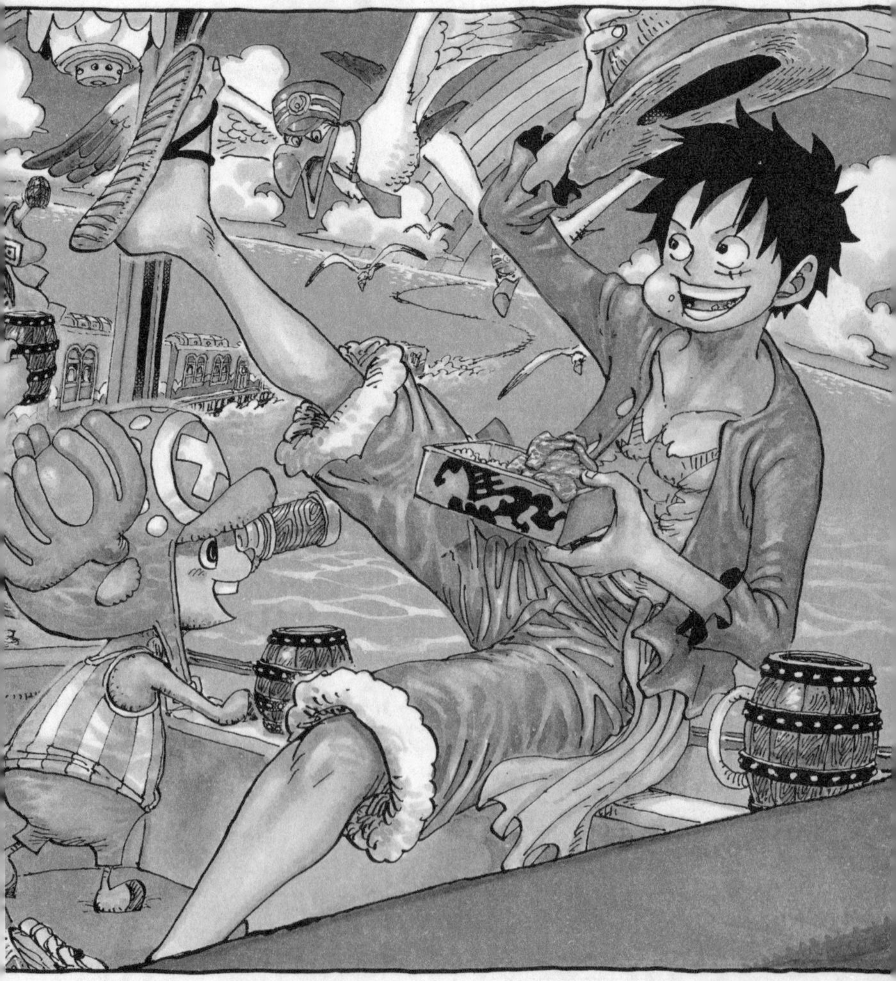

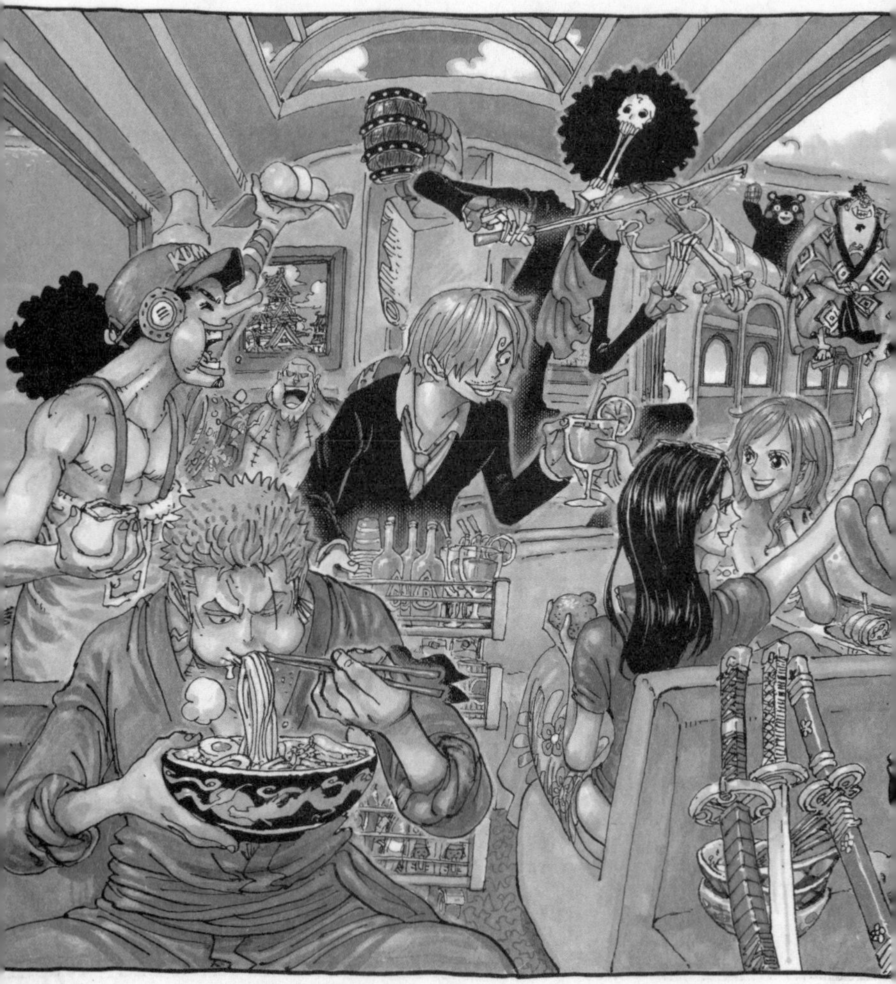

vol.98
ONE PIECE

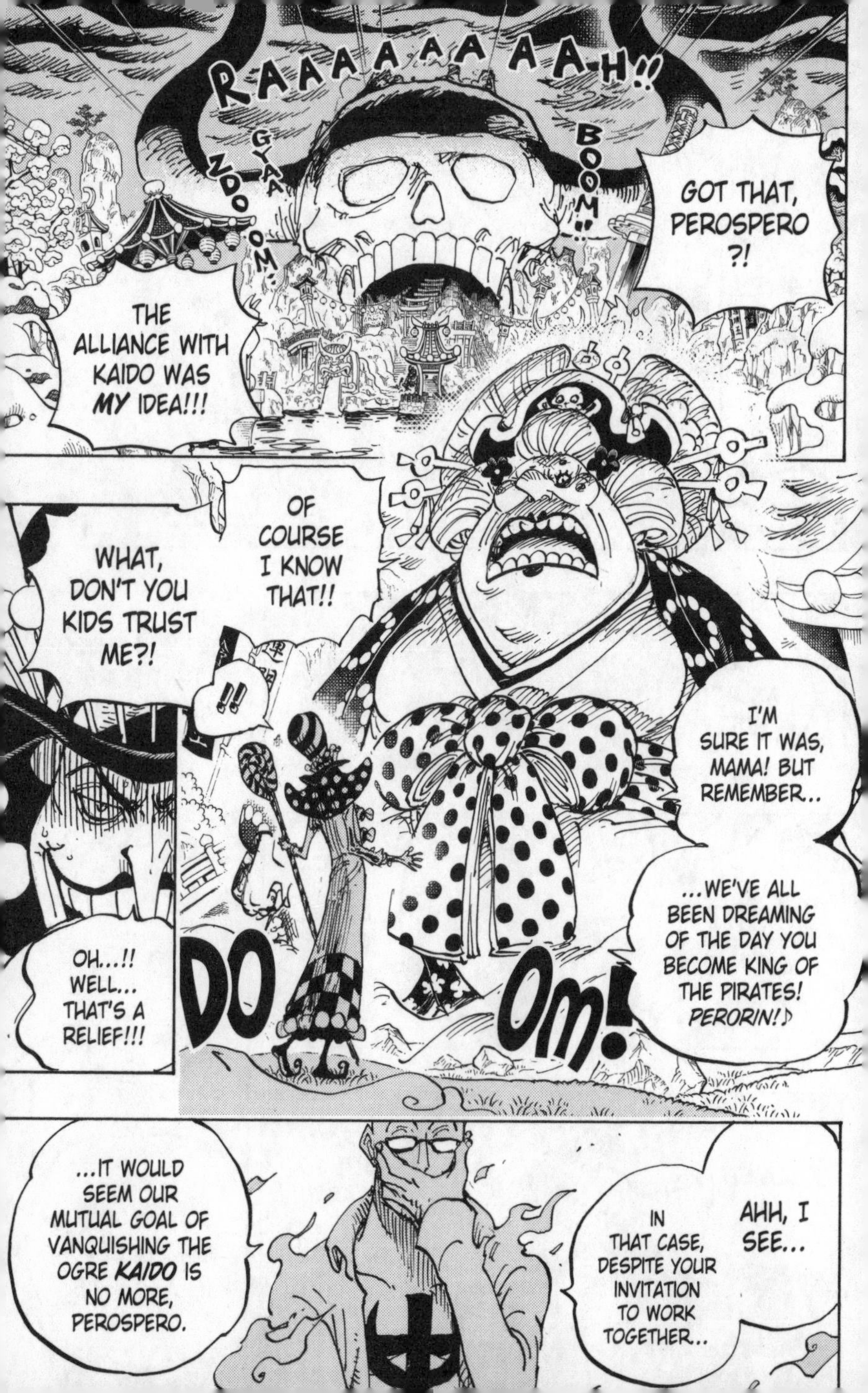
RAAAAAAAH!!
ZDOOOOM
GYAA
BOOM!!
GOT THAT, PEROSPERO ?!
THE ALLIANCE WITH KAIDO WAS *MY* IDEA!!!
OF COURSE I KNOW THAT!!
WHAT, DON'T YOU KIDS TRUST ME?!
!!
I'M SURE IT WAS, MAMA! BUT REMEMBER..
...WE'VE ALL BEEN DREAMING OF THE DAY YOU BECOME KING OF THE PIRATES! *PERORIN!*♪
DOOM!
OH...!! WELL... THAT'S A RELIEF!!!
AHH, I SEE...
IN THAT CASE, DESPITE YOUR INVITATION TO WORK TOGETHER...
...IT WOULD SEEM OUR MUTUAL GOAL OF VANQUISHING THE OGRE *KAIDO* IS NO MORE, PEROSPERO.

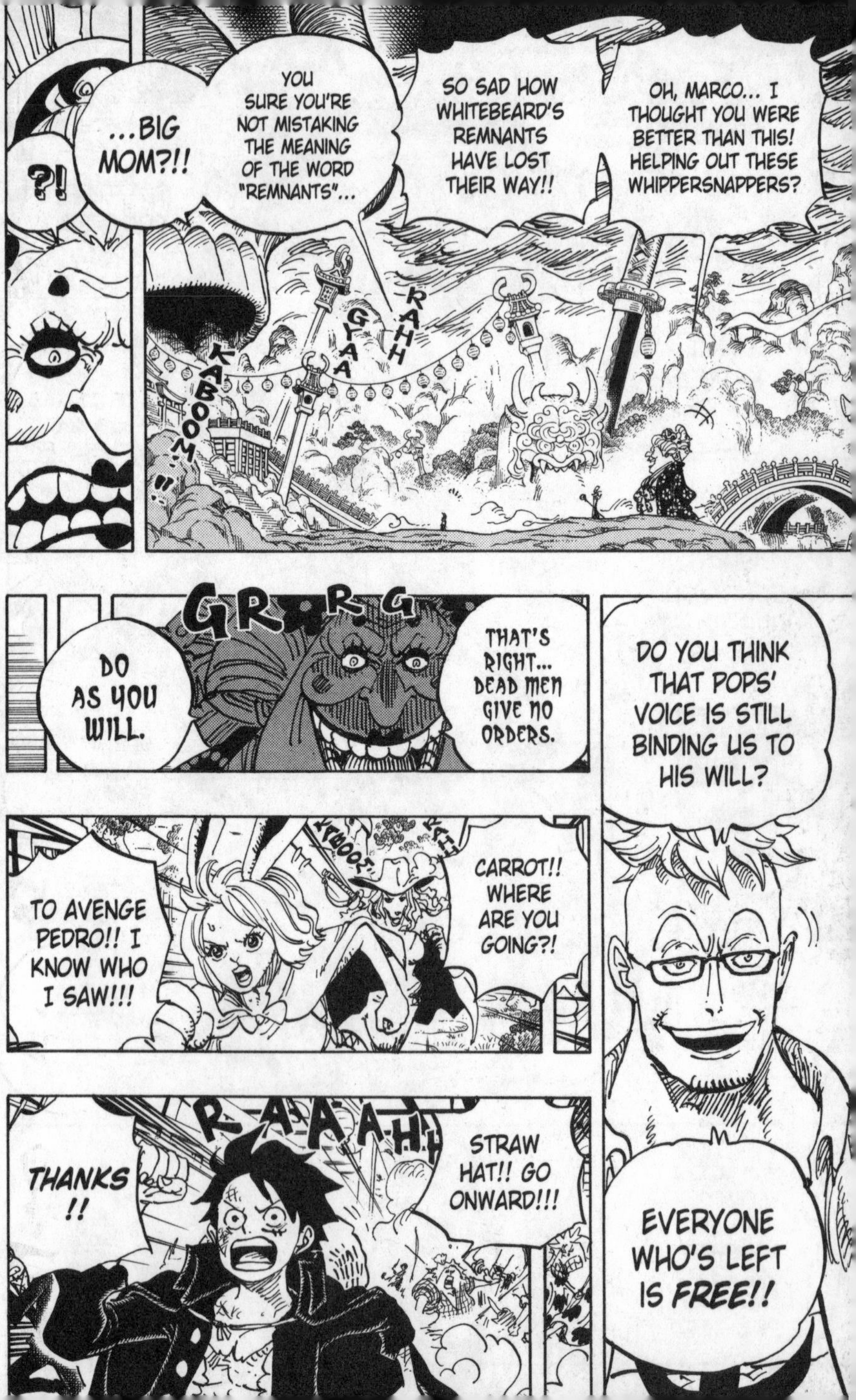
OH, MARCO... I THOUGHT YOU WERE BETTER THAN THIS! HELPING OUT THESE WHIPPERSNAPPERS?
SO SAD HOW WHITEBEARD'S REMNANTS HAVE LOST THEIR WAY!!
YOU SURE YOU'RE NOT MISTAKING THE MEANING OF THE WORD "REMNANTS"...
RAHHH
GYAAA
KABOOM!!
...BIG MOM?!!
?!
DO YOU THINK THAT POPS' VOICE IS STILL BINDING US TO HIS WILL?
EVERYONE WHO'S LEFT IS FREE!!
GRRRG
THAT'S RIGHT... DEAD MEN GIVE NO ORDERS.
DO AS YOU WILL.
CARROT!! WHERE ARE YOU GOING?!
TO AVENGE PEDRO!! I KNOW WHO I SAW!!!
STRAW HAT!! GO ONWARD!!!
RAAAAH
THANKS!!

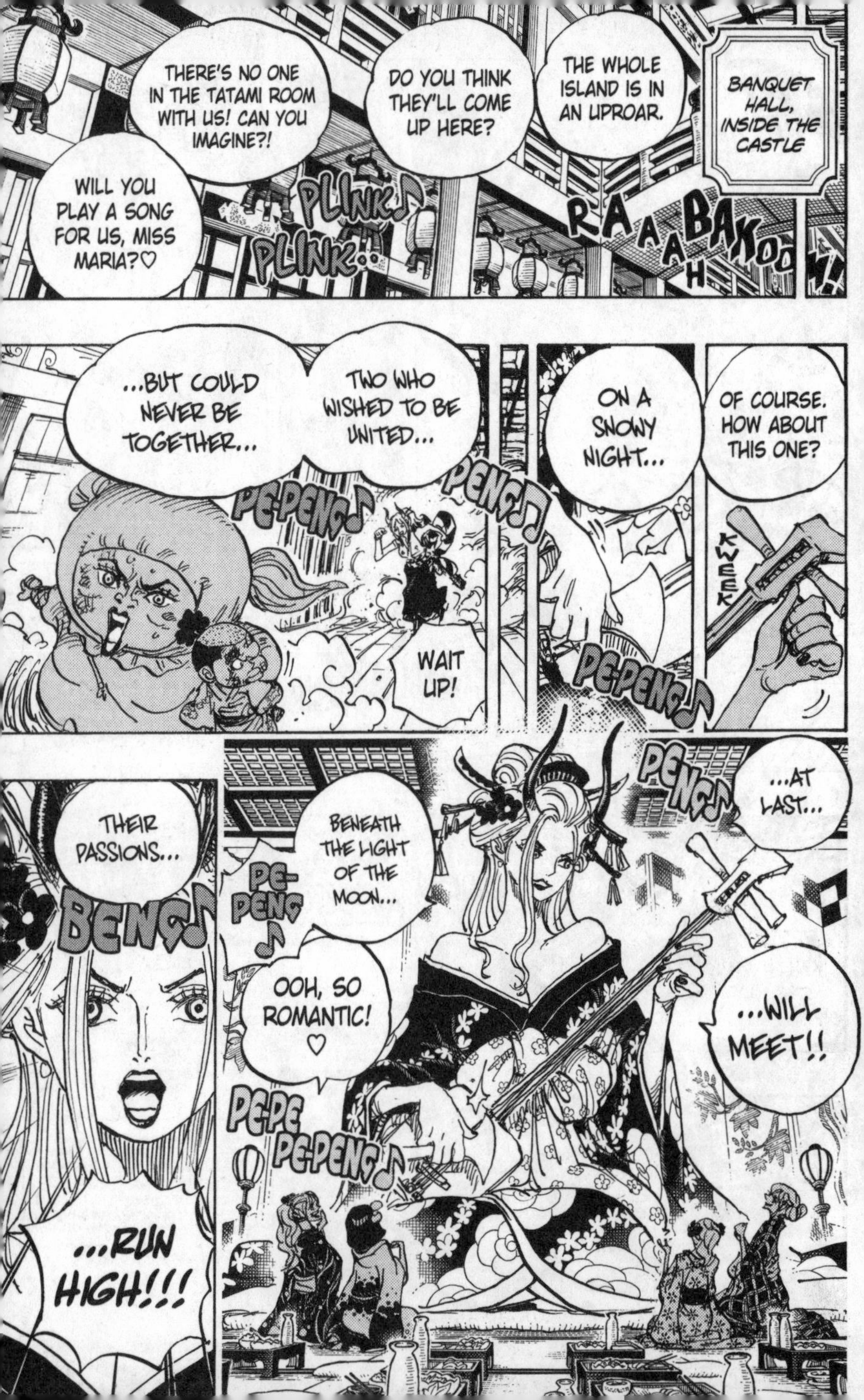

BANQUET HALL, INSIDE THE CASTLE
RAAAAH
BAKOOM!!
THE WHOLE ISLAND IS IN AN UPROAR.
DO YOU THINK THEY'LL COME UP HERE?
THERE'S NO ONE IN THE TATAMI ROOM WITH US! CAN YOU IMAGINE?!
PLINK♪
PLINK..
WILL YOU PLAY A SONG FOR US, MISS MARIA?♡
OF COURSE. HOW ABOUT THIS ONE?
KWEEK
ON A SNOWY NIGHT...
PE-PENG♪
TWO WHO WISHED TO BE UNITED...
PENG♪
...BUT COULD NEVER BE TOGETHER...
PE-PENG♪
WAIT UP!
PENG♪
...AT LAST...
BENEATH THE LIGHT OF THE MOON...
PE-PENG♪
...WILL MEET!!
OOH, SO ROMANTIC! ♡
PE-PE PE-PENG♪
THEIR PASSIONS...
BENG♪
...RUN HIGH!!!

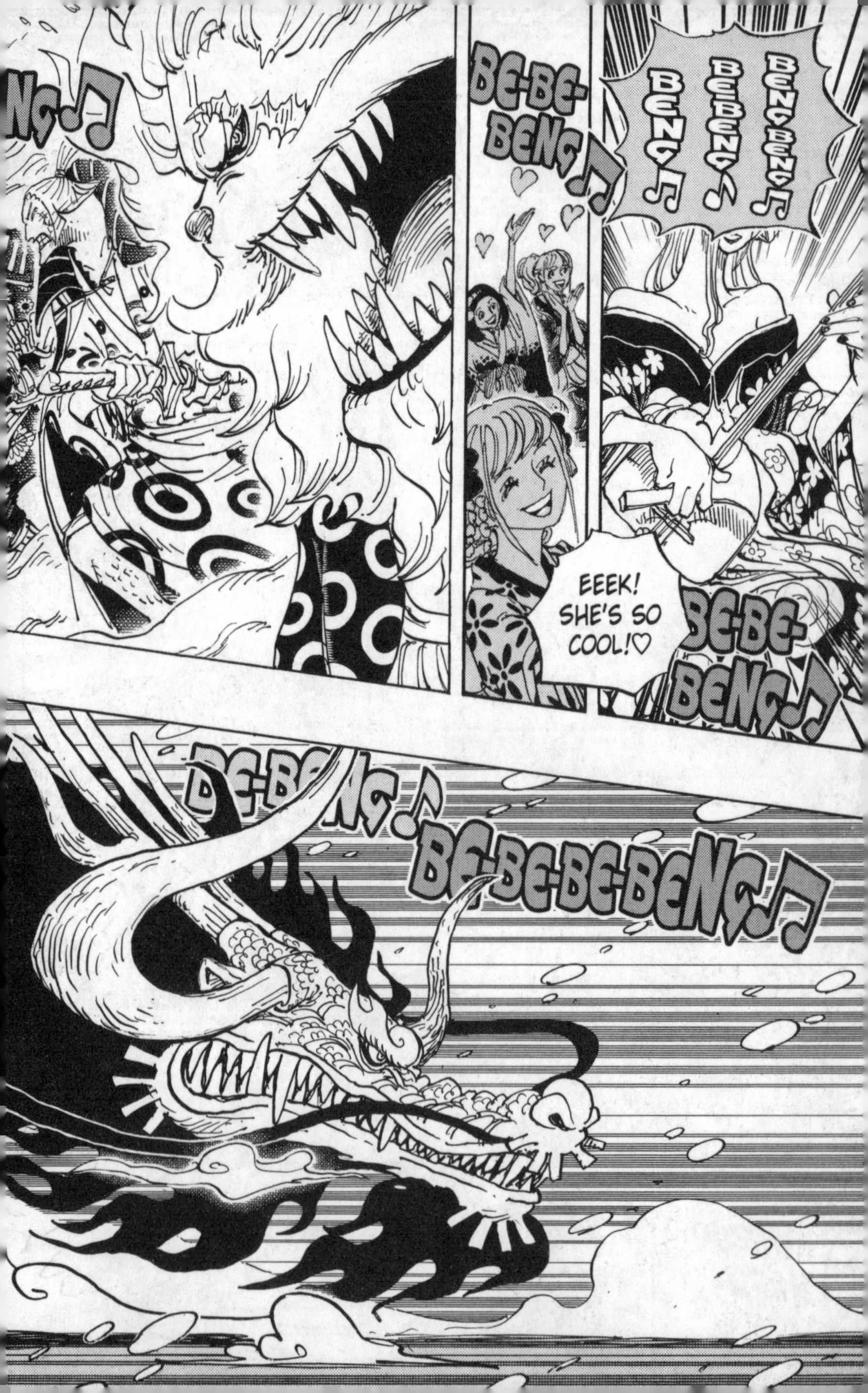
BENGBENG♫
BEBENG♫
BENG♫
BE-BE-BENG♫
BE-BE-BENG♫
EEEK! SHE'S SO COOL!♡
NG♫
BE-BENG♫
BE-BE-BE-BENG♫

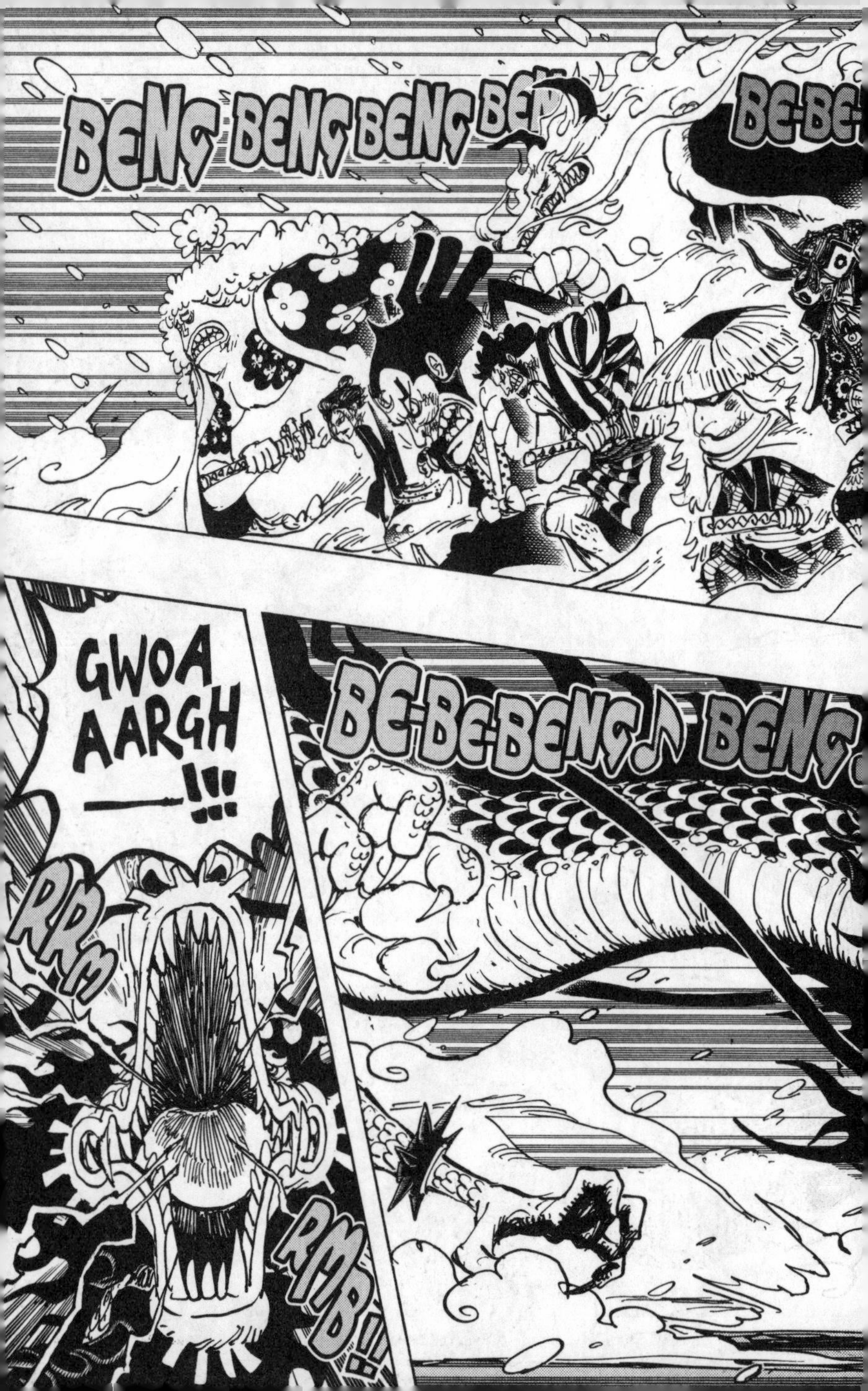
BE-BE-
BENG BENG BENG BEN
BE-BE-BENG♪ BENG
GWOA AARGH —!!!
RRM
RMB!!

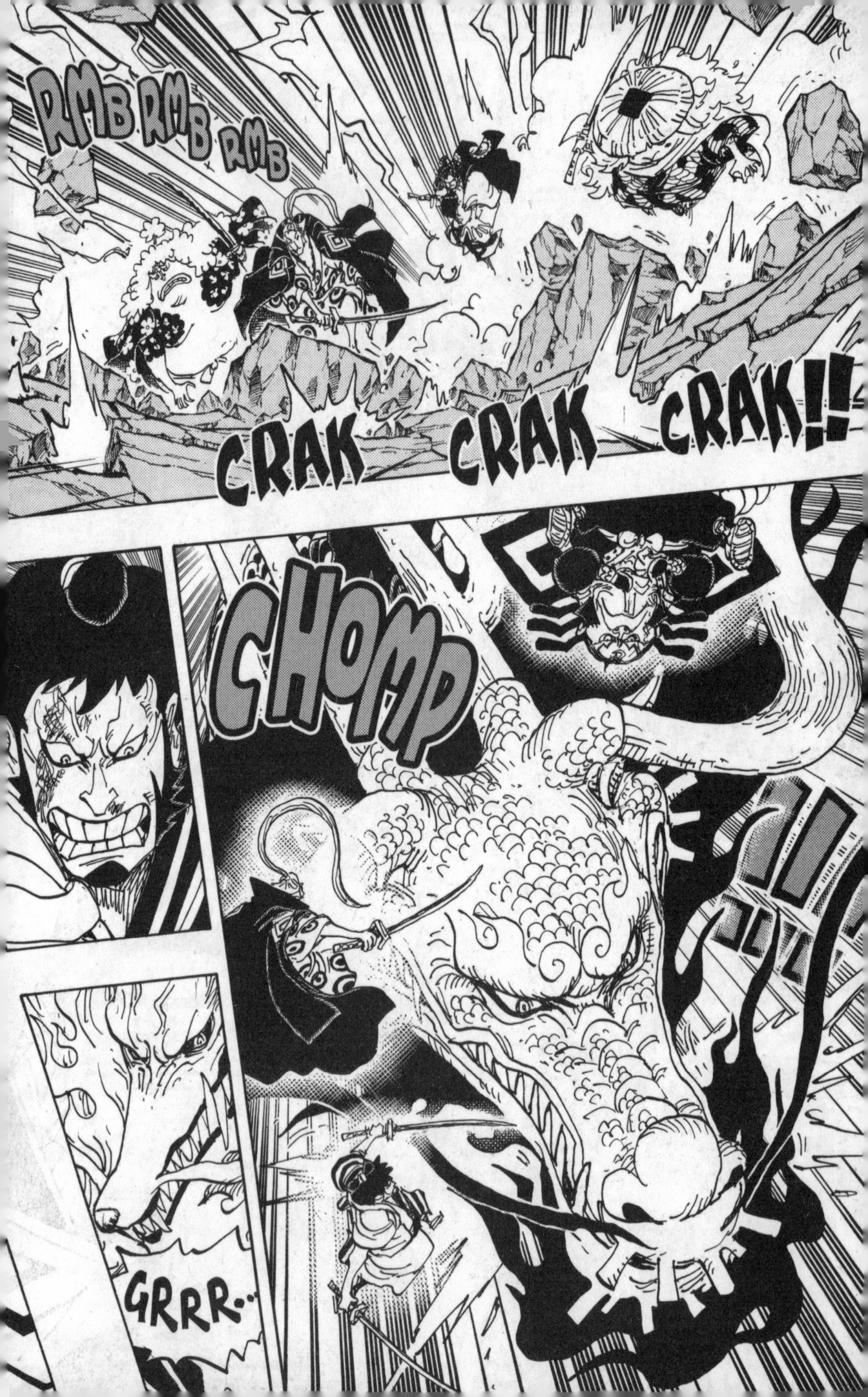
RMB RMB RMB
CRAK CRAK CRAK!!
CHOMP
GRRR...

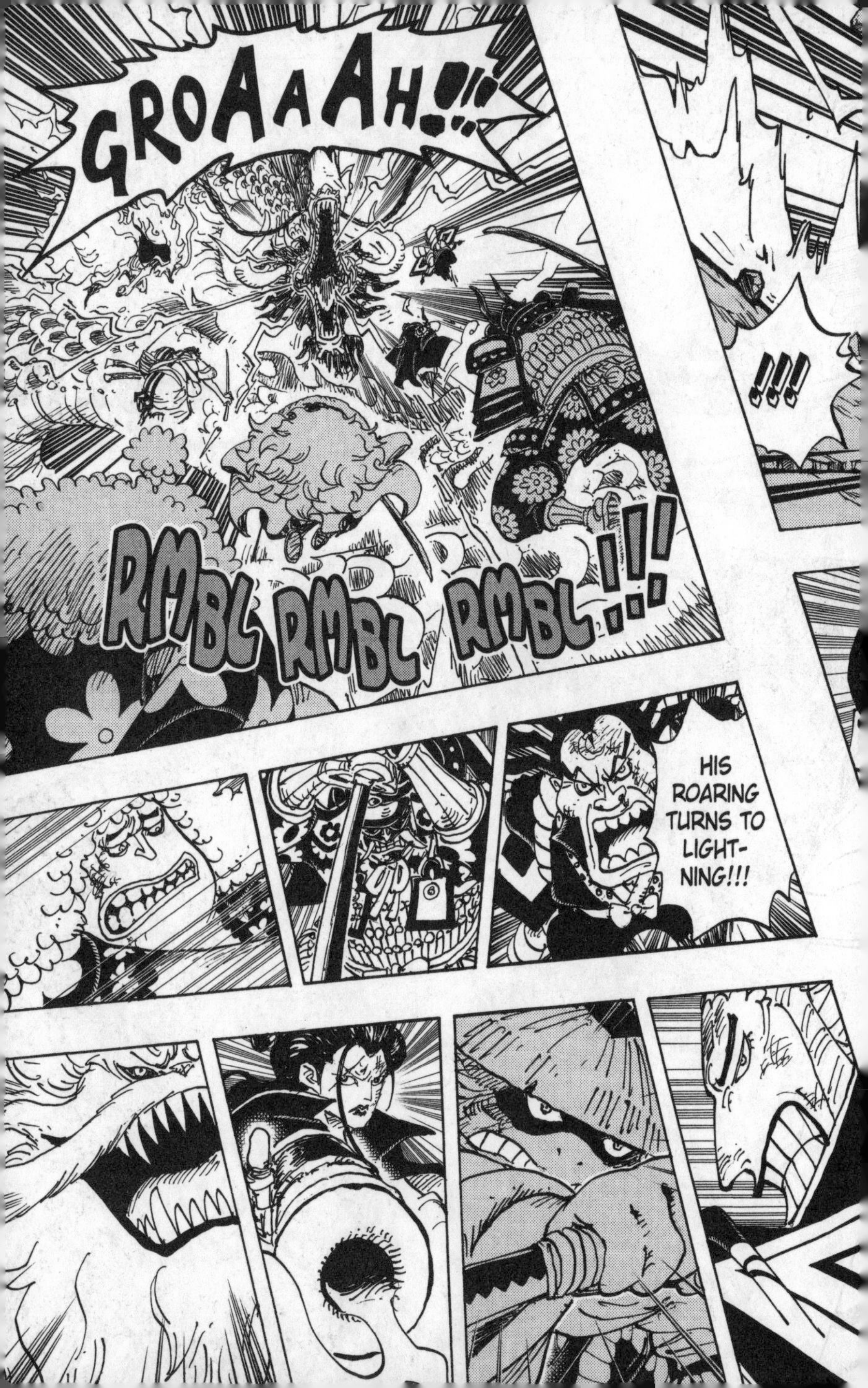
GROAAAH!!!
!!!
RMBL RMBL RMBL!!!
HIS ROARING TURNS TO LIGHT-NING!!!

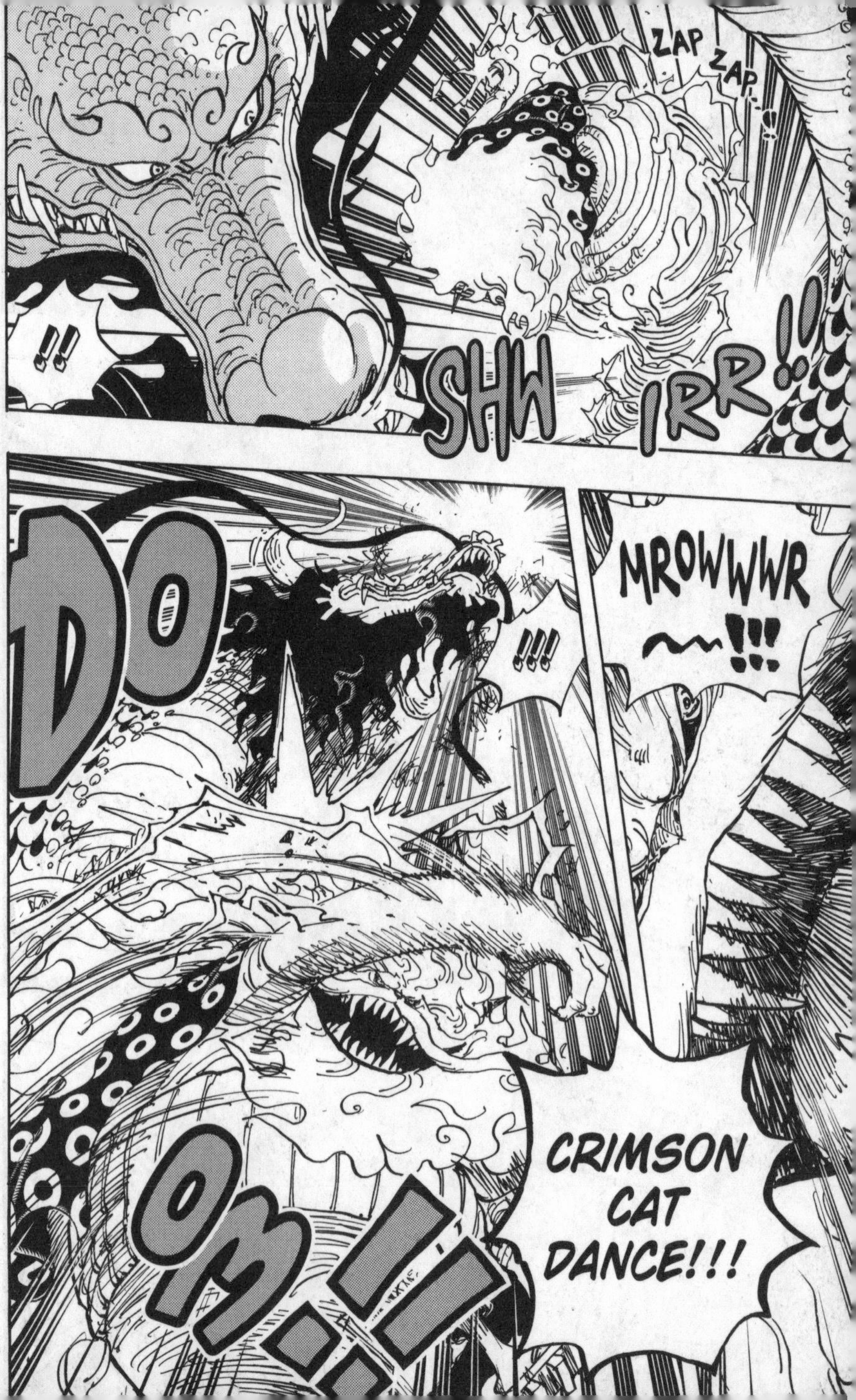
ZAP ZAP
SHWIRR!!
!!
MROWWWR ~~!!!
CRIMSON CAT DANCE!!!
!!!
DOOM!!

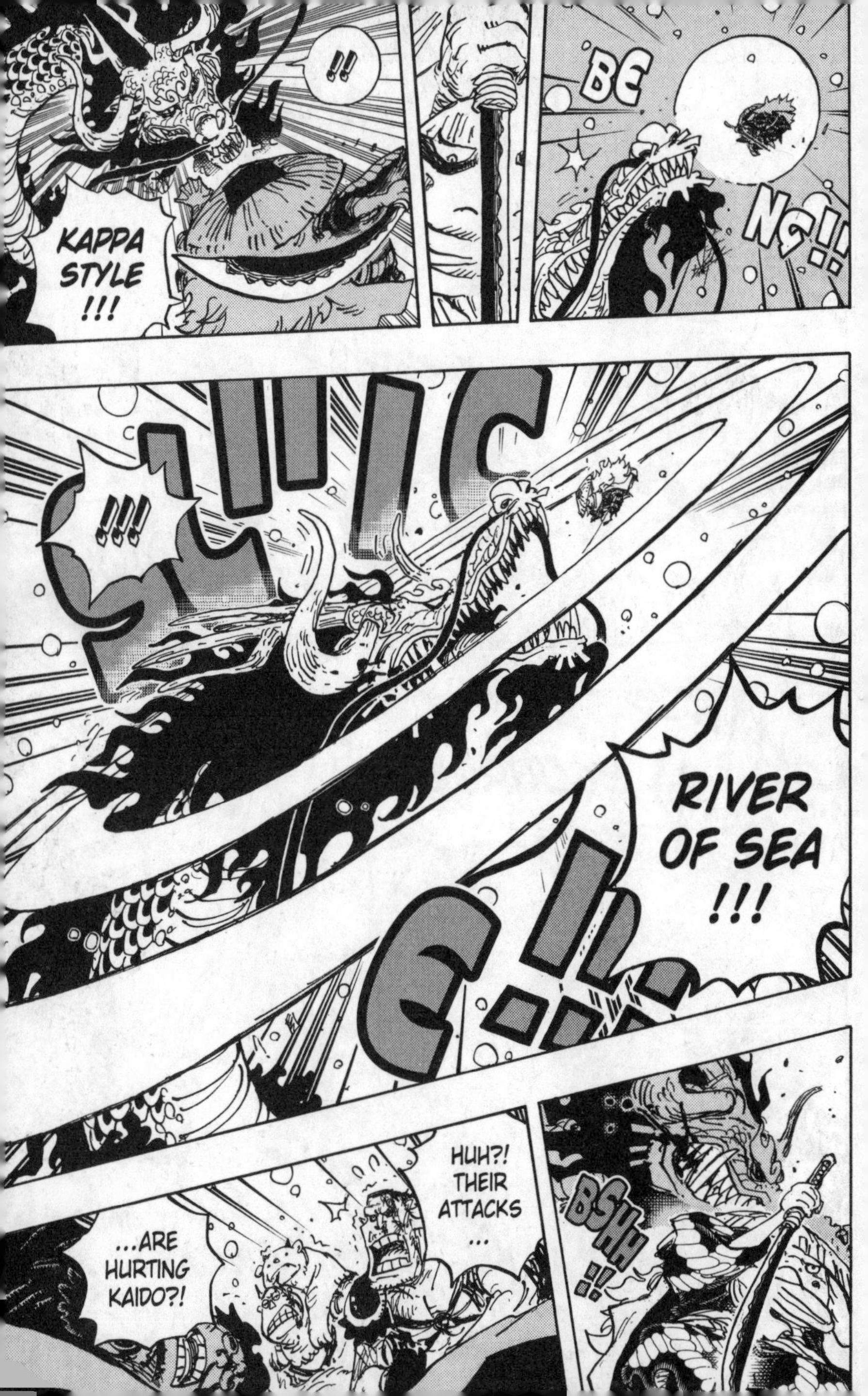
BENG!!!
!!
KAPPA STYLE!!!
RIVER OF SEA!!!
!!!
BSHH!!
HUH?! THEIR ATTACKS...
...ARE HURTING KAIDO?!

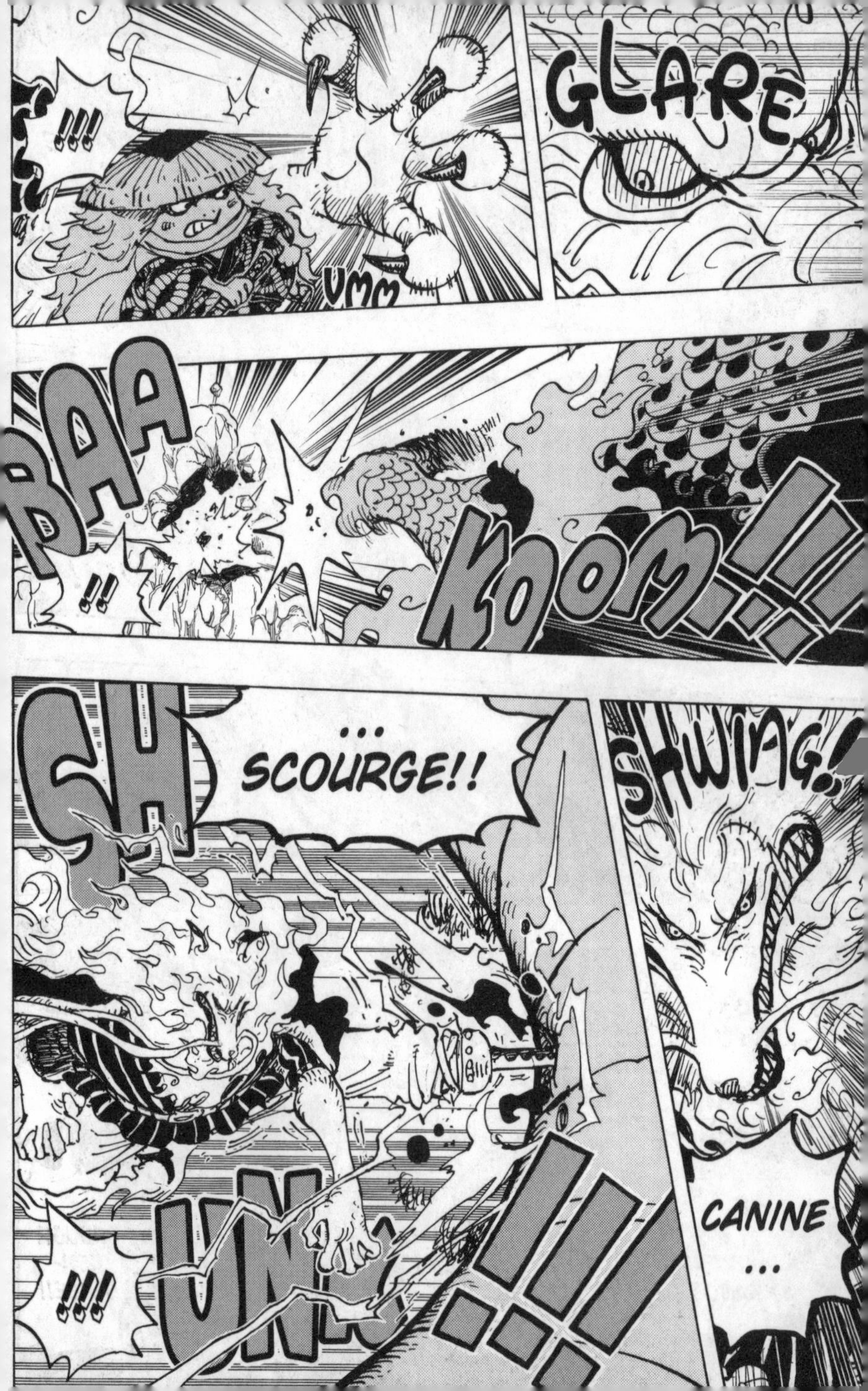
GLARE
!!!
UMM
KOOM...!!!
BAA
!!
SHWING!!
CANINE ...
... SCOURGE!!
SH
UN
!!!

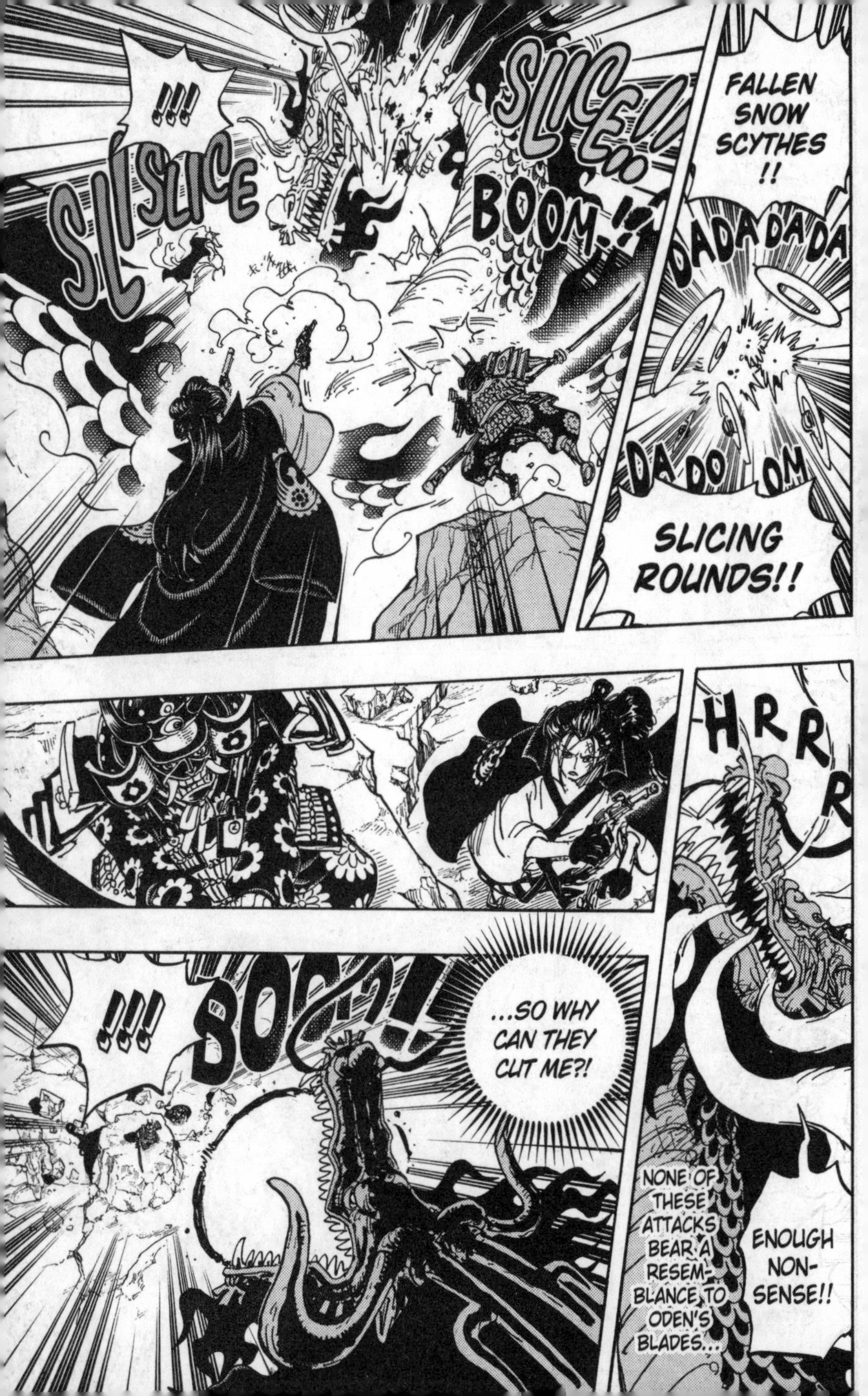
FALLEN SNOW SCYTHES!!
DADADADADA
DA DO OM
SLICING ROUNDS!!
SLICE!!
!!!
BOOM!!
SLISLICE
HRRRR
NONE OF THESE ATTACKS BEAR A RESEM-BLANCE TO ODEN'S BLADES...
ENOUGH NON-SENSE!!
...SO WHY CAN THEY CUT ME?!
!!!

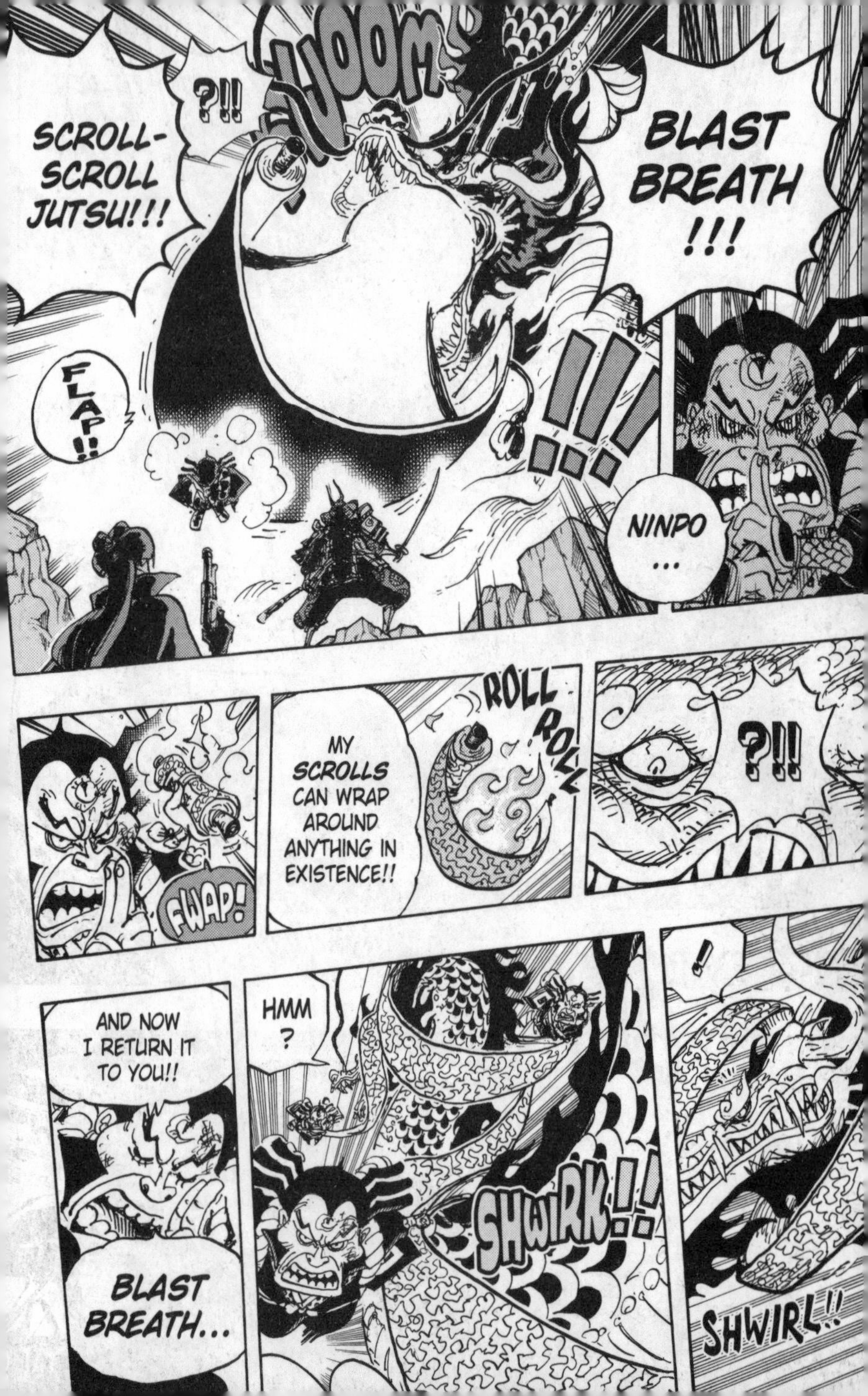
WOOM
BLAST BREATH!!!
!!!!
NINPO...
?!!
SCROLL-SCROLL JUTSU!!!
FLAP!!
?!!
ROLL ROLL
MY SCROLLS CAN WRAP AROUND ANYTHING IN EXISTENCE!!
FWAP!
!
SHWIRL!!
HMM ?
SHWIRK!!
AND NOW I RETURN IT TO YOU!!
BLAST BREATH...

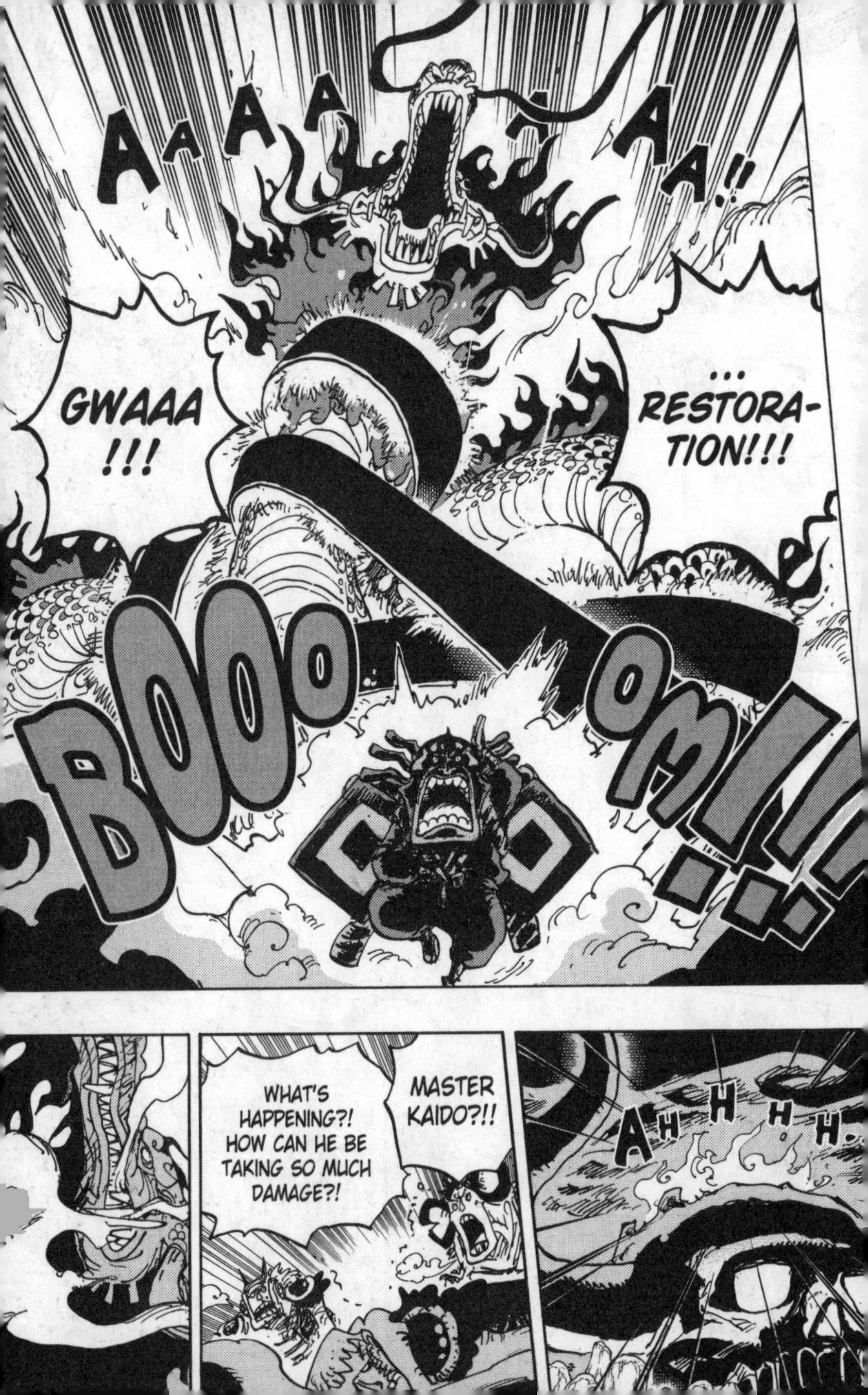
AAAAAAAA!!
... RESTORATION!!!
GWAAA!!!
BOOOOOM!!!!
AHHHH.
MASTER KAIDO?!!
WHAT'S HAPPENING?! HOW CAN HE BE TAKING SO MUCH DAMAGE?!

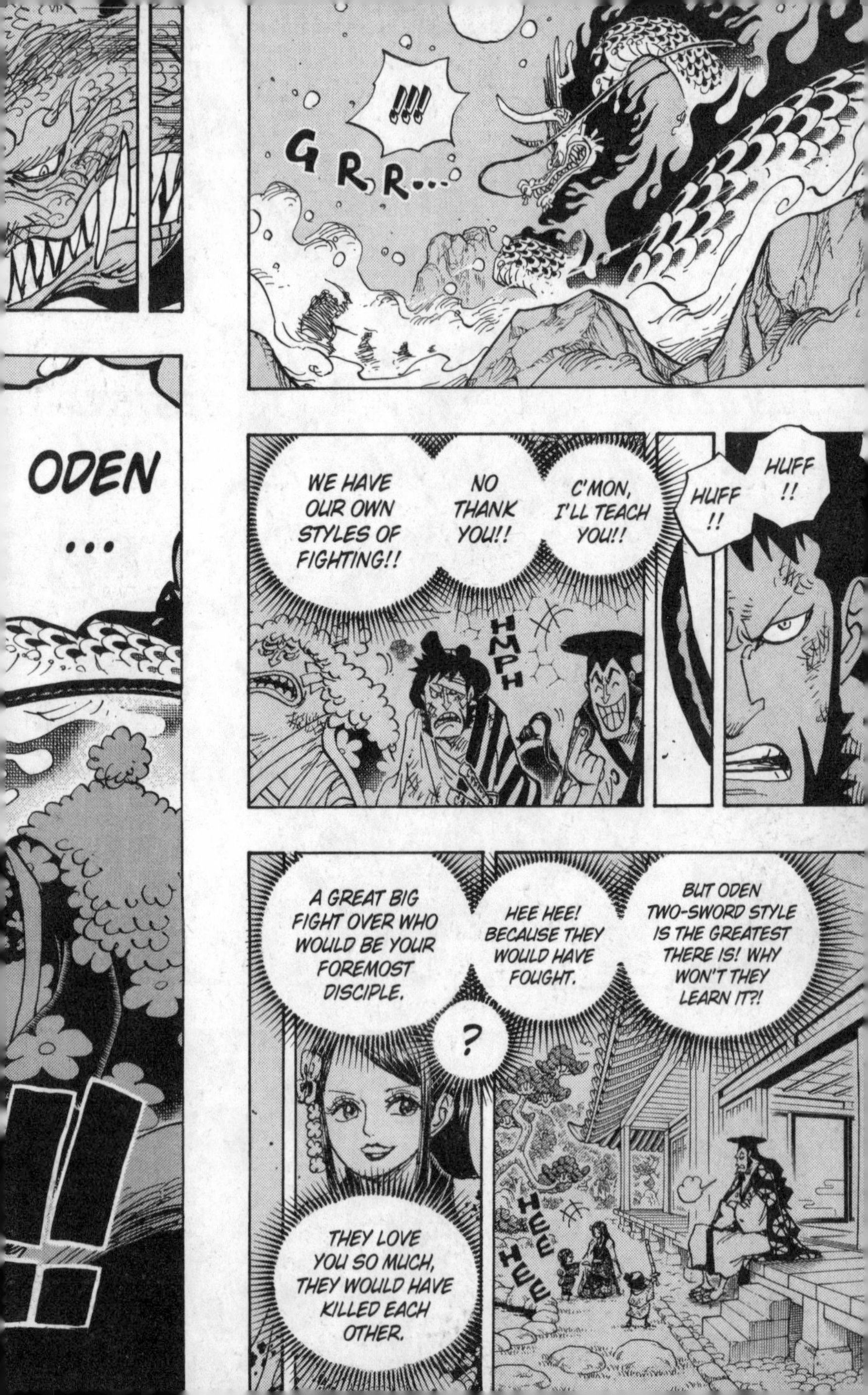
!!!
GRR...
HUFF !!
HUFF !!
C'MON, I'LL TEACH YOU!!
NO THANK YOU!!
WE HAVE OUR OWN STYLES OF FIGHTING!!
HMPH
BUT ODEN TWO-SWORD STYLE IS THE GREATEST THERE IS! WHY WON'T THEY LEARN IT?!
HEE HEE
HEE HEE! BECAUSE THEY WOULD HAVE FOUGHT.
A GREAT BIG FIGHT OVER WHO WOULD BE YOUR FOREMOST DISCIPLE.
?
THEY LOVE YOU SO MUCH, THEY WOULD HAVE KILLED EACH OTHER.
ODEN ...
!!

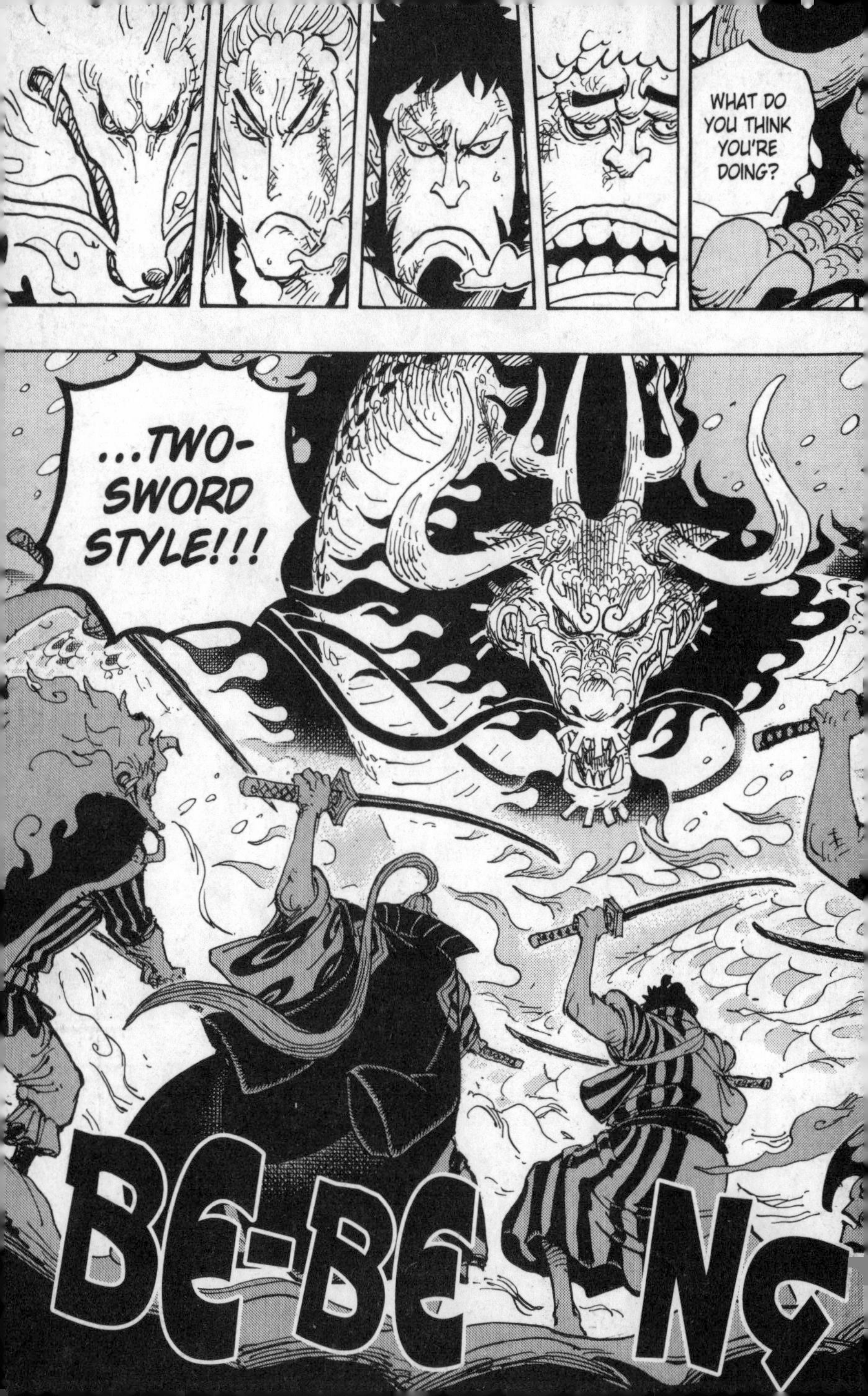
WHAT DO YOU THINK YOU'RE DOING?
...TWO-SWORD STYLE!!!
BG-BG-NG

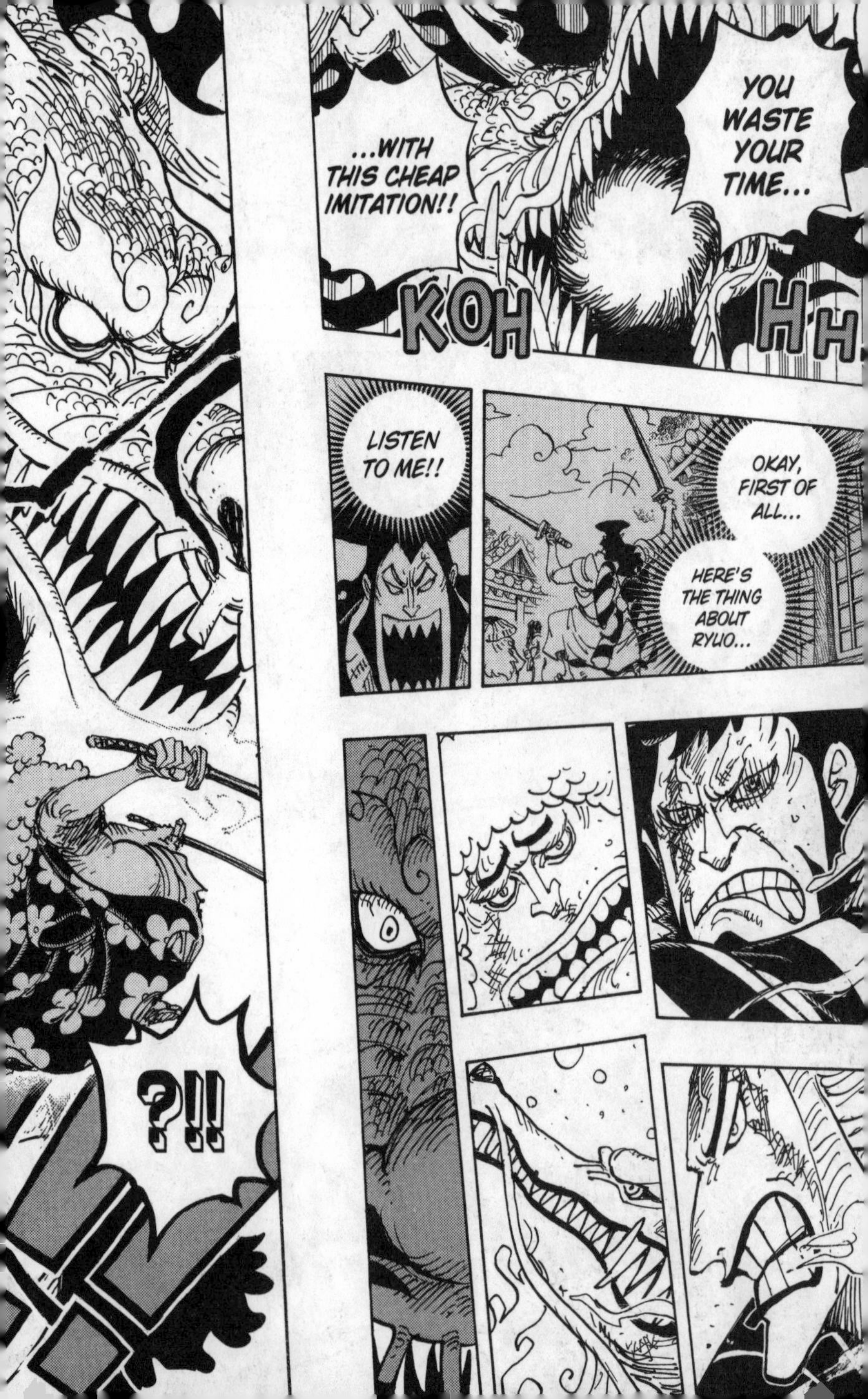
YOU WASTE YOUR TIME...
...WITH THIS CHEAP IMITATION!!
KOH
HH
OKAY, FIRST OF ALL...
HERE'S THE THING ABOUT RYUO...
LISTEN TO ME!!
?!!

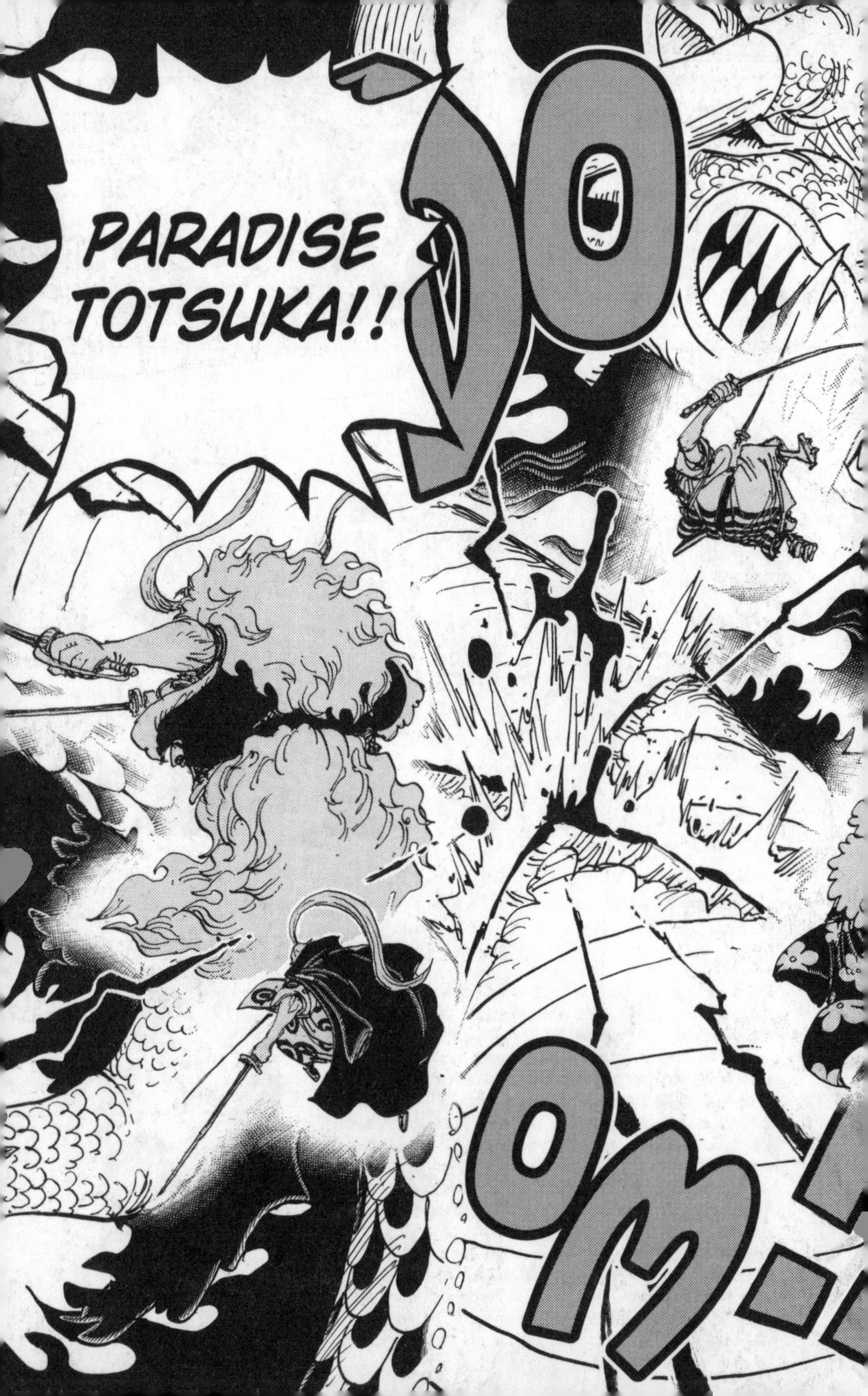
PARADISE TOTSUKA!!

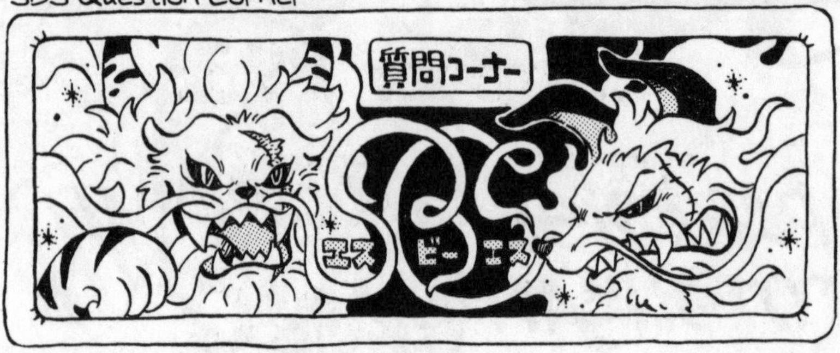
質問コーナー
エス ビー エス

(I ♡ OP, Ishikawa)

Q: Please draw the future versions of the pervy cook…I mean, Sanji at age 40 and age 60.

--Gum-Flame Fruit

A: Okay. I got lots of requests for this one. Here you go!

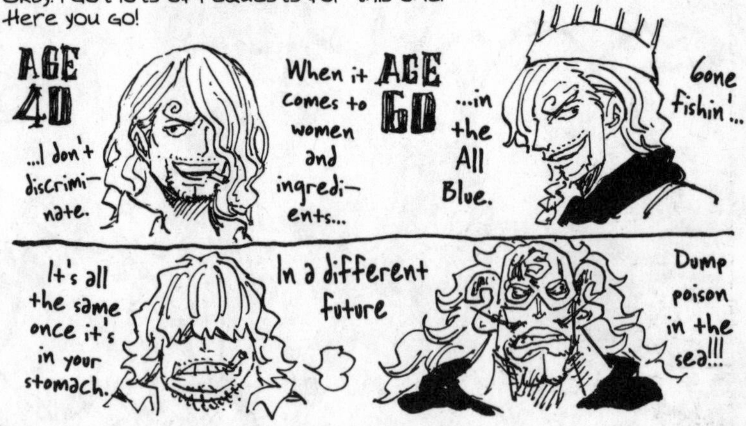
AGE 40
...I don't discrimi-nate.
When it comes to women and ingredi-ents...
AGE 60
...in the All Blue.
Gone fishin'...
It's all the same once it's in your stomach.
In a different future
Dump poison in the sea!!!

Q: Odacchi!! Question for you!! In chapter 962, "Daimyo and Vassals," young Izo is shown with a katana, and young Kiku with a gun. That's the opposite from what they use now! Was there a meaning behind this?

--Yuu-kun

A: In that panel, Kiku's just holding her brother's gun for him. That's a real small detail for you to pick out! Anyway, after their father was tried as a criminal, these two siblings had to work as entertainers and suffer the abuse and manipulation of cruel adults. They could only survive by relying on each other. One of their skills was sharpshooting, and Izo was a master at it. But he was never confident with the katana. Later, when they were on Whitebeard's ship, Izo was hitting targets to entertain the crew, when Vista the Flower Sword said to him, "Use your best skill to protect your master!!" If a samurai is sworn to protect his master, why fixate on the sword if you're not good at it? "Samurai" is meant to be a way of life. So Izo put down the sword and picked up the gun instead.

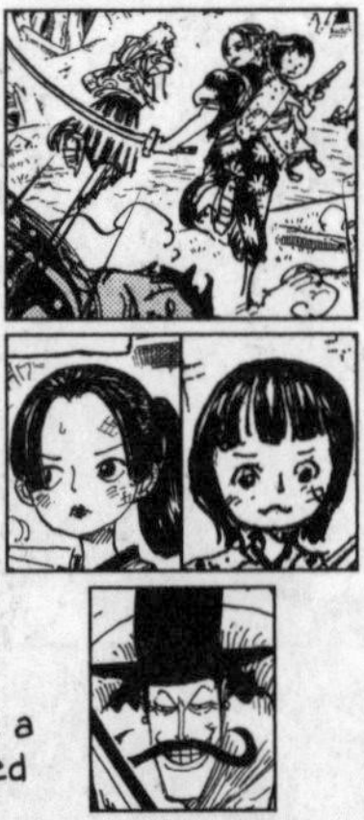

Chapter 993:

THE DREAM OF WANO

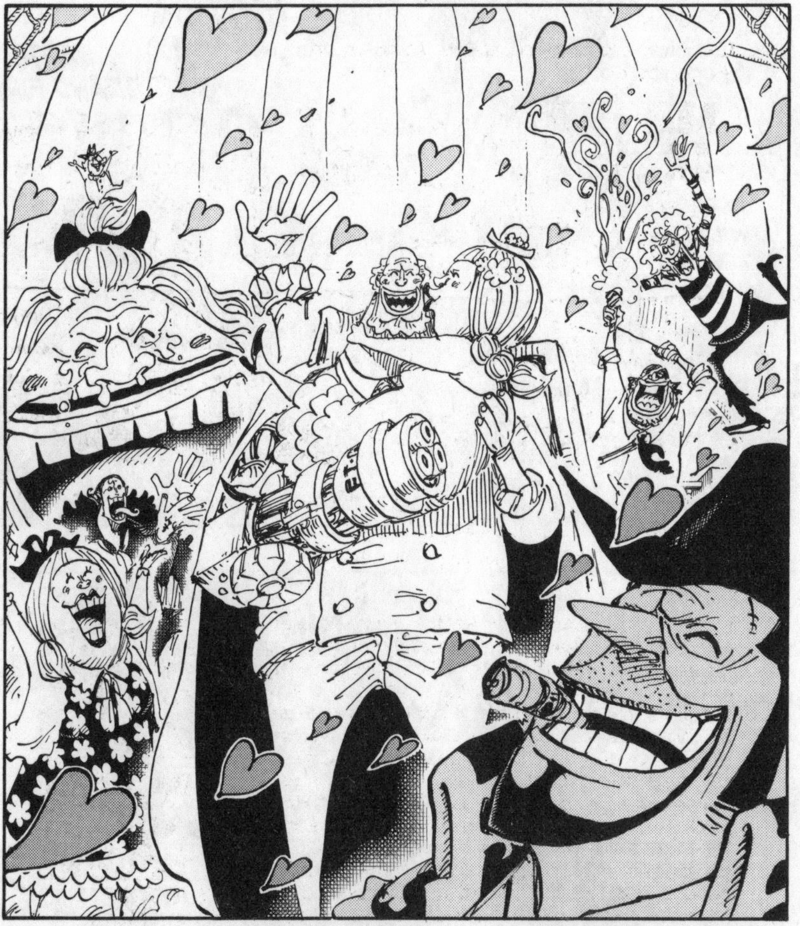

GANG BEGE'S OH MY FAMILY
VOL. 36: "GOTTI AND LOLA'S WEDDING♡"

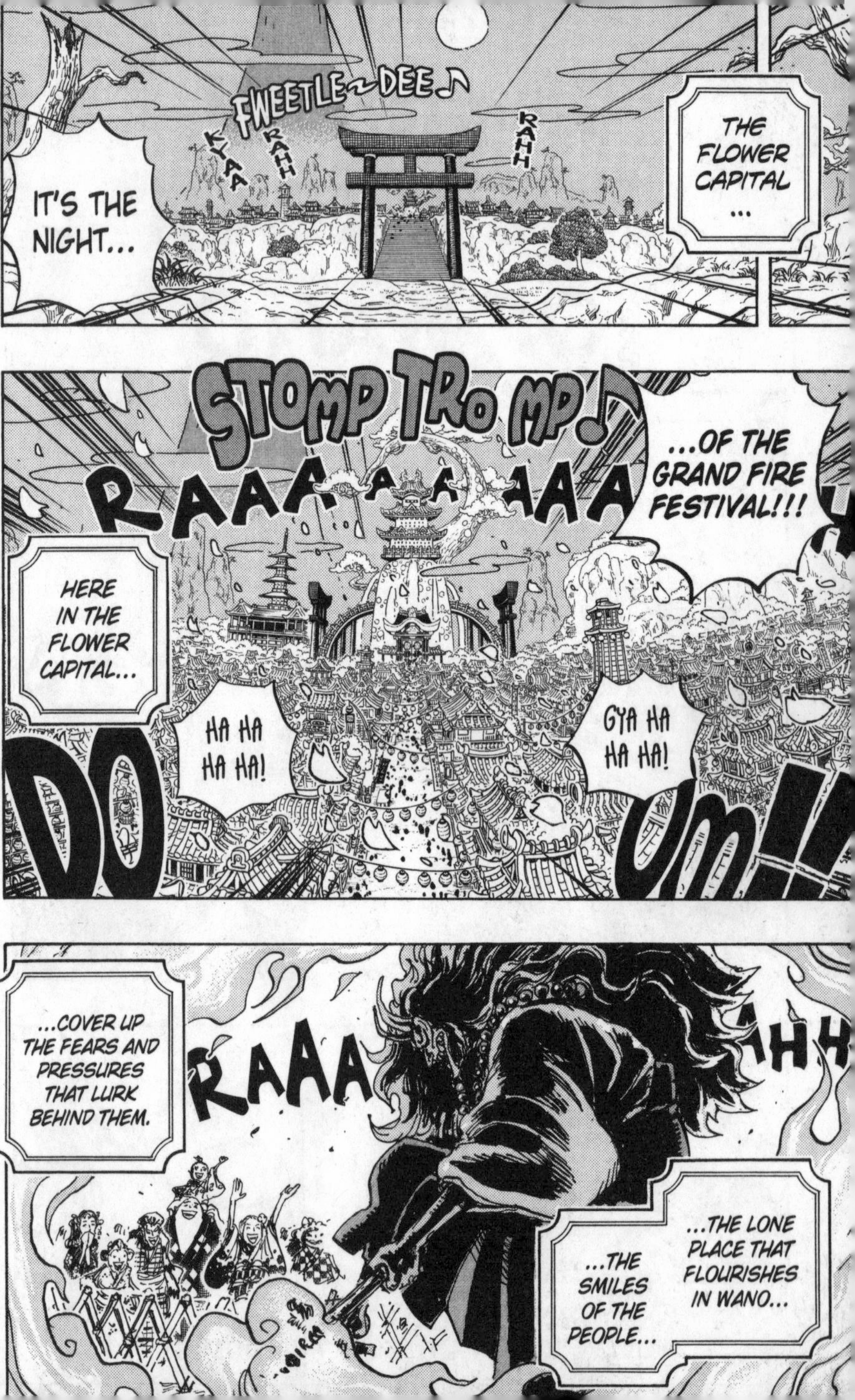
THE FLOWER CAPITAL ...
FWEETLE~DEE♪
RAHH
RAHH
KYAA
IT'S THE NIGHT...
STOMP TROMP♪
...OF THE GRAND FIRE FESTIVAL!!!
RAAAAAAAA
HERE IN THE FLOWER CAPITAL...
GYA HA HA HA!
HA HA HA HA!
DO
UM!!
...THE LONE PLACE THAT FLOURISHES IN WANO...
...THE SMILES OF THE PEOPLE...
AHH
RAAA
...COVER UP THE FEARS AND PRESSURES THAT LURK BEHIND THEM.

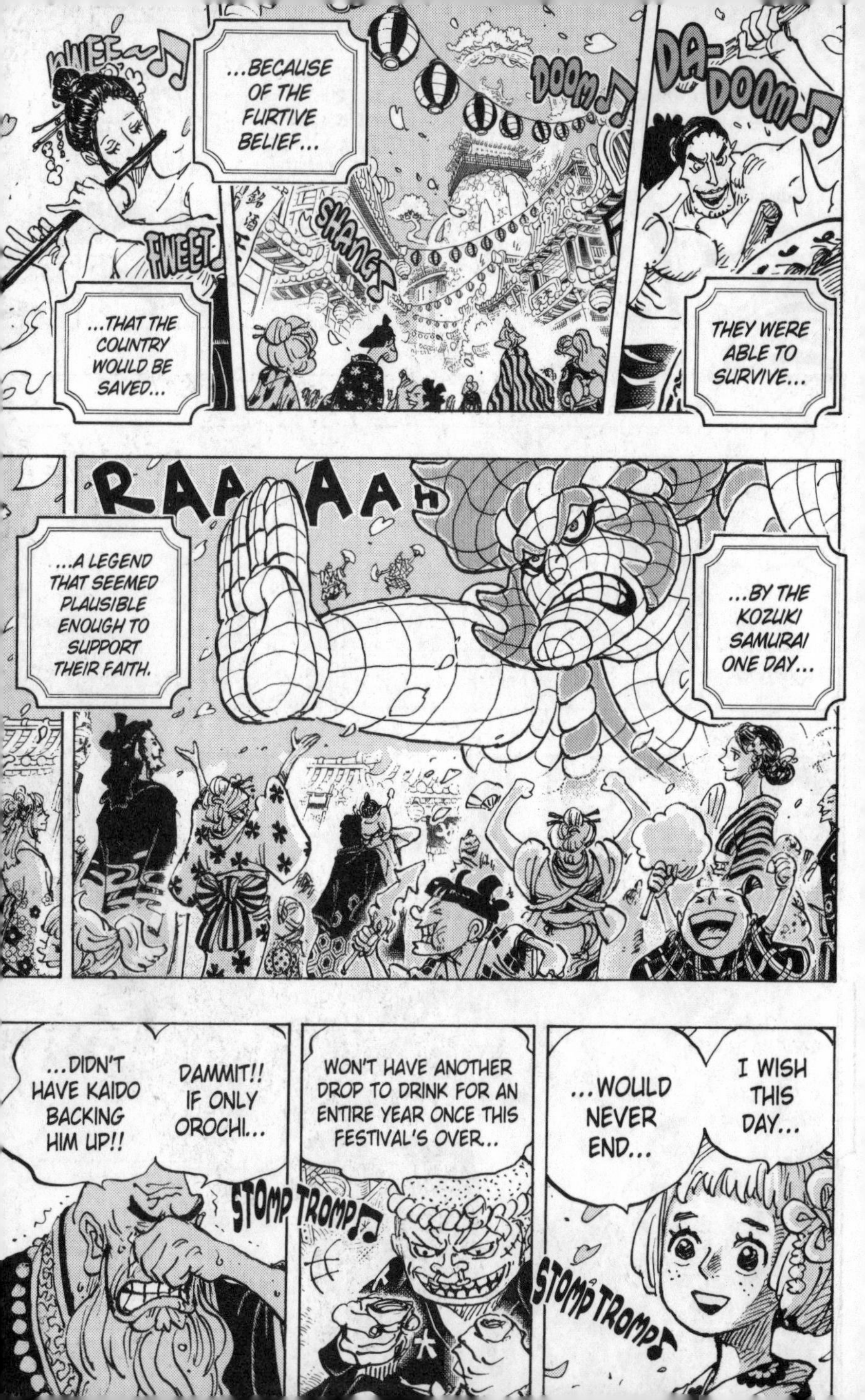
DA-DOOM♪
THEY WERE ABLE TO SURVIVE...
DOOM♪
...BECAUSE OF THE FURTIVE BELIEF...
SHANG♪
WHEE~♪
FWEET♪
...THAT THE COUNTRY WOULD BE SAVED...
RAAAAAH
...BY THE KOZUKI SAMURAI ONE DAY...
...A LEGEND THAT SEEMED PLAUSIBLE ENOUGH TO SUPPORT THEIR FAITH.
I WISH THIS DAY...
...WOULD NEVER END...
STOMP TROMP♪
WON'T HAVE ANOTHER DROP TO DRINK FOR AN ENTIRE YEAR ONCE THIS FESTIVAL'S OVER...
STOMP TROMP♪
DAMMIT!! IF ONLY OROCHI...
...DIDN'T HAVE KAIDO BACKING HIM UP!!

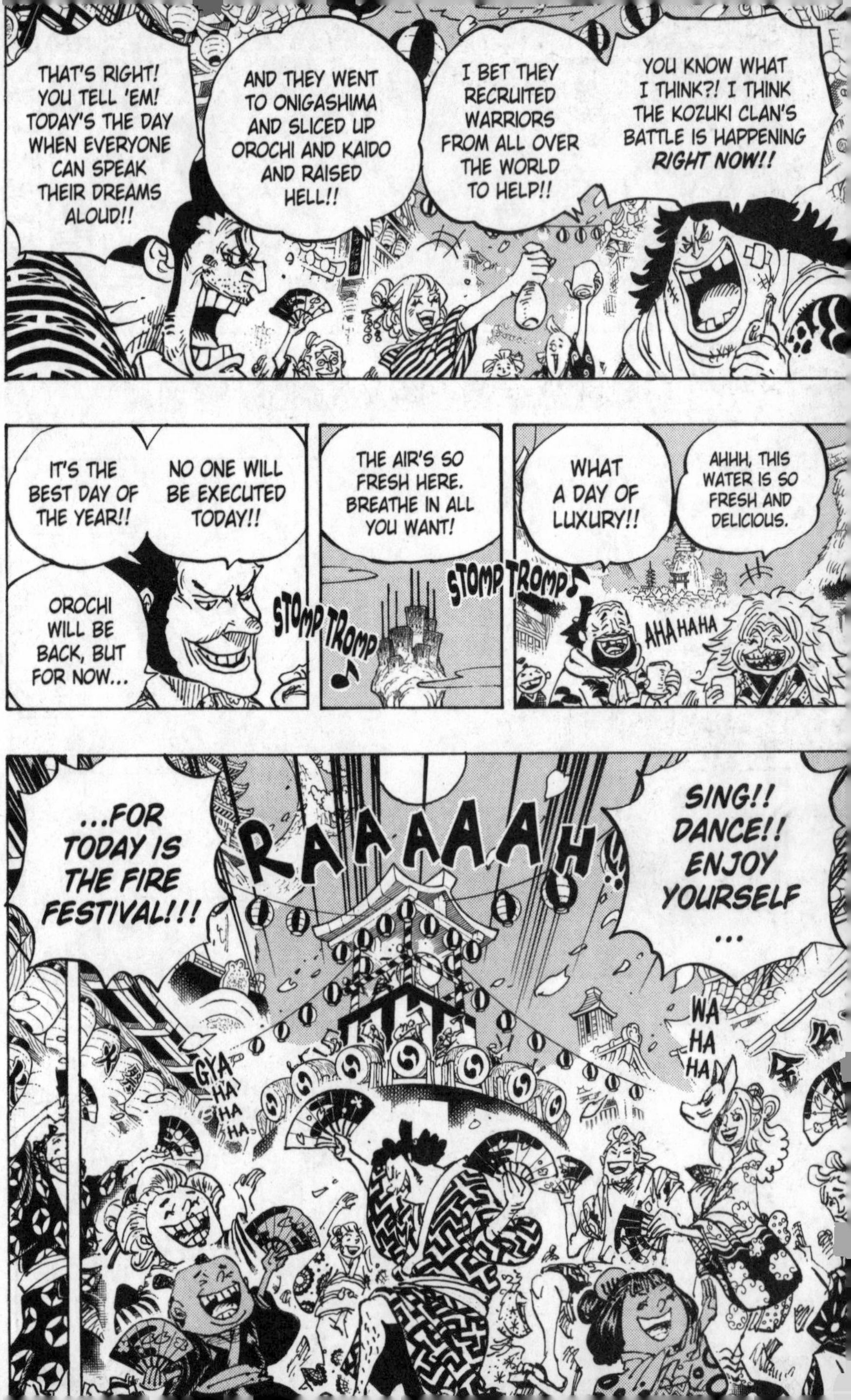
YOU KNOW WHAT I THINK?! I THINK THE KOZUKI CLAN'S BATTLE IS HAPPENING *RIGHT NOW!!*
I BET THEY RECRUITED WARRIORS FROM ALL OVER THE WORLD TO HELP!!
AND THEY WENT TO ONIGASHIMA AND SLICED UP OROCHI AND KAIDO AND RAISED HELL!!
THAT'S RIGHT! YOU TELL 'EM! TODAY'S THE DAY WHEN EVERYONE CAN SPEAK THEIR DREAMS ALOUD!!
AHHH, THIS WATER IS SO FRESH AND DELICIOUS.
WHAT A DAY OF LUXURY!!
AHAHAHA
STOMP TROMP
THE AIR'S SO FRESH HERE. BREATHE IN ALL YOU WANT!
STOMP TROMP
NO ONE WILL BE EXECUTED TODAY!!
IT'S THE BEST DAY OF THE YEAR!!
OROCHI WILL BE BACK, BUT FOR NOW...
SING!! DANCE!! ENJOY YOURSELF ...
RAAAAAH
...FOR TODAY IS THE FIRE FESTIVAL!!!
WA HA HA
GYA HA HA HA

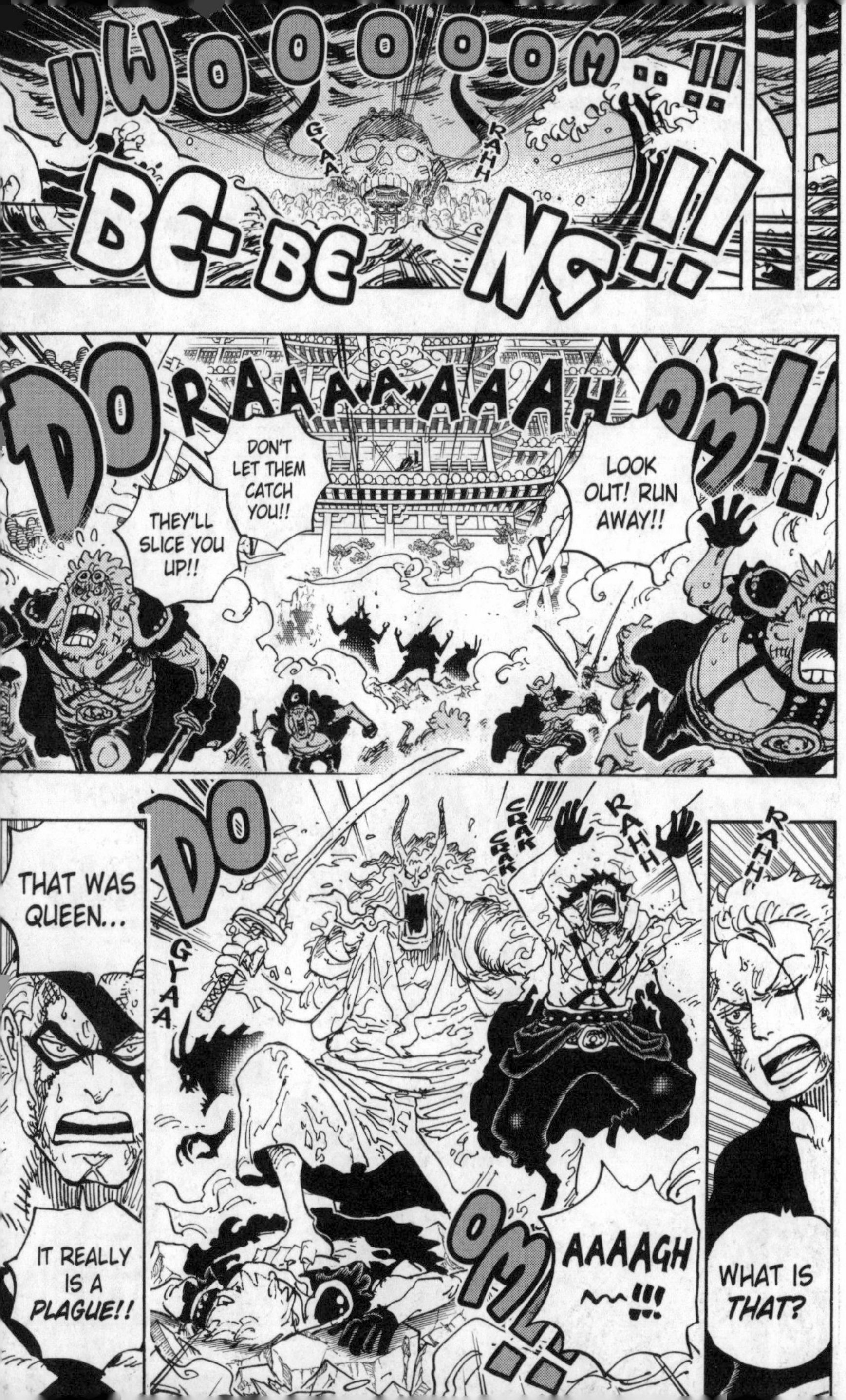
UWOOOOOOM..!!
RAHH
GIYAA
BE-BE-NG..!!
DORAAAAAAHOM!!
LOOK OUT! RUN AWAY!!
DON'T LET THEM CATCH YOU!!
THEY'LL SLICE YOU UP!!
RAHH
WHAT IS *THAT?*
DO
OM..!!
RAHH
CRAK CRAK
GYAA
AAAAGH~!!!
THAT WAS QUEEN...
IT REALLY IS A *PLAGUE!!*

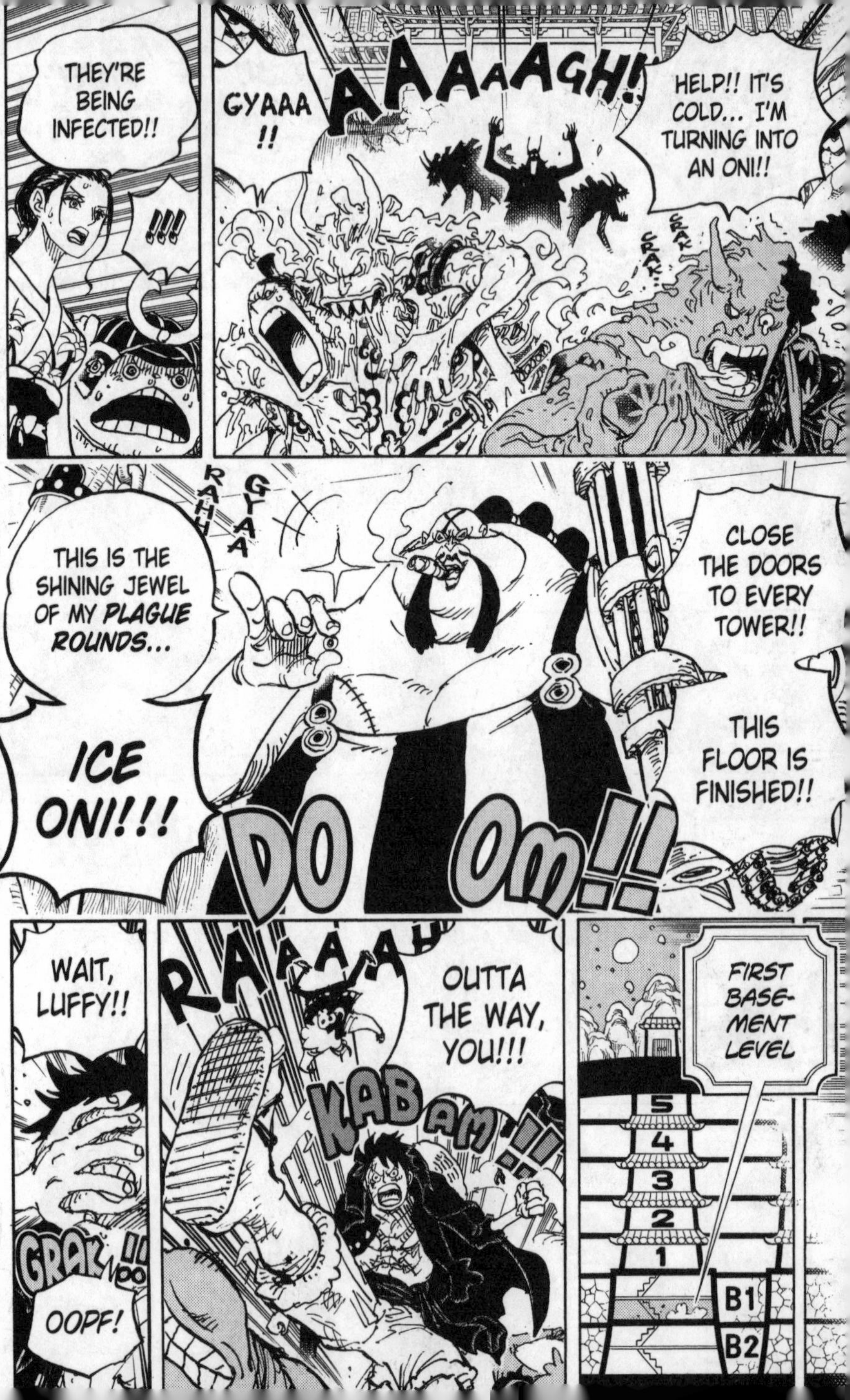
HELP!! IT'S COLD... I'M TURNING INTO AN ONI!!
CRAK CRAK
AAAAAGH!!
GYAAA !!
THEY'RE BEING INFECTED!!
!!!
CLOSE THE DOORS TO EVERY TOWER!!
THIS FLOOR IS FINISHED!!
DOOM!!
GYAAA
RAHH
THIS IS THE SHINING JEWEL OF MY PLAGUE ROUNDS...
ICE ONI!!!
FIRST BASEMENT LEVEL
5
4
3
2
1
B1
B2
RAAAAAH
OUTTA THE WAY, YOU!!!
KABAM!!
WAIT, LUFFY!!
GRAK!!
OOPF!

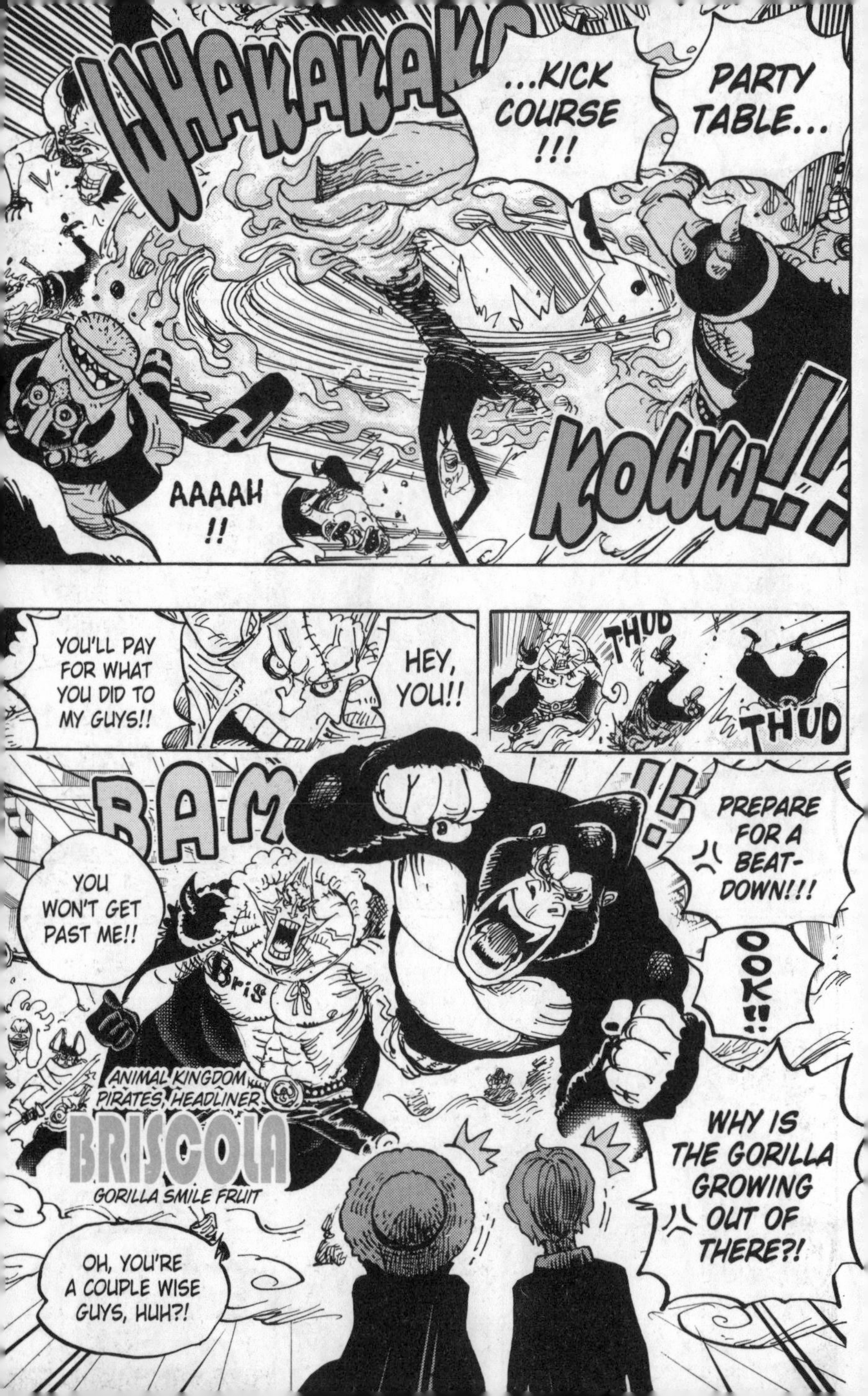
PARTY TABLE...
...KICK COURSE!!!
WHAKAKAK
KOWW!!!
AAAAH!!
THUD
THUD
HEY, YOU!!
YOU'LL PAY FOR WHAT YOU DID TO MY GUYS!!
PREPARE FOR A BEAT-DOWN!!!
OOK!!
BAM!!
YOU WON'T GET PAST ME!!
ANIMAL KINGDOM PIRATES, HEADLINER
BRISCOLA
GORILLA SMILE FRUIT
WHY IS THE GORILLA GROWING OUT OF THERE?!
OH, YOU'RE A COUPLE WISE GUYS, HUH?!

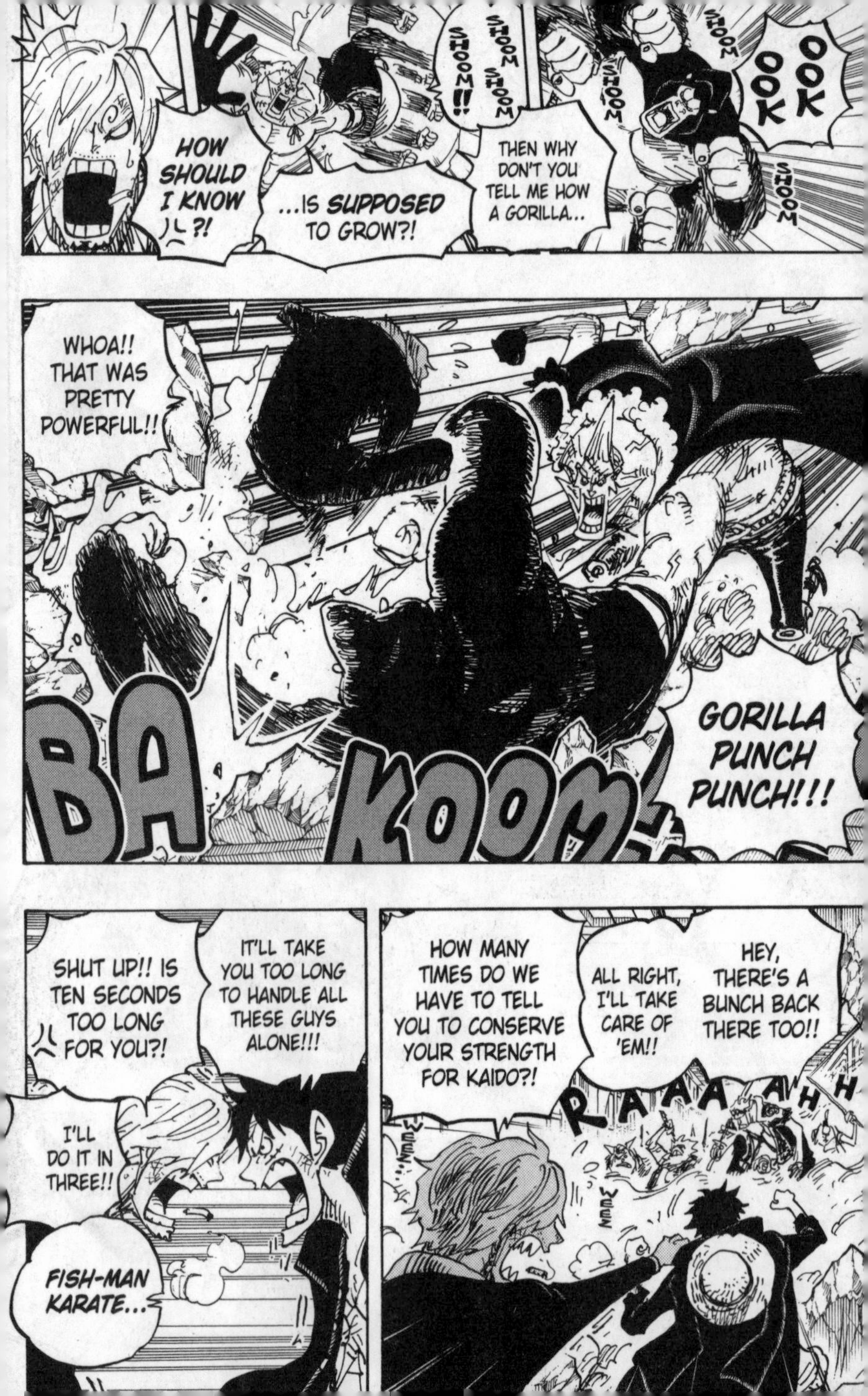
OOK OOK
SHOOM
SHOOM
SHOOM
THEN WHY DON'T YOU TELL ME HOW A GORILLA...
...IS SUPPOSED TO GROW?!
SHOOM SHOOM SHOOM
SHOOM!!
HOW SHOULD I KNOW?!
GORILLA PUNCH PUNCH!!!
WHOA!! THAT WAS PRETTY POWERFUL!!
BA
KOOM
HEY, THERE'S A BUNCH BACK THERE TOO!!
ALL RIGHT, I'LL TAKE CARE OF 'EM!!
HOW MANY TIMES DO WE HAVE TO TELL YOU TO CONSERVE YOUR STRENGTH FOR KAIDO?!
RAAAAH
IT'LL TAKE YOU TOO LONG TO HANDLE ALL THESE GUYS ALONE!!!
SHUT UP!! IS TEN SECONDS TOO LONG FOR YOU?!
I'LL DO IT IN THREE!!
FISH-MAN KARATE...

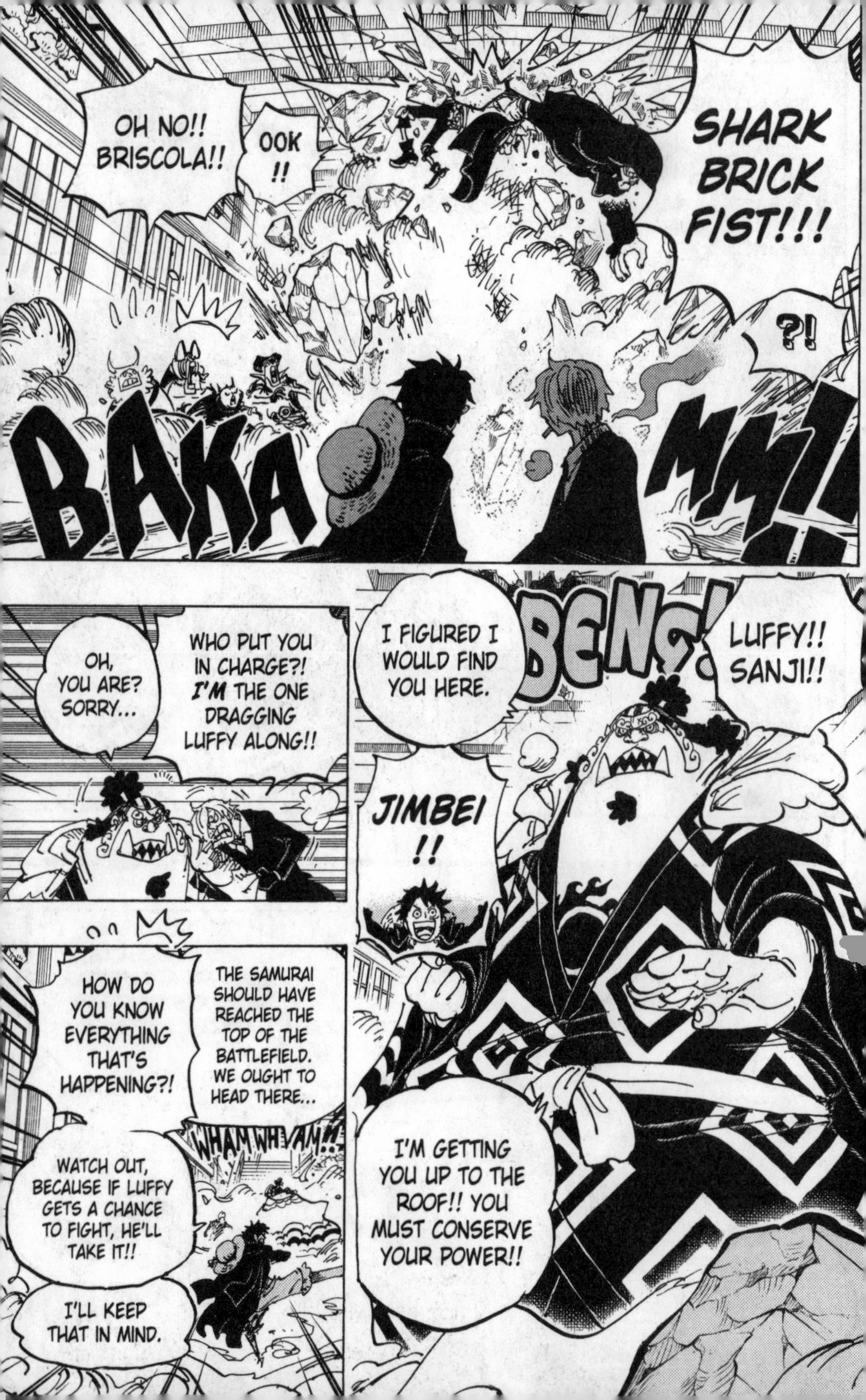
SHARK BRICK FIST!!!
OOK !!
OH NO!! BRISCOLA!!
?!
BAKAMM!
LUFFY!! SANJI!!
BENG!
I FIGURED I WOULD FIND YOU HERE.
JIMBEI !!
I'M GETTING YOU UP TO THE ROOF!! YOU MUST CONSERVE YOUR POWER!!
WHO PUT YOU IN CHARGE?! *I'M* THE ONE DRAGGING LUFFY ALONG!!
OH, YOU ARE? SORRY...
THE SAMURAI SHOULD HAVE REACHED THE TOP OF THE BATTLEFIELD. WE OUGHT TO HEAD THERE...
HOW DO YOU KNOW EVERYTHING THAT'S HAPPENING?!
WHAM WHAM!!
WATCH OUT, BECAUSE IF LUFFY GETS A CHANCE TO FIGHT, HE'LL TAKE IT!!
I'LL KEEP THAT IN MIND.

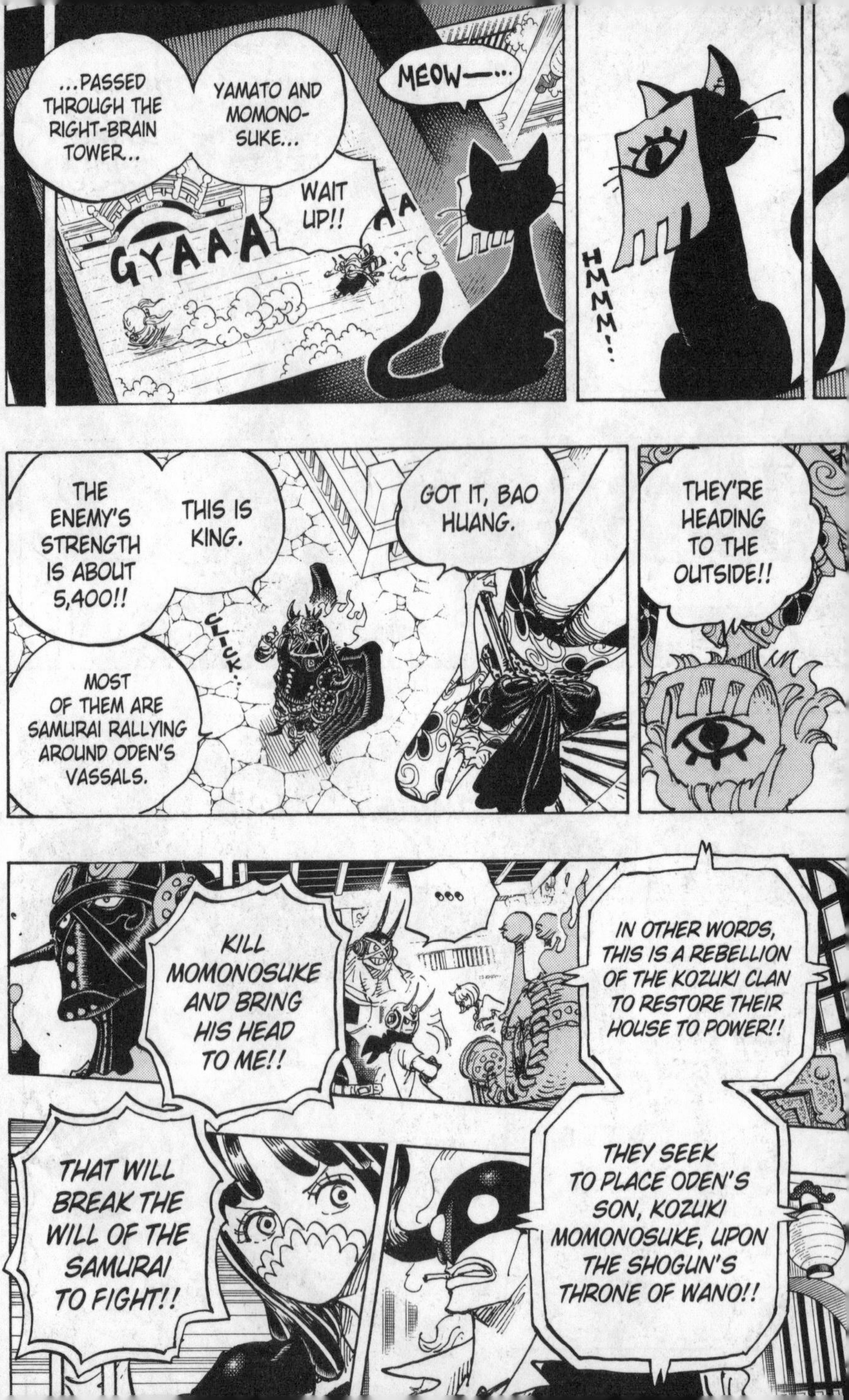
HMMM!!
MEOW—...
YAMATO AND MOMONOSUKE...
...PASSED THROUGH THE RIGHT-BRAIN TOWER...
WAIT UP!!
AA
GYAAA
THEY'RE HEADING TO THE OUTSIDE!!
GOT IT, BAO HUANG.
THIS IS KING.
THE ENEMY'S STRENGTH IS ABOUT 5,400!!
CLICK...
MOST OF THEM ARE SAMURAI RALLYING AROUND ODEN'S VASSALS.
IN OTHER WORDS, THIS IS A REBELLION OF THE KOZUKI CLAN TO RESTORE THEIR HOUSE TO POWER!!
...
KILL MOMONOSUKE AND BRING HIS HEAD TO ME!!
THEY SEEK TO PLACE ODEN'S SON, KOZUKI MOMONOSUKE, UPON THE SHOGUN'S THRONE OF WANO!!
THAT WILL BREAK THE WILL OF THE SAMURAI TO FIGHT!!

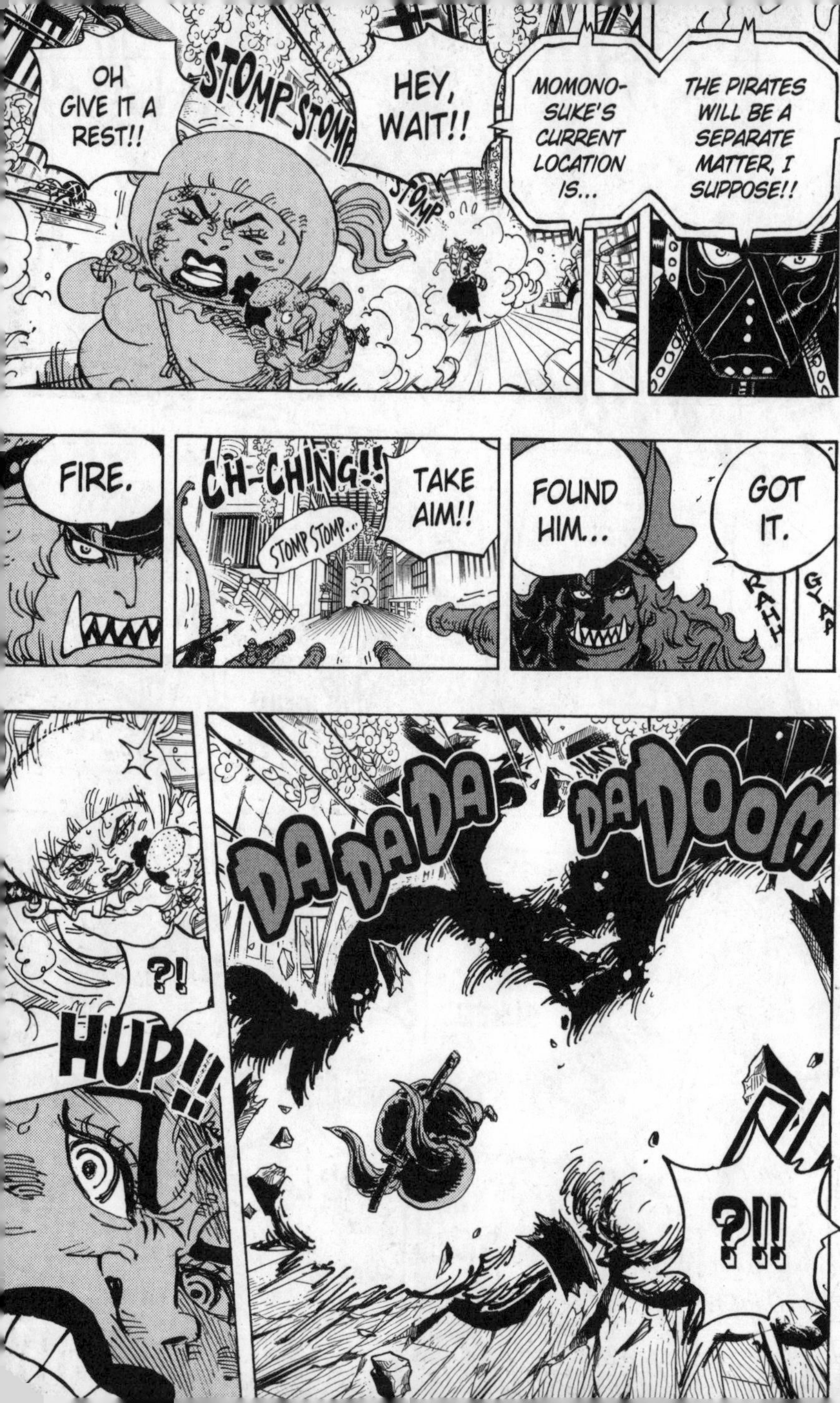
THE PIRATES WILL BE A SEPARATE MATTER, I SUPPOSE!!
MOMONOSUKE'S CURRENT LOCATION IS...
HEY, WAIT!!
STOMP STOMP
OH GIVE IT A REST!!
STOMP
GOT IT.
GYAA
FOUND HIM...
RAHH
TAKE AIM!!
CH-CHING!!
STOMP STOMP...
FIRE.
DA DA DA DA DOOM
?!!
?!
HUP!!

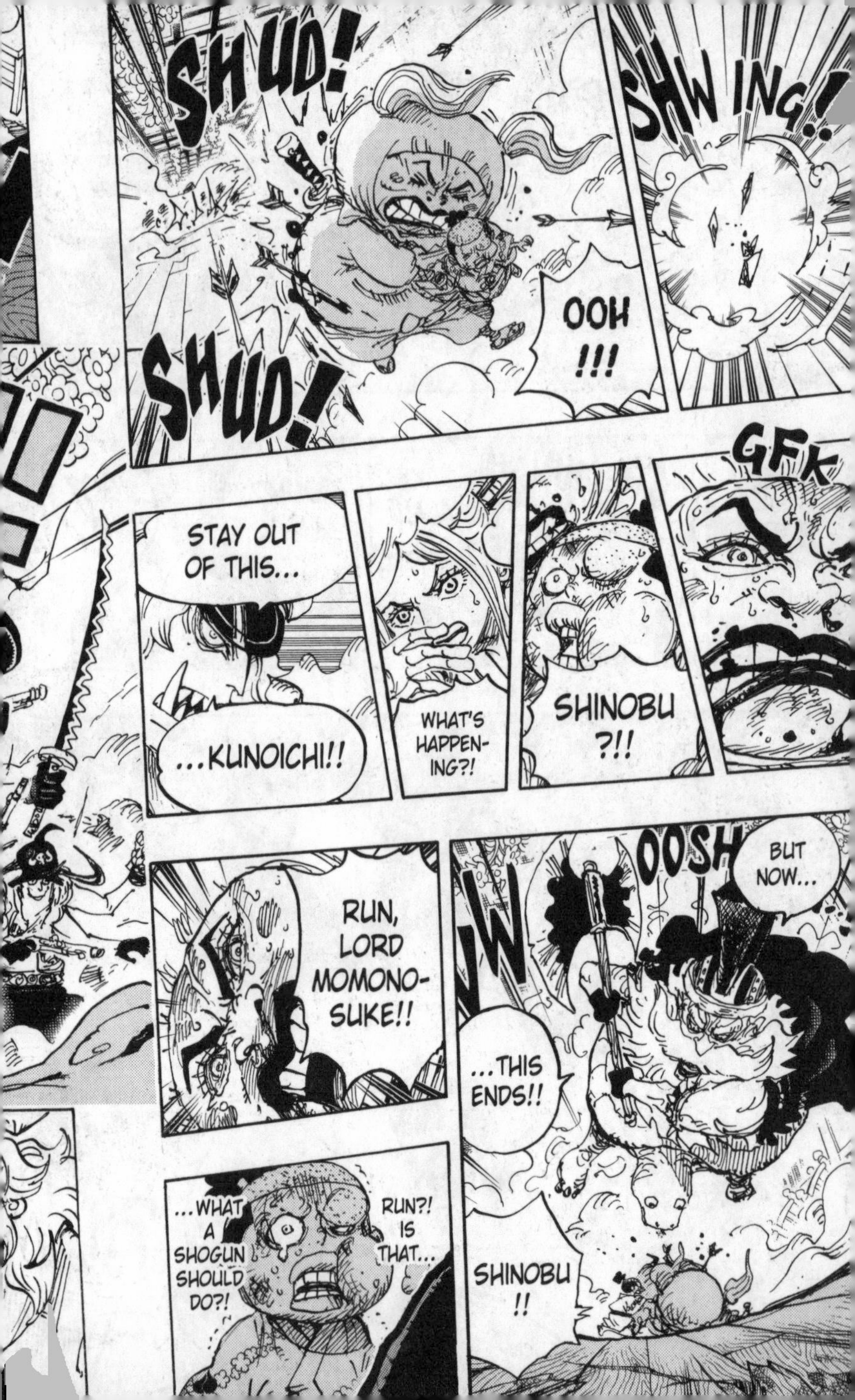

SHWING!!
SHUD!
OOH !!!
SHUD!
GFK
SHINOBU ?!!
WHAT'S HAPPEN-ING?!
STAY OUT OF THIS...
...KUNOICHI!!
OOSH
BUT NOW...
...THIS ENDS!!
SHINOBU !!
RUN, LORD MOMONO-SUKE!!
RUN?! IS THAT...
...WHAT A SHOGUN SHOULD DO?!

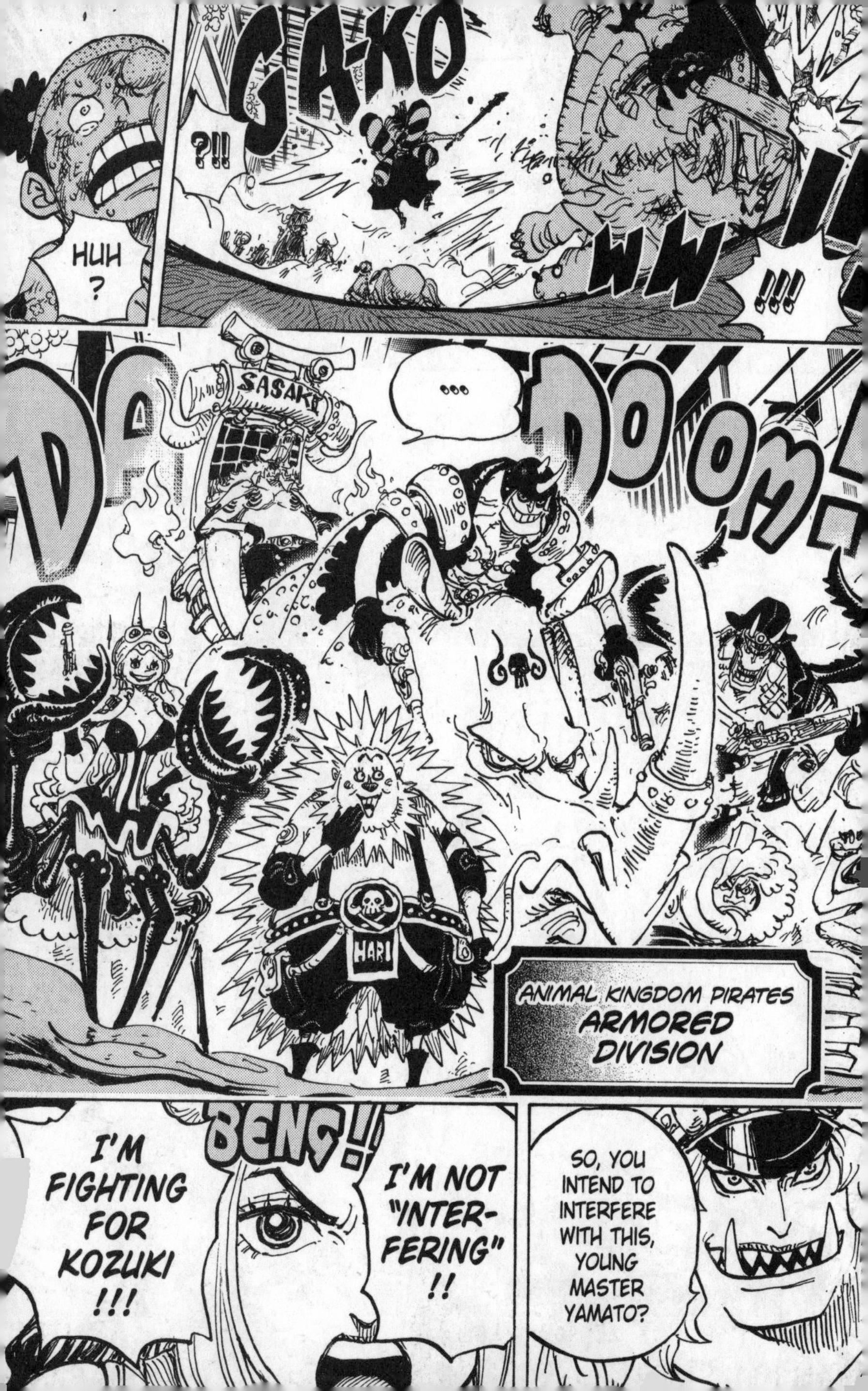
GA-KO
?!!
!!!
HUH ?
DOOM
...
SASAKI
HARI
ANIMAL KINGDOM PIRATES ARMORED DIVISION
SO, YOU INTEND TO INTERFERE WITH THIS, YOUNG MASTER YAMATO?
BENG!!
I'M NOT "INTER-FERING" !!
I'M FIGHTING FOR KOZUKI !!!

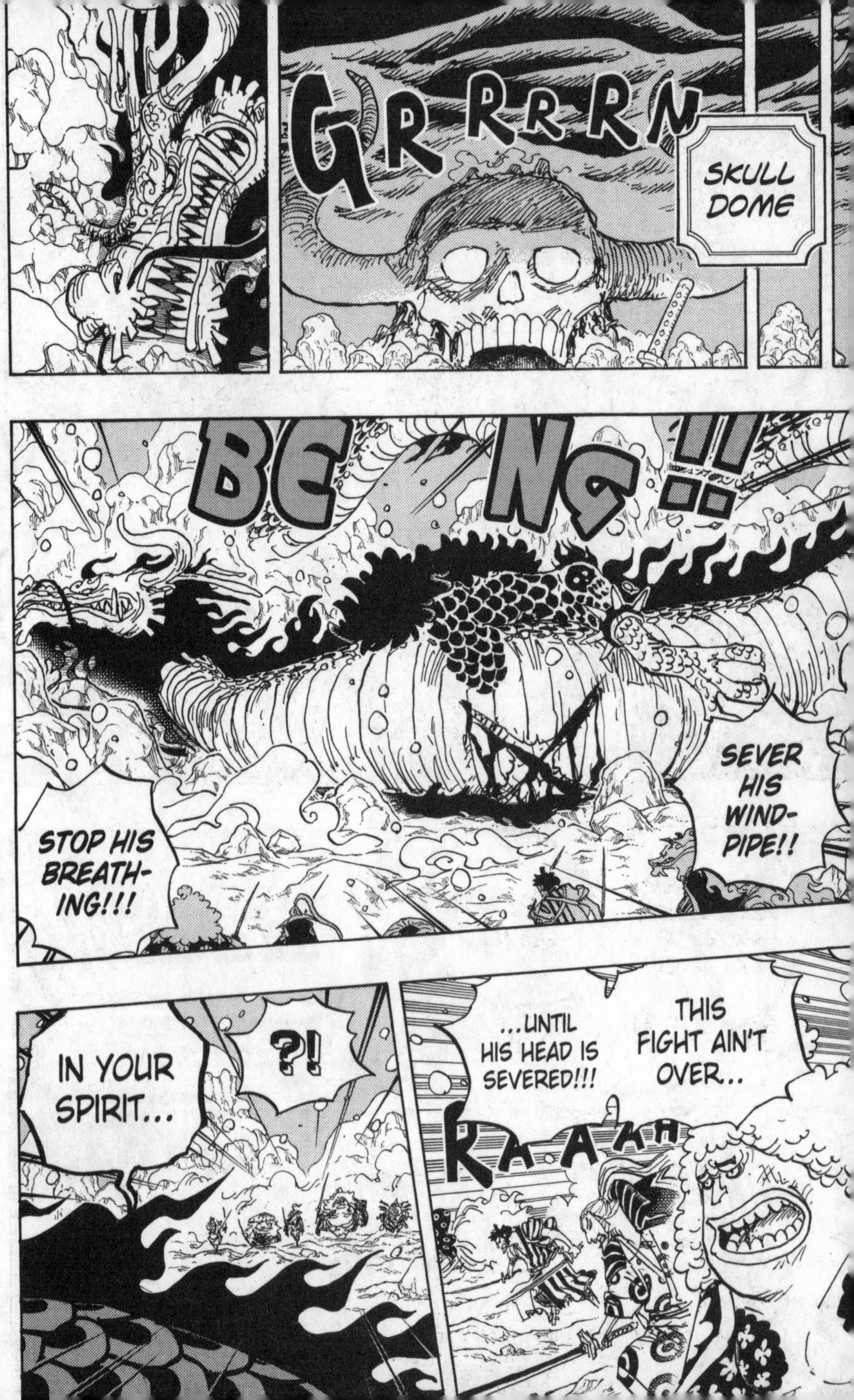
SKULL DOME
GRRRRRN
BENG!!
SEVER HIS WINDPIPE!!
STOP HIS BREATHING!!!
THIS FIGHT AIN'T OVER...
...UNTIL HIS HEAD IS SEVERED!!!
RAAAAH
?!
IN YOUR SPIRIT...

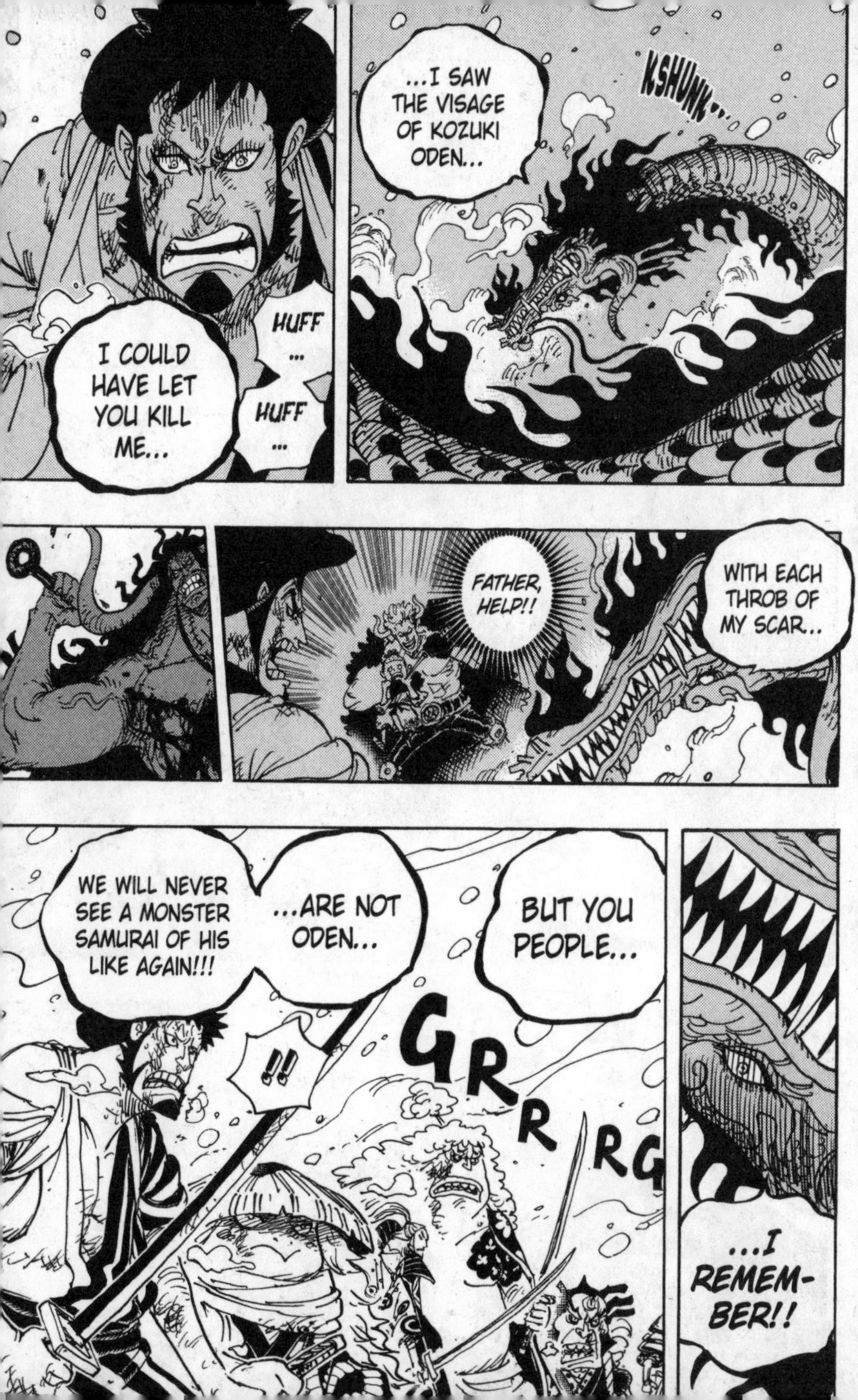
...I SAW THE VISAGE OF KOZUKI ODEN...
KSHUNK...
HUFF ... HUFF ...
I COULD HAVE LET YOU KILL ME...
WITH EACH THROB OF MY SCAR...
FATHER, HELP!!
...I REMEM-BER!!
BUT YOU PEOPLE...
...ARE NOT ODEN...
WE WILL NEVER SEE A MONSTER SAMURAI OF HIS LIKE AGAIN!!!
GRRRRG
!!

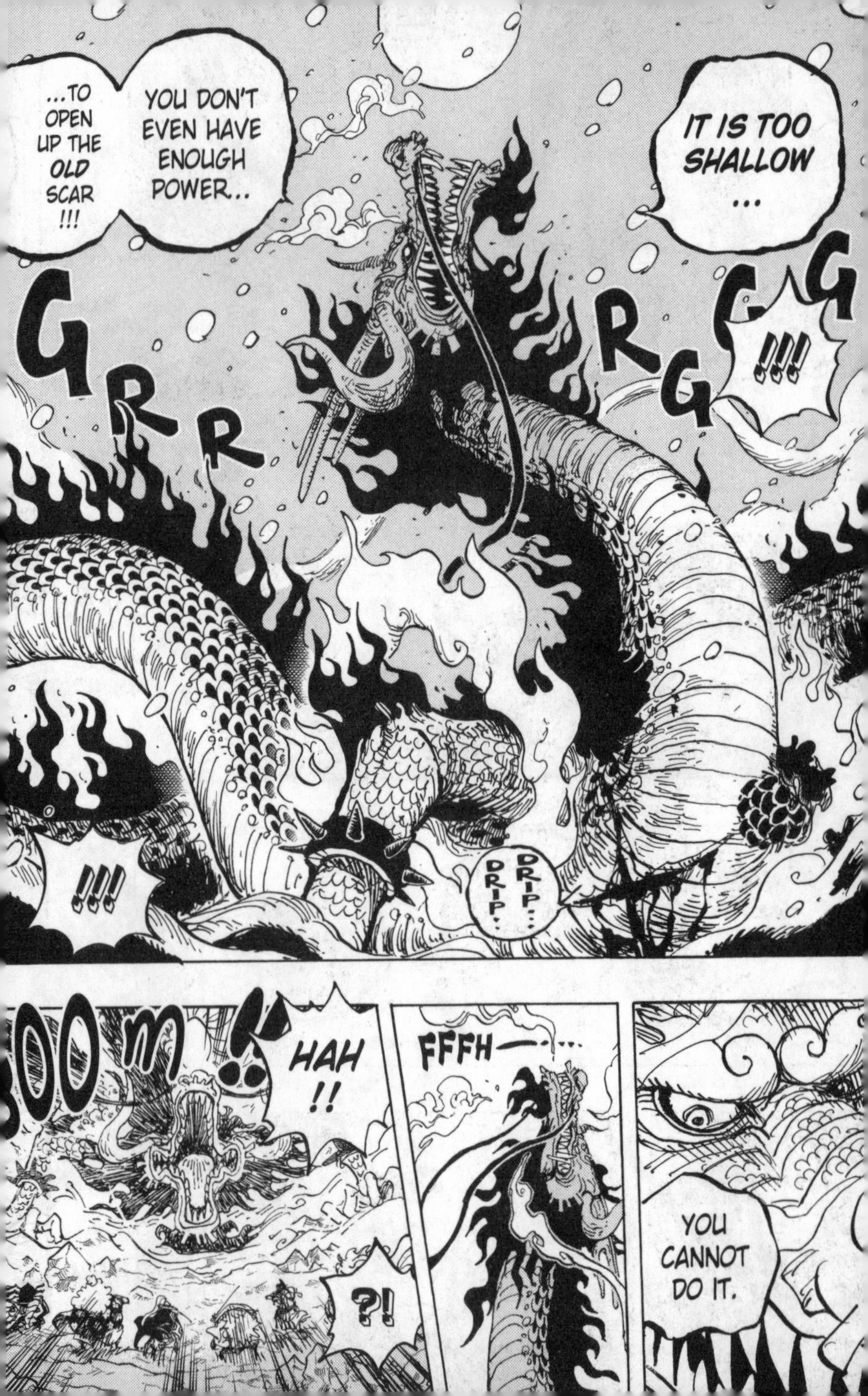
IT IS TOO SHALLOW ...
YOU DON'T EVEN HAVE ENOUGH POWER...
...TO OPEN UP THE OLD SCAR !!!
GRRRRGGG
!!!
DRIP... DRIP...
!!!
YOU CANNOT DO IT.
FFFH—...
HAH !!
?!

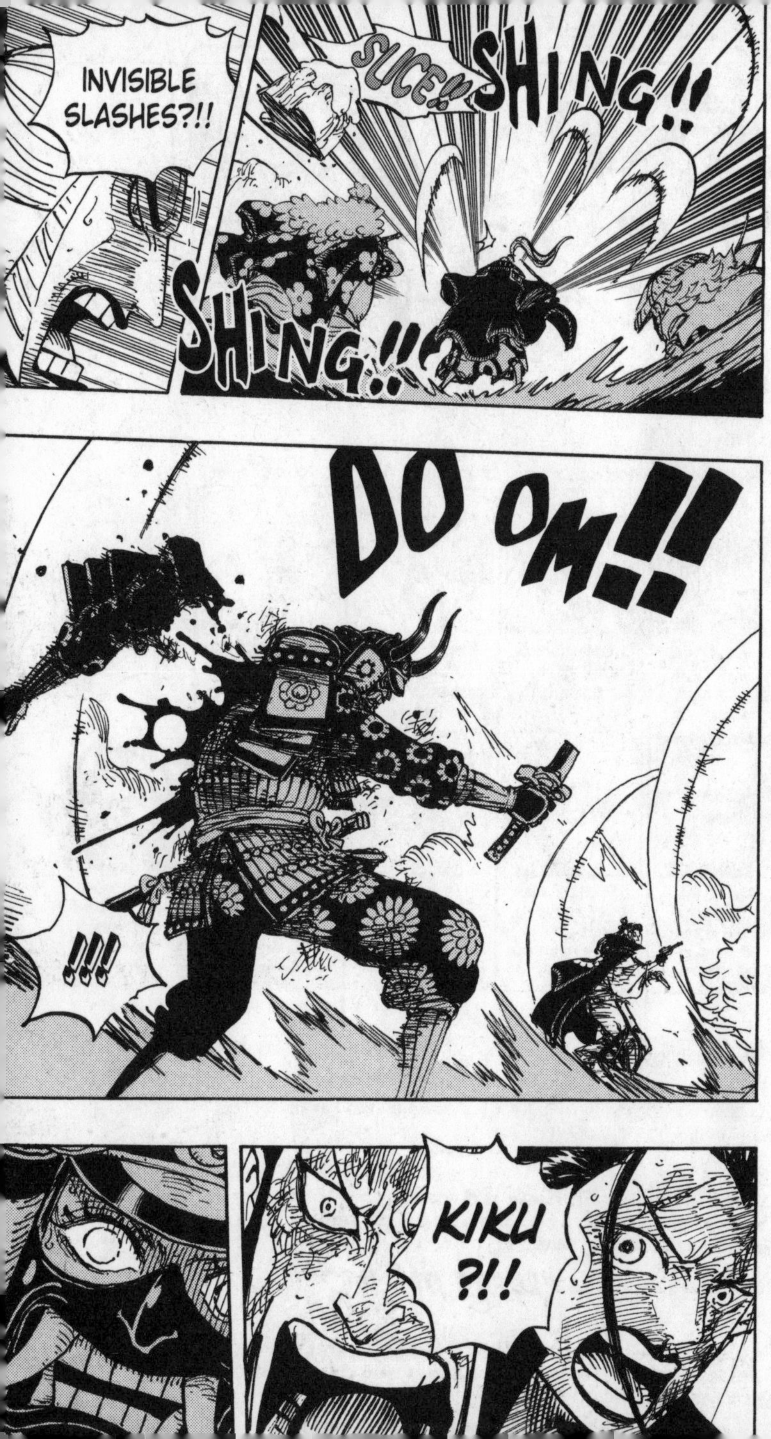
SHING!!
SLICE!!
INVISIBLE SLASHES?!!
SHING!!
DOOM!!
!!!
KIKU ?!!

SBS Question Corner

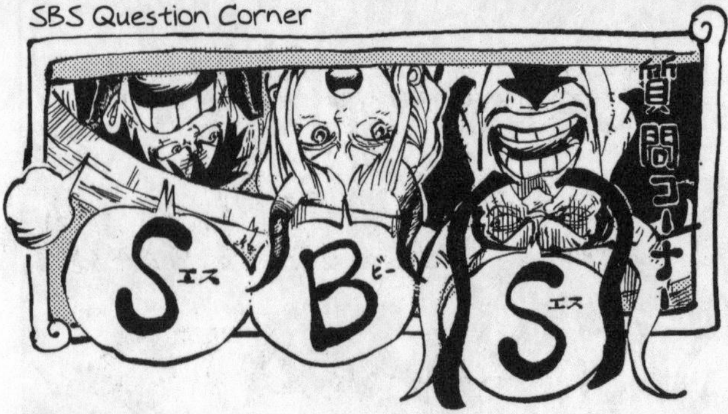

S
B
S

(Rashad, America)

Q: If Zolo, Nami, Usopp, Sanji and Franky had Devil Fruit Powers, which fruit would each of them eat?

--420 Land

A: Ooh, that's an interesting question. Here's what I want to see...

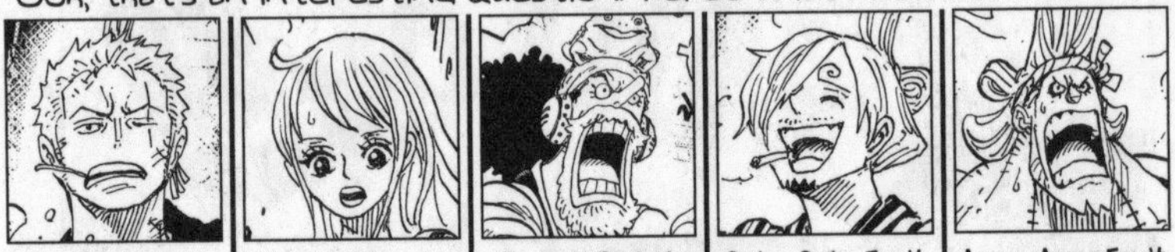

Fish-Fish Fruit, Mythical Type, Azure Dragon Model

Rumble-Rumble Fruit (Lightning Woman)

Pocket-Pocket Fruit (Unlimited pockets on your body)

Swim-Swim Fruit

Arms-Arms Fruit

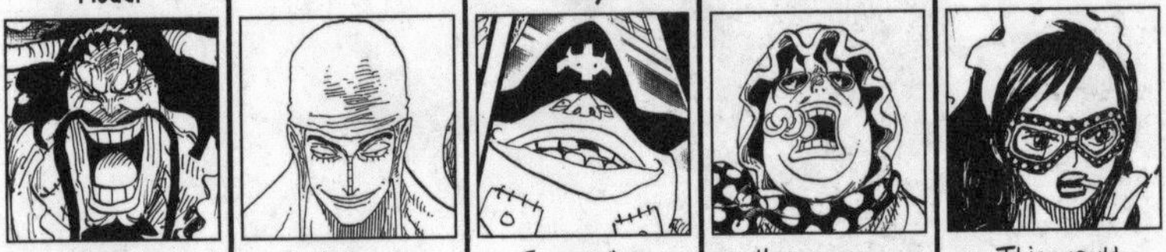

What if the sword turns into the dragon, rather than Zolo? I think that would be awesome.

She'd be the invincible weather girl. (To everyone but Luffy)

Seems like the perfect fit for Usopp with all his gadgets and tools.

He can pass through walls and swim under the ground. A dangerous power in Sanji's hands.

This would be the best possible power for Franky.

Q: Is the vassal tasting Momonosuke's food for poison in chapter 971 the same person who was reporting on Oden's controversial deeds to Sukiyaki in chapter 960? Then he's been serving the Kozuki Clan for generations... I actually cried a little when I realized this.

--Higuma

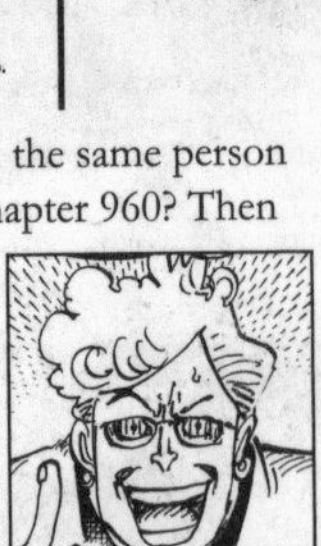

A: Yes, that's right. His name is Banzaburo. He was taken in by Sukiyaki at a young age, and feels a lifelong debt to his master.

Q: Here's what I want to ask: **"LEAVE OR LIFE?"**

--Negibozu

A: Hey, that's terrifying!! What?! No, you can't have my life! I choose leave! I'm leaving!! That's the end of the SBS! See you next volume!! Zoooom!!

Chapter 994:
MY OTHER NAME IS YAMATO

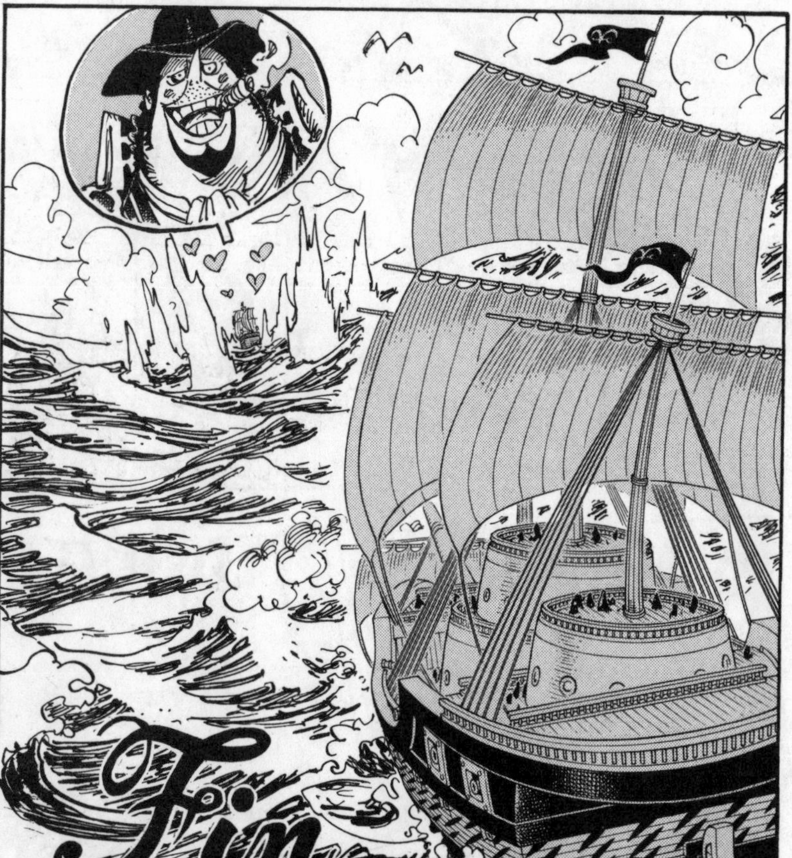
Fin

GANG BEGE'S OH MY FAMILY
FINAL VOL.: "THE BLISSFUL SHIP SAILS ON THROUGH CELEBRATION CANNONS"

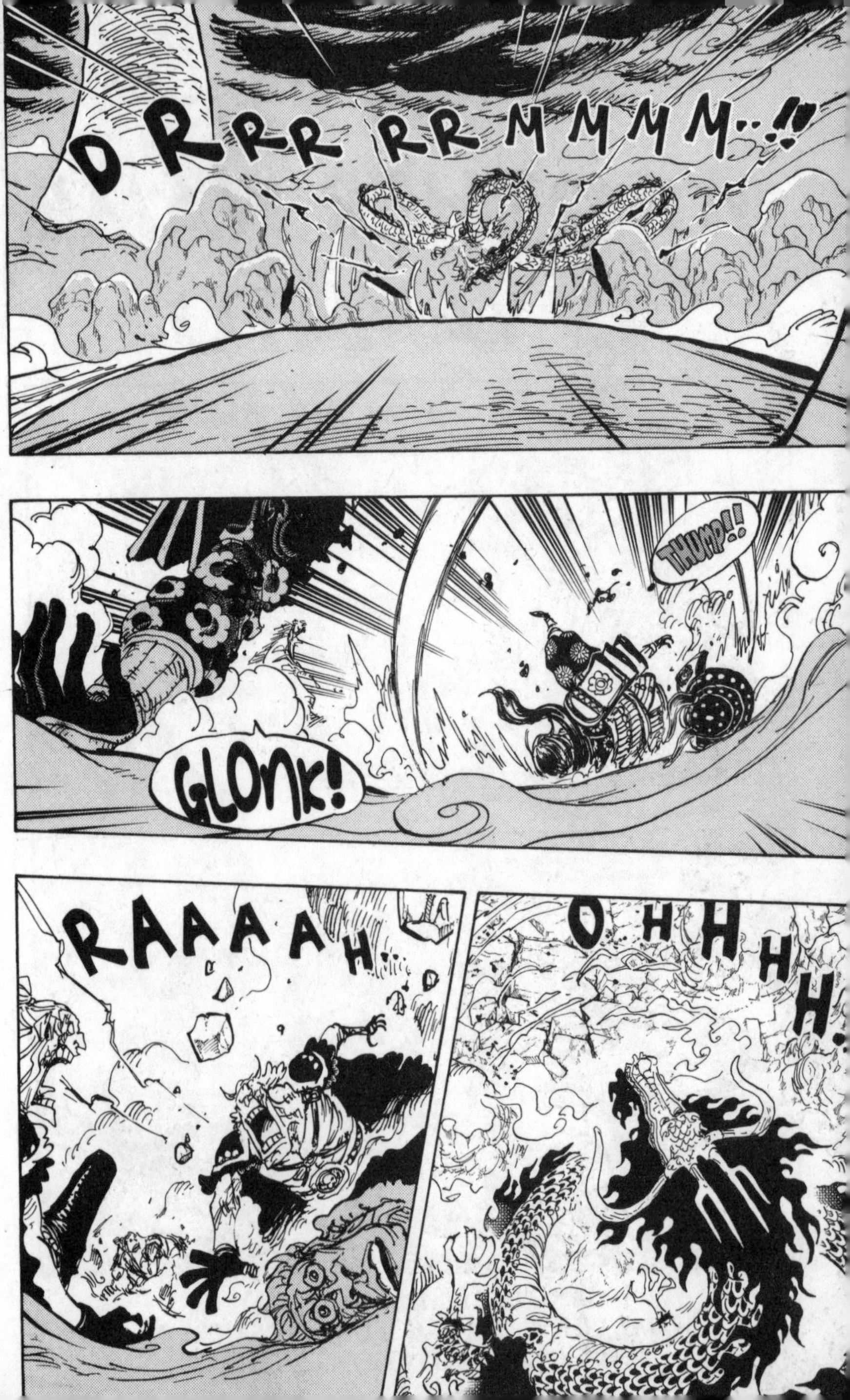
DRRRRRMMMM..!!
THUMP!!
GLONK!
OHHHH.
RAAAAH

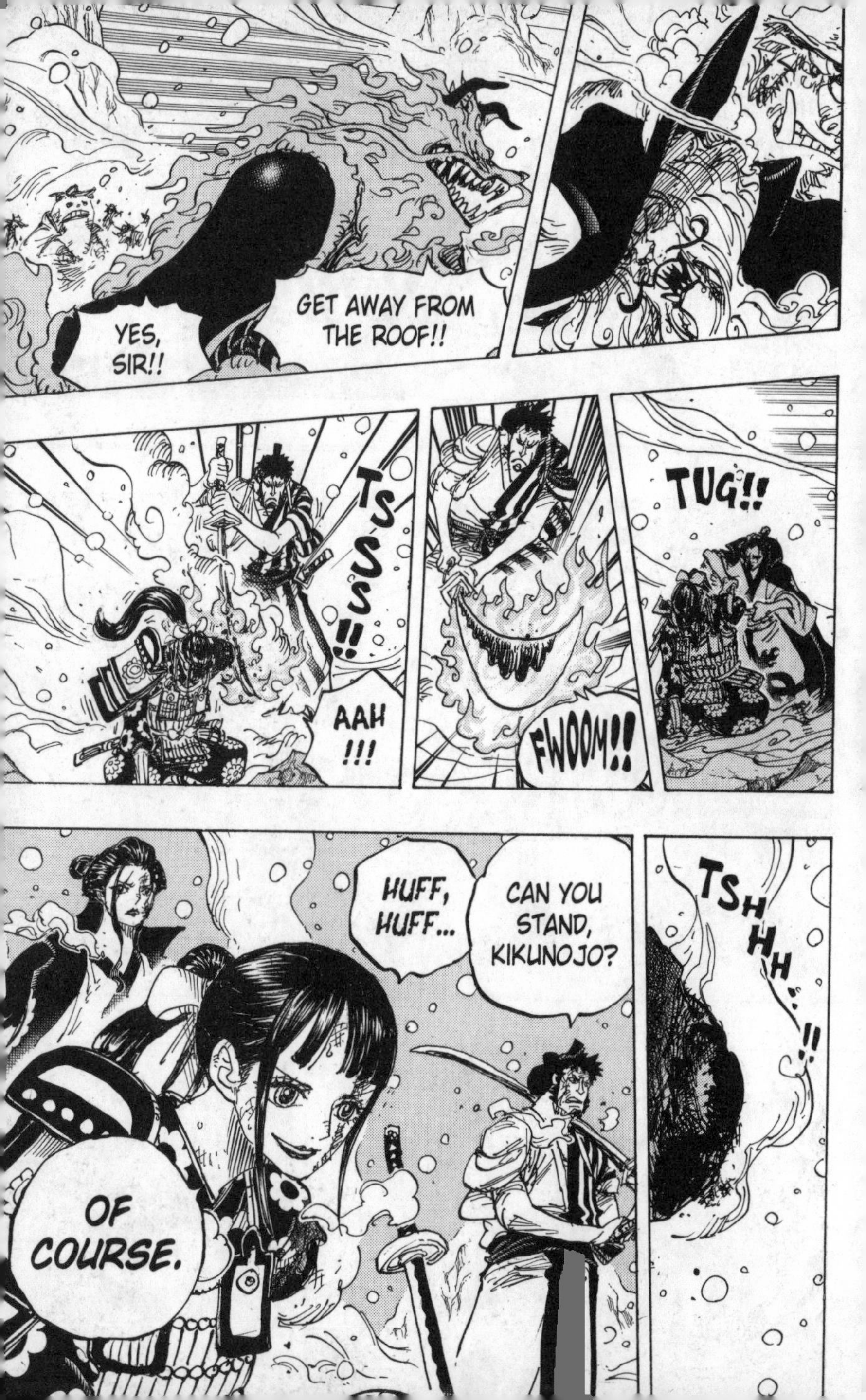
GET AWAY FROM THE ROOF!!
YES, SIR!!
TUG!!
FWOOM!!
TSSS!!
AAH!!!
TSHHH..!!
CAN YOU STAND, KIKUNOJO?
HUFF, HUFF...
OF COURSE.

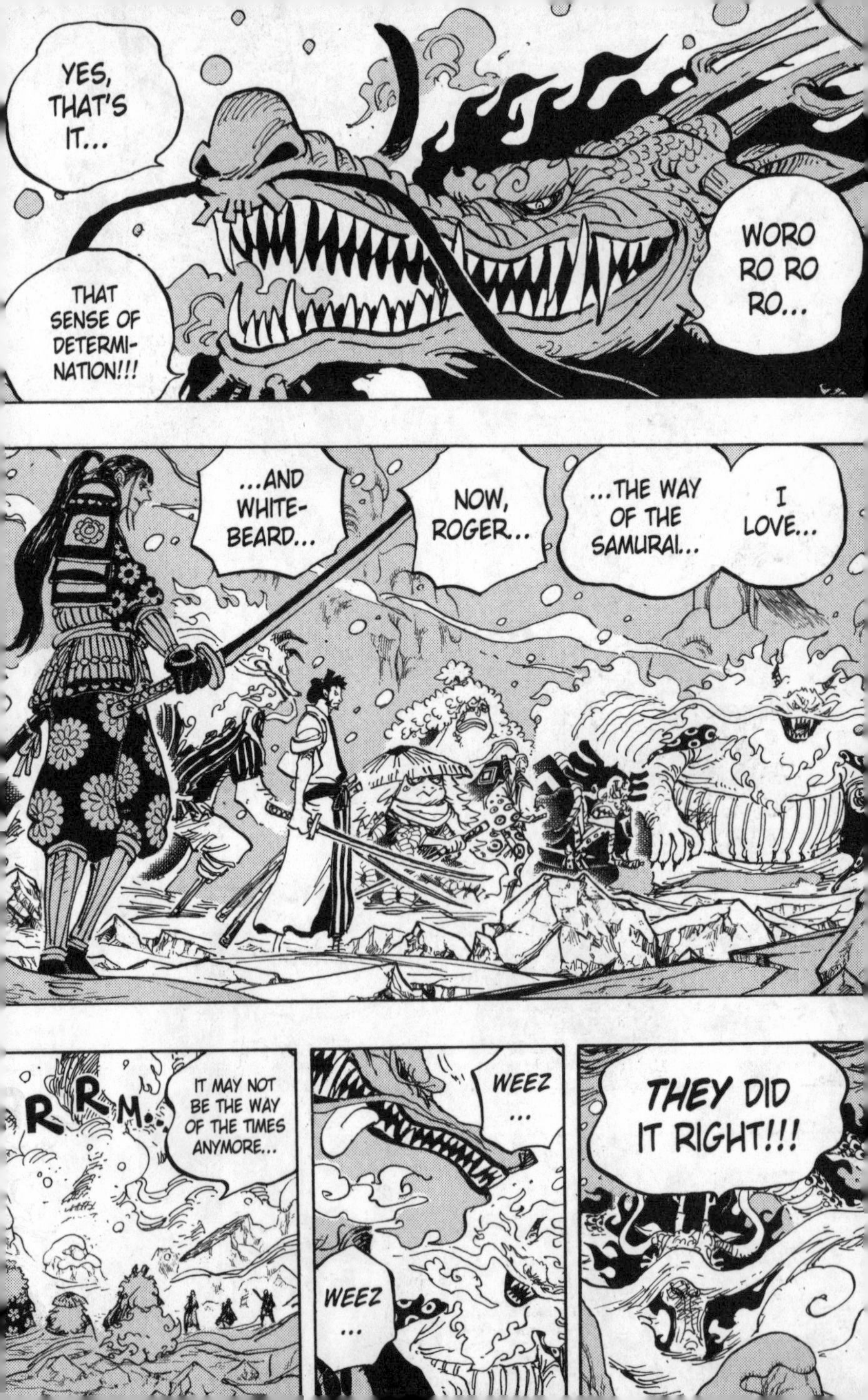
WORORO RO RO...
YES, THAT'S IT...
THAT SENSE OF DETERMINATION!!!
I LOVE...
...THE WAY OF THE SAMURAI...
NOW, ROGER...
...AND WHITEBEARD...
THEY DID IT RIGHT!!!
WEEZ...
WEEZ...
IT MAY NOT BE THE WAY OF THE TIMES ANYMORE...
RRM.

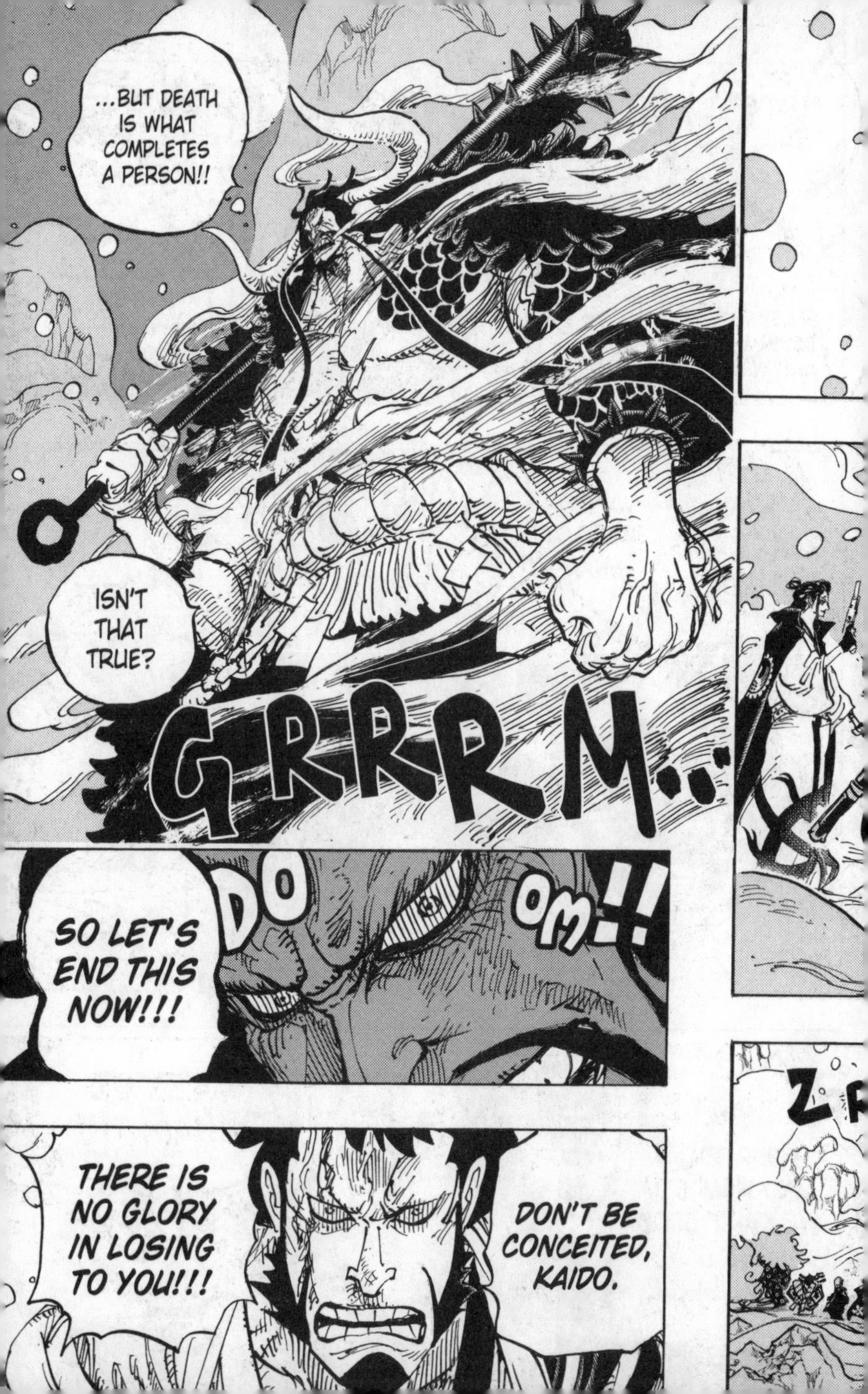
...BUT DEATH IS WHAT COMPLETES A PERSON!!
ISN'T THAT TRUE?
GRRRM..
DOOM!!
SO LET'S END THIS NOW!!!
DON'T BE CONCEITED, KAIDO.
THERE IS NO GLORY IN LOSING TO YOU!!!

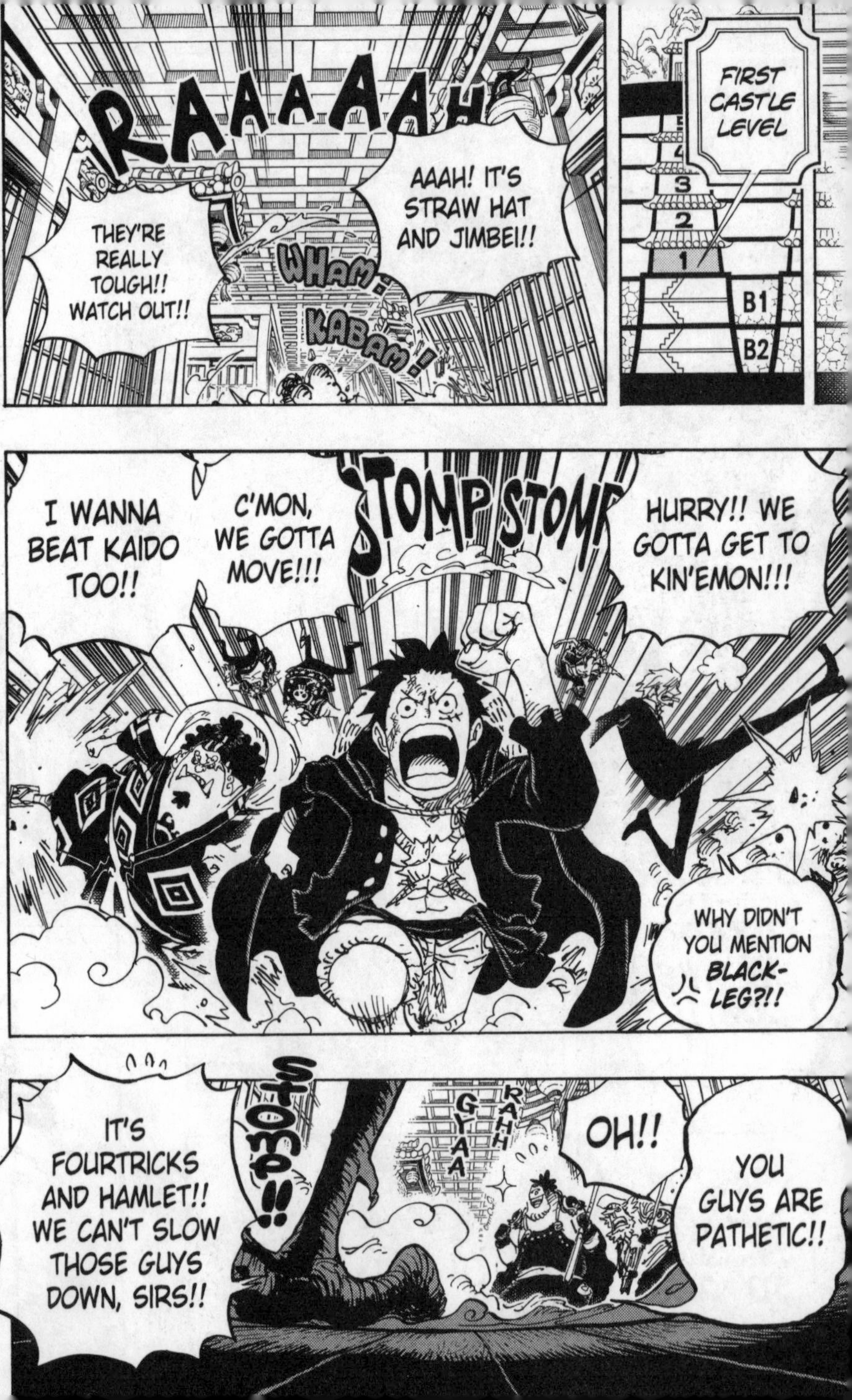
FIRST CASTLE LEVEL
4
3
2
1
B1
B2
RAAAAAH
AAAH! IT'S STRAW HAT AND JIMBEI!!
THEY'RE REALLY TOUGH!! WATCH OUT!!
WHAM!
KABAM!
HURRY!! WE GOTTA GET TO KIN'EMON!!!
STOMP STOMP
C'MON, WE GOTTA MOVE!!!
I WANNA BEAT KAIDO TOO!!
WHY DIDN'T YOU MENTION BLACK-LEG?!!
YOU GUYS ARE PATHETIC!!
OH!!
RAHH
GYAA
STOMP!!
IT'S FOURTRICKS AND HAMLET!! WE CAN'T SLOW THOSE GUYS DOWN, SIRS!!

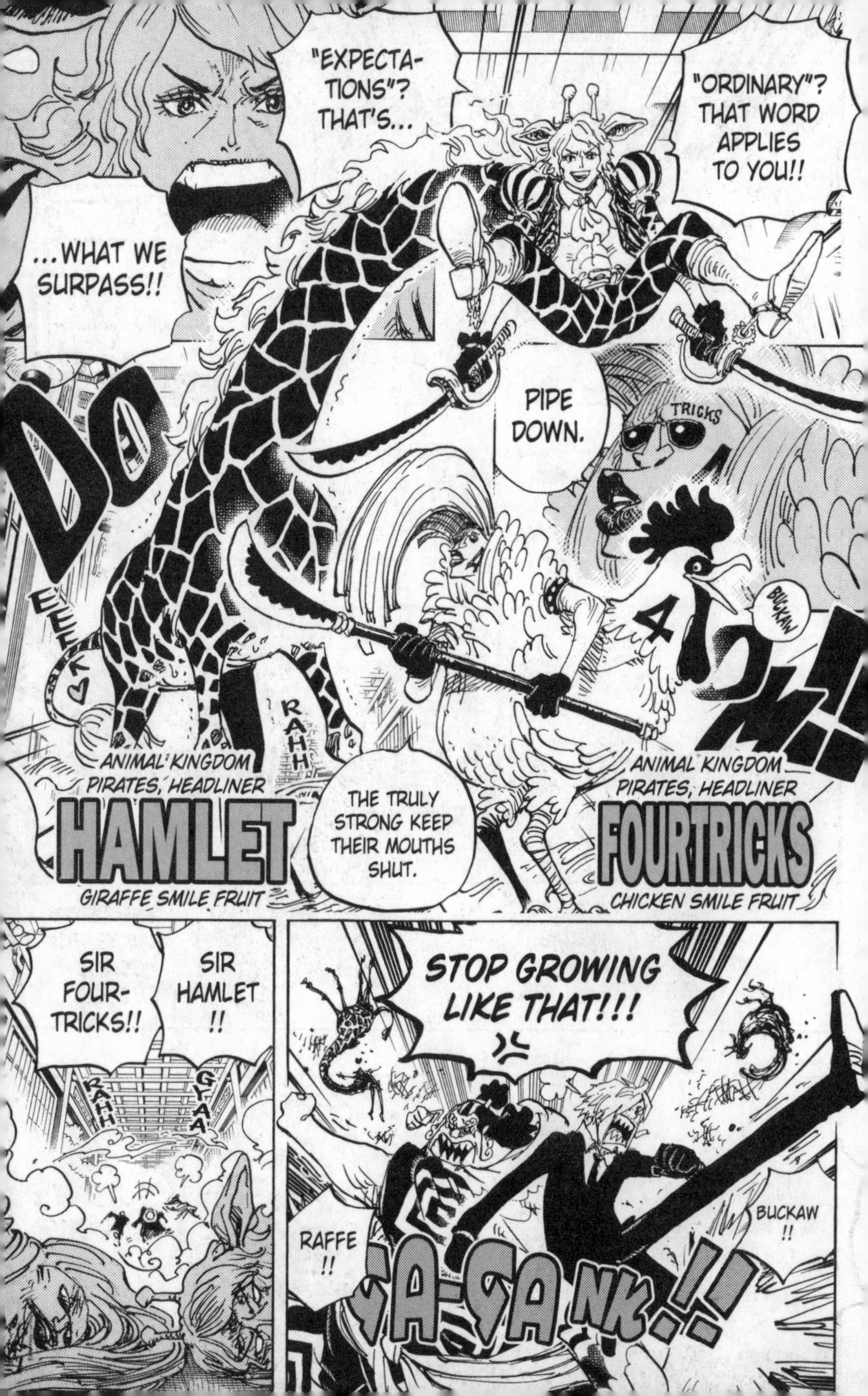
"ORDINARY"? THAT WORD APPLIES TO YOU!!
"EXPECTATIONS"? THAT'S...
...WHAT WE SURPASS!!
TRICKS
PIPE DOWN.
BUCKAW
DO
EEEK♥
RAHH
ANIMAL KINGDOM PIRATES, HEADLINER
FOURTRICKS
CHICKEN SMILE FRUIT
THE TRULY STRONG KEEP THEIR MOUTHS SHUT.
ANIMAL KINGDOM PIRATES, HEADLINER
HAMLET
GIRAFFE SMILE FRUIT
STOP GROWING LIKE THAT!!!
BUCKAW !!
RAFFE !!
A-GANK!!
SIR HAMLET !!
SIR FOUR-TRICKS!!
GYAA
RAHH

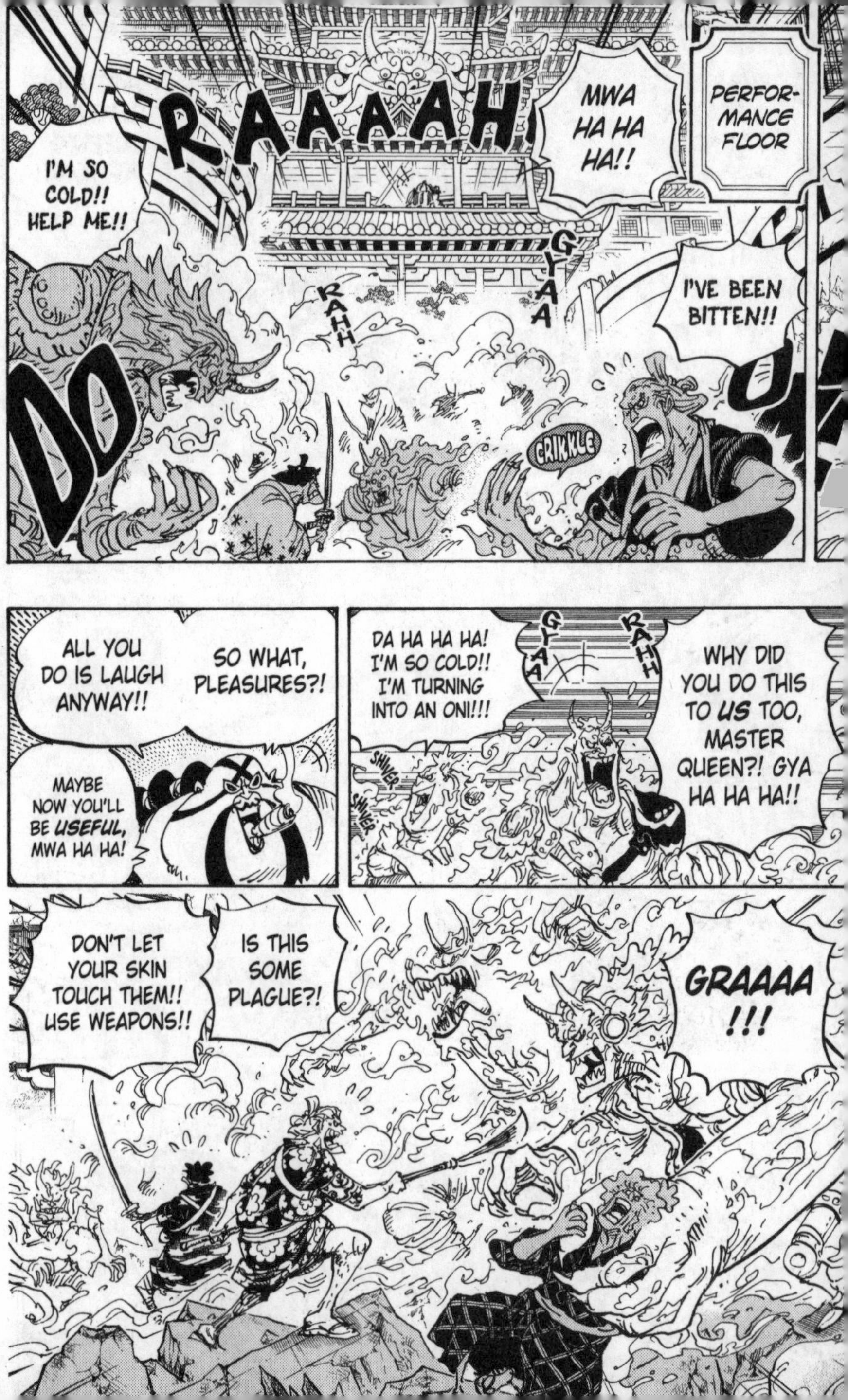
PERFORMANCE FLOOR
MWA HA HA HA!!
RAAAAH
I'M SO COLD!! HELP ME!!
I'VE BEEN BITTEN!!
GYAA
RAHH
CRIKKLE
DO
WHY DID YOU DO THIS TO US TOO, MASTER QUEEN?! GYA HA HA HA!!
RAHH
GYAA
DA HA HA HA! I'M SO COLD!! I'M TURNING INTO AN ONI!!!
SHIVER
SHIVER
SO WHAT, PLEASURES?!
ALL YOU DO IS LAUGH ANYWAY!!
MAYBE NOW YOU'LL BE USEFUL, MWA HA HA!
GRAAAA!!!
IS THIS SOME PLAGUE?!
DON'T LET YOUR SKIN TOUCH THEM!! USE WEAPONS!!

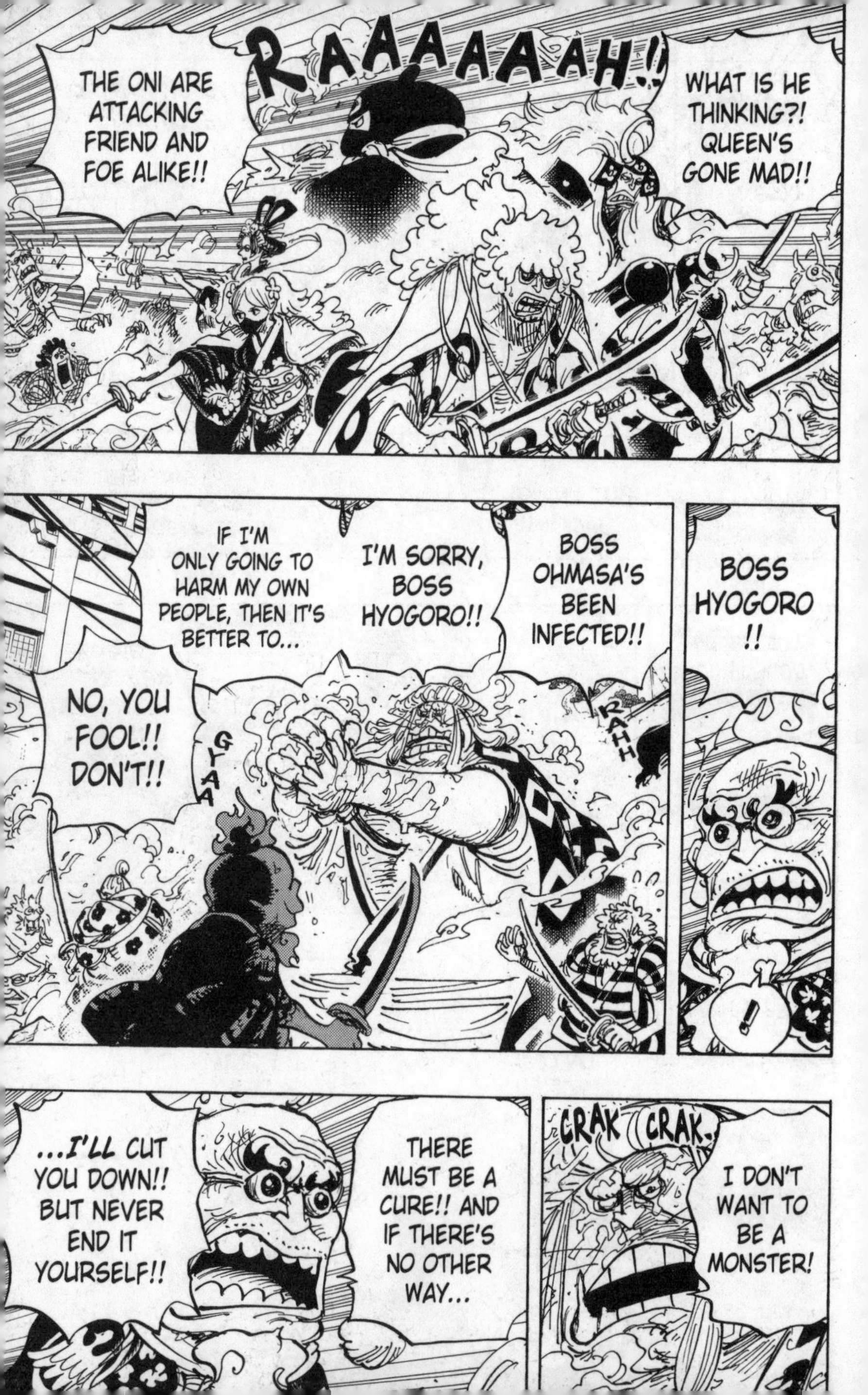
WHAT IS HE THINKING?! QUEEN'S GONE MAD!!
RAAAAAAH!!
THE ONI ARE ATTACKING FRIEND AND FOE ALIKE!!
BOSS HYOGORO !!
BOSS OHMASA'S BEEN INFECTED!!
RAHH
I'M SORRY, BOSS HYOGORO!!
IF I'M ONLY GOING TO HARM MY OWN PEOPLE, THEN IT'S BETTER TO...
GYAA
NO, YOU FOOL!! DON'T!!
CRAK CRAK
I DON'T WANT TO BE A MONSTER!
THERE MUST BE A CURE!! AND IF THERE'S NO OTHER WAY...
...*I'LL* CUT YOU DOWN!! BUT NEVER END IT YOURSELF!!

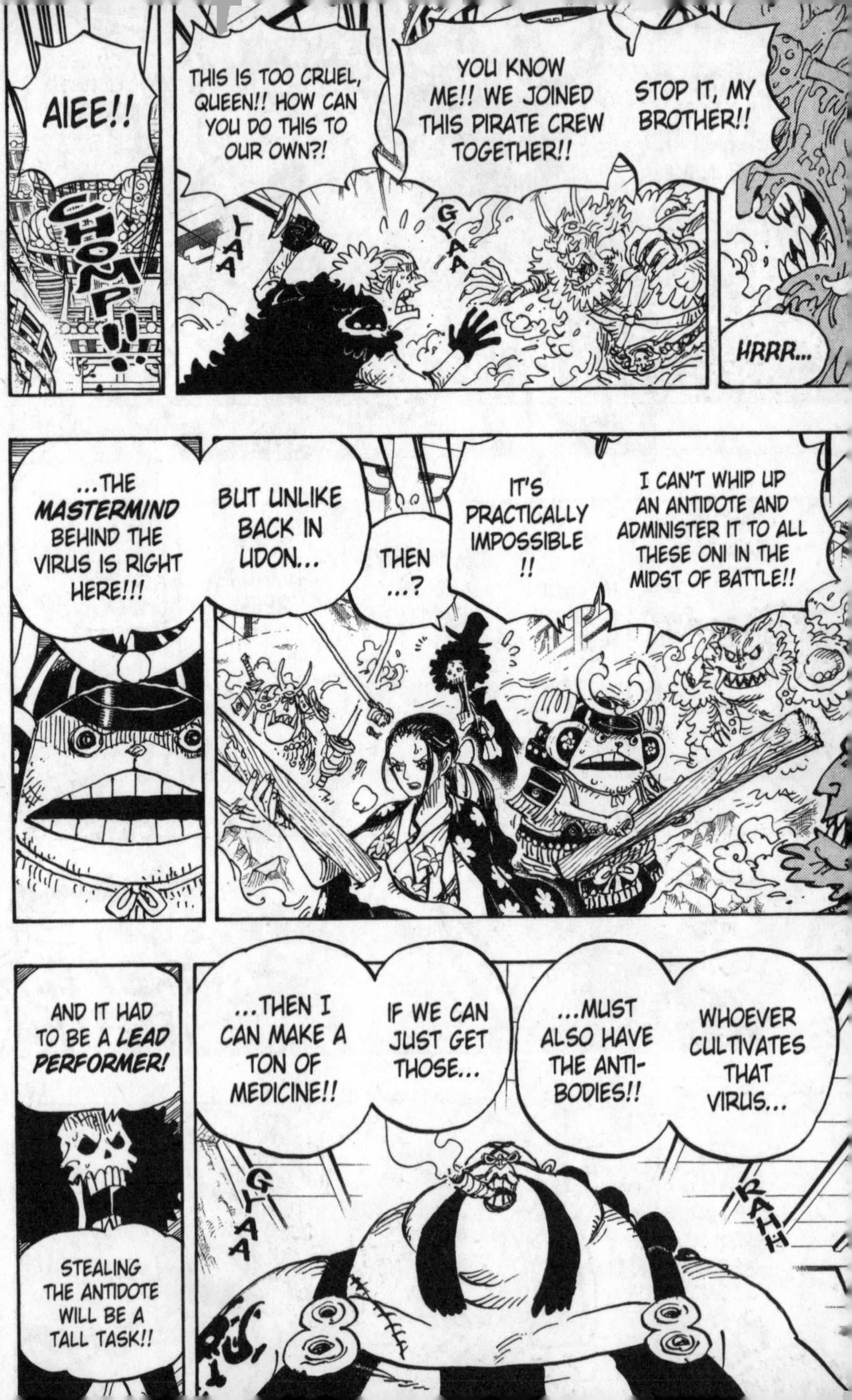
STOP IT, MY BROTHER!!
HRRR...
YOU KNOW ME!! WE JOINED THIS PIRATE CREW TOGETHER!!
THIS IS TOO CRUEL, QUEEN!! HOW CAN YOU DO THIS TO OUR OWN?!
GYAA
YAA
AIEE!!
CHOMP!!
I CAN'T WHIP UP AN ANTIDOTE AND ADMINISTER IT TO ALL THESE ONI IN THE MIDST OF BATTLE!!
IT'S PRACTICALLY IMPOSSIBLE!!
THEN ...?
BUT UNLIKE BACK IN UDON...
...THE *MASTERMIND* BEHIND THE VIRUS IS RIGHT HERE!!!
WHOEVER CULTIVATES THAT VIRUS...
...MUST ALSO HAVE THE ANTIBODIES!!
IF WE CAN JUST GET THOSE...
...THEN I CAN MAKE A TON OF MEDICINE!!
RAHH
GYAA
AND IT HAD TO BE A *LEAD PERFORMER*!
STEALING THE ANTIDOTE WILL BE A TALL TASK!!

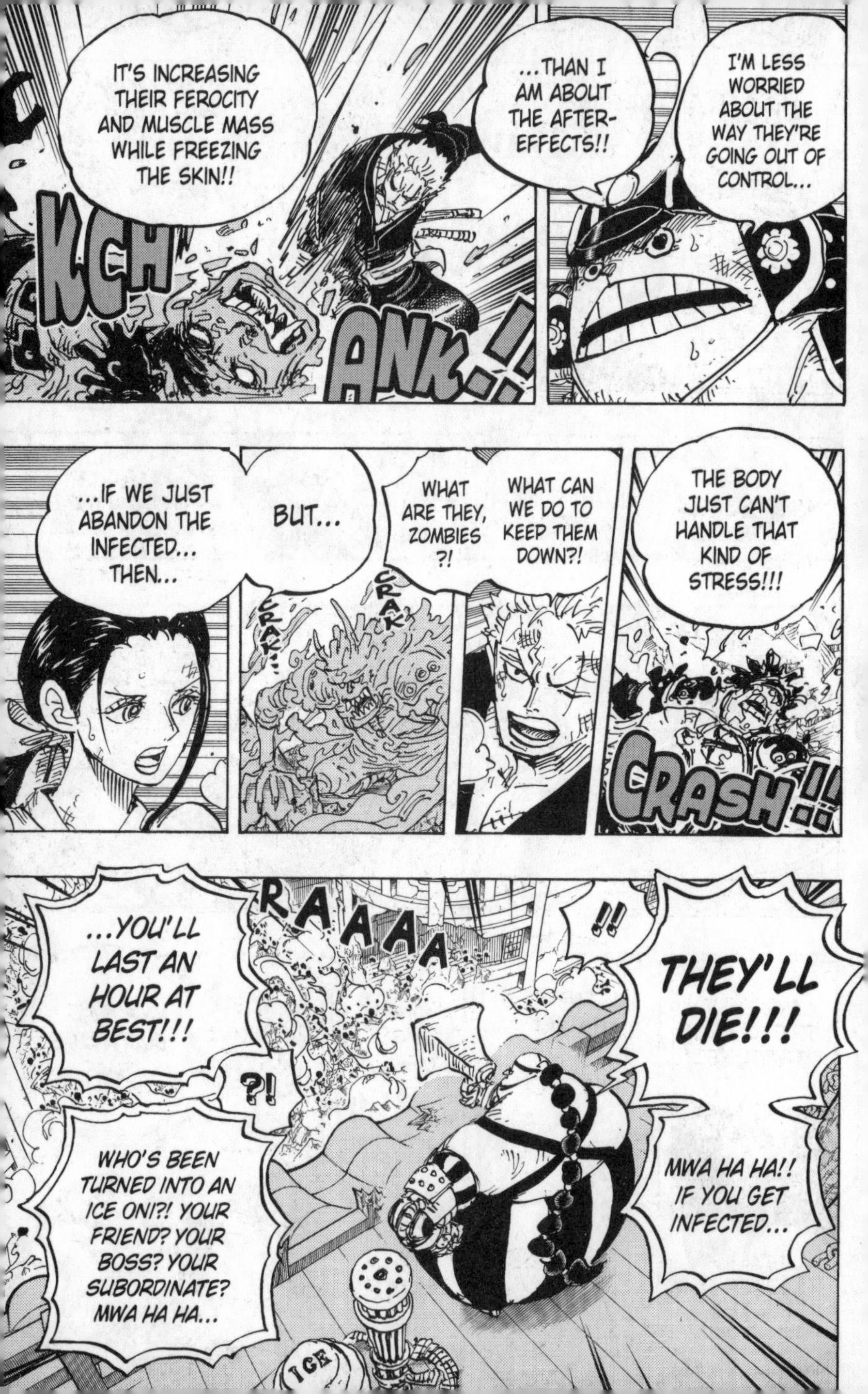
I'M LESS WORRIED ABOUT THE WAY THEY'RE GOING OUT OF CONTROL...
...THAN I AM ABOUT THE AFTER-EFFECTS!!
IT'S INCREASING THEIR FEROCITY AND MUSCLE MASS WHILE FREEZING THE SKIN!!
KCH
ANK!!
THE BODY JUST CAN'T HANDLE THAT KIND OF STRESS!!!
CRASH!!
WHAT CAN WE DO TO KEEP THEM DOWN?!
WHAT ARE THEY, ZOMBIES?!
CRAK
CRAK
BUT...
...IF WE JUST ABANDON THE INFECTED... THEN...
THEY'LL DIE!!!
!!
RAAAA
MWA HA HA!! IF YOU GET INFECTED...
...YOU'LL LAST AN HOUR AT BEST!!!
?!
WHO'S BEEN TURNED INTO AN ICE ONI?! YOUR FRIEND? YOUR BOSS? YOUR SUBORDINATE? MWA HA HA...
ICE

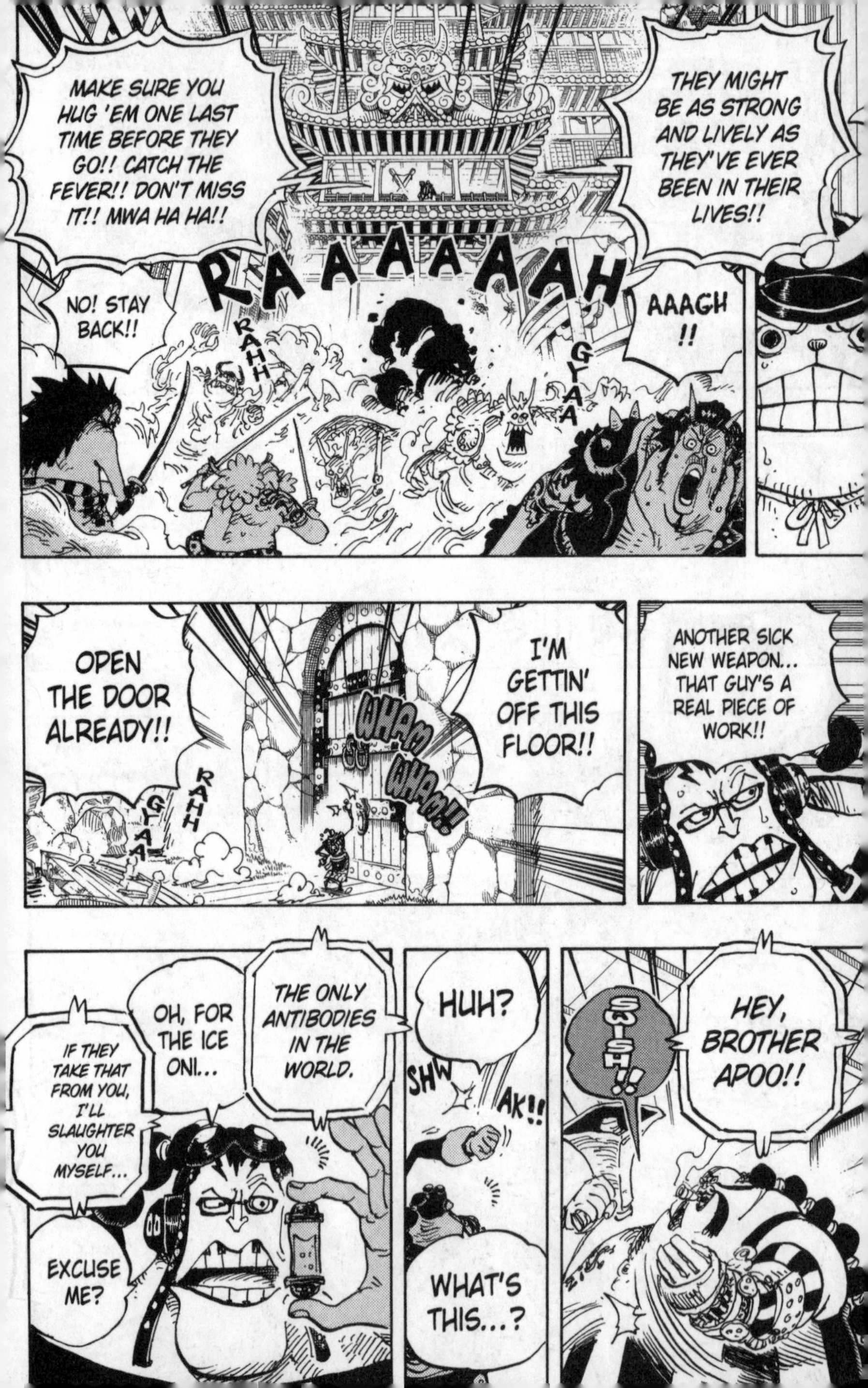
THEY MIGHT BE AS STRONG AND LIVELY AS THEY'VE EVER BEEN IN THEIR LIVES!!
MAKE SURE YOU HUG 'EM ONE LAST TIME BEFORE THEY GO!! CATCH THE FEVER!! DON'T MISS IT!! MWA HA HA!!
RAAAAAAH
AAAGH!!
GYAA
RAHH
NO! STAY BACK!!
ANOTHER SICK NEW WEAPON... THAT GUY'S A REAL PIECE OF WORK!!
I'M GETTIN' OFF THIS FLOOR!!
WHAM
WHAM!!
OPEN THE DOOR ALREADY!!
RAHH
GYAA
HEY, BROTHER APOO!!
SWISH!!
HUH?
SHWAK!!
WHAT'S THIS...?
THE ONLY ANTIBODIES IN THE WORLD.
OH, FOR THE ICE ONI...
IF THEY TAKE THAT FROM YOU, I'LL SLAUGHTER YOU MYSELF...
EXCUSE ME?

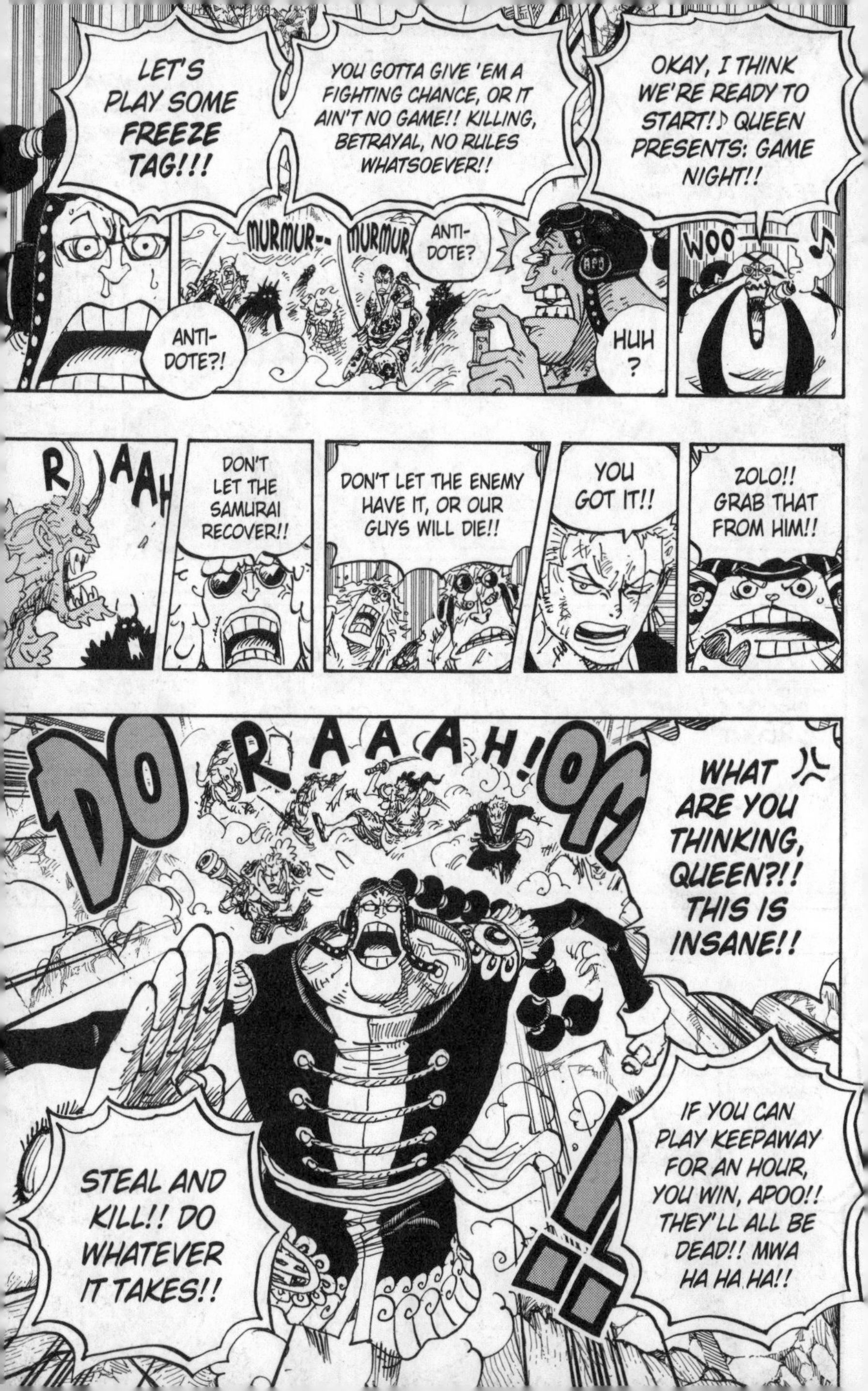

OKAY, I THINK WE'RE READY TO START!♪ QUEEN PRESENTS: GAME NIGHT!!
WOO
YOU GOTTA GIVE 'EM A FIGHTING CHANCE, OR IT AIN'T NO GAME!! KILLING, BETRAYAL, NO RULES WHATSOEVER!!
LET'S PLAY SOME FREEZE TAG!!!
HUH ?
ANTI-DOTE?
MURMUR-- MURMUR
ANTI-DOTE?!
ZOLO!! GRAB THAT FROM HIM!!
YOU GOT IT!!
DON'T LET THE ENEMY HAVE IT, OR OUR GUYS WILL DIE!!
DON'T LET THE SAMURAI RECOVER!!
RAAH
WHAT ARE YOU THINKING, QUEEN?!! THIS IS INSANE!!
DO RAAAH!!
IF YOU CAN PLAY KEEPAWAY FOR AN HOUR, YOU WIN, APOO!! THEY'LL ALL BE DEAD!! MWA HA HA HA!!
STEAL AND KILL!! DO WHATEVER IT TAKES!!

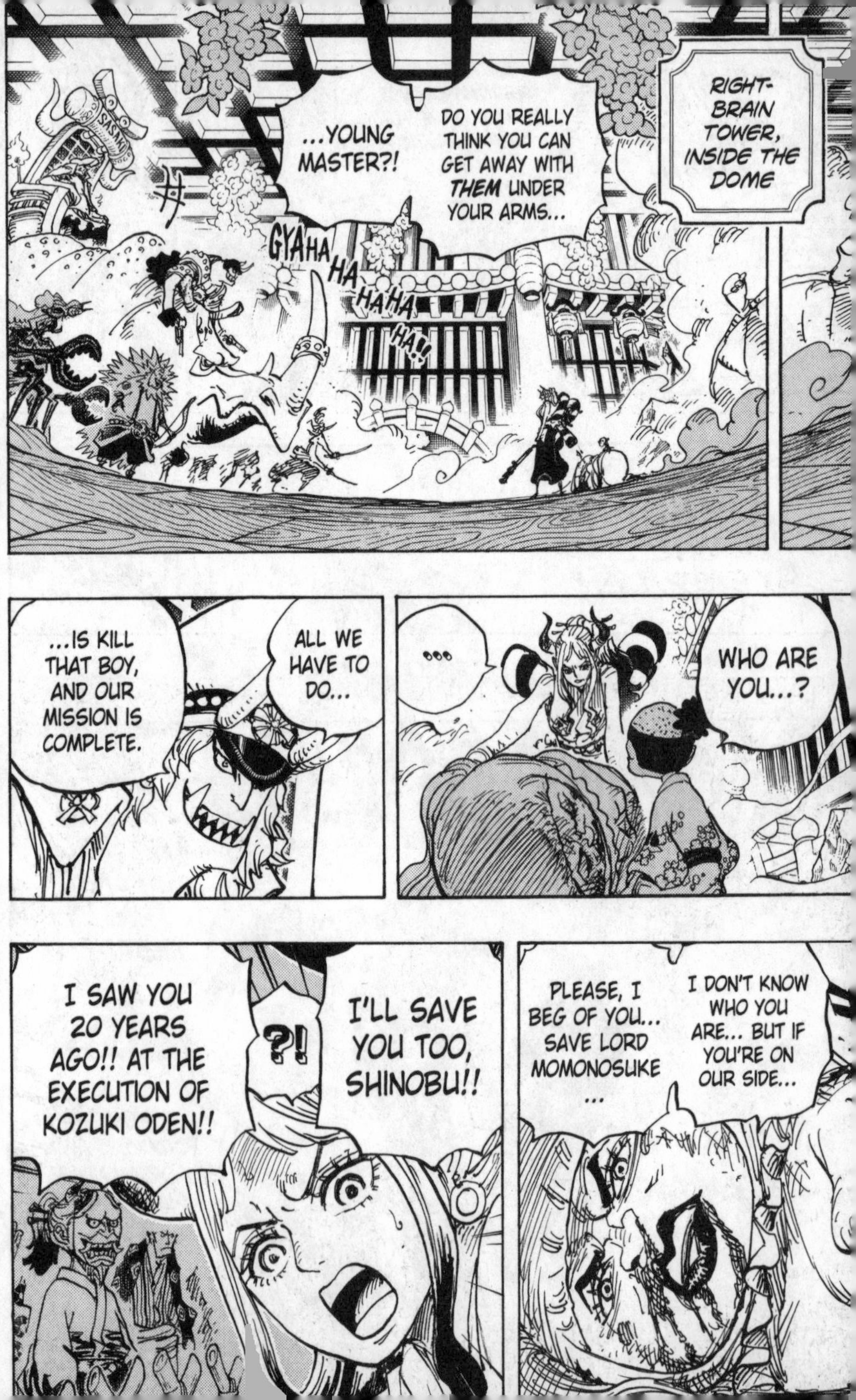
RIGHT-BRAIN TOWER, INSIDE THE DOME
DO YOU REALLY THINK YOU CAN GET AWAY WITH *THEM* UNDER YOUR ARMS...
...YOUNG MASTER?!
GYAHAHAHAHAHA!!
WHO ARE YOU...?
...
ALL WE HAVE TO DO...
...IS KILL THAT BOY, AND OUR MISSION IS COMPLETE.
I DON'T KNOW WHO YOU ARE... BUT IF YOU'RE ON OUR SIDE...
PLEASE, I BEG OF YOU... SAVE LORD MOMONOSUKE...
I'LL SAVE YOU TOO, SHINOBU!!
?!
I SAW YOU 20 YEARS AGO!! AT THE EXECUTION OF KOZUKI ODEN!!

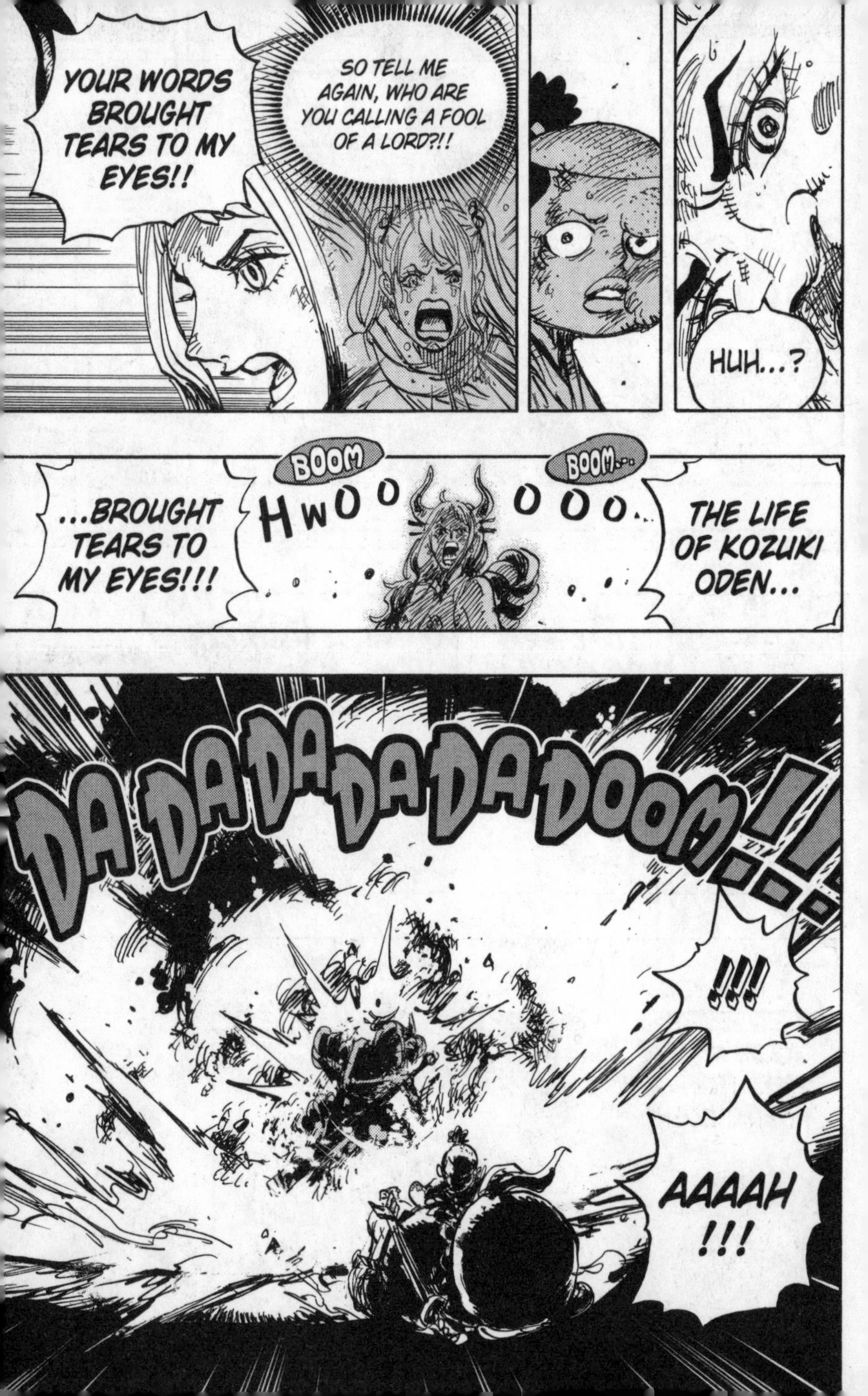
HUH...?
SO TELL ME AGAIN, WHO ARE YOU CALLING A FOOL OF A LORD?!!
YOUR WORDS BROUGHT TEARS TO MY EYES!!
THE LIFE OF KOZUKI ODEN...
BOOM
HWOOOOOO...
BOOM
...BROUGHT TEARS TO MY EYES!!!
DA DA DA DA DA DA DOOM!!!
!!!
AAAAH!!!

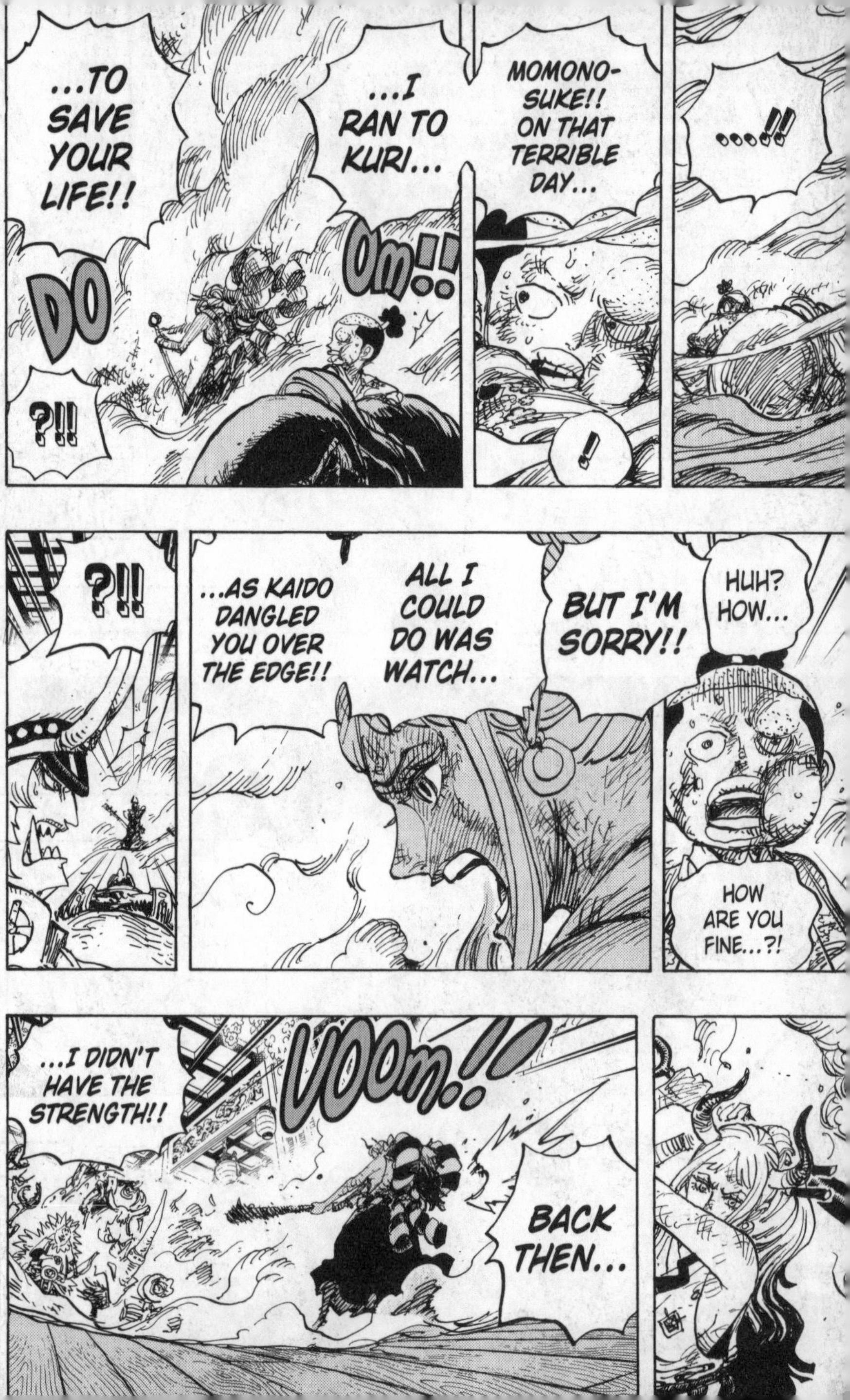

....!!
MOMONOSUKE!! ON THAT TERRIBLE DAY...
!
...I RAN TO KURI...
Om!!
...TO SAVE YOUR LIFE!!
DO
?!!
HUH? HOW...
HOW ARE YOU FINE...?!
BUT I'M SORRY!!
ALL I COULD DO WAS WATCH...
...AS KAIDO DANGLED YOU OVER THE EDGE!!
?!!
BACK THEN...
VOOm!!
...I DIDN'T HAVE THE STRENGTH!!

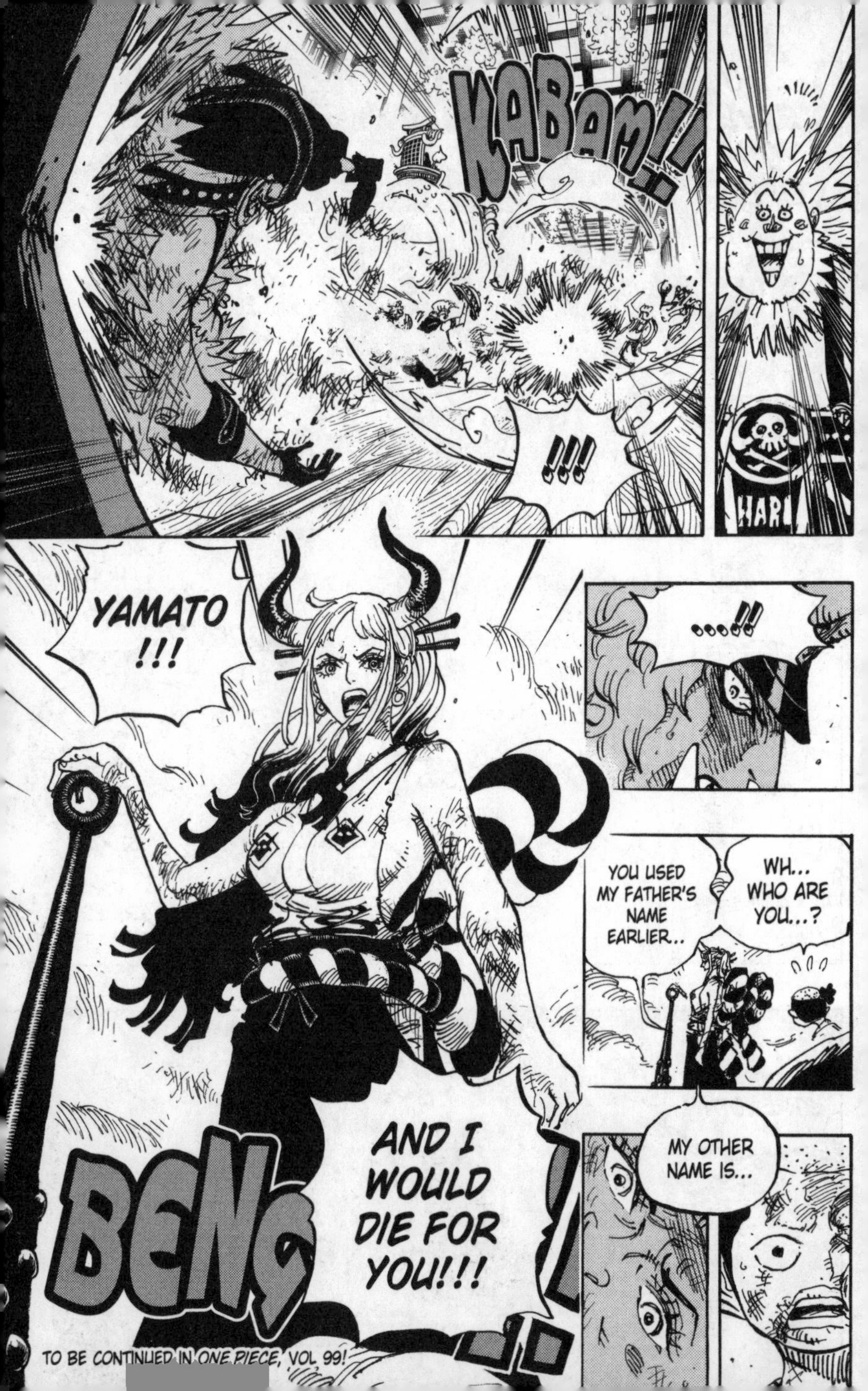

HARI
KABAM!!
!!!
....!!
WH... WHO ARE YOU...?
YOU USED MY FATHER'S NAME EARLIER...
MY OTHER NAME IS...
YAMATO !!!
AND I WOULD DIE FOR YOU!!!
BENG

TO BE CONTINUED IN ONE PIECE, VOL 99!

COMING NEXT VOLUME:

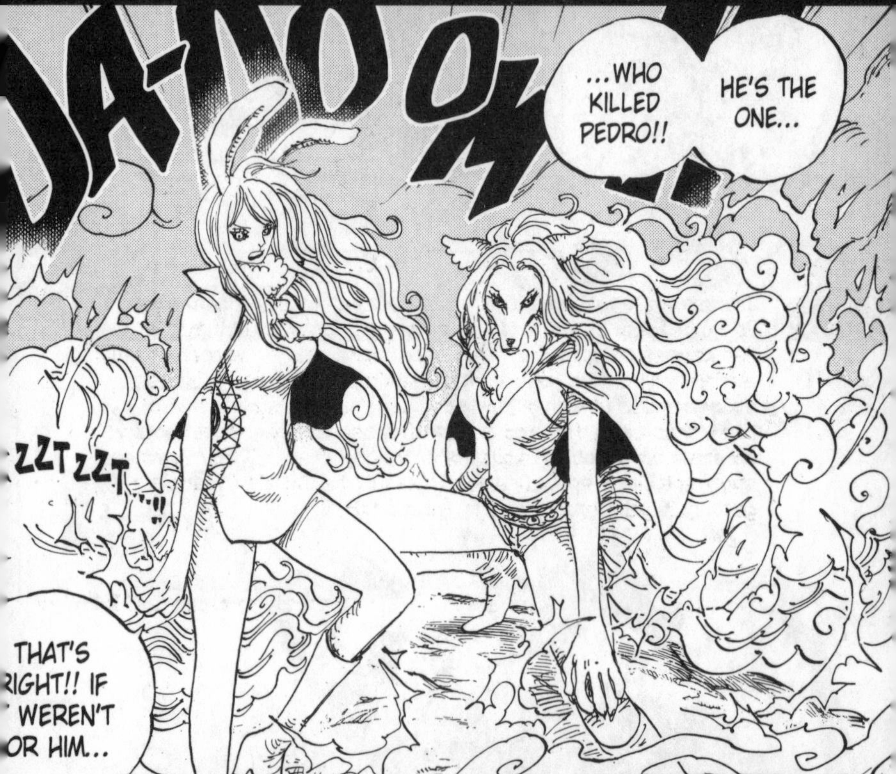

HE'S THE ONE...
...WHO KILLED PEDRO!!
ZZT ZZT
THAT'S RIGHT!! IF WEREN'T OR HIM...

Things are getting crazy as the Straw Hats and their samurai allies battle against the combined might of Kaido and Big Mom. Luffy and his crew are gonna need to level up if they hope to make it off the island alive!

ON SALE MAY 2022!

尾田栄一郎

There's an insect called a "spiky beetle" in Japanese. They found a spiky beetle without spikes, so they called that a "spikeless spiky beetle," and then there was a member of that subfamily that did have spikes, making it a "spiky spikeless spiky beetle." I'm thinking that there are probably some of them that can't fly, and a few of those are particularly quick to move on to other situations, making them "flighty flightless spiky spikeless spiky beetles." Meanwhile, here's "Wano's getting mighty breathless in volume 98!"

Let's go!!!

—Eiichiro Oda, 2021

iichiro Oda began his manga career at the age of 17, when his one-shot cowboy manga **Wanted!** won second place in the coveted Tezuka manga awards. Oda went on to work as an assistant to some of the biggest manga artists in the industry, including Nobuhiro Watsuki, before winning the Hop Step Award for new artists. His pirate adventure **One Piece**, which debuted in **Weekly Shonen Jump** in 1997, quickly became one of the most popular manga in Japan.

ONE PIECE VOL. 98
WANO PART 9

SHONEN JUMP Manga Edition

STORY AND ART BY EIICHIRO ODA

Translation/Stephen Paul
Touch-up Art & Lettering/Vanessa Satone
Design/Yukiko Whitley
Editor/Alexis Kirsch

Printed in Canada

Published by VIZ Media, LLC
P.O. Box 77010
San Francisco, CA 94107

10 9 8 7 6 5 4 3 2 1
First printing, December 2021

viz.com

DEMON SLAYER
KIMETSU NO YAIBA

Story and Art by
KOYOHARU GOTOUGE

In Taisho-era Japan, kindhearted Tanjiro Kamado makes a living selling charcoal. But his peaceful life is shattered when a demon slaughters his entire family. His little sister Nezuko is the only survivor, but she has been transformed into a demon herself! Tanjiro sets out on a dangerous journey to find a way to return his sister to normal and destroy the demon who ruined his life.

BORUTO
=NARUTO NEXT GENERATIONS=

CREATOR/SUPERVISOR **Masashi Kishimoto**
ART BY **Mikio Ikemoto** SCRIPT BY **Ukyo Kodachi**

A NEW GENERATION OF NINJA IS HERE!

Naruto was a young shinobi with an incorrigible knack for mischief. He achieved his dream to become the greatest ninja in his village, and now his face sits atop the Hokage monument. But this is not his story... A new generation of ninja is ready to take the stage, led by Naruto's own son, Boruto!

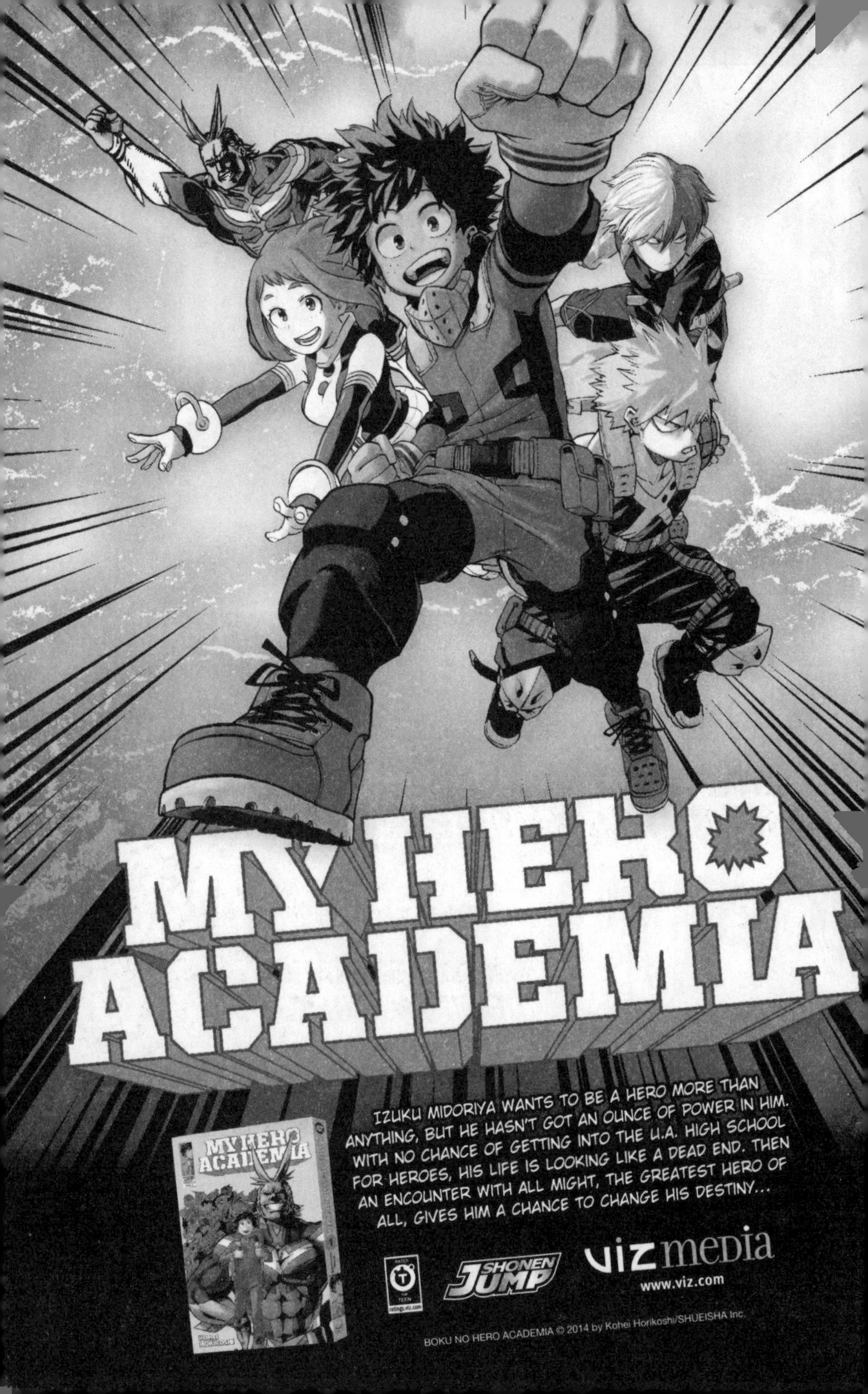
MY HERO ACADEMIA
IZUKU MIDORIYA WANTS TO BE A HERO MORE THAN ANYTHING, BUT HE HASN'T GOT AN OUNCE OF POWER IN HIM. WITH NO CHANCE OF GETTING INTO THE U.A. HIGH SCHOOL FOR HEROES, HIS LIFE IS LOOKING LIKE A DEAD END. THEN AN ENCOUNTER WITH ALL MIGHT, THE GREATEST HERO OF ALL, GIVES HIM A CHANCE TO CHANGE HIS DESTINY...
MY HERO ACADEMIA
KOHEI HORIKOSHI
RATED T TEEN
ratings.viz.com
SHONEN JUMP
viz media
www.viz.com
BOKU NO HERO ACADEMIA © 2014 by Kohei Horikoshi/SHUEISHA Inc.